Hermann Kinder and
Werner Hilgemann

The Anchor Atlas of World History

Volume I

From the Stone Age to the Eve of the French Revolution

Translated by
Ernest A. Menze
with maps designed by
Harald and Ruth Bukor

D0001779

Anchor Press
Doubleday
New York London Toronto Sydney

DTV-ATLAS ZUR WELTGESCHICHTE Vol. 1 was originally published by Deutscher Taschenbuch Verlag

Copyright © 1964 by Deutscher Taschenbuch Verlag GmbH & Co. KG. München (Deutschland)

Anchor Books edition: 1974

Library of Congress Number: 72:90090

ISBN: 0-385-06178-1

Copyright © 1974 by Penguin Books Ltd.

Filmset in Great Britain by Typesetting Services Ltd, Glasgow

Printed in Great Britain by Hazell Watson & Viney Limited
Member of BPCC plc Aylesbury Bucks

Anchor Press

Published by Bantam Doubleday Dell Publishing Group, Inc.,
666 Fifth Avenue, New York, New York 10103

'Anchor', 'Doubleday'.

The portrayal of an anchor is a trademark of
Doubleday, a division of Bantam Doubleday Dell
Publishing Group, Inc.

8 9

Contents

Symbols and Abbreviations

●	City, town	▲▲▲	Barrage, blockade
■	Large city, or cultural centre	⌒⌒⌒	Defensive wall
■	Capital city	🔥	Insurrection, revolution
‡	Archbishopric	⚡	Site of conflict, theatre of operations
✝	Bishopric	✕	Battlefield
✣	Former bishopric	♛	Monarch (emperor, king, prince)
♠	Monastery, abbey	▲	Head of state, president
♣	Castle, palace	Ⓢ	Legislature
✦	Fortress, stronghold	⬛	Parliamentary institution
☀	Siege	GB	Political power
✤	Conference site		League, alliance
◉	Treaty site	Ⓕ	League partner
◡	Destroyed town	⊢⊣	Personal union
✕	Mountain pass	◯◯	Marriage

acc.	according	Belg.	Belgian
addit.	additional	Bened.	Benedictine
admin.	administration	bib.	biblical
Ach.	Achaean	Boh.	Bohemian
Akk.	Akkadian	bp	bishop
Alb.	Albanian	bpc	bishopric
Albig.	Albigensian	Brit.	British
Alp.	Alpine	Bulg.	Bulgarian
Amer.	American	Burg.	Burgundian
anon.	anonymous	Byz.	Byzantine
approx.	approximately		
art.	artistic	c.	circa
Assyr.	Assyrian	cap.	capital (city)
attr.	attributed	cal.	called
Arab.	Arabic	Calv.	Calvinist
Aram.	Aramaic	Carm.	Carmelite
archbp	archbishop	Carol.	Carolingian
archbpc	archbishopric	Carth.	Carthaginian
Athen.	Athenian	Castil.	Castilian
August.	Augustinian	Cath.	Catholic
Aust.	Austrian	Celt.	Celtic
aut.	autonomous	cen.	central
		cent.	century
b.	battle	cf.	compare
Balk.	Balkan	Chin.	Chinese
Bav.	Bavarian	Cist.	Cistercian

Clun.	Cluniac	kdm	kingdom
colon.	colonial	km.	kilometre
comp.	comparative		
const.	constitutional	l.	livres
Cret.	Cretan	Lang.	Langobard
Corin.	Corinthian	Lat.	Latin
ctr(s).	culture(s)	lib.	liberation
cult.	cultural	lit.	literary
		Lith.	Lithuanian
d.	died	loc.	located
Dan.	Danish	Luth.	Lutheran
der.	derived	Lyd.	Lydian
dest.	destroyed		
Domin.	Dominican	m.	metre
Dor.	Doric	Maced.	Macedonian
dyn.	dynastic	mar.	married
		Mauret.	Mauretanian
E.	east	Med.	Median
eccles.	ecclesiastical	Medit.	Mediterranean
econ.	economic	Merov.	Merovingian
ed.	edition	Mess.	Messenian
Egy.	Egyptian	mil.	million
Eng.	English	milit.	military
esp.	especially	Min.	Minoan
est.	established	miss.	missionary
Etrus.	Etruscan	mod.	modern
Eur.	European	monast.	monastic
exc.	except	Mongol.	Mongolian
excl.	excluding	Mor.	Moravian
		mt(s)	mountain(s)
fd	founded	mus.	musical
Fin.	Finnish	Myc.	Mycenaean
fl.	flourished		
Flor.	Florentine	N.	north
Fr.	French	nat.	national
Frank.	Frankish	NE.	north-east
Fris.	Frisian	Nor.	Norwegian
		Norm.	Norman
Gen.	Genoese	nr	near
geog.	geographical	N.T.	New Testament
Ger.	German	NW.	north-west
Germ.	Germanic		
Gk	Greek	Orient.	Oriental
gm(s)	gram(s)	Orth.	Orthodox
Goth.	Gothic	Ostro.	Ostrogothic
gvt	government	O.T.	Old Testament
gvtl	governmental	Ott.	Ottoman
Hellen.	Hellenistic	Palest.	Palestinian
hered.	hereditary	Pers.	Persian
Hit.	Hittite	Phoen.	Phoenician
Hung.	Hungarian	Phryg.	Phrygian
		Pol.	Polish
Illyr.	Illyrian	polit.	political
imp.	imperial	pop.	population
incl.	including	prob.	probably
incorp.	incorporated	Prot.	Protestant
infl.	influence	prov.	provincial
ind.	independent	Prus.	Prussian
inh.	inheritance	Pur.	Puritan
int.	international		
Ion.	Ionian	recog.	recognized
Iran.	Iranian	relig.	religious
Isl.	Islamic	rest.	restoration
		Rom.	Roman
Jap.	Japanese	Rum.	Rumanian
Jes.	Jesuit	Rus.	Russian
Jew.	Jewish		

s.	south	Swed.	Swedish
Sard.	Sardinian	Syr.	Syrian
Scand.	Scandinavian		
Scyth.	Scythian	territ.	territorial
SE.	south-east	Theb.	Theban
sec.	secular	Thrac.	Thracian
Sem.	Semitic	Thur.	Thuringian
sep.	separate	Turk.	Turkish
Sicil.	Sicilian		
Slav.	Slavic	Ukr.	Ukrainian
soc.	social		
Sp.	Spanish	var.	various
Spart.	Spartan	Varan.	Varangian
sq.	square	Venet.	Venetian
strat.	strategic	vict(s).	victory(ies)
sub.	subordinate	Visi.	Visigothic
subs.	subsequently	vol(s).	volume(s)
subj.	subjugated		
Sum.	Sumerian	w.	west
sw.	south-west		
		yr(s)	year(s)

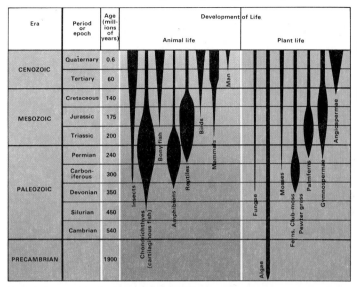

Era	Period or epoch	Age (millions of years)	Development of Life Animal life	Plant life
CENOZOIC	Quaternary	0.6		
	Tertiary	60	Man	
MESOZOIC	Cretaceous	140		Angiospermae
	Jurassic	175	Bony fish / Birds	
	Triassic	200	Mammals	
PALEOZOIC	Permian	240	Reptiles	Gymnospermae
	Carboniferous	300		Mosses / Palmferns
	Devonian	350	Insects / Amphibians	Fungae / Ferns, Club-moss / Pewter grass
	Silurian	450	Chondrichthyes (cartilaginous fish)	
	Cambrian	540		
PRECAMBRIAN		1900		Algae

Geological eras and the development of organic life

Era	Australopithecus	Pithecanthropus (Homo erectus)	Homo sapiens (Neanderthalensis)	Unclassified finds	Homo sapiens
UPPER PLEISTOCENE		Ngandong	Monte Circeo Gibraltar Engis-Spy La Chapelle La Ferrassie Lake Eyassie Tabun Krapina Saccopastore Ehringsdorf	Broken Hill Saldanha	Mt Carmel Fontéchevade
MIDDLE PLEISTOCENE		Chou Kou-tien Trinil Casablanca Ternifine Rabat Montmaurin Mauer Modjokerto Oldovai	Neanderthal	Swanscombe Steinheim	
LOWER PLEISTOCENE	China South Africa			Note: Neither table is organized to represent an exact chronological scale; they are intended to be approximations only.	

Important Hominid finds in the Pleistocene era

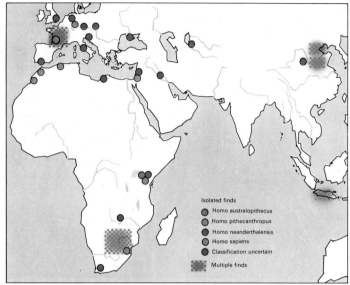

Pleistocene sites of human remains

Isolated finds
- Homo australopithecus
- Homo pithecanthropus
- Homo neanderthalensis
- Homo sapiens
- Classification uncertain

Multiple finds

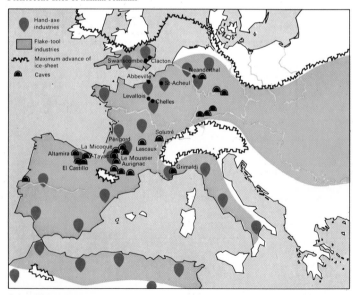

Palaeolithic industries

Hand-axe industries

Flake-tool industries

Maximum advance of ice-sheet

Caves

Swanscombe   Clacton
Neanderthal
Abbeville   St-Acheul
Levallois   Chelles
Solutré
Périgord
La Micoque   Lascaux
Altamira   Tayac   Le Moustier
El Castillo   Aurignac   Grimaldi

Man in the Palaeolithic (Old Stone Age)

Pre-hominids are known from the Late Tertiary (c. 6 mil. yrs ago); the earliest finds of man are c. 2.6 mil. yrs old and known as **Australopithecus** or **Homo australopithecus** (named by the discoverer RAYMOND DART in 1924, who made the first find at Taungs, Transvaal). Evidence of intelligence (tool-making and using) associated with early remains classifies them as primitive hominids. They are associated with pebble-tool industries. Man gradually developed during the Pleistocene; **Pithecanthropus** (Homo erectus) is associated with early hand-axe industries, and knew the use of fire (earliest evidence from China).

Neanderthal man (H. sapiens neanderthalensis) first appears in the Middle Pleistocene, associated with Mousterian industries. Other human remains are known which are not easily classified, but resemble Homo sapiens (e.g. from Broken Hill, Saldana, Swanscombe and Steinheim). These early hominids were replaced in the last Ice Age (Würm) by Homo sapiens sapiens (Cromagnon, Grimaldi, Chancelade, Oberkassel, Predmost, Lautsch, Combecapelle, Brünn, etc.).

At the end of the Pleistocene period the major **human races** were in existence: the Mongoloids (Asia), Negroids (Central Africa), Caucasoids, and the Australians.

The **Pleistocene** is divided into Glacial (cold) and Interglacial (mild) periods (in thousands of yrs B.C.):

600–540	1st Ice Age (Günz)
540–480	1st Interglacial period (Günz–Mindel)
480–430	2nd Ice Age (Mindel)
430–240	2nd Interglacial period (Mindel Riss = Great Interglacial)
240–180	3rd Ice Age (Riss)
180–120	3rd Interglacial period (Riss–Würm)
120–10	4th Ice Age (Würm), followed by the post-glacial period

Archaeologically the Pleistocene is divided into 3 periods:

600–100	Lower Palaeolithic (Older Old Stone Age)
100–50	Middle Palaeolithic (Middle Old Stone Age)
50–10	Upper Palaeolithic (Upper Old Stone Age)

Industries: Palaeolithic industries are usually named after the original find-spots (e.g. Clacton, Clactonian). The most important raw material, stone (usually flint), was struck in various ways to make tools of predetermined shapes, which served to work wood and bone, and as weapons (clubs, hatchets and points).

The worked stones fall into 4 main groups of industries.

1. Tools made from small lumps of stone or pebbles – pebble-culture: S. and E. Africa, Siam, Burma, Malaya, Java, China. Working the pebbles results in chopping-tools, choppers, and early forms of the hand-axe.

2. Tools derived from stone cores, usually bifacial (hand-axe). **Abbevillian** (Abbeville on the Somme), earlier cal. Chellean (Chelles on the Marne): Africa, India, Java, Western Europe.
Acheulian (St-Acheul, nr Amiens): Africa, India, W. and Cen. Europe.
Micoquean (La Micoque, Dordogne): Africa, India, W. and Cen. Europe, Palestine, Syria.

3. Tools made from unilaterally worked flakes, struck from a core by direct percussion.
Clactonian (Clacton, Essex): W. and Cen. Europe, Africa, India.
Levalloisian (Levallois-Peret, nr Paris): Africa, Europe, N. India.
Tayacian (Tayac, Dordogne): Palestine, Syria, N. Africa, W. Europe.
The technical traditions of the hand-axe and flake-tool ctrs were fused in the **Mousterian** (Le Moustier, Dordogne): fine points, carefully finished choppers. The dead were buried, occasionally with artefacts or natural objects.
For these industries there is much evidence for stone tools; evidence of artistic activity is slight, as is information about dwelling structures, diet, etc.

4. Tools derived from struck-off fragments (flakes): blade industries (points, drills, scrapers, cutters).
Perigordian (Périgord): the 'Chateiperron-point', later the Gravette point.
Aurignacian (Aurignac): bone-tools, weapon points, awls and engraving scrapers. Development of art, female figurines ('The Venus of Willendorf'); engravings on stone, bone, and ivory: **paintings and drawings** in the caves of Altamira, El Castillo, et al.
Homo sapiens pushes N. from the Near East.
Solutrean (Solutre): tools with finished surfaces, laurel-leaf points, needles.
Magdalenian (Abri la Madelene, nr Tursac): bone-tools, spear-throwers, harpoon-points, long blades.
The high point of cave art (c. 120 sites), e.g. at Altamira (1879) and Lascaux (1940). Smaller art objects were made from bone, antler, ivory and stone (engravings and sculptures). With the end of the Magdalenian period there is only slight evidence preserved for man's artistic activity.
Men lived in groups, hunting both small and large animals and gathering a wide range of vegetable foods.
They dwelt in caves, huts, skin tents, or under rocky overhangs.
Religion: possible evidence for hunting-cults, magic, and a belief in the gods. Burial of the dead with gifts of food, tools and ornaments.

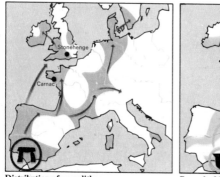

Distribution of megaliths

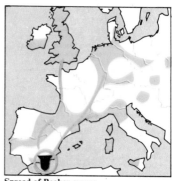

Spread of Beaker groups

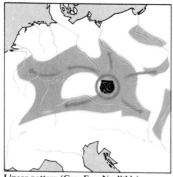

Linear pottery (Cen. Eur. Neolithic)

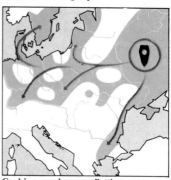

Cord-impressed ware or Battle-axe ctr.

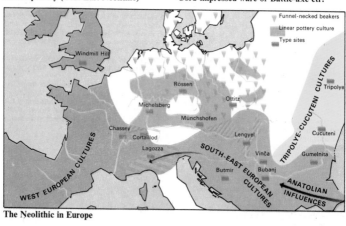

The Neolithic in Europe

The Mesolithic (Middle Stone Age)
This cult. period begins *c.* 10,000 B.C. with the retreat of the ice-sheets northwards. In the s. it was soon followed by the Neolithic, but in Northern Europe the Mesolithic way of life persisted in remote areas into the 2nd millennium B.C. The econ. way of life of the Mesolithic hunters, fishers and gatherers was similar to that of the preceding Palaeolithic period. But the warmer climate provided different living conditions for man, with the spread of forests (birch, willows, hazel, firs, then oak with ash). Subsistence was based on hunting, fowling, fishing and extensive gathering of wild plants. In Europe, settlement took place, mostly along the coasts, to exploit marine food sources, and by rivers, streams and lakes with rich sources of shellfish (settlements marked by very large shell-middens). Settlements were generally of small groups, and the camp site was shifted quite often, sometimes to exploit seasonal foods. Men lived in rock shelters, in caves and in brushwood huts. The Mesolithic is characterized by microliths – very small flints (e.g. small points and blades) often used in composite tools; technical innovations include the axe and pick (unpolished stone at first, later ground and polished for a strong cutting edge). Some raw materials had a restricted distribution, and were traded over long distances (evidence for travel in boats and sledges with runners). Decoration often consisted of abstract designs. Domesticated dogs (Star Carr). Agriculture and pottery adopted at the end of the period. Mesolithic ctrs expanded in Europe, N. Africa (Capsian, Oranian, Sebilian) and Palestine (Natufian).
Mesolithic ctrs: The Azilian, developed into the **Sauveterrian** (geometric flint microliths).
Maglemosan, concentrated on lakeshores (NW. Europe), fishing in lakes and rivers, using curved fishhooks and building weirs; wooden canoes and skin-covered boats, paddles.
Ertebölle: spread along the Scandinavian coast; deep sea-fishing, connected with barter. Hunting of large game animals, later replaced by small ones.
Division of labour: probable responsibility of women for collecting the plant foods (wild cereals, waterplants, etc.). Domestic dogs.
Tardenoisian: small settlements. The industry may have been derived from the Aegean; trapezoidal microliths.
Natufian (Near East): flint tools, microliths, sometimes made into sickles to harvest wild grain. In the later stages brick buildings evolved, e.g. at Jericho. At Jarmo, evidence for the development of primitive farming.

The Neolithic in Europe
Western Europe: megaliths (monuments built of very large stones) spread over Spain, France, England, Ireland, Switzerland, and parts of Italy. Characteristics: dolmen, burial chambers of stone constructed in post and lintel form, long barrows, later round barrows with 'false vaults' created by projecting overhangs. Most common in **Brittany**, where menhirs were aligned in stone alleys (200 to 1,500 m long

at Carnac), or in circular arrangement (as at Stonehenge, in Southern England); an anthropomorphic character is suggested by some engravings. The Bell-beaker ctr. (characterized by pots shaped like upside-down bells) spread through Spain and Western and Cen. Europe. Society consisted of small groups engaged in hunting with bows and arrows; primitive farming; and rudimentary metallurgy.
The Balkans: elevated houses, painted pottery figurines (mainly female). Eastern infl. leads to the erection of mud-brick walls and fortifications. Rectangular buildings of the Gk Megaron type, with main hall and porch, occur. Horses were domesticated and battle-axes in use.
The Tripolye ctr. (loc. between the Carpathians and the Dnieper in the Ukraine): rectangular longhouses were arranged in a circle around an empty cen. space. Much further to the E. the Pontic-Aral Sea neolithic is characterized by burial finds which included no burial gifts but were marked by extensive use of ochre.
Linear pottery Neolithic: pottery covered with bands of decoration (spiral-, meander-, and angular geometrical designs); D-sectioned polished stone axe-edge blades common. Area of concentration: Bohemia, Moravia, Cen. Germany; from here expansion to the E. to the Theiss and Vistula rivers, to the W. to the Rhine, to the S. into the region of the River Drave, and to the N. along the line Cologne–Hanover–Magdeburg. Type of settlement: villages protected by walls and ditches with large buildings 30–40 m. long and 5–7 m. wide.
Northern Europe (Poland, Cen. Germany, Denmark, Southern Sweden). 2 groups: (a) **Funnel-necked beaker ctr.** The origin of the funnel-necked beaker people, who lived in longhouses with room-like subdivisions, is unknown, though it has elements of linear pottery, Neolithic and local Mesolithic. (b) **Cord-impressed ware or battle-axe ctr.** Vessels were decorated by cord impressions. (Expansion in Saxony, Thuringia, Schleswig-Holstein, and at the mouth of the Oder.) The **battle-axe** was the most important weapon. Horses were bred. The people of the cord-impressed ware ctr. (battle-axe people) were prob. not Indo-Eur. in origin.
Summary: there was close contact between the var. ctrs by means of active and extensive trade (e.g. grinding stones, amber, flint). Travel on rivers in dugout canoes or skin-covered boats, on land, roads or paths, solidified by branches and logs in wet places, wagons with solid wheels, drawn by oxen and reindeer and later by horses. **Religions:** probable belief in life after death; belief in the return of the dead may be shown by the fact that bodies were burned or tied; there were ancestry and fertility cults. Belief in a heavenly god, often identical with the god of thunder and lightning, as well as in magic and evil spirits.
Econ. life: hunting and gathering important at first, but the emphasis on farming increases steadily. Intensive agriculture led to soil exhaustion and the movement of settlements into new land; once the vacated land had recovered it could be repopulated.

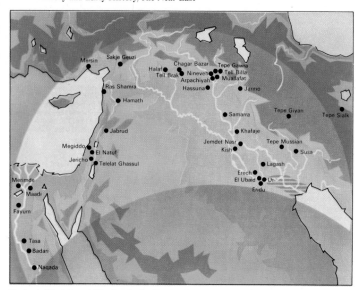

Centres of incipient civilization in the 'Fertile Crescent'

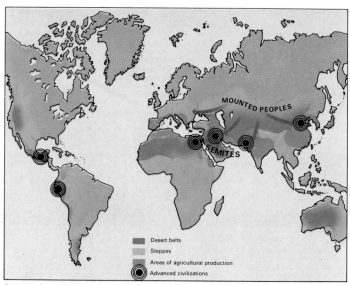

Centres of advanced civilization

Neolithic (New Stone Age)

Within the Neolithic ctrs., characterized by settlements on graduated plateaux, or on the fringes of mts where rainfall is high, important innovations (building with bricks, polished stone tools, pottery, the potter's wheel) and econ. change took place: **the transition to farming as a way of life** – and thereby to a productive econ. life – with agriculture (the planter) and the raising of animals (the herdsman) both being practised by the end of the Neolithic (cal. the **Neolithic revolution** by GORDON CHILDE). Wild grains were cultivated (wheat, barley, millet) and sheep, goats, pigs and asses were domesticated. People settled in villages, later in cities, fortified by walls. Jericho (between 8000 and 6000 B.C.) may be considered as a preliminary step on the road to highly developed urban ctr. Rectangular buildings were constructed in succession to roundhouses. At first they were made of reed, fortified with mud, later of unbaked clay, and then of **dried brick. Art:** jewellery in the beginning was made from shells and stones, later from precious metals and stones. The painted pottery, produced with the aid of the potter's wheel, was skilfully decorated with geometrical designs and abstract and naturalistic representations of humans and animals. (The high point of this development is found at Susa in Iran.) Small sculptures (female figurines) were produced. Sealstones were introduced. Copper became an important raw material. (At first it was hammered into shape, later cast as well.) The first **sacred buildings** were erected at Eridu, Tepe Gawra and Uruk. Temples were built in large areas reserved for sacred purposes. (The outer walls of temples were artistically proportioned by moulded pillars.) The first clay tablets with writing on them (econ. accounts of temple affairs) were found at Uruk; the picture language evolved into a language of words and sounds. All ctrs made provisions for the dead. During the earlier period, important sites were: Hassuna, Jarmo (Eastern Iraq), Sialk I (Eastern Iran), Jericho and Sakje Geuzi (Syria); during the middle period: Halaf, Samarra, Sialk II, Arpachiyah, Tepe Gawra, Hissar, Tasa, Badari, Merimde, and Fayum; during the later period: El Ubaid, Susa (Elam), Telelat Ghassul, Sialk III, Hissar (I B-C), Amrah and Gerseh.

c. 3000 the **'Great Deluge'** took place (prob. in the form of several floods and catastrophic events). Dams and canals were built in Egypt (Nile) and in Mesopotamia (Tigris and Euphrates). The bib. account corresponds with the Gilgamesh epic.

The Development of Advanced Civilizations

The historical epoch begins with the development of advanced urban civilizations (cal. by WITTFOGEL 'hydraulic societies'), which followed the 'Neolithic revolution'. Advanced ctrs develop into riverine civilizations in Egypt along the Nile, in Mesopotamia along the Euphrates and the Tigris, in India in the Indus valley and in China along the Hwang Ho (for early Amer. civilizations, see p. 223). A factor in this development may have been a change in climate, which began in the Mesolithic period and led to the dehydration of large areas (with desert-belts stretching from W. to E.: from the Sahara to the steppes of Kirghizia). With increasing pop. after the inception of farming, the inhabitants of the regions in question migrated to the fertile river valleys. A condition for existence in the river valleys was the solution of common problems on a soc. basis. Since changes in the economy freed part of the pop. from the need to engage in subsistence farming, more men now became available to pursue other tasks (i.e. crafts, defence, relig. life, admin. and technology). This led to the stratification of society along the various levels of occupation and, thereby, the development of a **differentiated society** – a process which was aided by the complication of methods of production and increasing trade specialization. **The city** – an important characteristic of civilization – became a centre for the production and exchange of goods, for trade and markets. Power over the city in Mesopotamia rested with the priest-king (to whom, as the representative of God, the city belonged). In Egypt the Pharaoh governed, and was revered as God's son or even as God himself (charismatic leadership). A state religion was the basis and support of his rule. The centralization of the state and the hierarchical ordering of society into sharply differentiated classes (rulers, priests, warriors, officials, craftsmen, traders, peasants, slaves) enabled the Egyptians to solve the problems which confronted every riverine civilization. So did the organized admin:, which brought about the development of writing, because of necessary accounting procedures. Among its tasks were the organization of the economy through the division of labour (allocation of *corvées* and duties; food-supply for the pop.) and the planning of agriculture in the region belonging to the city. The most important role of the admin. was to prepare irrigation projects and control the recurring floods: digging of ditches and canals, erection of dikes and the construction of aqueducts and reservoirs for drinking-water. All civilizations tended to expand their territories; the city-states became empires. Common language, ctr. and religion led to common ways of thought and feeling. Expanding trade connections (cities as markets) led to inter-urban infls., and widened intellectual horizons.

Common characteristics of these early civilizations: metal-working, bricks, square-hewn stones (the primary element of architecture), polygonal wall-construction, working in precious metals and stones, production of thin-walled vessels, writing, large sculptures, polished stone, irrigation, urban settlement.

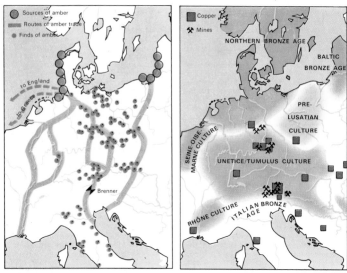

Amber trade and distribution of finds

The Middle Bronze Age

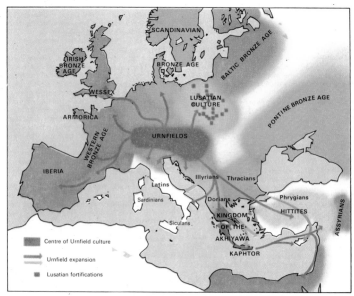

The European Bronze Age and Urnfield expansion

The Bronze Age Technology (c. 3500–800 B.C.)
Development of metallurgy: metal-working developed in the Near East, with Late Neolithic ctrs. making and using a few metal tools and ornaments. These were mostly of copper; gold, silver and lead were also known. Later, more complex bronze-working developed. In Europe metallurgy developed in the Balkans in the 4th millennium B.C. with the production of tools and weapons as well as simple ornaments. **Copper Age:** the resurgence of metal-working in Europe was influenced by 3 main cult. groups:
1. The Beaker groups in Cen. Europe.
2. The Corded Ware groups in Northern Europe.
3. The Eastern Eur. groups, which had cult. links with the earlier Balkan metallurgy (e.g. Baden, Vucedol, Laibach, Altheim).

In the later 3rd millennium B.C., these groups were producing simple copper artefacts, such as knives, daggers and pins. The metal was obtained from surface deposits of ore, and by mining. Once extracted, the ores were smelted to obtain the metal, which was stored as ingots and cast in simple open moulds to make artefacts; copper could also be hammered into shape, esp. native copper. Experimentation with alloys led to the production of bronze, which made more complex casting possible and gave a harder cutting edge to tools and weapons.

Sources and probable phases of exploitation in the Early Bronze Age: access to sources of the new raw material (copper and tin ores) influenced the development of Early Bronze Age ctr. groups, and the possession and use of metal artefacts became important politically. Many Early Bronze Age groups produced elaborate decorative gold-work, possibly indicative of soc. status.
1. Sources: Alp., Carpathian and Slovakian ores.
   Cultures: Alp. Early Bronze Age, mid-Danubian Early Bronze Age, Slovakian Early Bronze Age.
2. Sources: Cen. Ger. Highlands, Boh. ore mts., Ital. ores.
   Cultures: Unetice (Cen. Ger. Early Bronze Age) and Ital. Early Bronze Age.
3. Peripheral groups which developed Early Bronze Age ctrs.: Rhône, Armorica (Brittany), Wessex (Britain), Ireland, Iberia.

Larger cult. spheres developed with a more clearly structured society (industry, the crafts and trade were now carried on along with agriculture and the raising of animals). Amber found in Jutland and Samland became an object of barter. The trade lanes followed the Saale, Main and Elbe rivers from the Danube to Jutland, and along the Oder to the Baltic. Trade followed the S.–N. direction of general expansion. Amber was found in the beehive tombs of Mycenae; pearls from Fayum in Egypt, on the other hand, were found in England. In the Early Bronze Age the dead were mainly buried in a squatting position; after the Middle Bronze Age they were cremated.

The Most Important Ctrs.
1. The **Unetice ctr.** of the Early Bronze Age: Cen. Germany, Bohemia, Lower Austria. The 'princely tombs' of Cen. Germany are well known (esp. the mortuary mound of Leubingen with its rich treasure of gold). Because of its central geographical position as a region of transition between the Mediterranean and the N., the Unetice ctr. had extensive trade connections. Related ctrs. which were also strongly influenced by the **Bell-beaker** groups were that of Staubingen in Bavaria (which exploited rich ore-deposits) and the Adlerberg ctr. of the Middle Rhine.
2. **Tumulus (Cairn) ctr.** of the Middle Bronze Age: the area of settlement was circumscribed by the Meuse, the Seine, the Alps, the Oder and Lower Saxony. The dead (prob. only those of the upper classes) were buried under mortuary mounds (tumuli) with gifts of weapons and jewellery. Econ. basis: raising of domestic animals and some agriculture. The intermediate position of the area in the trade between N. and S. was important.
3. The **Urnfield ctr.** (after 1300): the dead were cremated, and their ashes interred in urns in large cemeteries ('urnfields'). Expansion from the Middle Danube to the s., along the Danube to Bohemia, Poland (the Lusatian ctr.), and Cen. Germany; also to Western France, Cen. Italy and Northern Spain. The Venetii and the Illyrii had features in common with the Urnfield ctr. There is evidence for cult. upheaval as the Urnfield ctr. expanded (hoards of bronze and of jewellery confirm this observation). Society became more structured, and peasants and tradesmen were more clearly differentiated by increasing specialization. Links with the Near East decreased gradually and Europe became culturally and economically more independent. The advance of the Urnfield ctr. to the s. influenced the following events:
   (a) The centres of Mycenae and the Late Minoan ctr. of Crete came to an end;
   (b) Asia Minor was invaded (the Empire of the Hittites came to an end, p. 35);
   (c) Northern Italy and Latium were invaded;
   (d) Maritime peoples invaded Egypt (p. 25; the Philistines entered Palestine, p. 37).
4. **The Northern Bronze Age.** The inhabitants of Northern Germany and Scandinavia lived in rectangular homes with 'porches' (Gk megaron; for the early history of the Germ. tribes, cf. p. 109). Artistic evidence from Scandinavia suggests connections with Greece by way of the Urnfield ctr. and with the British Isles. At the beginning of the Bronze Age, metal objects were copied in stone; eventually the local manufacture of bronze objects developed. The people of the Northern Bronze Age had horse-drawn war-chariots; they buried their dead under large mortuary mounds (e.g. richly provided tombs nr Upsala and Seddin); later they changed to cremation.
Religion: the cult of the sun, 'the Sun-chariot of Trundholm', 'sun-boats' of gold, and rock-engravings. These engravings include representations of ships, sun-disks and images of the gods: figures with spears, axes, hammers, etc.

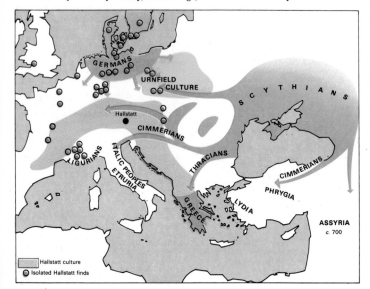

Hallstatt cultures

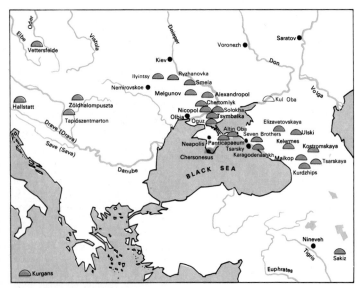

Kurgans of the Scythians in the Black Sea area

The Iron Age (from 800 B.C.)

The final Bronze Age ctr. of Hallstatt, so called after the cemetery found nr Hallstatt in the Salzkammergut of Austria, and based on the Urnfield ctr., developed into the Early Iron Age. A prerequisite for this development was the multiple deposits of iron ore which made possible the development of iron production and industries. The second most important industry was salt-mining at Hallstatt itself and at Dürnberg nr Hallein. In these quickly developing econ. centres an ever-increasing soc. differentiation into peasants, craftsmen and traders took place, as work processes became more complex.

Expansion of Hallstatt ctrs. in the Iron Age:
Croatia, Bosnia, s. and w. Germany, the Alp. regions, Switzerland, Eastern and Southern France, and Northern Spain. The most important aristocratic urban civilization developed at Ateste in Venetia and at the upper end of the Adriatic Sea, where strong Corin. and Etrus. infls. are noticeable. In the other areas, late forms of the Urnfield ctr. still existed. The main characteristics of the Hallstatt ctrs. are the so-called Hallstatt swords, which were long swords of bronze, later of iron. The large straight pins of the Urnfield ctr. were replaced by a new form of pin with a catch, resembling our safety pin.

Burial customs: at first, especially during the later period of the Urnfield ctrs., cremation was practised; gradually this was replaced by burial of the whole body. The dead were occasionally placed on wagons under mortuary mounds; in the later period women and servants were sometimes killed after the death of a man and buried with him (prob. due to Scyth. infl.). Princely tombs are usually found near fortified estates (Heuneberg, Mont Lassoix-Vix). In North-eastern Germany the urns, covered by inverted bell-shaped vessels, were buried in stone boxes. The urns were sometimes shaped like houses or barns and decorated with pictures of hunting-scenes, men on horseback or horsedrawn wagons.

The La Tène ctr. (the Later Iron Age) after 450 B.C. constituted the high point of the Iron Age. It was influenced by the Scythians (via the Hallstatt ctr.), by the Greeks (via Massilia up the Rhône), by the Etruscans ('along the path of the Argonauts': i.e. along the Po, through the mt. passes of Switzerland to the Rhine and Rhône rivers). La Tène groups (who were probably connected with the Celts) brought urban civilization to culturally less advanced areas like Bohemia, the British Isles, and the Iberian Peninsula. (For the expansion of the Celts, see p. 77.) The native populations of the invaded areas show evidence of strong Celt. acculturation.

The Cimmerians and the Scythians

During the Late Bronze Age, 2 nomadic Indo-Eur. peoples spread from the eastern steppes to the w. and s.:
1. Expanding (c. 750) from the Crimean Peninsula through the Caucasus southward into Asia Minor, **the Cimmerians** threatened the Assyrian Empire. Allied with the Assyrians they dest. the kdm of Urartu (also cal. Van, see p. 35). However, they were subs. pushed westward and moved through Asia Minor, defeating the Phryg. kdm and king GYGES OF LYDIA (killed defending his land). The Cimmerians were followed by:
2. **The Scythians** who, coming out of Turkestan, drove them on and subjugated them. Pursuing the Cimmerians into Asia Minor, the Scythians struggled with the Assyrians and the Medes, and were pushed back by the Med. king, CYAXARES, in 628 B.C. CYRUS THE GREAT and DARIUS I OF PERSIA campaigned against the Scythians (DARIUS from 514–512 B.C.), who had settled N. of the Black Sea. Crossing the Dniester, the Scythians advanced along the lower Danube into the Balkans, and into the Pannonian Plains and the area s. of the Carpathians. An additional advance brought them into Brandenburg (find at Vettersfelde). Apart from the advances southward into the areas of the early riverine civilizations, the attacks also thrust to the w. The Scythians and Cimmerians reached Eastern Germany, Bavaria and – with the Thracians (as shown by finds of bridles) – Northern Italy.

The supremacy of the Scythians was founded on the **battle techniques of the steppes.** Lightly armed horsemen carried a short, composite ('Turk.') type of bow made of bone and tendons; the arrows had triangular heads of stone, bone, bronze and iron. After the conquest of Asia by the Scythians, armies of horsemen were formed throughout the Middle East, determining battle techniques for years to come.

Econ. life: raising of domestic animals (for milk and wool), and trade in prepared skins (markets in Bactria, Assyria and Greece), meat, grain and slaves (market in the Pontic (Black Sea) area).

Religion: worship of TABITI (the 'Great Goddess'), PAPEUS (the 'God of the Heavens'), APIA (the 'Earth Goddess'), OETOSYRUS (the 'Sun God') and ATIMPAASA (the 'Goddess of the Moon'). Shamans practised sorcery and witchcraft utilizing the magic power of amulets (use of rattles and clattering tins). Augury was practised with the aid of magic wands and the tearing of bast threads. There were no temples or altars.

Burial practices: princes were buried under mortuary mounds (Kurgans); the most magnificent of these are situated in Southern Russia (Western finds: Bessarabia, Wallachia, Dobrudja, Hungary, Eastern Germany). Women, servants and horses were killed and their bodies placed in the princely grave; the deceased was also supplied with abundant gifts of precious metal.

The Cimmerians, adopting the Tauric (Crimean) ctr., had strong infl. on the older Hallstatt ctr. and thus transmitted cult. elements from Asia Minor; the Scythians influenced the younger Hallstatt ctr. and the La Tène ctr.

The Venetii, Illyrii and Thracians already occupied their historic habitats.

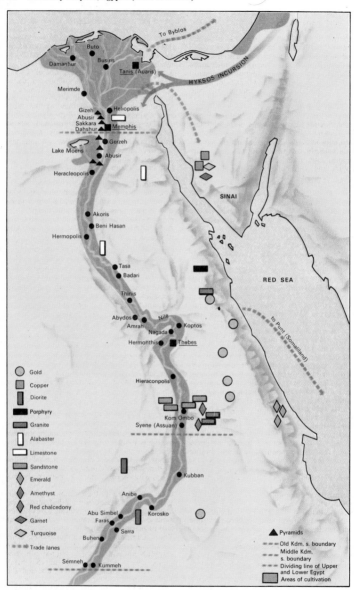

To Byblos

Buto
Damanhur
Busiris
Tanis (Auaris)
HYKSOS INCURSION
Merimde
Heliopolis
Gizeh
Abusir
Sakkara
Dahshur
Memphis
Gerzeh
Lake Moeris
Abusir
Heracleopolis
SINAI

Akoris
Beni Hasan
Hermopolis
RED SEA

Tasa
Badari
Thinis
to Punt (Somaliland)
Abydos
Nile
Amrah
Koptos
Nagada
Hermonthis
Thebes

Hieraconpolis

Gold
Copper
Diorite
Porphyry
Granite
Alabaster
Limestone
Sandstone
Emerald
Amethyst
Red chalcedony
Garnet
Turquoise
Trade lanes

Kom Ombo
Syene (Assuan)

Kubban

Anibe
Abu Simbel
Koroско
Faras
Serra
Buhen

Semneh
Kummeh

▲ Pyramids

Old Kdm, s. boundary
Middle Kdm,
s. boundary
Dividing line of Upper
and Lower Egypt
Areas of cultivation

Old Kingdom and Middle Kingdom

Egypt (acc. to HERODOTUS 'the gift of the Nile') is loc. in the fertile valley of the Nile (the 'black earth'), which is approx. 1,000 km. long, 10 to 20 km. wide, and to the E. and W. surrounded by desert (the 'red earth'). The periodic floods, occurring between July and October and carrying rich mud and silt, were the basis of the country's fertility. Subsequent to the pre-historic ctrs. of Badari ('Badarian villages'), Merimde and Nagada, the kdms of Upper and Lower Egypt developed c. 3000 B.C. The 2 kdms were united under NARMER and AHA (acc. to Gk tradition under MENES) and the cap. was founded at Memphis (the 'White Wall').

The Old Kdm (2850–2052)

2850–2650 The Thinis Period (Dynasties I–II). During this period the state was isolated from other peoples and alien influences were eliminated. Struggles with the Bedouins of the Sinai Peninsula took place and copper mines were obtained there. Excursions to Byblos (Lebanon) were undertaken (here cedar was obtained); advances into Nubia made; royal tombs constructed (*Mastaba* (Arab.) = 'bench').

2650–2190 The Age of the Pyramids (Dynasties III–VI). The polit. centre was at Memphis under the first king, ZOSER, who is buried in the step-pyramid of Sakkara (constructed by the architect and doctor, IMHOTEP, and consisting of 6 *mastabas* built one upon the other). Dynasty IV: **the pyramid builders:** SNEFRU (pyramids of Dahshur and Medum), CHEOPS, CHEPHREN and MYCERINUS (the pyramids at Gizeh, W. of Cairo). Dynasty V: the solar religion (RE of Heliopolis) became the state religion (sacred shrines with obelisks dedicated to the sun). Dynasty VI: with the increasing impotence of the Pharaohs, the power of feudal lords increased. Soc. changes quickened the breakdown of the unitary state and the S. gained its independence. Struggles among local feudal lords promoted the increasing undermining of law and order; uprisings took place, tombs were dest. The intellectual crisis is reflected in the literature of the time.

2190–2052 1st Intermediary Period (Dynasties VII–X = the Age of Heracleopolis). Of the local feudal lords, only the regional rulers of Heracleopolis attained great importance. The princes of Thebes struggled for unification.

The State: as incarnation of the god HORUS ('the Hawk'), the Pharaoh (Egyp. = 'Great House') was the absolute, hered. king. From the 4th Dynasty he was revered as the son of the Sun-God, RE. **Centralized admin. of the State.** Officials (cal. 'writers'), serving under a chief minister, were chosen from the nobility (which had lost power) by the king and appointed by him. The kdm was divided into districts and regional princes named. There was no standing army. Econ. life was based on the exchange of natural produce. Apart from taxation (grains and domestic animals) subjects were obliged to contribute labour services (*corvées*). Legal order was preserved by courts of law.

Religion: in the beginning there was a multiplicity of cults. Gods were represented as animals or as the heads of animals. During the historic period the **solar religion** was of great importance. Development of centres of important cults: RE-ATUM at Heliopolis, PTAH at Memphis and THOTH at Hermopolis. OSIRIS, the God of Fertility, became the God of the Underworld. There was belief in judgement after death and existence after death, which explains the sacrificial gifts.

The Hieroglyphs: hieroglyphic writing consisted of pictographic writing with symbols for words, groups of consonants, and single consonants; there were no vowels. Apart from this the cursive hieratic form of writing and the conventionalized 'demotic' script developed (c. 700 B.C.). The calendar (which began in mid July, i.e. at the time of the great annual flood) had 365 days ($12 \times 30 + 5$). Leap years were not considered, which explains the difference from the solar year. Later Sirius was observed and the 'Sirius year' was found to have 365 and a $\frac{1}{4}$ days.

The Middle Kdm (2052–c. 1570)

The unification of Egypt proceeded from Thebes under MENTUHOTEP II after milit. conflicts.

1991–1786 Dynasty XII. Renewed centralization of the admin. and lessening of the power of the provincial princes. The defence of Egypt was secured by the building of fortifications in the Eastern Delta and at the 2nd Cataract. Large temple complexes were erected at Karnak, the shrine of the new Imp. God, AMON. The greatest extension of the kdm and its most glorious period.

1878–1841 under Sesostris III Egyp. infl. reached into Lower Nubia (with its goldmines); trade routes developed, leading to the Red Sea, the Sinai Peninsula, Somaliland, Crete and Byblos (Lebanon). Under AMENEMHET III the Fayum was opened by the creation of Lake Moeris, and the building of the pyramid and the mortuary temple of Hawwara was undertaken ('Labyrinth'). Sculptures: the aged SESOSTRIS III, AMENEMHET III, and the royal sphinxes. A new type of statue, the crouched figure with pulled-up knees and a long gown covering the feet, was developed. Literature: 'The Maxims of King Amenemhet', 'The Tale of Sinuhe'.

1778–c.1610 2nd Intermediary Period (Dynasties XIII–XIV). Domestic polit. problems encouraged the

c. 1650 invasion by the Hyksos, a group of peoples prob. composed of Churrit (Hurrians) and Sem. tribes (Hyksos, Egyp. *hekachesut* = 'Chiefs of Foreign Lands' – refers to their upper class). The invasion resulted from the migration of peoples caused by the advances of the Indo-Eur. peoples c. 2000 B.C. The invaders formed a ruling élite and dominated Upper Egypt from their cap. Auaris in the Eastern Delta by means of their **new battle technique, utilizing horses and chariots** (Dynasties XV–XVI); however, the Hyksos conformed to the superior Egyp. ctr.

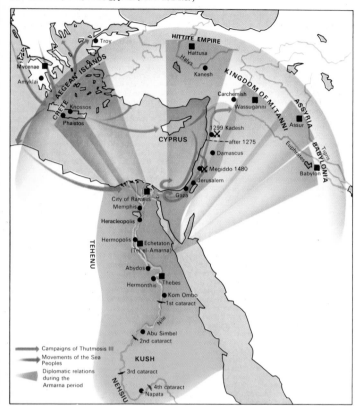

The map legend:
- Campaigns of Thutmosis III
- Movements of the Sea Peoples
- Diplomatic relations during the Armarna period

The Empire (New Kingdom)

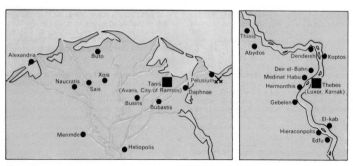

The delta region during the Late Period

Middle Egypt

The Empire (the New Kdm) (1570–715)

AMOSIS drove the Hyksos from their residence, pursued them into Palestine, and founded the New Kdm (Dynasty XVIII). Under his successors, AMENOPHIS I and THUTMOSIS I, Egypt became the leading major power: campaigns were waged into Asia to the Euphrates and into Nubia up to the 3rd Cataract. The greatest expansion of power occurred under

1501–1480 Queen Hatshepsut. War was avoided. Trade expeditions to Somaliland and vigorous building activity under the direction of her minister and favourite SEMNUT (the Terrace Temple at Deir el-Bahri) mark the period. After her (perhaps violent) death her husband (up to then 'prince consort')

1480–1448 Thutmosis III followed her on to the throne. Under him Egypt experienced its greatest territ. expansion (from the Euphrates to the 4th Cataract of the Nile).

1480 With the destruction of the Syr.–Palest. coalition at Megiddo through the use of mercenary troops and horse-drawn chariots, Phoenicia and Palestine were conquered and the Mitannian state became a neighbour (p. 35). The heirs continued the successful foreign policy of THUTMOSIS III.

1413–1377 Amenophis III, mar. to TEJE, a woman of non-noble origins, reigned luxuriously. Despite clever dyn. marriages, active diplomacy and trade with the Mitannian state, Babylonia, Crete, Cyprus, Assyria, the Hit. Empire, and the Aegean Islands (recorded on the clay tablets of el Amarna in the Akk. 'diplomatic' language), the downfall of Egyp. world-power began.

1377–1358 Amenophis IV, the 'Heretical King', mar. to NEFERTITI, introduced the worship of ATON, the sun disk (monotheism of the sun). (Hymn: 'Song of the Sun'.) The cap. was moved to Akhetaton (= 'the source of Light of Aton' – better known as el-Amarna); later AMENOPHIS adopted the name IKHNATON. Since little attention was given to foreign policy, Egyp. authority in Asia diminished. Reaction after the death of IKHNATON eliminated his relig. innovations. His sons-in-law SAMENKHKARE and TUTANKHAMEN (famous because of the richly endowed tomb found in 1922) returned the cap. to Thebes. HAREMHAB, a former general of IKHNATON, made himself king, successfully fought against the Hittites in Syria, and created internal order by tough legislation. The relig. rest. was completed, the ancient cults restored and the Amarna period condemned.

1345–1200 (Dynasty XIX): SETHOS I and RAMSES II fought the Hyksos and reconquered Syria (b. of Kadesh, 1299). c. 1275 a treaty of friendship between RAMSES II and HATTUSILIS III, the king of the Hittites, was concluded. The balance of power in Syria was restored and the boundary was again loc. along the Orontes. Egypt's new cap. during this period was the City of Ramses in the Nile delta.

1234–c. 1220: MERNEPTAN campaigned in Palestine (first mention of the tribe of Israel in the Israeltele), and against the Libyans, who were allied with the Sea Peoples (Greeks, Philistines, *et al.*).

1197–1165 Ramses III. Repeated attacks by the 'Sea Peoples' and Libyans were repulsed; prisoners taken in the battle were settled in the Delta. Under RAMSES' successors internal unrest set in. Palestine and Nubia were lost and the land was impoverished; however, a **concentration of econ. power** formed around the **large temples.**

Art: during the New Kdm enormous temple structures were erected: the temples to AMON at Karnak, Luxor and Medinet Habu. 'Amarna' art developed (the sculptured heads of IKHNATON and NEFERTITI, 'family' likenesses). Under the Ramsesides the great pillared hall of Karnak, the rock-temple of Abu Simbel, colossal statues and the mortuary temple at Medinet Habu were created.

After struggles with the priests of AMON at Thebes and the leaders of Libyan mercenary troops,

Shoshenk (c. 950, cal. SHISHAK in the Bible), proceeding from Bubastis in the Delta, obtained power. Subs. some of their priests migrated to Nubia, where their successors founded a theocratic state with its cap. at Napata (c. 750).

c. 950 Shoshenk invaded Palestine and plundered Jerusalem.

The Late Period (715–332)

715–663 Foreign rule by Ethiopia, ended by incursions of the Assyrians who, under ESSARHADDON, advanced to Thebes (671), but were pushed back by the Ethiopians.

662 Conquest of Egypt by ASSURBANAPAL (p. 31). **Egypt became an Assyr. province.** Provincial princes ruled as governors, among them the founder of the 26th Dynasty.

663–609 Psamtik, who freed Egypt from Assyr. rule and suppressed the power of the priests of AMON and the Lib. mercenaries. **Ion. mercenaries** were settled in the Delta region and Ion. trading stations were founded (Naucratis). Final blossoming of the Empire under

569–525 Amasis. Egypt became a sea power in the Eastern Mediterranean and entertained relations with the Gk islands and the Gk colonies in Cyrenaica. Defensive alliances with CROESUS OF LYDIA and POLYCRATES OF SAMOS against the Persians failed. AMASIS' son PSAMTIK III was defeated by the Pers. king CAMBYSES at Pelusium in

525. Egypt became a Pers. province (p. 45).

332 Alexander the Great conquered Egypt (p. 65). After 304, rule of the Ptolemies (p. 67). 30 B.C., beginning of Rom. domination.

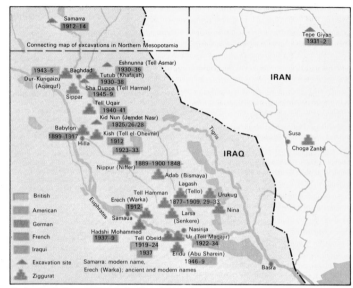

Archaeological excavations in Southern Mesopotamia

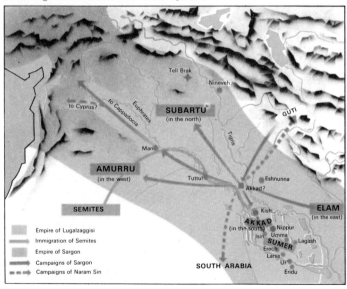

Sargon's Akkadian Empire

Sumer

c. 3200–2800 the **Sumerians** settled in Southern
Mesopotamia (= land between the streams).
Their origin is unknown; it is possible that
they came from the E. and were related to the
creators of the Indus Valley civilization. The
land was divided into city-states. The centres
of the cities were the monumental temples,
erected on rising terraces of bricks, the walls
decorated with coloured plugs of clay in
mosaic fashion. They were loc. in districts
dedicated to the god to whom the land
belonged. Possessors of polit. power and the
chief of the high priests were the **local princes**
(*Lugal* = 'great man'). They dominated both
priesthood and city. **Writing** (first pictographs,
later abstract symbols, scratched into tablets
of soft clay with slate-pencils = **cuneiform**) was
used in the admin. of the temple. **Art:** cylinder
seals took the place of stampseals (official seals
used to seal vessels containing supplies in the
temple district); small sculptures were created
of clay, stone and metal. There were also **early
manifestations of large sculptures** ('The Lady
of Warka'). **Religion:** the oldest Sum. trinity
were ENLIL, ANU and ENKI; next to them there
were UTU, the Sun-God, NANNA, the Goddess
of the Moon, and INNIN (ISTAR), the Goddess
of Love. The sexagesimal numerical system
divided the time of the day (24 hours, 60
minutes, 60 seconds) and the circle (360°).

2800 – 2500 Early Dyn. Period. Gradual infiltration by Semites. MESILIM of KISH was the
first king. Nippur became the relig. centre.
'State Socialism' associated with religion
was discontinued (state and temple were no
longer linked). The polit. power of the
palace stood independent, next to the power
of the temple. Cities were surrounded by
walls (by GILGAMESH at Erech). The temple,
erected on rising terraces, was expanded
into the Ziggurat. The Ziggurat consisted of
several storeys, connected by stairs; the
temple at the top formed the 'temple-tower'.

From 2500 Dynasty I of Ur, founded by
MESANNEPADDA. It is famous for the royal
tombs, excavated in 1922. There are 16
tombs of kings and princesses and priestesses
with rich burial gifts. The tombs also contained those who voluntarily (by poison)
followed the princes into death. This custom
was probably the consequence of the 'sacred
marriage' of the Goddess INNIN (represented
by the high priestess) to TAMMUZ, the God
of the Underworld (represented by the king).

c. 2500–2360 Dynasty I of Lagash. The ruler
URNANSHE threw off the domination of
Kish. The first historical document, the so-
called 'Stela of the Vultures', recorded the
deeds of his son EANNATUM. EANNATUM's
successor, ENTEMENA, fought the infl. of the
priesthood. The priesthood helped the fourth
ruler, UGALANDA, to ascend the throne. The
usurper, URUKAGINA, introduced soc.
reforms (through a 'contract' with the deity,
NINGIRSU, the income of the priests was cut,
and widows and orphans were protected).
LUGALZAGGISI ('King of the Lands') OF
UMMA conquered Lagash, with the aid of the
dissatisfied priesthood; he also conquered
Ur, Erech, Larsa, Kish and Nippur, and
advanced to the Mediterranean. The Empire
of Akkad rose against LUGALZAGGISI, the
last of the Sum. rulers.

The Akk. Empire

2350–2300 Sargon I of Akkad, 'ruler of the
four quarters of the world', conquered
Mesopotamia, parts of Syria and Asia
Minor, and Elam. The innovative, mobile
battle technique of the Akkadians (desert-
fighting technique), utilizing spears as
projectiles as well as bows and arrows, was
superior to the slow-moving phalanges of
the Sumerians with their long lances and
mighty shields. Sargon founded a major
centralized state and built a new cap. at
Akkad. Official inscriptions now appeared
in the Akk. language. **The ruler was considered divine.** New Akk. gods were ISTAR
ANU and the Sun-God, SAMAS. Uprisings
followed SARGON's death.

2270–2230 His grandson, NARAMSIN, 'the
God of Akkad', renewed the power of the
Empire. There was fighting in Southern
Arabia and in the Zagros mts. (recorded in
the 'Stela of the Battle'). With NARAMSIN's
death the Empire decayed.

2150–2050 Alien rule by the Gutians, who
came out of Iran and were in turn driven
out by UTUKHEGAL, king of Erech. The
Sumerians were restored to power.

2050–1950 Dynasty III of Ur (rulers: URNAMMU,
SHULGI, BURSIN, SHUSIN, IBBISIN). Rest.
of the Empire and temples of Sumer and
Akkad. The kings of city-states became
prov. governors of the New Empire under
SHULGI. By the 'sacred marriage' (see above)
SHULGI became God. He erected a mausoleum for himself and his parents in the royal
cemetery of Ur. During the rule of SHUSIN
w. Sem. tribes advanced and a line of fortifications was built at mid-course of the
Euphrates. Trade connections with India
were taken up. As a result of struggles with
the Elamites and the king of Isin, the
Empire was destroyed. Though there were
no new motifs demonstrated in **pictorial art,**
Sum. **literature** reached its highest stage
during this period. The reign was supported
by a highly developed temple and state
economy, which involved a vast bureaucratic
apparatus. At the beginning of the 3rd
Dynasty of Ur **Gudea of Lagash** attempted
to restore classical Sum. civilization. Wealth
obtained through trade made the construction of great complexes dedicated to relig.
cults possible.

After 2000 the Sem. Canaanites invaded the
Empire and considerable semitization was
the consequence. States were created at
Isin, Larsa and Babylon (*Babili* = God's
gate). Still, Sumerian survived as the
language of a cult. Sum. civilization experienced a last period of polit. and cult.
flowering under RIMSIN of LARSA (1758–
1698).

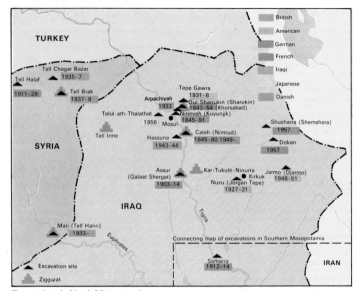

Excavations in North Mesopotamia

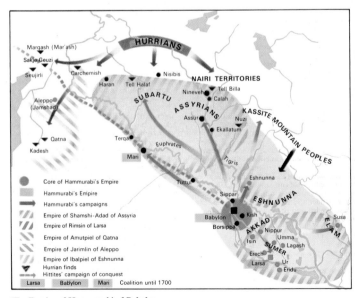

The Empire of Hammurabi of Babylon

The Old Assyr. Empire (1800–1375)

c. 2500 the **Assyrians** settled at the Upper Tigris and Greater Zab rivers. They were a tough, warlike people who had been formed by the mixing of the non-Sum. original pop. (of the Tell Halaf and Samarra ctrs.) and Sem. immigrants, and were culturally dependent on the s. The cap. and the country received their names from **Assur**, the supreme God. Assur rose following the fall of the 3rd Dynasty of Ur and conquered the Northern Babylonian territory (c. 1800). An invasion by the Hittites interrupted trade connections with the N. and NW., lessening the state income and decreasing the power of Old Assyria. The throne was regained by **Shamshi-Adad** (King of the Whole, 1749–1717) after foreign rule by NARAMSIN OF ESHNUNNA (famous for his set of laws). Shamshi-Adad's Empire included parts of the nt. regions as well as parts of Mesopotamia and Mari. He maintained an extended system of alliances. The reign was one of patriarchal absolutism. His son ISME-DAGAN was defeated by RIMSIN OF LARSA and later became a vassal of HAMMURABI. Little is known of the history of Old Assyria until 1450, when it became a vassal state of Mitanni.

Babylon

1728–1686 Hammurabi of Babylon. At his ascension to power 6 states were rivals for predominance: Larsa, Eshnunna, Babylon, Qatna, Aleppo and Assur. The 3-power league of Larsa, Mari and Babylon existed for 15 yrs to wage war with Eshnunna, Elam, the mt. peoples and Assur. With the victorious conclusion of the wars against the neighbouring peoples HAMMURABI overcame his allies, RIMSIN OF LARSA and ZIMRILIM OF MARI. During the reign of the latter the famous palace of Mari, where an archive of 20,000 clay tablets has been found (the tablets recorded the appearance of prophets at the sites of sacred cults), was completed.

HAMMURABI's concern for the life and property of his subjects was shown by the **Code of Hammurabi,** which contained reforming laws, following the principle of 'talion' ('An eye for an eye, a tooth for a tooth'). Punishments: whippings, maiming, execution (impaling, burning, drowning). The language of admin. and cult. life was Akk. The major work of ancient Mesopot. literature in its Babylonian manifestations is: *The Epic of the Creation of the World* (and the *Gilgamesh Epic*), hymns, psalms, prayers. Major deities: MARDUK of Babylon, the Sun-God, SAMAS, and the Goddess of Love, ISTAR. Under the successors of HAMMURABI the s. seceded and there were struggles with the Kassites and the Hurrians.

1531 Sack and burning of Babylon by the Hit. king, MURSILIS I (p. 35).

1530–1160 Kassite Period (the Kassites were a tribe originating in Iran).

1160 Sack of Babylon and overthrow of Kassite power by the Elamites.

From 1137 temporary great-power status of Babylon under NEBUCHADNEZZAR I (4th Babylonian Dynasty). He created a nat. monarchy and liberated the country from Elamite rule. Babylonia subs. fell under Assyr. infl.

The Hurrians

During the 2nd millennium the Hurrians migrated from the region of Lake Van into Northern Mesopotamia. From there they undertook campaigns into Assyria, Mesopotamia, Asia Minor, Syria and Palestine. Everywhere they formed an **upper class.** (*Marjanni* = knight, cf. Ind. *marj* = young hero). Landed property was hered. and could not be sold, but these regulations were circumvented by means of 'adoptions' and 'bequests'. The Hurrians were superior in battle because of their horse-drawn chariots.

Religion: the major gods were TESUD (God of the Weather), CHEPAT (Goddess of the Sun) and KUMARBI (Father of the Gods). The Arian upper classes revered the Ind. gods INDRA, MITRA and VARUNA.

Art: stone slabs incised with relief (orthostats) arranged in rows. The Hurrians built the rectangular longhouse. Their pictorial art was practised on a monumental scale.

The Middle Assyr. Empire (1375–1047)

1390–1364 ERIBA-ADAD, in alliance with the Hittites, obtained the independence of Assyria from Mitanni (p. 35). His son ASSURUBALLIT I (1364–1328) cal. himself 'Brother of the Pharaoh'. Wars of conquest in the service of the god ASSUR continued under SHALMANESER I (1273–1244) and TUKULTI-NINURTA I (1243–1207). **Brutal warfare.** Mass-deportations were carried out to destroy the substance and the nat. consciousness of the subj. peoples. Extended building programmes were carried out at Assur and Nineveh. Assyr. power declined with the invasions of the Arameans and the fall of the Hit. kdm.

Assyr. power was restored under **Tiglath-pileser I (1112–1074).** Struggles against the Nairi countries extended northward up to the region of the Black Sea. The Syrian dynasties were forced to pay tribute. TIGLATHPILESER's heirs struggled with the Arameans and Assyr. territory shrank to the core region.

Warfare: the centre point was held by the charioteers; there was also infantry, and shock troops with helmets, mail and shields. Iron was introduced after 1200 because of the enforced settlement of Hit. blacksmiths (the Assyrians possessed the iron-ore deposits of Asia Minor).

Law. Barbarically severe punishments: puncturing of ears; severance of ears, lower lips and fingers; castration; destruction of faces by the application of boiling asphalt.

Econ. life: land was owned by the temple, the crown and the nobility. Agriculture reached a high point of development (technically improved ploughs), as did gardening.

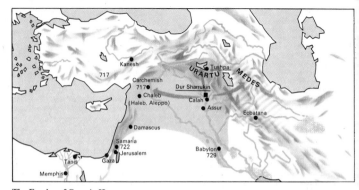

The Empire of Sargon II

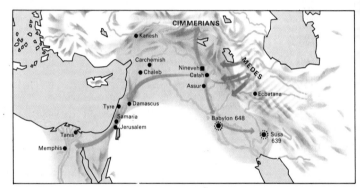

The Empire of Assurbanapal

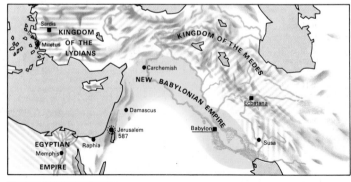

The New Babylonian Empire

The New Assyr. Empire

ADADNIRARI II engaged in conflicts in Northern Mesopotamia (909–889).

883–859 his great-grandson ASSURNASIRAPLI II, **the cruellest of the Assyr. kings**, subs. created an empire which corresponded to that of TIGLATHPILESER I in size. The resistance of neighbouring peoples was broken by annual campaigns which used **cavalry** for the first time in the history of warfare. Cruel methods of subjugation put the conquered into a state of fear: impalement, scourging and mass-executions. A new residence with a gigantic palace was est. at Calah, populated by deportees. ASSURNASIRAPLI's son

858–824 SHALMANESER III cemented overlordship in Syria and Palestine so as to control the trade routes from the Euphrates and Tigris to the Mediterranean Sea. The subjugation of Damascus, the Aramean cap., was not accomplished. At this time (835) the Medes and Persians were first mentioned. A revolt towards the end of SHALMANESER's reign was suppressed by his son SHAMSHIADAD V, but only with the aid of Babylon. Again with Babylonian aid, Assyria was able to stand its ground against the Medes, who est. themselves in the region of Lake Urmia (p. 45).

810–806 SAMMURAMAT (Gk Semiramis) carried out a successful domestic and foreign policy during the minority of the heir to the throne. Her son ADADNIRARI III conflicted with the Babylonians, the Medes, and esp. the kdm of Urartu (Ancient Armenia, sometimes cal. the Vannic kdm; p. 35). The autocratic conduct of the Assyr. governors and the weakness of the crown were overcome by

745–727 Tiglathpileser III, founder of Assyr. world-dominion. SARDURI II of Urartu was defeated and Northern Syria, Damascus and Gaza were conquered. Under the name PUL he became king of Babylon (729). Under his successor SHALMANESER V there was unrest in Syria and Palestine as well as disputes with the priesthood. SHALMANESER V was assassinated during the siege of Samaria.

722–705 SARGON II (*Sharrukin* = 'Just ruler'). He revived the privileges of aristocracy and priesthood: The last of the Hit. states were subj., the kdm of Urartu defeated; struggles with the Medes took place, and the Babylonians were overcome; the Egyptians were defeated at Raphia (Rafah). SARGON built a residence at Dur Sharrukin ('Sargon's palace'). His son

704–681 SENNACHERIB was an extravagant despot. He subj. Judea in 701 (siege of Jerusalem) and dest. Babylon. Utilizing enormous armies of forced labourers, he transformed Nineveh into the country's cap. (double walls 25 m. high with 15 gates). A canal 50 km. long, conducted over an aqueduct 280 m. long and 22 m. wide, was dug to supply water for the city. His severity, opulence and brutal conduct brought about his murder. His younger son

680–669 ESARHADDON suppressed an uprising by his brothers and ordered the rebuilding of Babylon. Allied with the Scythians, he pushed the Cimmerians back and conquered Egypt, short of Nubia. **Under him Assyria achieved its greatest territ. expansion.**

668–626 ASSURBANAPAL dest. Thebes. Supported by all Assyria's enemies, his brother SHAMASHSHUMUKIN rose against him, making it impossible for him to hold on to Egypt, a task also made difficult by the long distances involved. In 648 Babylon was conquered. In 639 Susa (Elam) was dest. The large library at Nineveh was est. (it contained over 22,000 clay tablets, incl. poetry, lit., historical, philosophical, medical and astronomical texts as well as records of business transactions). Internal unrest and Scyth. incursions weakened the state. CYAXARES OF MEDIA and NABOPOLASSAR OF BABYLONIA **conquered and dest. all Assyr. cities** (Ashur 614, Nineveh 612, Charran (Haran) 608). The pop. was wiped out, the land laid waste.

Art: enormous palace-structures with ornamental sculptures in scale at Nineveh, Calah, Dur Sharrukin and Ashur ('historical pictography' represented in scenes of the hunt, war and relig. cults worked in relief).

The New Babylonian Empire (625–539)

Continued attempts by the Chaldeans to obtain Babylon were successful only after the death of ASSURBANAPAL.

625–605 NABOPOLASSAR king of Babylonia, Elam, Western Mesopotamia, Syria and Palestine.

604–562 NEBUCHADNEZZAR II, a skilled diplomat, caused the Empire to flourish. He enlarged Babylon, building the 'Processional Avenue', the 'Istargate', and the cen. temple 'Esagila' ('House of the Risen Head') with 'Etemenanki', the terraced tower ('House of the Creation of Heaven and Earth' = the legendary Tower of Babel, total height 90 m.). A balance of power between the great powers was est.

598 Occupation of Jerusalem because of the alliance between Judea and Egypt (1st Deportation; p. 37). 587 Destruction of Jerusalem (p. 37). Subs. signs of decay became apparent and there was conflict with the priests of Marduk, who helped NABONIDUS, the 'archaeologist on the throne', to become king (555–539). Unwise measures against the priesthood forced the king to leave Babylon for Tema, a city loc. on an oasis. For the final decade Babylon was under the regency of BALSAZER.

539 Conquest of Babylonia by the Pers. king CYRUS II, making it a Pers. province.

331 Alexander the Great conquered Babylonia (p. 65).

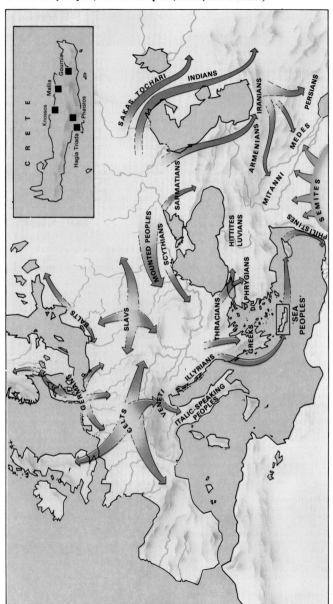

Expansions of the Indo-Europeans, Crete

The Indo-Europeans

The existence of the Indo-Europeans is demonstrated not so much by archaeological evidence as by their language. All Eur. peoples, with the exception of the Basques and the Finno-Ugrians, speak Indo-Eur. languages, which include Celtic, Germ., Italic, Slav. and Baltic. Illyrian, Venetian, Thracian, Phryg., Hit., Luwian, Tocharian and Old Ind. are extinct. Gk, Armenian and Iran. exist to this day. The Indo-Eur. languages are divided into **2 groups:** the Satem and the Kentum (the E. and W. group). The difference lies in the pronunciation of the palatal 'k-sound', in some languages pronounced 's', e.g. the number 100 = Old Ind. *sata, awest. satem;* Gk *hekaton;* Lat. *centum.*

The home of the Indo-Europeans was prob. the region between Cen. Europe and Southern Russia (in earliest times they prob. lived in the Kirghiz steppes of Western Kazan, which explains their relationship to the Ural-Altaic linguistic group). It is therefore wrong to simplify and speak of Indo-European as a primordial language, or of the Indo-Eur. people as primordial people and of their home as the original home of man. But a distinction between the Eastern and the Western group may be made. The **development of Indo-European into distinct languages** does not have to be explained as the separation into single units; rather, it may be accounted for by the intermingling of alien linguistic elements. An Indo-Eur. community prob. existed during the Neolithic; the separation into distinct peoples took place c. 2000.

Econ. life: a comp. view of the early period of the Indo-Eur. peoples shows that gold, silver and copper (Lat. = *aes*) were known. The Indo-Europeans raised domestic animals: horses, cattle, sheep, dogs, goats and pigs. This suggests that raising animals was the predominant occupation. Agriculture was introduced only later following advancement into regions having a superior ctr. Pottery and weaving were practised.

Society: large families were organized on the basis of patriarchal law. A broad lower class was dominated by the lords and their retinue, who mostly occupied themselves with the hunt and the pursuit of warfare. Weapons: axe, bow and arrow.

Religion: a hierarchy of gods, the God of the Heavens the supreme deity.

Expansion: the advance of the **Cord-impressed ware** or **Battle-Axe people** into Cen. Germany is prob. linked to the expansion of the Indo-Eur. peoples, for the cult. make-up of the earliest Indo-Eur. peoples first applied to them. **The migrations of the Indo-Eur. peoples** began c. 2000, leading to the establishment of the first Indo-Eur. states in Asia Minor and India (aristocratic society with horse-drawn chariots).

Crete

Cretan civilization – following the outline of its discoverer, SIR ARTHUR EVANS – is divided into the Early, Middle, and Late Minoan periods. Each of these periods is again subdivided into 3 chronological segments (Early Minoan I–III, Middle Minoan I–III, Late Minoan I–III). The Neolithic and sub-Neolithic age is followed by the

2600–2000 Early Minoan period (I–III), known for the harbour-cities erected in Eastern Crete and the circular tombs in the Mesara (*tholoi* = burial chambers). Archaeological finds: seals, copper and bronze daggers, and gold jewellery. Min. civilization fl. *c.* 2200 (the age which witnessed the destruction of Troy II).

2000–1570 Period of the first ('older') unfortified palaces (Middle Minoan I–II) at Knossos, Phaistos and Mallia. The palaces were centres of **econ. life** with vast storage space for oil, grain and wine. The inhabitants traded with the Gk mainland and the Syr. and Egyp. ports. Pictographic writing developed as a result of Egyp. infl. There were no conquests. **Applied arts:** production of **ceramics** fl. at Kamares: vessels of stone and faience (glazed earthenware). At the time of the Hyksos invasion of Egypt (p. 23) the first palaces were dest. **Religion:** no images; ecstatic rites in natural shrines and sacred caves. Worship of a Mother/Earth Goddess (as mistress of the animals, the Serpent Goddess, and the Goddess of the Shield), and male gods.

1570–1425 Flowering of the ('younger') palaces (Middle Minoan III–Late Minoan II) at Knossos, Phaistos and Hagia Triada (with grandiose structures surrounding a cen. courtyard). This period witnessed the establishment of an empire with the development and improvement of a cen. admin. and an economy following the Egyp. model. Unchallenged **maritime supremacy** (Thalassocracy). Active barter with Middle Kdm Egypt. Pictographic script replaced by Linear A (pre-Gk language). Women held a privileged position in society. During the 16th cent. B.C. the palace of Knossos was twice damaged by earthquakes, but was each time rebuilt. During the 15th cent. the Achaeans from the mainland began to settle. They quickly gained infl. The original inhabitants left the palaces of Mallia, Hagia Triada and Phaistos. The conquerors now used as script Linear B, already being used for the Gk language on the mainland. **Art:** changes in the repertoire of ornamental forms (Tektonik). Last flowering of Knossos: the 'palace style' in ceramics and the painting of frescoes.

c. 1425, the destruction of the palace of Knossos by fire occurred during an unsuccessful revolt of the Cret. pop. against their new masters from Mycenae. Definitive establishment of Ach. dominance (p. 47).

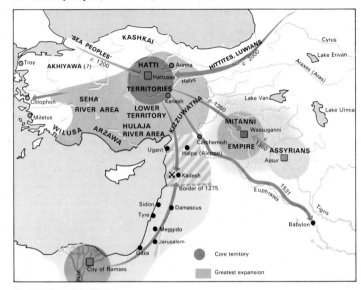

The Kingdom of the Hittites

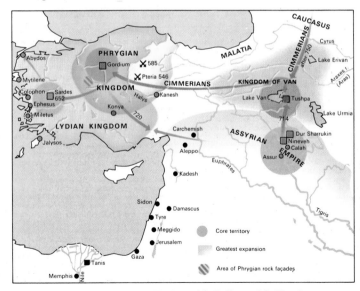

The Kingdom of Van (Urartu) and the Kingdoms of the Lydians and the Phrygians

The Hittites

The most ancient people of Indo-Eur. ctr., the Hittites, invaded with the Luwians the area of Cen. Asia Minor – settled then by proto-Hatti peoples – *c.* 2000 B.C. (Languages: Hattic, the language of the Hatti of Asia Minor; Luwian, the language of the Luwians; and Kanesian, the language of the Hittites.) The name 'Hittite' ·is not of Indo-Eur. origin, but is known from the O.T. and from Assyr. historiography. The polit. beginnings of the kdm are unknown. Following severe fighting with the native pop., a kdm was est. in Anatolia with its cap. at Kussar.

1640–1380 The Old Hit. Kdm, founded by LABARNAS, whose name became the title of succeeding Hit. kings. Under his successor HATTUSILIS I the polit. centre of the state was removed to Khatusas. An advance into Syria was undertaken. His successor MURSILIS I defeated Aleppo and conquered Babylon (1531). After his murder the kdm was weakened by domestic unrest (royal assassinations). The reforms of TELEPINUS (*c.* 1460) restored order in the interior: the order of succession was regulated by law; the privileges of the nobility were retained. Under his successors the kdm was strengthened.

1380–1200 The New Hit. Kdm.

1380–1346 Under SUPPILULIUMAS the Hit. kdm was recognized as a great power. Large areas of Asia Minor were subj., and the **Mitanni kdm,** which had experienced its period of flowering 1450–1350, was dest. The Mitanni cap. was at Wassuganni. The most important Mitanni ruler was SAUSHSATAR, whose territory reached from the Zagros mts to the Mediterranean, and from Lake Van to Assur. Under TUSRATTA, the Assyrians and Hittites attacked the Mitanni. Ugarit, Aleppo and Carchemish in Syria became Hit. dependencies. The Hit. king MURSILIS II fought successfully in the E. and the W. MUWATALLIS (1315–1290) defeated the Egyptians at Kadesh in Syria (p. 25). *c.* 1200 the kdm collapsed under the stormy attacks of the 'Sea Peoples'. After the time of SUPPILULIUMAS there was contact with the **Achaeans (Akhiyawa).**

Religion: adoption of Khurrish and proto-Hit. gods (the Sun-Goddess of Arinna). From Babylon the Hittites learned of ritual, omen and magic.

Society: at the head of the feudal state was the king (*Labarna*), whose succession to the throne in each case was determined by his predecessor; after death he was deified. He was the supreme judge, priest and war-lord. The queen occupied a strong position (*Tawananna*); there was also the nobility (a free estate of warriors), the infl. of which was later diminished by bureaucratic officials. War was rarely conducted in brutal fashion. Legislation was humane: monetary fines and jail sentences; the rights of men and women were protected.

Van, Phrygia and Lydia

Vannic kdms were est. in Eastern Anatolia during the 13th cent. They had predominantly Khurrish populations. The attempts of the Assyrians to gain polit. infl. in these areas failed. As Assyr. power receded

c. 835–825 SARDURI I founded the kdm of Van or Urartu (bib. Ararat) in the region of Lake Urmia and Lake Van. The wealth of the country was based on the production of iron and copper. These people were active traders. Their cap. was loc. at Tushpa (later Van). Under SARDURI's successors, Van became a major power. The boundaries of the state were defined by the Euphrates, Lake Urmia, Aleppo and Lake Erivan. An advance across the Tigris and Euphrates was made under SARDURI II, but he was defeated by TIGLATHPILESER III.

714 Victory of Assyria over Van. From 620, incursion by the Scythians from Southern Russia. After 600, immigration of the Indo-Eur. Armenians. From 610 Van was part of the Median Empire (p. 45).

The kdm was administered by bureaucratic officials; at the head was the king, the servant of CHALDI, the nat. deity. Media was the country most advanced in metal work techniques. Grain, wine and fruits were grown: irrigation systems.

c. 800 the Phryg. kdm was est. in Anatolia (cap. Gordium). The most important ruler was MIDAS (Assyr. MITA), famous in Gk mythology for his legendary treasures of gold. MIDAS mar. a Gk princess. The Phrygians struggled with the Assyrians. In 709 they concluded peace and began paying tribute to SARGON II. During the 7th cent. the Cimmerians entered Phrygia and subjected it to their rule (p. 21).

Religion: orgiastic cult of the 'Great Mother' (CYBELE) and of her lover ATTIS; worship of SABAZIUS (DIONYSIUS), the god of wine.

Following on the collapse of the Phryg. kdm, the Lyd. kdm under the Mermnadae dynasty gained in importance.

680–652 GYGES dethroned KANDAULES and subj. Western Asia Minor; but he fought without success against the Gk cities, conquering only Colophon. GYGES was killed in the defensive struggle against the Cimmerians. His son ARDYS restored Lyd. power and continued the struggle against the Gk cities (Priene fell).

605–560 Alyattes, who made Lydia into a major power, expanded the frontiers of the kdm to the River Halys (585). *c.* 575 Smyrna was dest. 585–546 balance of power between Media, Babylonia, Lydia and Egypt.

560–546 Croesus, his son, subj. all the Gk cities of Asia Minor, exc. Miletus. He made rich gifts to the Gk temples. A preventive war against the Persians failed.

546 Defeat at Pteria. **Lydia became a province of Persia** (p. 45). The most important contribution of the Lydians to civilization was the **development of coined money** (7th cent.).

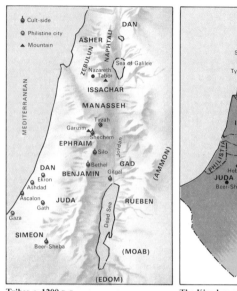

Tribes, c. 1200 B.C.

The Kingdom of David

The Kingdoms of Israel and Judah

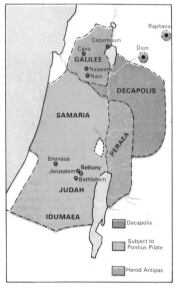

Palestine in the time of Christ

After 1500, contemporaneously with the migrations of the Arameans into that region, **the Israelite tribes advanced into Palestine.** c. 1250, under the leadership of Moses, some of the tribes left Egypt (God's revelation on Mt Sinai: the pact between God and the chosen Israelite tribes; Jehovah the only Lord; the Ark of the Covenant the focal point of relig. life). Ties were est. with the tribes already in Palestine.

c. 1200 the **League of the 12 Tribes** was formed (Amphictyony: the polit. and cult. union of the inhabitants of the region for the protection of a centrally loc. shrine). The league was founded on the common origins and relig. worship of the tribes. The Judges (tribal leaders) watched over relig. worship and the observation of God's law (1200–1000).

From 1200 the coast of Palestine was settled by the Philistines (part of the stormy attacks of the 'Sea Peoples'), and a league of city-states est. (Ashdad, Ascalon, Ekron, Gaza, Gath). During the 11th cent. there was strong pressure by the Philistines and the Ammonites (Eastern Jordan); **the kdm of Israel** was est. as a defensive measure.

c. 1010 **Saul,** the leader in the struggle against the Ammonites, was proclaimed king. After a brief reign he was defeated by the Philistines on the plain of Jezreel. Saul's son Ishbaal ruled briefly in the N. In the s.

c. 1006–966 **David** was anointed king at Hebron. Judah and Israel were united. The Philistines were defeated. Jerusalem was captured, and was made the relig. and polit. cap. (here the Ark of the Covenant was kept and a strict admin. was est.). Using mercenaries, David successfully fought the Moabites, Ammonites and Edomites. With the conquest of the remaining Canaanite city-states, a major Palest. state was est. David's successor was the son of his wife Bathsheba.

c. 966–926 The son-in-law of a Pharaoh, **Solomon** was a great diplomat. But he lost the Aram. provinces despite his capabilities. The Edomite kdm was re-established. Great building projects were carried out at Jerusalem (the palace, the Temple of Jehovah), financed by the wealth obtained in trade with Arabia in cooperation with Hiram of Tyre (p. 39). A centralized state was created with a system of taxation and labour services. The land was divided into 12 provinces, each of which had to assume the expenses of the court one month in the year. A fleet of chariots was maintained. With the death of Solomon

926 **The kdm divided** into a southern kdm (Judah, cap. Jerusalem) under Rehoboam, and a northern kdm (Israel, cap. Shechem, later Tirzah and Pnuel, then Samaria) under Jeroboam, who elevated the ancient shrines of Dan and Bethel to royal shrines.

926–722 **The Kdm of Israel.** Following internal unrest and struggles with Egypt, Aram. Damascus and the Philistines, the army advanced its leader (878–871) Omri to the throne. Stabilization of power in the interior. Samaria, a milit. strong-point, became the relig. and polit. cap. Moab was again incorp. into the state.

871–852 Ahab, Omri's son, succeeded and mar. the Phoen. princess Jezebel. His daughter Athaliah mar. King Joram of Judah. Phoen. deities were introduced and worshipped. The prophet Elijah became leader of a Jehovic counter-movement against the 'House of Omri'.

845–817 Jehu was anointed king by a delegate of the prophet Elisha. The Omrites were eliminated and the cult of Baal suppressed. Tribute was paid to the Assyrians. During the unrest of the subsequent period, Amos and Hosea appeared as representatives of the pure Jehovic religion and predicted Israel's demise (outrage over exploitation of the poor).

722 Sargon II **dest. Samaria** after a 3-year siege (p. 31). Resettlement of many Israelites in Media and Mesopotamia. Israel became an Assyr. province. The remaining pop. mingled with new arrivals: the Samaritans.

925–587 **The Kdm of Judah.** The relationship of Judah to the northern kdm under the early rulers was tense. Close relations were est. under Joram (852–845). Athaliah (845–839) ruled tyrannically after the elimination of the Omrites. The House of David was eradicated. The worship of Baal was introduced. Athaliah was murdered in 839. Her successor was Jehoash. His son Amaziah paid tribute to Damascus. Judah was defeated by the Israelites and the treasure of the Temple was stolen. Appearance of the prophet Isaiah, who gave polit. counsel.

725–697 Strengthened by an alliance with Egypt, Hezekiah attempted to break away from Assyria. Sennacherib (p. 31) defeated the Egyptians, subjected Judah and threatened Jerusalem (701). Hezekiah's son Manasseh was once again a vassal of Assyria. Under his great-grandson

639–609 **Josiah** a spiritual regeneration set in after an ancient text of laws (prob. the Book of Deuteronomy) was found in the Temple. The Temple was purified and all other sacred symbols were dest.
The prophet Jeremiah appeared, but his message of impending doom was rejected. Internal and foreign conflicts (succession struggles and the war between Egypt and Babylonia) led to the siege by Nebuchadnezzar II, which lasted 1½ yrs.

587 It culminated in the **conquest and destruction of Jerusalem.**

586–538 The 'Babylonian captivity' (p. 31). Subs. the Diaspora (Gk = 'dispersal') became the fate of the **Jews** (a term now applied to the people as a whole instead of 'Israelites' and 'Hebrews').

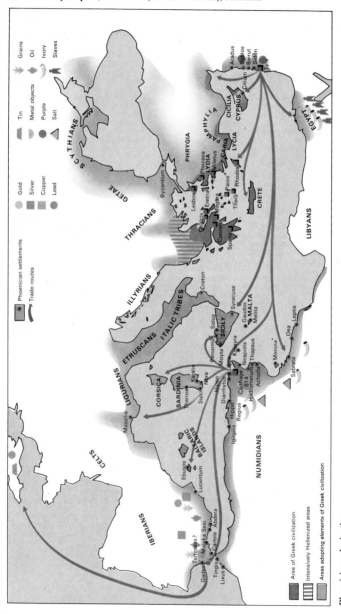

Phoenician colonization

Grains
Oil
Ivory
Slaves

Tin
Metal objects
Purple
Salt

Gold
Silver
Copper
Lead

Phoenician settlements
Trade-routes

Area of Greek civilization
Intensively Hellenized areas
Areas adopting elements of Greek civilization

CELTS

IBERIANS

Tartessos?
Gades Malaka Sexi
Tingis Carteia Abdera
Lixus

Ebusos
BALEARIC ISLANDS
Lucentum

LIGURIANS

Massilia

CORSICA

SARDINIA
Tharros Nora
Karalis
Sulcis

NUMIDIANS

Iglgilis
Hippo
Regius

ETRUSCANS

ITALIC TRIBES

Croton

Panormus
Solus
SICILY
Motya Neapolis
Kossyra Thapsus
Hippo
Diarrhytus Achollla
Carthage Hadrumetum
814

Gaudos
Melita
MALTA

Meninx

Oea Leptis
Sabrata

LIBYANS

ILLYRIANS

THRACIANS

GETAE

SCYTHIANS

Byzantium

PHRYGIA

Lesbos
Chalcis Phocaea
Eretria Miletus
Megara LYDIA
Corinth Paros CARIA
Thera Rhodes LYCIA
Sparta PAMPHYLIA
CRETE CILICIA

CYPRUS
Citium

Aradus
Byblos
Berut
Sidon
Tyre

EGYPT

Israel

539 With the conquest of the New Babylonian Empire by CYRUS II, **Palestine** became **part of the Pers. Empire.** The Temple was reconstructed and some of the deported returned. A polit. and relig. revival began under NEHEMIAH and EZRA (the city walls were rebuilt, the agrarian pop. resettled, debts forgiven and the inhabitants of Judah prohibited from marrying members of alien peoples). Jerusalem was not only the sacral centre of the post-exile community, but also the polit. focal-point of the province of Judah (seat of the governor). A law promulgated by EZRA (458 (?), Pentateuch, Sacred Law, the Priests' Writ, the first 5 books of the O.T.) formed the basis of the religion of the Law (the Law was the gift of God). All life was governed by the Law. Its knowledge, exposition and interpretation by scholars therefore became necessary in the synagogues (schools). The foundation for religiously and politically active Judaism was thereby laid. The high priest led the Jerusalem relig. community. The sacrificial rites were performed by the Zadokian priests; lesser services were performed by the Levites.

From 332 Palestine was under the **rule of Alexander the Great.** The Samaritans separated from the Jews and created their own shrine at Mt Gerizim (the Samaritan Schism). They adopted the books of Pentateuch as their Holy Writ.

c. 200 the O.T. was translated into Gk ('Septuaginta'). Another centre of Judaism developed in Egypt (Alexandria). Under Hellen. infl., the community split into Hellen. and Orth. factions, the latter adhering to the laws.

168 **Revolt of the Hasmoneans** (Maccabees) (MATTATHIAS and his sons, esp. JUDAS MACCABEUS) against the Seleucids to regain relig. and polit. freedom (Religious War). Although the overlordship of the Seleucids was acknowledged from 142, the Jews retained a large measure of polit. independence.

140–137 Kdm of the Hasmoneans.

Development of relig. groups: the **Pharisees,** loyal to the Law but believing in the separateness of Jew. life; the **Saducees,** a strongly conservative group who rejected belief in immortality; and the **Essenes,** who believed in preparation for a messianic kdm through ascetic living, rites of purification and monast. communities (Chirbet Qumran, after 1947 discoveries at Wadi Qumran the 'Dead Sea Scrolls')).

63 **Pompey** incorp. Palestine into the Roman Empire (Conquest of Jerusalem, imposition of tribute duties).

39–4 B.C. **Herod the Great** appointed king of the Jews by the Rom. senate. With the tacit approval of the Romans, he eliminated the Hasmoneans and took possession of Jerusalem (37). His kdm was divided between his sons: ARCHELAUS received Judah, Samaria and Idumaea (in A.D. 6 he was banished and PONTIUS PILATE appointed Rom. governor); HEROD ANTIPAS received Galilee and Pereae. JOHN THE BAPTIST was murdered during the reign of HEROD ANTIPAS.

Appearance of Christ. Annunciation of the beginning of the Kdm of God. CHRIST was executed by crucifixion after being convicted for blasphemy (c. A.D. 33).

A.D. 66–70 Revolt of the Jews after the Romans demanded adherence to the cult of the Emperor and erected an imp. shrine in Jerusalem.

70 Conquest and **destruction of Jerusalem** by TITUS, son of VESPASIAN (p. 97).

133 Suppression of a Jew. revolt by HADRIAN. Jews were no longer allowed to reside in Jerusalem; a new relig. centre was est. in Jamnia.

Phoenicia

Kasios in the N., Mt Carmel in the S., and the Lebanon range in the E. formed the boundaries of Phoenicia. The kdm consisted of politically autonomous **city-states** under the overlordship of a king (leading families participated in the gvt of the cities). The chief cities were Aradus, Byblos, Beirut, Sidon and **Tyre,** the leading power between 1000 and 774.

969–936 HIRAM I. Extensive trade in the Red Sea and the Mediterranean provided wealth (cooperation with SOLOMON).

During the 8th cent. the Phoen. cities were dependent on Assyria.

701 Conquest of Phoenicia (exc. Tyre) by SENNACHERIB (p. 31).

From 586 Phoenicia belonged to the New Babylonian Empire; only Tyre was able to withstand a siege of 13 yrs (585–573). Under Pers. rule vassal kdms were est. Later they submitted to ALEXANDER THE GREAT without resistance.

332 Tyre was, however, only conquered after a 7-month siege.

Commerce: Following upon the collapse of Cret.–Myc. power (c. 1200), the Phoenicians took over Medit. trade. Export goods: glassware, cloth dyed with purple, metal articles manufactured in factories utilizing motifs created in Mesopotamia and Asia Minor. **Phoen. writing,** adopted by the Greeks as the 'Phoen. symbols', developed c. 1000. The Lat. alphabet, the basis of our Rom. characters, proceeded from the Gk.

814 Tyre **est. Carthage** ('New City'). After the home cities were conquered by the Assyrians, Carthage gained polit. power in the Western Mediterranean. From 650, Carthage possessed its own fleet and armies (later mercenaries) and became the protector of the western Phoen. colonies. Carthage had an aristocratic constitution; but there were conflicts between the council and the elected milit. leader. Supreme deities: BAAL, HAMMON and ASTARTE. Human sacrifice.

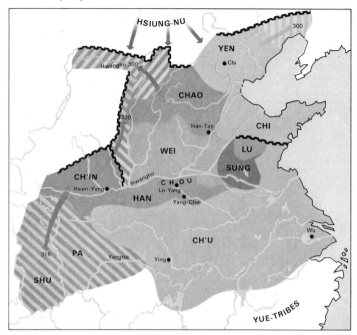

The 'Epoch of the Warring States'

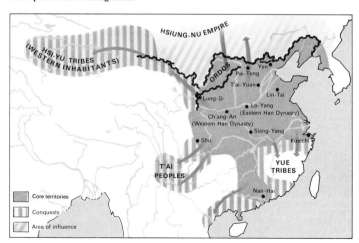

China during the Han Dynasty

The Neolithic ctrs. of Kansu, Yang-shao (Western Honan) and Lung Shan, and the as yet not clearly defined ctr. of Northern Hopei, were followed by the legendary Hsia Dynasty (c. 1800–1500).

1500–1000 The Shang Dynasty est. a feudal state in North-eastern Honan under a king who also had priestly functions. The cities, incorporating temple structures, were fortified by walls. Symbolic script was developed and used by oracular priests. The chariot was in use. The site of the royal residence was moved several times and there were struggles with neighbouring tribes.

Religion: at the centre was the Tao (= the way), the principle governing the ordered universe; besides the Tao, the 'sublime heavens', nature, and the spirits of ancestors were worshipped; a cult of sacrifice and the reading of oracles were also practised.

1000–770 Western Chou Dynasty. This was a purely feudal state: the king's land was loc. in the centre, surrounded by the domains of his vassals, which again were bordered by smaller feudal states. Consequently, cen. power had no chance to expand; the vassals therefore grew strong and summoned nomads into the land. A high proportion of royal land was lost following the relocation of the cap. at Loyang (770).

770–256 Eastern Chou Dynasty. The power of the kings waned, the independence of the feudal lords increased. Larger principalities were est. which allied with one another in defence against the nomads. The country was distressed by continual wars, which led to impoverishment for some of the nobility. The peasants gained in importance, since they now became the determining factor in the conduct of warfare (the peasants deciding the outcome of battles rather than the noble charioteers). The merchant class became the most important element sustaining the state; merchants collected from vassals the duties-in-kind so important to sustain the cities.

551–479 Confucius founded an ethical system, strengthened by religion, which stressed confidence in human inclinations to morality and humanitarianism.

6th cent. Lao-tze. The heart of Lao-tze's mystic teaching was the Tao, the source and fountain of all being and truth. Human society was to be governed by the wise man. During the 5th cent., Mo Ti called for 'universal love'. Condemnation of all wars of aggression.

403–221 Chan-kuo period ('Epoch of the Warring States'). Division of China into sep. states. Admin. of the states through professional bureaucrats. Increasing importance of the cities as centres of admin., and growth of a bourgeoisie.

221 Cheng, the ruler of Ch'in, annexed the remaining 6 states of Han, Chao, Wei, Ch'u, Yen and Ch'i. Introduction of cavalry, adopted from the w.; utilization of iron replaced bronze weapons. Among the states competing for power, the well-organized border-state of Ch'in gradually gained ascendency.

221–206 Ch'in Dynasty. Title of the ruler: 'First most Sublime Ruler of the Ch'in'. A unitary centralized state, governed by officials, was est. Territ. division of the country into departments and prefectures. A reform measure standardized weights, measures, coins and script; regional differences were thereby eliminated and trade improved. Chancellor Li Ssu ordered 'book-burning' to destroy feudal traditions (213). Milit. advances were made to the N. (against the Huns – building of the 'Great Wall' which, however, consisted mainly of earthen mounds) and to the s. Opposition to centralization led to conflicts and the formation of the

206 B.C.–A.D. 9 Western Han Dynasty, which adopted the administrative system of the Ch'in, but integrated it with the feudal organization of the Chou. Constitution and admin. were democratized and a bureaucratic state est. with the following functions: to raise taxes, administer irrigation systems and direct commerce and traffic. Defence against the Huns, who had united their tribes during the 3rd cent., was the objective of foreign policy. The pinnacle of power was reached under

140–87 Emperor Wu Ti, who fought the Huns victoriously. The Empire thereby gained its largest territ. extension. The feudal power of the nobles was eliminated. Transcontinental trade flourished on the 'silk-roads'. Still, wars caused internal econ. difficulties. Under Wu Ti's successors the strength of the Huns was broken (they migrated westward). The great noble families fought between themselves. The representatives of one of these families

A.D. 9–23 Wang Mang raised himself to the throne, but was not successful with his polit. reform programme. The loss of the Cen. Asiatic provinces and natural catastrophes provoked numerous uprisings; among them the revolt of the 'red eyebrows'.

25–250 Eastern Han Dynasty, founded by Liu-Hsiu, a descendant of the Han emperors, who took the name of Kuang Wu-ti on becoming Emperor. A new flowering of the Empire followed: overseas trade was initiated from Nan-hai (Canton). Chin. silk was exported to the Rom. Empire. By the end of the 1st cent. A.D., China had regained the power position of the time of Wu-ti: Turkestan was conquered and the Pers. Gulf reached. Paper was invented c. 100. During the 1st cent. Buddhism spread from India. Internal struggles at the imp. court subs. (184) led to the popular rebellion of the 'yellow turbans' (the problems at the imp. court concerned questions of succession, the power of the empresses and their retinues, and the infl. of the eunuchs).

220 Ts'ao P'ei (founder of the Wei Dynasty) forced the last of the Han rulers to resign.

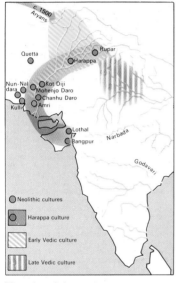

The early period

Neolithic cultures

Harappa culture

Early Vedic culture

Late Vedic culture

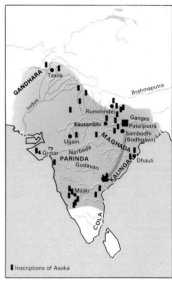

The Empire of Asoka

Inscriptions of Asoka

India, c. A.D. 150

Roman trading ports

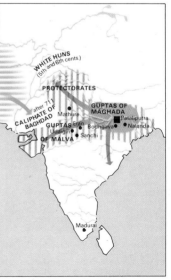

The Gupta Empire, c. A.D. 400

c. 3000 B.C. Neolithic Indus ctrs. in NW. India (Amri, Nal, Quetta, Kulli, Nundara). The most important ctr. of India's early history was

2500–1800 the Harappa ctr. Ruled by kings (rajahs), and superior kings (maharajahs), the Harappa civilization was marked by cities constructed to a chequerboard plan (a castle hill dominating the city) with brick houses and canal systems. Trade was carried on along the river. Seals depicting animal figures were in use (among them a seal with a male figure seated in the yoga position, surrounded by animals and representing SHIVA). Possibly contact existed with the Sumerians (p. 27).

c. 1500 the Aryans ('Arya'), a people of Indo-Eur. origin, migrated from the NW. into the Ganges valley.

1500–1000 The Early Vedic period. The Aryans, who used the chariot, were militarily superior to the original inhabitants (the Dravidians). A peasant ctr. with individual homesteads, herds of animals, but little grain production, developed.

1000–600 The Late Vedic period. Gradual expansion in the region of the Ganges and advance into the area of present-day Delhi. Struggles between the Aryan tribes.

Religion: the Vedas (cf. Lat. vidi = 'I have seen, I know'; sacred 'knowledge') are the world's most ancient sacred writings. They were written in Sanskrit, an Indo-Eur. language. c. 1000 the Rigveda was composed (the Samaveda, the Yajurveda and the Atharvaveda were composed later). In addition to impersonal power, represented by RITA (= truth), the gods VARUNA (the God of Human Obligations) and MITHRA (the God of Contracts) were revered; also certain natural forces were conceived of as deities: USHAS (the aurora), AGNI (fire), SURYA (the sun). The nat. deity was INDRA, the most imp. sacrifice was the Soma-sacrifice (a festival involving the use of intoxicants). There was belief in life after death. The Vedas were interpreted by priests in the Brahmanas (a form of early scientific commentary of the 8th cent.) and by priests and laymen in the Upanishads (mystical writings), which were related to the Brahmana texts and later led to the practice of yoga. A strong longing for salvation was at the core: a yearning for union with the most sublime reality.

Development of the caste-system (a 'divine institution'): warriors (Kshatryas), priests (Brahmins), peasants (Vaishias), subj. peoples and those of mixed blood (Shudras), and those without caste (Pariahs).

c. 560–483 Gautama Buddha ('the Enlightened One') proclaimed salvation by reincarnation through self-improvement. By means of the 'noble eightfold path', the faithful, purified by moral conduct, could ultimately enter Nirvana.

c. 540–468 Vardhamana the Mahavira ('great hero') and Jina ('the victor'). Teachings: the suffering of the world is the consequence of the fusion of spirit and matter. Liberation is attained through self-punishment: ascetic living, self-castigation and fasting. His followers call themselves Jains (after Jina).

512 Gandhara and Sind were incorporated into the Pers. Empire (DARIUS I).

327–325 Campaign of Alexander the Great to India. Subjugation of Gandhara and victory over POROS at the banks of the Hydaspes (mod. Jhelum); the return (p. 65). Subs. Gk ctr. was transmitted to India through the kdm of Bactria (Gandhara art).

321–185 The Maurya Dynasty, founded by

321–297 Chandragupta, who defeated the last king of the Nanda dynasty (the Maghada kdm), expanded the state territorially and held his own against SELEUCUS NICATOR (312–282).

272–231 His grandson Asoka became the founder of the first Ind. Empire (cap. Pataliputra). Impressed by the terrible cruelty accompanying the conquest of Kalinga, ASOKA embraced Buddhism (at Kalinga 100,000 people were killed and 150,000 deported. The rule of the 'Prince of Peace' was tolerant to other religions, and marked by a deep moral earnestness; it made use of an extended administrative apparatus. After ASOKA's death, the empire was divided and its power declined.

From 170, small Gk principalities were est. in the Punjab via Bactria, only to be conquered by the Sakas (75 B.C.), who were in turn defeated by the Parthians. Three kdms were est. in the s. of India: Kerala, Pandya and Cola.

c. A.D. 50. The invasion of the 5 tribes of Yüeh-chih from Bactria and their unification resulted in the formation of the Kushana Empire of Northern India, which experienced its greatest flowering under KANISHKA. KANISHKA promoted Buddhism and combined the extension of trade with miss. activity. The Empire was made a dependency by the Sassanids c. A.D. 240.

c. A.D. 50. The Satavahana Dynasty began its rule over the Andhra kdm in the Northwestern Deccan; it decayed c. 195. Saka nobles, giving way to the Parthians, est. a Satrap-state, which lasted until approx. 405.

c. 320–535 The Gupta Empire. The empire (cap. Pataliputra) gained its predominant position under the first 3 rulers. The territory was expanded to the N. and s. and cult. life thrived (as the creator of epics and dramas, KALIDASA became India's greatest poet).

From 430, incursions of the White Huns (Hephthalites). Conquest and partition into Western and Eastern kdms brought about the decay of the Gupta Empire.

c. 527, the power of the White Huns collapsed. In addition to the founding of the empire of the later Gupta (Malwa), the subsequent period saw the establishment in Northern India of the Empire of Kanauj, ruled by HARSHA. After 647, HARSHA's empire broke up into small states ruled by Rajput clans.

From 700, Buddhism gradually driven out of India by Hinduism.

From 711, incursions by the Arabs.

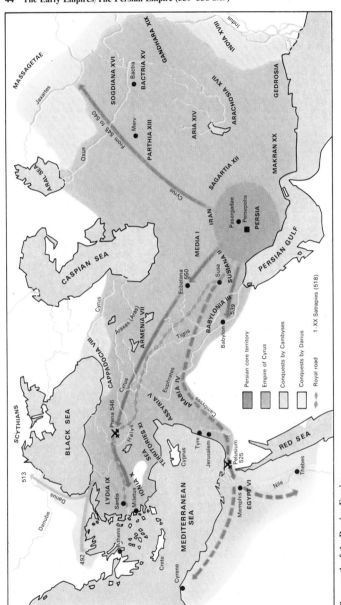

Legend:

- Persian core territory
- Empire of Cyrus
- Conquests by Cambyses
- Conquests by Darius
- Royal road
- 1–XX Satrapies (518)

The growth of the Persian Empire

Labels on map: MASSAGETAE, SOGDIANA XVI, BACTRIA XV, GANDHARA XIX, INDIA XVIII, Indus, Bactra, Jaxartes, PARTHIA XIII, ARIA XIV, ARACHOSIA XVII, GEDROSIA, Merv, Oxus, From 545 to 540, SAGARTIA XII, MAKRAN XX, Cyrus, ARAL SEA, IRAN, Pasargadae, Persepolis, PERSIA, PERSIAN GULF, MEDIA I, Ecbatana 550, Susa 550, SUSIANA II, CASPIAN SEA, Cyrus, Araxes (Aras), ARMENIA VII, Tigris, BABYLONIA III, Babylon 539, CAPPADOCIA VIII, Euphrates, ASSYRIA V, ARABIA IV, Cyrus, Cambyses, BLACK SEA, SCYTHIANS, Pteria 546, Halys, LYDIA IX, PHRYGIA XI, IONIA, Sardis, Miletus, Athens, Tyre, Cyprus, Jerusalem, Pelusium 525, RED SEA, 513, Danube, Darius, 492, Crete, MEDITERRANEAN SEA, Memphis, EGYPT VI, Nile, Thebes, Cyrene

Iran ('Land of the Aryans'): geographically, the plateau between the ancient areas of civilization in Iraq and the Punjab. After 1500 the Iranians immigrated in two waves, first the Bactrians and Sogdians, then the Medes and Persians.

The Medes

835 Persia (Parsua) and Media (Mada) on Lake Urmia are mentioned by the Assyr. king SHALMANESER III. The Medes were able to retain their land in continual struggles with the Assyrians.

715 Capture of DAYUKKU, who, acc. to HERODOTUS, was the founder of the Med. Empire.

c. 700, the Achaemenians began their rule of Persia; though they had to acknowledge Med. overlordship.

647–625 PHRAORTES fell in the struggle against the invading Cimmerians and Scythians.

625–585 CYAXARES, who **made Media a major power,** drove out the Scythians, and Cimmerians. With Babylonian aid, he dest. Assyria (p. 31; Ashur fell in 614, Nineveh in 612). The Halys river formed thereafter the boundary in Asia Minor. Overawed by a solar eclipse predicted by THALES OF MILETUS, CYAXARES broke off the undecided battle with ALYATTES OF LYDIA here (28 May 585). The Pers. vassal-king CYRUS II OF ANSHAN, son of CAMBYSES of the royal house of the Achaemenians, rose against CYAXARES' son ASTYAGES (585–550).

The Pers. Empire

559–529 CYRUS II conquered the Med. kdm and strengthened his rule over Iran.

546 He defeated the Lyd. king CROESUS, subj. the Gk cities of Western Asia Minor, and conducted campaigns in Eastern Iran.

539 Conquest of Babylonia. Return of the Jews to Palestine (p. 39).

529 Death of CYRUS II in the struggles against the Massagetae in Eastern Iran.

529–522 CAMBYSES II killed his brother BARDIYA upon ascending the throne. In 525, he conquered Egypt and advanced to Nubia and Libya. The sorcerer GAUMATA, pretending to be the murdered BARDIYA, instigated a revolt.

522 CAMBYSES II d. in Syria.

521–486 **Darius I,** the son-in-law of CYRUS II and descendant of a branch of the Achaemenian family (mar. to ATOSSA), killed GAUMATA (16 Oct. 521) and suppressed the revolt. He was the creator of the Pers. Empire. In 518 he campaigned in Egypt. In 513 he subj. the Indus river region. In 512 he was unsuccessful in a campaign against the Scythians across the Bosporus to the Lower Danube; but he forced Thrace and Macedonia to become dependencies.

500–494 Suppression of the initially successful revolt of the Gk cities of Western Asia Minor. 494 Miletus dest. The punitive expedition against the Gk city-states failed at Marathon in 490 (p. 57). DARIUS d. while preparing a campaign against Greece.

486–465 XERXES I beat down uprisings in Babylonia and Egypt.

480–479 **The campaign against Greece** failed. Subs. there were revolts in the suppressed territories and uprisings in the satrapies. As state power decreased, the eunuchs gained in importance.

387 Western Asia Minor was returned to Persia by the 'King's Peace' (also named after ANTALCIDAS, Sparta's delegate to the negotiations) (p. 63).

330 After the assassination of DARIUS III by the satrap BESSUS, Iran was part of the empire of ALEXANDER THE GREAT (p. 65).

Aims of Pers. policies: defence of the northeastern boundary against the peoples of the steppes who lived beyond the Jaxartes river; possession of the opposite shores of the Aegean and the Black Sea (Scyth. territory). These aims were over-ambitious through insufficient manpower and material.

The Pers. army's superiority over the peoples of Asia Minor was due to a battle technique adopted from the peoples of the steppes, i.e. an attack of mounted warriors armed with bows and arrows. The Persians formed the core of the army, and among them was the famous guard, the 'Imperishable Ten Thousand'.

Admin. and constitution: division of the country into 20 administrative districts (satrapies). Taxation in fixed amounts. The basis of the currency was the gold daric. High administrative positions were filled by members of the royal family, but also by native rulers and tyrants. Tasks of the satrapies: to maintain standing armies and supply labour for public works. Traffic between the provinces and the cen. admin. was conducted along royal roads, the most famous being the road from Sardes to Susa. The canal connecting the Nile with the Red Sea was restored and used for maritime traffic between Persia and Egypt. Aram. was the administrative language. The bureaucracy was watched by 'listeners' ('the ears of the king').

Religion: Zarathustra (ZOROASTER) appeared during the 6th cent., founding a new religion based on a revelation. **Ahura Mazda** was the creator and master of the world. Man had the power to decide between good and evil, to choose truth or untruth. At the end of the world awaited the day of Last Judgement. The teachings were proclaimed in the 16 Gathas (hymns). The conception of the conflict between good and evil was exaggerated during later times. The moral law changed into polit. commitment (under DARIUS, enemies were represented as prevaricators, he himself as the representative of the truth). The Persians tolerated the religions of suppressed peoples.

The Pers. Empire was the first major Indo-Eur. power, but it became an **Orient. despotism** (under XERXES) introducing Eastern court ceremonial, *proskynesis* (prostration), and treating subjects as slaves.

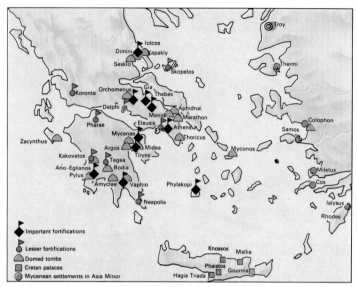

The Mycenaean epoch

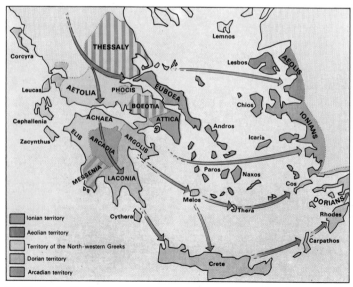

The 'Greek migrations'

The Early and Middle Helladic Epochs (2500–1600)

2500–1850 The Early Helladic Epoch. Formation of var. ctrs. in the Aegean region. In Greece a **peasant ctr.** developed which est. itself in Thrace, Phocis, Boeotia, Attica, Argolis and Corinth (characterized by a special kind of pottery, very early ceramics). Traces of this ancient Medit. pop. are shown in linguistic evidence: place-names with the endings '-nthos' and '-ssos' were not of Indo-Eur. origin (terms designating plants and metals, and terms of navigation and fishery, were adopted by the Greeks).

1850–1600 The Middle Helladic Epoch. **Immigration of Indo-Eur. tribes** (the 'Proto-Greeks'): Ionians and Aeolians (Achaeans). This immigration did not take place in one great milit. campaign, but rather by gradual infiltration of tribes and splinter-groups of tribes (peaceful co-existence alternated with warlike conflicts). The fusion with the original Medit. pop. prepared the ground for transition to the

1600–1150 Late Helladic Epoch (the Myc. Epoch). Society: noble lords (Aristoi) who were charisteers **resided in monumental fortresses** with the Megaron at the centre ('Cyclopic walls'). There is evidence of warlike conflicts among the Myc. lords (cantons as spheres of influence), but also of peaceful co-existence under one overlord (the ruler of 'Golden Mycenae' in the Argolis). Precondition for the construction of the fortified castles was the ownership of large numbers of slaves. Warfare, the chase and court festivities made up the noble's life. During the

15th cent. Mycenae's power was extended to Asia Minor (Miletus), Melos and Crete (predatory raids). Techniques used in the making of Min. ceramics and domed tombs were adopted to serve the ancestor cult of the noble class. Destruction of the 'younger palaces' (p. 33). Settlement on Crete, Rhodes and Cyprus.

1400–1150 Late Myc. Epoch. Construction of gigantic **domed tombs** and fortifications (Mycenae, Tiryns, Pylos, Gha, Athens). The 'Lion's Gate' and the 'Treasury of Atreus' (with its dome 14·5 m. in diameter) at Mycenae are famous. During the 13th cent. the fortifications were expanded monumentally to aid defence against the tribes intruding from the Balkans.

c. **1250 a new wave of immigration (the 'Aegean Migrations').** Consequences: rise of the Middle Assyr. Empire and of the Phoenician city-states. Appearance of the Etruscans in Italy. Destruction of Troy VIIa.

c. **1150 destruction of the Myc. fortified castles.**

The **'Gk Migrations'** (1200–1000) (also called the 'Dorian Migration') were initiated by the advance of the Illyrians to the Mediterranean Sea. North-western Greeks settled in Epirus, Aetolia, and Acarnania; the Dorians reached Crete and south-western Asia Minor by sea and the Peloponnesus via the land route. They drove the Achaeans to the Ion. Islands. Attica, Euboea and the Cyclades, untouched by the migrations, remained in Ion. hands. Settlement of the western coast of Asia Minor. The course of the migrations is reflected in the spreading of the most important dialects of the Gk tribes: Ion., Ach. (Aeolian) and Dorian. The invaders were militarily superior because of their new battle technique: **mounted warriors with weapons of iron against chariotseers with weapons of bronze.**

Gradual development of a new polit. order:

1. Continued settlement around ancient Myc. castles (*polis*) led to the development of the city-states.

2. Settlements in newly conquered territories developed into villages which gave up the old milit. order (the assembly of king and free warriors) and a new property-owning (noble) class was formed.

3. The monarchical form of gvt was retained in the border regions of Greece (Epirus, Macedonia).

A basis of cult. cohesion for the Greeks was their form of **writing and alphabet**, which they adopted from the Phoenicians and developed further (vowels were represented by means of superfluous consonant symbols, amounting to the first pure form of phonetic writing). The myths of the Myc. epoch ('The Atrides', 'Perseus', 'Oedipus', 'Seven Against Thebes', 'Helena' and 'Menelaus') were antecedents for the Homeric epics. Gk religion made use of sacred shrines important to all Greeks (Delphi, Delos, Samos, Olympia). The athletic contests which grew out of them made this religion into a pan-Hellen. institution (contest = Gk *agon*); the Olympic Games were dedicated to Zeus: victors were recorded from 776 b.c.; the Pythian Games were held in honour of Apollo at Delphi; the Isthmian Games were held at Corinth in honour of Poseidon; and the Nemean Games were held at Nemea in the Argolid in honour of Zeus. The opposing concepts of **Hellenes** (participants in Gk civilization) and **Barbarians** were developed.

Art: two previous areas of art influenced the 'geometric' epoch of Gk art: Cret.–Myc. art (from the beginning of the 3rd millennium to c. 1400), and Myc. art (c. 1600–1200). During the period of post-Myc. art (12th and 11th cents.) distortion and impoverishment of Myc. form set in; the proto-geometric period (1050–950) again experienced a deterioration of traditional motifs; however, there also was a new beginning (geometric art). During the geometric period (950–700) an ornamental cosmos was created from simple geometric designs (lines, meander, half-circles) on the amphora (vase). The work of art was strengthened by stringent structuring (tectonic = the relationship of horizontal and vertical lines to one another). Abstract forms of representation were introduced (statuettes).

Greek city-states

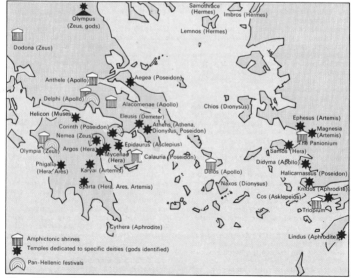

Sites of Greek religious cults

Polit. Structure

The **polis**, the city- or communal state, developed from urban settlements and their surrounding communal lands. The polis was characterized by internal and external independence (autonomy and eleutherism), econ. self-sufficiency (autarky), and local cults (polit. and relig. community). Polit. relations between the city-states were regulated by peace treaties and alliances. The polis was not named after its location, but after the name of the inhabitants, which derived from the location. The polis was protected by a deity and governed by the laws it decreed. Areas of city-states: Attica 2,500 sq. km., Corinthium 880 sq. km., Argos 1,400 sq. km., 22 city-states in Phocis together occupied 1,650 sq. km.

At first the monarchical form of gvt of the conquered was adopted (*basileus* = 'the king', a word of non-Gk origin). The king did not of himself have absolute power; he was endowed with it by ZEUS (image of the shepherd and his flock). With the conquest by the Gk tribes completed, strict royal power and uniform leadership were no longer required. The monarchical form of gvt, with limited powers, continued to exist in Laconia, Argos, Arcadia, Elis and Macedonia. Based on its landed property and large retinue of dependants and slaves, the aristocracy deprived the kings of their power in the other regions. **Aristocracy** was the reign of caste by the large landowners (the warrior caste). The life of the aristocracy consisted of warlike tournaments, chariot races, the chase and leisure. The mark of the aristocrat was the breeding of horses. **Oligarchy** (rule of the few) was introduced; the 'many' (free men, semi-free men and slaves) and the poor were dominated. During the 7th and 6th cents. usurpers, aided by dissatisfied minor citizens, rose from the aristocracy and made themselves autocratic rulers (**tyranny**). During the struggle against the large landowners and important citizens they accorded favourable treatment to artisans and peasants. **Democracy** ('rule of the people') was the final stage of the development, as steadily broadening layers of society received rights of citizenship (rights were demanded for assuming duties). Democracy was made possible by the introduction of slavery, which provided the necessary leisure for polit. activity by free citizens.

Greek religion

Two cult. spheres contributed to the relig. conceptions of the Greeks:

1. The **Old Medit. (peasant) sphere**: gods of fertility and mother goddesses (close to the earth and the nether world) and the dying God of Spring; also peasant cults.
2. The **Indo-Eur. sphere** (var. waves of invasion, 2000–1100): ZEUS, the God of Weather and Light, Protector of the Law and Divine Creator; perhaps HESTIA, Goddess of the Hearth (Lat. Vesta).

Old Medit. and Indo-Eur. conceptions of religion fused after 1600 in the aristocratic world of Crete and Mycenae, strongly infl.

by Min. civilization. During this period ZEUS, HERA, POSEIDON, ATHENA, PAEAN (= APOLLO), ILITHYIA (ERLEITHYIA) and, perhaps, DIONYSUS were worshipped. A further development of this feudalistic religion, which corresponded to the hierarchically structured aristocratic society of the Myc. castles, resulted from the diffusion of **aristocratic religion** by **Homer:** ZEUS, God of the Heavens; his wife HERA, Goddess of the Hearth and Matrimony; DEMETER, Goddess of Mother Earth; POSEIDON, God of the Seas; HEPHAESTUS, God of Fire and Metalwork; ARES, God of War; APOLLO, God of Light, Purity and Insight; his sister ARTEMIS, Goddess of the Chase; APHRODITE, Goddess of Love; HERMES, God of Thieves and Merchants; ATHENA, Protectress of the Crafts, Arts and Sciences. Apart from these there was **popular religion** in the form of local deities, old fetishes, incarnations of natural forces, heavenly bodies (the sun and moon), and abstract concepts such as conflict and hope. Dogmas, magic, priests and superstition were unknown. HESIOD's *Theogony* revealed earnest morality and a naïve faith in justice (ZEUS as the divine judge). New relig. concepts were developed by the adherents of the **Orphic cult** and the **Pythagoreans** (thoughts of reward and punishment in the hereafter) and by the **mystery cults** (the Eleusinian mysteries), which promised the initiated (*mystes*) life after death.

Coming from Thrace, the concept of DIONYSUS, the God of Wine, entered Greece during the 7th cent. With his acceptance by APOLLO at Delphi, the last of the gods joined the Olympic pantheon.

During the 4th cent. the cult of ASCLEPIUS, God of Medicine, was introduced. **Relig. syncretism** was the **characteristic of the Hellen. period** (dissolution of the relig. and polit. community of the polis). The physical existence of the Olympic gods and the many local deities was doubted, but atheism did not gain prominence; Greek man's imagination, prodded to relig. speculation by personal problems or polit. disruptions (such as the Celt. invasions), was unresponsive to it. TYCHE, the Goddess of Blind and Cruel Fortune, to whom all were subject, was revered. Beside the ancient mystery cults (DEMETER and DIONYSUS) there now appeared the new and mysterious cults of ISIS, BAAL and CYBELE, considered to be incarnations of ancient Gk gods (*Interpretatio Graeca*).

Artificial creation of a cult: the Egypt. imp. god SARAPIS (from OSIRIS-APIS) was accepted as God of Salvation and Oracles; later he was connected with ISIS, the Queen of the Gods.

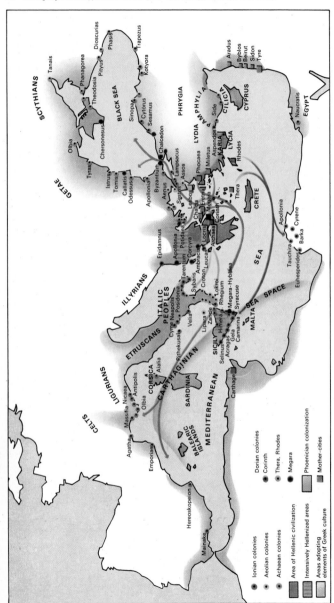

Greek colonization, 750–550 B.C..

Dorian colonies
● Corinth
● Thera, Rhodes
● Megara

Phoenician colonization
Mother-cities

Ionian colonies
Aeolian colonies
Achaean colonies

Area of Hellenic civilization
Intensively Hellenized areas
Areas adopting elements of Greek culture

Gk Colonization (750–550 B.C.)

Colonization was the basis for the development of an overall 'Gk' consciousness; it was brought about by: development of crafts, expansion of maritime trade, pop. surplus (advice of HESIOD to limit oneself to one child; the exposure of newly born children to the ravages of nature), indebtedness of the peasantry, polit. emigration, soc. conflicts (Megara, Corinth and Athens). However, and not least, colonization was the manifestation of a new consciousness of life asserting itself with elemental power. The founding of a colony was effected by a mother-city which – often influenced by an oracle – appointed a founder (oecist); colonies were also founded by centrally loc. seaports. Centralized planning did not exist. There were two types of colony: **trading** and **agrarian.** They possessed polit. autonomy but retained contact with the mother-city through common cults and customs. **Border countries were Hellenized.** Expansion proceeded westward because of advancement by the Assyrians into the E.: Campania, Sicily, Lower Italy, Southern Gaul. However, Carthage obstructed peaceful colonization in the Western Mediterranean. Cyrene and Naucratis on the northern shore of Africa gained in importance as trade centres (p. 25).

Ionia

As the mother-city of more than 90 urban settlements along the coasts of the Black Sea, **Miletus** became the leading polit. and cult. centre and the most important transit port for trade with the Orient.

c. 750 the older heroic epics of the Trojan wars were transformed by **Homer** into the *Iliad* and *Odyssey* ('the primer of Gk youth'). Ion. civilization was closely intertwined with the history of the Near East.

From 700 contact was est. with the Phryg. and Lyd. kdms. **The Ionians adopted money economy** (talent, mina). Warfare with GYGES and ALYATTES OF LYDIA (p. 35).

From 650 soc. and polit. unrest in the Ion. cities led to the **crowding-out of the nobility of birth** and to the ascendency of great merchant families. The people gained increasing infl., often under the leadership of tyrants.

560 Subjugation of Ionia by CROESUS OF LYDIA (p. 35). Consequence: the autonomy of the cities was preserved. Trade was est. with the interior of Lydia; the city-states were obliged to contribute milit. service.

546 **Beginning of Pers. dominance. Sardis** became cap. of the Ion. satrapy (517). The Ion. fleet assisted DARIUS in his campaign against the Scythians. The emigration of the Ion. philosophers to Lower Italy was an important consequence of these events.

537–522 With the aid of LYGDAMIS OF NAXOS the **Tyranny of Polycrates of Samos** was est. Samos flourished culturally and politically and dominated the Aegean Sea (Thalassocracy). Alliance with AMASIS OF EGYPT (p. 25).

Art: 700–600 period of orientalization. Incursion of naturalistic elements from the East (fables, plants, animals). Because of its trade with Ionia, **Corinth** became an important mediator. Other centres of art were Attica, Chalcis and Rhodes. Eastern influence led to monumental structures being erected (the Heraion of Samos, the Zeus temple of the Peisistratidae). Late-geometric temples were erected at Sparta, on Samos and Thermos (the structure of the temple was derived from the ancient Gk noble residence, the Megaron). This period also witnessed the beginning of **small-scale artistic works:** metalworks decorated with relief, small sculptures, and weapons. **Early sculptures:** the statuette of Auxerre; the Kouros of POLYMEDES OF ARGOS. The Cretan, DAEDALOS, is considered the 'inventor' of large-scale sculpturing. Large-scale sculptures may be considered as the symbolic representation of man; monumental architectural projects (i.e. the stone-temple surrounded by a colonnade = peristyle) may be understood as the symbolic representation of the polis.

Ion. lyric: (1) iambic poetry, accompanied by stringed instruments: ARCHILOCUS OF PAROS; HIPPONAX OF EPHESUS. (2) Elegy, accompanied by the flute (mourning): KALLINOS OF EPHESUS, TYRTAEUS, MIMNERMUS OF COLOPHON. (3) The lyric of Lesbos: TERPANDER OF LESBOS (the inventor of the 7-stringed lyre), ALCAEUS and SAPPHO OF LESBOS, ANACREON OF TEOS. (4) Choir lyrics: ALCMAN OF SARDIS, STESICHORUS OF HIMEAR.

Philosophy: separation from the myth. tradition of Miletus led to the development of **Ion. natural philosophy.** The search for the 'beginning', the 'Arché' = prime matter/ cause/mover. For THALES (*c.* 624–546), the *arché* was water; for ANAXIMANDER (*c.* 611–546), the *Apeiron* was something limitless and uncertain; for ANAXIMENES (*c.* 586–525), the air (*aer, pneuma*) was uniform, infinite, indestructible matter. A school of philosophy was founded by XENOPHANES OF COLOPHON at Elea in Lower Italy (570–after 480): conception of unity and global nature of the universe. Being was at the heart of all thought for MARMENIDES OF ELEA (540–470). A fraternity-like association was formed at Croton by PYTHAGORAS OF SAMOS (580–500): the harmony and order of the world was to be discovered with the aid of mathematics, physics, acoustics and astronomy. Arithmetic, music and polit. theory. The migration of souls taught. For HERACLITUS OF EPHESUS (*c.* 535–470), the first principle of the world was not being, but becoming (change); change, however, acc. to a determined rhythm, cal. the order and reason of the world.

Econ. life: extension of Ion. trade to Asia Minor. Coinage replaced trade-in-kind (barter) with a money economy. Development of a merchant class. The slave-trade first appeared at Chios.

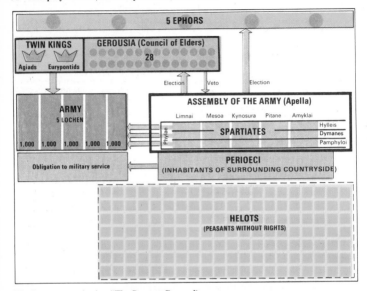

The Spartan constitution ('The Spartan Cosmos')

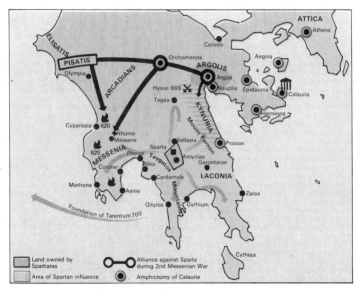

The Peloponnesus to 500 B.C.

Sparta

c. 900 Sparta was founded when 4 villages (Limnai, Mesoa, Kynosura, Pitane) were consolidated into a single settlement in the Eurotas river valley.

740–720 1st Messenian War. Occupation of the mountain fastness Ithome and conquest of Messenia by king THEOPOMPUS.

706 Founding of Tarentum.

680–650 King Pheidon of Argos est. his predominance in that city in the north-eastern Peloponnesus after struggles with Tegea and Sparta (dispute over the area of Kynuria, b. of Hysiae 669). PHEIDON introduced standard weights and measures (the pheidonic foot; obolus, drachma). The establishment of the amphictyony of Calauria strengthened his already leading position.

660–640 (?) 2nd Messenian War. Assisted by Achaea, Elis and Argos, the Messenians revolted. The loss of the Messenian Spartiate lands led to severe polit. and econ. tensions in Sparta.

640 By utilizing the **new battle technique of arranging hoplites in phalanges** (hoplites = mail-clad foot-soldiers armed with spears, swords, round shields, hauberks and leg-protectors), Sparta subj. the Messenians. Sparta developed into a milit. state, a form of state called 'hoplite-polity' in many cities of Greece.

Consequences of the war: unscrupulous suppression of the helots, isolation of the Spart. people from the outside world (iron bars used as domestic currency), cult. decay and rule by a minority: the 9,000 Spartiates as full citizens.

550 The Peloponnesian League was est. under the milit. domination of Sparta **(hegemony).** All Peloponnesian states, exc. Achaea and Argos, were obliged to render milit. assistance; but they retained their autonomy. Sparta subs. became the strongest milit. power in Greece, fighting against the tyrannies (intervention in Samos, Athens and Sicyon) and the *demos* (people); however, there were no conquests by Sparta after the mid 5th cent. and the *status quo* was maintained (no pop. surplus).

Constitution and State

Acc. to legend, the constitution of Sparta (the so called 'Great Rhetra') was the work of LYCURGUS; actually, it was the result of centuries of development. It provided for kings, the 'Council of Elders' (*Gerousia*), and the assembly of the army. After the admission of Amyclae into the Spartan League of Settlements, the **Lacedaemonian state** was est.; later the constitution was reformed through the creation of the board of ephors, which limited royal power to control of the army. During the second half of the 6th cent. the ephors gained control of domestic and foreign policy.

Organized in 3 phylae, the Spartiates lived in male communities. Young men aged 14 to 20 were educated by the state; 20- to 30-yr-old men lived in communities of warriors, the older ones in communities organized around common mess-halls (*syssitia*). Econ. life was based on the division of the land into non-transferable, hered. estates (*kleroi* = landless) worked by the helots (servile peasants). The helots had to deliver half their harvest; they were secretly (*krypteia*) spied on and a season of war was waged against them each year. The Dor. inhabitants of Lacedaemonia and Messenia (living in *c.* 100 cities) belonged to the *perioeci* (inhabitants of the surrounding country), whose rights were curtailed, but who were obliged to render milit. service. They did not take part in the Assembly of the Army or benefit from state education.

Culture: strong influence of Ion. ctr. through the lyrical poets (lyrists) of Eastern Greece: TERPANDER OF LESBOS, ALCMAN OF SARDIS and TYRTAEUS (songs, hymns, choirs).

Development in the Rest of Greece

c. **700 Hesiod of Ascra** in Boeotia: the *Theogony* (myths of the gods strongly orientated towards ZEUS); the *Erga* ('Works and Days') (describing the downfall of humanity over the span of 5 ages, instructions for peasants and sailors).

c. the turn of the 7th cent. the hitherto oral tradition of **law** was **recorded in writing,** contributing to the development of legal institutions and legal concepts (often against the wishes of the aristocracy).

During the 7th cent. **tyrannies were est.** in var. Gk city-states as a result of conflicts within the aristocracy (first at Corinth, Megara and Sicyon, later also in Ionia). Consequences: strong gvtl power, determined domestic and foreign policy.

657–580 The Tyranny of Corinth: CYPSELUS, PERIANDER and PSAMMETICHUS. Greatest flowering of Corinth as the foremost sea-power of Greece. Peasants were given favourable treatment over the aristocracy (large estate owners). Trade relations were expanded with Miletus, Lydia and Egypt.

600–570 The Tyranny of Cleisthenes of Sicyon. Following polit. reorganization, the Delphian amphictomy was assisted in the first 'Holy War' against the Phocians. The transit tolls for pilgrims on their way to Delphi were eliminated by the destruction of Cirrha. **Delphi became the most important sacred shrine in Greece.**

582 Reorganization of the Delphian Games.

Art: 600–500 the Archaic Epoch. The Dor. regions were at first in the lead (Corinth) of artistic production; later the Ionic (Athens) moved up. Statues of **nude youths** (Kouroi) and **gowned girls** (Korai) served as sacred symbols at relig. services. Vase painting with black figures representing the myths reached its climax with EXEKIAS (*c.* 550–520); from 530 vase painting with red figures flourished, finding its greatest exponent in the Attican master EUPHRONIOS. Temple sculptures (pediment, metope, frieze). **The perfection and termination of mature Archaic art occurred in Athens.**

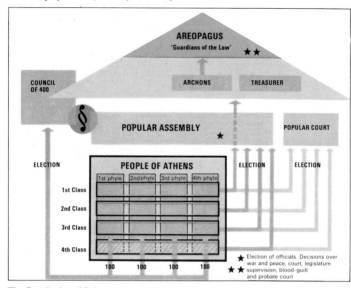

The Constitution of Solon

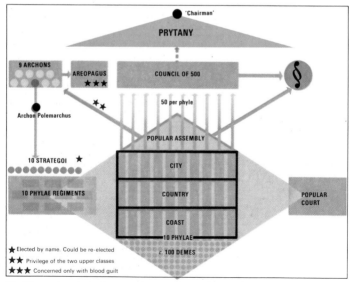

The Constitution of Cleisthenes

To begin with there was a kdm to which the noble lords of Attica subjected themselves. Following their settlement in the city of Athens (urban aristocracy), royal power was gradually curtailed.

683 Monarchy was replaced by the **archonship.** Archons were officials serving for 1 yr. Jurisdictions: the Archon Basileus was responsible for the cult of DIONYSUS, the Archon Eponymos was the ancient overseer of the city of Athens, and the Archon Polemarchos was leader of the army. Indebtedness of the peasants led to a crisis of the state which

c. 624 was to be alleviated by **the legislation of Dracon** ('Draconian punishment'). Six additional archons (*thesmothetai*) were appointed and vendetta was outlawed. Soc. tensions led to the aggravation of the domestic situation: the peasants were in econ. distress (bondage resulting from indebtedness); maritime trade brought about a growth of the importance of the middle class, which led to polit. demands on the aristocracy.

594 Solon was appointed archon with dictatorial powers to serve as 'conciliator'. He brought about:

1. **Emancipation of the peasantry.** Debts on landed property (*hypothec*) were eliminated and personal bondage (*seisachtheia*) abolished; the land was not redistributed, but a limit was set to the size of holdings.

2. **Curtailment of aristocratic power.** Property-owning citizens were divided into 4 classes: the *pentakosiomedimnoi* (500 bushels of grain), the *hippeis* (300–500 bushels of grain), the *zeugitai* (peasants rendering services with teams of draft animals), serving in the choir of hoplites, and the *thetes* (the propertyless class). **Timocracy** (rule by those owning property) prevailed (a class system focusing on agricultural production and land yield).

3. **Reform of the currency** by transition from Aeginaean to Euboean-Miletan coinage.

4. **Codification of the law.** Each citizen entitled to bring his case publicly to court.

Basic principles of Solon's code:

1. Emancipation of the individual; the individual was no longer rooted in the clan; rather, he was made a member of the polity.

2. Promotion of trade and crafts.

The Constitution: The popular assembly (*ecclesia*) elected the archons and the keeper of the treasury from the members of the first class; the 'Council of 400' (corresponding to the 4 ancient *phylae*) was elected from the members of the 3 upper classes. The *thetes* took part in the popular assembly and the popular court (*heliaea*). The laws did not achieve polit. stabilization; rather, they renewed unrest and divided the people into 2 factions: the aristocracy of the interior, and the inhabitants of the coast (under the leadership of the Alcmaeonids). The peasants of the mountains supported in

560 **the establishment of the Tyranny of** Peisistratus. Athens experienced a period of polit. and cult. advance. The peasantry received favourable treatment. The ruler was protected by bodyguards. SOLON's laws were not abolished. Coins of the state showed the image of ATHENA and the owl. The cult of DIONYSUS was promoted.

527–514 HIPPIAS and HIPPARCHUS followed PEISISTRATUS as tyrants.

519 Alliance of Plataea with Athens against Thebes.

514 HARMODIUS and ARISTOGEITON murdered HIPPARCHUS out of private vengeance.

510 **The Tyranny was overthrown** by the Alcmaeonid, CLEISTHENES, with the aid of the Delphic oracle and a Spart. army under CLEOMENES.

509–507 **Reforms of Cleisthenes:** a new arrangement of the phylae est. democracy by means of **isonomy** (equality of polit. rights for all citizens). The citizenry was organized into 10 phylae composed each of 3 groups (*trittys*) coming in equal numbers from the 3 regions (city, country and coast). This selection was effected by lot. Each phyle sent 50 representatives to the 'Council of 500'. The Council (as the *Prytaneis*) took care of the business of the city-state for one council period (36 days) under the direction of a daily elected 'chairman' (*Prytanus*). Each trytts consisted of communes (*demes*) – autonomous administrative units – which kept a roll of citizens and made up the local basis of the constitution. Each citizen was a member of the popular assembly. The organization by phylae also applied to the army: there were regiments of the phylae under 10 elected *strategoi*, subject to the command of the Archon Polemarchos. The cup of hemlock was introduced as the means of capital punishment. Torture was abolished for free men. **Ostracism was introduced** as a means of banishing without loss of property or privileges citizens considered dangerous to the state.

508 CLEISTHENES was ostracized at Spart. instigation.

507 After CLEOMENES and the noble leader ISAGORAS had been besieged on the Acropolis by the Athen. people, CLEISTHENES was allowed to return.

506 The Spartans, Boeotians and Chalcidians were defeated by the Athenians. 4,000 Attican colonists (*cleruchies* = those who drew the lot) were settled at Chalcis. When CLEOMENES was defeated by Argos, democracy was introduced there too.

Poetry: high point of mature archaic lyric. THEOGNIS OF MEGARA: the elegies (aristocratic lament over social changes, symposion songs); ANACREON OF TEOS (570–488): songs of wine and love (love of young boys, symposion). ANACREON and IBYCUS OF RHEGIUM, the poets of passionate love, spent part of their lives at the court of POLYCRATES OF SAMOS. The choir-lyricists SIMONIDES (556–468) and BACCHYLIDES (505–450) were at the end of their lives at the court of Syracuse, where they met PINDAR OF THEBES, the greatest of the Gk choir-lyricists: cult songs (Paiane, dithyrambs, hymns), victory songs.

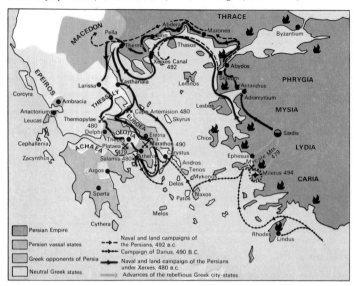

The Persian Wars

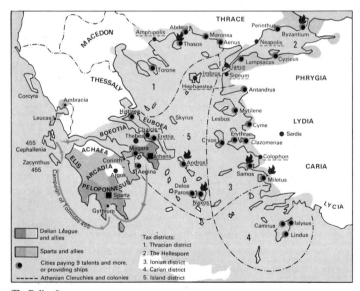

The Delian League

The Pers. Wars (500–479)

500–494 The Ion. Revolt under the leadership of ARISTAGORAS OF MILETUS – assisted only by Athens and Eretria – was beaten down by the Persians after initial successes (advance against Sardis; the Greeks defeated at Ephesus). Counter-attacking, the Persians reconquered Cyprus (497) and dest. the Ion. fleet nr Lade.

494 Destruction of Miletus. The inhabitants were deported to Mesopotamia.

493 THEMISTOCLES became Archon.

492 Conquest of Persia and Macedonia by the Persians under their commander MARDONIUS. MILTIADES THE YOUNGER, tyrant of Chersones, fled to Athens, where he was elected one of the 10 *strategoi*. A storm dest. the Pers. fleet at the rocky promontory of Mt Athos. Sparta and Athens rejected the Pers. demand to all Gk city-states to submit (i.e. to send tokens of water and earth).

490 1st Pers. Campaign under Datis and Artaphernes, accompanied by HIPPIAS. Destruction of Eretria and deportation of the inhabitants.

Sep. 490 b. of Marathon. The Athen. land army, led by MILTIADES, defeated the Persians (the vict. reported by the 'Marathon runner') by the use of superior Gk tactics. The Pers. fleet returned to Asia Minor. As champion of all Hellas, Athens was, after the vict., on its way to becoming a major power. Following the failure of his campaign against Paros, MILTIADES d. in prison (489).

487 Election of the archons by lot from 500 candidates of the 1st and 2nd classes. The office was thereby politically neutralized; receiving administrative and fiscal functions, the *strategoi* increased in polit. infl. (this was due also to the fact that they could be re-elected and had certain authoritarian powers).

487–483 Following the ostracism of polit. enemies (HIPPARCHUS (487), MEGACLES (486), XANTHIPPUS (484) and ARISTEIDES (483)), THEMISTOCLES was able to **carry through the fleet-building programme:** 180 triremes (= oars arranged by threes) were completed by 481. The ships were built by the state, their construction financed by the yields of the silver mines of Laurium; they were outfitted by wealthy citizens (liturgy). The *thetes,* as oarsmen, gained in polit. importance.

480 2nd Pers. Campaign: XERXES left Sardis with an army of more than 100,000. The mother-city, Tyre, commanded Carthage to **attack the Sicil. Greeks.**

480 b. of Himera. The Carthaginians were defeated by the tyrant GELON OF SYRACUSE; the Etrus. fleet was defeated by his brother HIERO OF SYRACUSE at the

474 naval **b. of Cyme** (Lat. Cumae, p. 73): the rise of Rome was made possible.

481 Under the leadership of Sparta **a defensive alliance** was concluded (Hellenic Symmachy). The naval **b.** of **Cape Artemisium** was indecisive.

Aug. 480 Subs. LEONIDAS, with 300 Spartiates

and 5,600 other warriors, d. at **Thermopylae** to secure the retreat of the Gk army. The Persians devastated Boeotia and Attica and sacked Athens. The pop. of Athens was evacuated to islands near by.

Sep. 480 Led by the Spartan EURYBIADES, who followed the plans of THEMISTOCLES, the **Greeks defeated the Pers. fleet nr Salamis.** Limited by the narrowness of the strait, the superior Pers. fleet had no manoeuvrability against the 310 Gk ships. Unpursued by the Greeks, the Pers. fleet withdrew to Asia Minor. MARDONIUS moved the Pers. army into winter quarters in Thessalia. Following the 2nd destruction of Athens in the spring of

479 in the **b. of Plataea** and the **naval vict. of Miletus** nr the **Mycale Mts,** the Greeks prevailed. THEMISTOCLES advised that Gk states which had been friendly to the Persians should suffer no reprisals and Greece enjoyed 20 yrs of peace.

Significance of the Pers. Wars: the Persians abandoned their expansionist aims. The polit. and intellectual independence of the Greeks was secured. The unfolding of Gk civilization was made possible.

479 Athens was surrounded by city walls despite the objections of Sparta.

478 The Ion. city-states were liberated by a Gk fleet under the Spartan PAUSANIAS. Because of his tyrannical conduct, PAUSANIAS was recalled by the ephors. Sparta appealed to the Ionians to settle in the Gk mother-country and withdrew from the war. Petitioned by the Ionians, Athens became their protector against the Persians.

The Delian League

477 Establishment of the Delian League (1st Attican Maritime Alliance, composed of Athens and the Ion. cities) as a defence against the Pers. danger. The allies had to make financial contributions (460 talents, stipulated by ARISTEIDES 'the Just'). Delos became cap. of the league. All members had an equal vote in the league council. Athens became the leading econ. power of Greece. Sparta and Athens were alienated.

470 THEMISTOCLES was ostracized (he d. a Pers. vassal at Magnesia on the Meander river). MILTIADES' son CIMON continued the war against the Persians, commanding the fleet of the League.

465 Double vict. of Cimon over the Pers. army and fleet at **Eurymedon** in Asia Minor. Sparta's hostility to the growth of Athen. power increased; the pop. of Sparta was reduced in numbers because of the catastrophic earthquake of 464 and the 3rd Messenian War (464–455). A supporting Athen. army, which had been requested to aid in the siege of the mt. fastness of Ithome, was sent back by the Spartans because they feared that it might spread democratic tendencies. For this reason

461 CIMON, who was well-disposed towards the Spartans, was ostracized from Athens.

Classical Art (5th/4th cents.)

The climax is found in the temple of ZEUS at Olympia and the temple of ATHENA (the Parthenon) on the Acropolis (ICTINUS and CALLICRATES). The leading sculptors were the Dorian **Polycleitus** (*doryphoros* = spear-carrier) and **PHIDIAS**. The former's work was distinguished by proportion and rhythm (discovery of 'counterpoint' (*contraposto*) = rest and movement of the human body, represented by the 'supporting' and the 'free' leg complementing one another). The latter was the creator of the Parthenon sculptures, and the ivory-gold representations of ZEUS and ATHENA. Nothing is preserved of the monumental frescoes of POLYGNOTUS OF THASOS. An idea of them may be had from the descriptions of PAUSANIAS and the contemporary Attican vase paintings. A precondition for the **art of the 4th cent.** was the dissolution of the polis and an increase in bourgeois attitudes. The great artists were **Praxiteles** (APHRODITE OF CNIDOS, HERMES), showing the humanity of the gods; **Scopas** (the 'maenad'): manifestation of pathos; **Lysippus** (the 'scraper'): creator of the hellen. type of man. All 3 artists were marked by a preference for contemporary motifs.

Literature

Gk **tragedy** grew out of the relig. worship of DIONYSUS (the chorus and the first 'responder' of THESPIS). The principal creators of Gk drama were:

Aeschylus (525–456), who introduced the second actor and reduced the chorus in size, lessening its importance in favour of dialogue. AESCHYLUS' tragedies were deeply religious and contained heroic elements of the archaic period: *The Persians* (472), *Seven against Thebes* (467), *The Oresteia* (458).

Sophocles (497–406) gave tragedy its classical form by introducing the third actor into the plot and strengthening the chorus. He drew the dramatic action from the internal lives of the characters (character tragedy): *Antigone* (442), *Oedipus Rex* (427), *Electra* and *Philoctetes*.

Euripides (480–406), using a psychological approach, attempted to alter the content of the epics by lessening the heroic image. He was the precursor of the bourgeois drama, which explains his strong infl. on world literature: *Medea* (431), *Hippolytos* (428), *Trojan Women* (415).

The high point of polit. satire in Athenian **comedy** was reached under CRATINUS (520–423), EUPOLIS (446–411) and

Aristophanes (445–385), the principal practitioner of the Athen. Old Comedy. He was concerned with soc. questions, criticized the politics of his city and fought against the Sophists: *The Clouds* (423), *The Wasps* (422), *The Birds* (414), *The Frogs* (405).

The principal practitioner of the younger, non-polit. comedy (the Athenian New Comedy) was MENANDER (343–290), with his bourgeois comedies of soc. criticism: *The Arbitrants*, *The Curmudgeon*.

The Writing of History

In his major work, *History* (*History of the Persian Wars*, or 'Description of the Exploration' = *Histories apodexis*), **Herodotus of Halicarnassus** (484–425), the 'Father of History' (acc. to CICERO), described the conflict between Europe and Asia (Hellenes and Barbarians); HERODOTUS' writing of history was rooted in moral and relig. factors, not in nationality (the historical process was explained in terms of deep faith in divine predestination).

Thucydides (460–396), the creator of objective historical science, wrote his *History of the Peloponnesian War* as a lesson for practical life (pragmatic historiography). The historical process was determined not by the gods, but by natural causes.

Xenophon (430–354) composed the *Anabasis* (describing the campaign of CYRUS and the retreat of the Greeks) and a history of his own times (*Hellenica*).

Philosophy

The **Sophists** (= teachers of wisdom) wanted to transmit general education to prepare young people for life with the aid of rhetoric, dialectics and civics. Knowledge was transmitted as a 'good'. Principal representatives: PROTAGORAS OF ABDERA: anticipation of subjectivism and relativism ('Man is the measure of all things'), doubts about knowledge (there is only one manner of thought), the right of the mightier; GORGIAS OF LEONTINI: teacher of a rhetoric which aimed at 'making the losing cause the winning one'; HIPPIAS OF ELIS: the independence of man from his environment.

Socrates (469–399) was the founder of anthropological philosophy. Using the inductive method (irony, *maieutic* . . 'midwife technique'), he attempted to arrive at a conceptual determination of the universal (the nature of virtue) so as to bring man to thoughtful contemplation and thereby to thoughtful action (virtue as knowledge can be taught). He warned of the confusion caused by an 'inner voice' (*daimon*).

Plato (427–347), founder of the Academy at Athens (387), moved from the Socratic manner of conceptualization ('the good', 'virtue') to the theory of ideas (= 'substantial', first form). He contrasted the world of existence with the world of appearance, which is only a manifestation of ideas. Inherent in the individual, ideas become apparent by recollection. PLATO's historical importance rests in his programmatic polit. works. Here he stressed wisdom, courage, sobriety and justice as the major virtues of man in a state of laws. Works: *The Apology*, *Crito*, *The Symposium*, *Phaedo*, *The Republic*, *The Laws*, etc.

Aristotle of Stagira (384–322), founder of the Lyceum at Athens, grasped all the knowledge of his time; he made some branches of philosophy independent and est. new disciplines of learning. His writings are marked by analytical thinking, empirical methodology (experimentation) and speculative construction.

The Perfection of Democracy

462 On the initiative of PERICLES and EPHIALTES, all polit. decisions and rights were placed in the hands of the Council (*Boule*), the courts (*heliaea*) and the Popular Assembly (*Ecclesia*); the powers of the Areopagus were thereby limited to matters of 'blood-guilt'. PERICLES continued the work of reform after the murder of EPHIALTES in 461.

461 Introduction of *per diem* allowances for members of the Council and the courts (paid by league taxes).

458 The democratic structure of the gvt was completed by the **admission of the 3rd class** (the *zeugitai*) to the archonship. The state was governed by the chairman of the Council (*Prytanus*). The loss of power by the aristocracy placed polit. responsibility in the hands of the people provided they were citizens.

451 The law governing the right of citizenship stipulated that both parents had to be Atticans. (Citizenship was an exclusive right; any Athenian whose mother was a foreigner was deprived of it; the few enjoyed such soc. privileges as allowances of money and grain.)

The Struggle with Sparta and Persia

461 Athens discontinued the alliance with Sparta, and instead concluded a treaty with Sparta's arch-enemy, Argos.

460–457 The 'long walls' were constructed which made Athens the greatest fortress of Greece.

460 After the Mess. helots had been settled with Athen. help in Naupactus, Athens concluded an alliance with Megara. Subs. the infl. of Athens over Corinth increased, leading the latter – like Aegina – to ally with Sparta.

457 Athens was threatened from the N. by Sparta's alliance with Thebes. The Spartans and Thebans were victorious at Tanagra, the Athenians at Oenophyta. The incorporation of Boeotia, Locris and Phocis into the Athen. alliance system est. **Athen. hegemony in Cen. Greece.**

456 Aegina was forced to join the Delian League (surrender of the fleet). Consequence: commercial competition was eliminated and Piraeus became the most important transit port of Greece.

Commercial considerations prompted Athens to support uprisings against the Persians such as that of INAROS in Egypt (at the time Egypt was, next to Sicily and Southern Russia, the richest granary). In the process the assisting Athen. fleet was dest., and in

454 the treasury of the Delian League was moved to Athens (one sixtieth of the tribute was given to the goddess ATHENA). The two-front war with Sparta and the Persians gradually exhausted the Athenians and in

451 resulted in the conclusion of a 5-yr armistice negotiated with the assistance of CIMON, who had returned from polit. exile.

449 CIMON d. on Cyprus shortly after the double vict. of the Athenians over the Persians at Salamis.

448 **Peace between Persia and Athens** (the Peace of Callias). Results: the Gk cities of Asia Minor and Cyprus remained within the Pers. Empire but retained their autonomy. Non-interference was pledged by both sides. The Aegean Sea was declared a Gk body of water.

448 The **transformation of the Delian League** – superfluous now since defence against Persia was no longer necessary – led to the establishment of the Athen. Empire. All former members of the Delian League gradually introduced Athen. coins, weights and measures. Tribute payments contd.

447 Summoned by PERICLES, a **general Gk peace congress** assembled at Athens. Its programme called for securing the peace, safety of sea lanes and rebuilding the shrines dest. by the Persians; Sparta's resistance led to the failure of the congress. Subs., uprisings against Athens took place (oligarchic revolt in Boeotia, 447; Euboea and Megara left the Athen. alliance, 446), and a Spart. army invaded Attica.

445 Athens was forced to conclude the Thirty Years Peace with Sparta and to recognize the hegemony of Sparta in the Peloponnesus. Next to **Persia and Carthage, Athens was now the 3rd great power in the Medit. world.** Rivalry continued between Sparta and Athens.

443–429 The Age of Pericles. After the elimination of his opposition (the ostracism of his opponent THUCYDIDES, 443), PERICLES was annually re-elected as a 'demagogue' ('popular leader') to the position of *strategos*. This position was the legal foundation of his dominant power; however, the real source of his power was in his infl. over the Athen. people, which surpassed that of his fellow *strategoi* (oratorical ability). A 'democracy in name, Athens was in reality the monarchy of the first citizen' (THUCYDIDES). Colonies and a number of cleruchies were est. to secure supplies for the immediate pop. Danger to the Athen. state: the transition from a productive to a 'welfare' state (the allowances). Athens followed coherent cult., foreign and domestic policies, which were attuned to each other. Polit. hegemony was tied to the Athen. cult. mission. The funds collected from the league members helped to construct the buildings on the Acropolis. This for years provided work and income for large numbers of people. But it was also a burden on Athen. finances. The cultured circle around PERICLES and ASPASIA included HERODOTUS OF HALICARNASSUS, ANAXAGORAS OF CLAZOMENAE, SOPHOCLES and PHIDIAS.

The Delian League was reorganized by the division of the cities into 5 fiscal districts and the establishment of democratic gvts in the member cities. The allies, who had been subordinated to the status of tribute-paying subjects, resisted Athens. (Samos left the league, 440, and was subs. conquered by PERICLES.) By 425 the league consisted of 400 city-states.

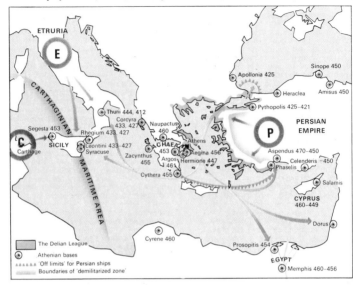

Athenian expansion during the 5th century

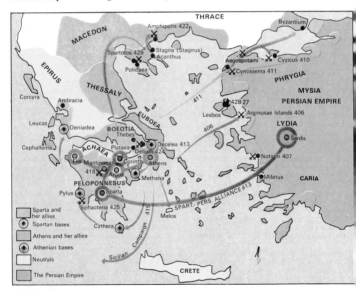

The Peloponnesian War

The Peloponnesian War (431–404)

Causes: the alliance of Corcyra with Athens against Sparta, the Athen. attack on Potidaea, and the Athen. commercial blockade of Megara; this led to Sparta's demand for autonomy for all the cities of the league.

432 Sparta and the Peloponnesians decided for war even though there was not much sympathy for war in Sparta at the time (the pop. had declined in numbers and there was fear of a renewed uprising of the helots; also, financial sources were lacking). **Pericles' war plan:** evacuation of the Atticans into the fortress Athens–Piraeus; use of the fleet against the Peloponnesus; avoidance of a land battle with the superior Spart. army. Since the financial edict of CALLIAS (434), the Athen. treasury had accumulated 6,000 talents.

431–421 The Archidamian War.

431–430 Two incursions by ARCHIDAMOS into Attica. Operations of the Athen. fleet along the coasts of the Peloponnesus.

429 Capitulation of Potidaea after a 2-yr siege, though the Athen. siege army was defeated by SPARTALOS. **Plague** broke out in Athens. A third of the Athen. pop. incl. PERICLES d. within 4 yrs. CLEON became the popular leader of Athens. While PERICLES had been alive, he had opposed the war policies; now he became one of their most ardent proponents: 'the politics of endurance'. The leader of the oligarchs was NICIAS,

429–427 The island of Lesbos left the Delian League and was punished. Two further incursions of ARCHIDAMOS into Attica took place. Plataea was conquered by the Spartans and the defenders executed.

425 The Spartans were defeated on the island of Sphacteria (120 Spartiates taken prisoner). CLEON rejected a Spart. peace proposal and advocated aggressive conduct of the war. After Athen. successes

424 the **Spart. army reforms of Brasidas** were carried out and the Spartans campaigned through Thrace (the cities of the coast left the Delian League). The Athen. fleet under CLEON rendered assistance to Sparta's enemies.

422 Defeat of the Athenians at Amphipolis. Deaths of CLEON and BRASIDAS.

421 A **50 Yrs Peace between Sparta and Athens** negotiated by NICIAS (the 'Peace of Nicias'). The *status quo ante* was restored. Sparta entered into a defensive alliance with Athens to oppose the alliance of the Peloponnesians with Argos. The policies of ALCIBIADES, an enemy of NICIAS, led to worsening relations between Athens and Sparta. Athens entered into alliance with Argos, Elis and Mantinea against Sparta, forced the adherence of Melos (416) and raided the coast of Laconia.

415–413 4th Sicil. Expedition. Segesta was assisted by Athens against Syracuse and Selinus. NICIAS advised against this policy. ALCIBIADES was accused of relig. blasphemy and ordered to return; he fled to Sparta. After initial successes by Athens, in

413 the Athen. fleet was dest. in the harbour of Syracuse; its army was dest. on the Asinaros; NICIAS was executed and the Gk prisoners were forced to work in stone quarries.

413–404 The Decelean War. Following the advice of ALCIBIADES, the Spartans occupied the fortress of Decelea so as to lay waste the Athen. lands. As a result some of the allies left the league and there was ill-feeling among the Athenians.

412 Sparta, surrendering the cities of Ionia, assured itself of Pers. financial assistance.

411 Athens introduced oligarchy (Council of 400, Popular Assembly of only 5,000 propertied citizens). Consequences: revolt of the Athen. army on Samos, and the return of ALCIBIADES. Overthrow of the oligarchy and broadening of democracy (the people received the right to sue in court).

410 ALCIBIADES, elected *strategos* in 411, was victorious at Cyzicus. A Spart. peace offer was rejected.

407 Return of ALCIBIADES to Athens. After the defeat of the Athen. fleet off Notium, ALCIBIADES was removed from office.

406 Athen. vict. at the b. of Arginusae; but, in spite of SOCRATES' plea, the leaders of the fleet were condemned to death (because shipwrecked crews had not been rescued).

405 The Spartans under LYSANDER were **victorious at Aegospotami.**

404 Siege and capitulation of Athens. Peace conditions: the 'long walls' had to be razed and the Delian League dissolved; the Athenians were obliged to render milit. service. Spart. hegemony was est. An oligarchy (the 'Thirty Tyrants') was est. in Athens. The final victor in the world-wide power struggle, involving Greece, Macedonia, Thrace, the Aegean, Asia Minor, Sicily and Lower Italy, was not Sparta but the Pers. Empire.

Sicily: after the defeat of the Athenians before Syracuse, the Carthaginians again intervened in Sicily.

409 The cities of Selinus and Himera were dest. by the Carthaginians. Following the conquest of Acragas (405), the Carthaginians advanced on Syracuse.

405–367 Under Dionysius I the Gk cities united and resisted. With the death of DIONYSIUS, his son DIONYSIUS II and the latter's cousin DION, a pupil of PLATO, began to quarrel.

344 Overthrow of DIONYSIUS II by the Corinthian TIMOLEON. Effective defence against the Carthaginians (341) and introduction of a democratic constitution (337).

307–288 Renewed flowering under **Agathocles**, who became tyrant with the aid of the Carthaginians and in 304 king of Sicily (following the example of the Diadochi). His reign was extended to Lower Italy. After his death, Syracuse was protected from Carth. attack by PYRRHUS (278).

274–215 HIERON II. After the Tarentinian War (p. 83), Lower Italy became Rom.

201 Syracuse incorp. into the Rom. province Sicilia.

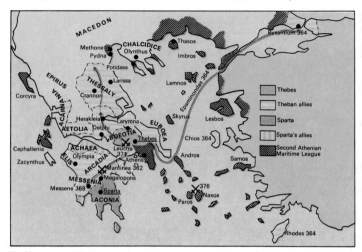

The Hegemony of Thebes

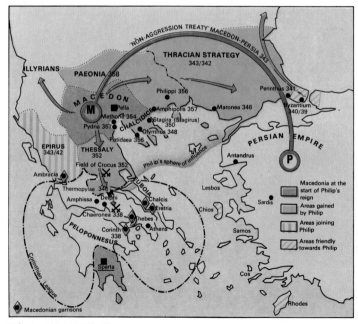

Macedonia under Philip II

Athens, Sparta, Thebes

Sparta controlled the oligarchies est. in Greece (there were garrisons under Spart. commanders = *Harmosts*). With Sparta's aid, the **'Thirty Tyrants' ruled briefly**; then, in 403, democracy was re-est. in Athens by THRACYBULUS (allowances paid for attendance at popular assemblies and theatrical performances after 392).

399 Socrates condemned to drink the poison hemlock (charge: corrupting youth and introducing new gods); re-est. democracy had become unsure of itself.

401 b. of Cunaxa. The death of the Pers. prince CYRUS ended his revolt against his brother, the Pers. king ARTAXERXES; return of the Gk auxiliaries ('Retreat of the 10,000') under the Athenian, XENOPHON.

399–394 War of the Spartans against Persia. Under AGESILAOS, Sparta renewed the war to free the Ion. cities.

395–387 The Corin. War: with Pers. support, Athens, Thebes, Corinth and Argos fought against Sparta. The Pers. fleet, reorganized by the Athenian CONON, defeated the Spartans in

394 at the b. of Cnidus; however, in the same yr the Athenians and Thebans were defeated by Sparta at Coronea. Because of the attempted reorganization of the Athen. Maritime League of cities and the reconstruction of the fortress Athens–Piraeus, Persia and Sparta negotiated; the Bosporus was blockaded by a Pers.–Spart. fleet to cut off Athen. grain imports from Southern Russia.

387 The King's Peace (the 'Peace of Antalcidas') between Athens and Sparta was mediated by the Pers. king: the Gk cities of Asia Minor came under the rule of Persia; the remaining Gk cities received autonomy, to be guaranteed by Sparta.

377 Establishment of the 2nd Athen. Naval League (having equal rights, the 60 members were autonomous) against Spart. encroachments (occupation of the Theb. citadel, the Cadmeia, by the Spartans in 382).

371 General peace between Athens and Sparta. Thebes refused to undo the unification of Boeotia, promoted since 379; Sparta therefore attacked.

371 b. of Leuctra. Defeat of the Spart. army by EPAMINONDAS (use of the 'oblique battle order'). This first defeat of a Spart. army in open battle marked the onset of Sparta's decline. The Thebans advanced to Laconia; Messenia and Arcadia were liberated.

369 Alliance of Sparta and Athens against Thebes, which was building its own fleet.

362 b. of Mantinea: the Thebans defeated Sparta and Athens; however, EPAMINONDAS was wounded and d. End of Theb. hegemony.

Macedonia

359–336 Philip II of Macedonia

Tri-partite organization of the state: the 'army kdm', the nobility (*hetairoi*), and the assembly of the army. Milit. superiority was the basis for success abroad: division of the aristocratic cavalry into regiments (*iles*). Major weapon: the couched lance. Formation of the Maced. phalanx ('*hetaerae* on foot'). Weapons: *sarissa* (long spears) and small round shields. Adoption of the 'oblique battle order' and coordination of the var. milit. branches. **Strategy of annihilation.** Cities were taken not by prolonged starvation, but by siege machines. The conquered gold mines of the Pangaeus mts E. of the Struma (Strymon) river provided the finance for milit. preparation.

With the **unification of Macedonia** (358), the object of PHILIP's foreign policy became obtaining access to the sea for his landlocked state. Advance to Amphipolis and Chalcidice (the Chalcidian peninsula) in 357. Chios, Rhodes, Cos and Byzantium left the 2nd Athen. Naval League; it was dissolved by **'the War of the Allies' (357–355).**

356–346 2nd Holy War against the Phocians, who were aided by the Athenians and Spartans, because of offence to the Delphic shrine. PHILIP intervened against the Phocians. He gained Potidaea, Methone, Stagirus and Olynthus, an ally of Athens. DEMOSTHENES in vain urged energetic assistance.

352 Thessaly conquered.

348 Euboea left the Athen. alliance under prodding from PHILIP.

346 The Peace of Philocrates between Macedonia and Athens based on the *status quo*: Athens remained the strongest sea-power with 30 triremes. Subs. PHILIP was victorious over the Phocians and **accepted into the Amphictomy of Delphi.**

343–342 Conquest of Thrace. At Athens, struggle between ISOCRATES (unite Greece under PHILIP against the Persians) and DEMOSTHENES (struggle against the 'barbarian' PHILIP).

340 Forming of the Hellenic League against PHILIP because of threats to shipping in the Black Sea and renewed intervention in Greece.

338 b. of Chaeronea. PHILIP's victory over the Greeks decided by the cavalry led by his son ALEXANDER. Severe punishment for Thebes, but milder peace for Athens ('friendship and alliance').

337 Corin. League of all Gk cities (with the exception of Sparta) under PHILIP's patronage. **Organization:** a League Council at Corinth, the Maced. king named leader (*hegemon*) and supreme general, autonomy for all members (guaranteed by PHILIP in purposeful contrast to the guarantee by the Pers. king in the 'King's Peace'). **Decision for war against Persia.**

336 Assassination of PHILIP.

Alexander's campaign

Alexander the Great (336–323)

Having secured Maced. rule over the Thracians and Illyrians, ALEXANDER suppressed the Gk revolt (Thebes, Athens, the Peloponnesus).

335 Destruction of Thebes and the enslavement of the inhabitants.

334 Beginning of the Pers. campaign: a Gk war of revenge and a Maced. war of conquest (30,000 infantry, 5,000 cavalry). After the crossing of the Hellespont in

May 334 the Pers. satraps of Asia Minor were defeated at the river **Granicus.** Next the Gk cities of the coast, then Caria, Phrygia (at GORDIUM the 'Gordian knot' was 'untied' by ALEXANDER's sword) and Cilicia were conquered. Maced. officers ruled the conquered territories as satraps.

Summer 333, set-backs from the premature dissolution of the Ion. fleet. The Persians conquered Chios and Mytilene.

Nov. 333 b. of Issus ('oblique battle order'). Victory of ALEXANDER over the Persians under DARIUS III CODOMANNOS. A Pers. plea for peace was refused.

332–331 Subjugation of Syria (conquest of Tyre, 332, after a 7-month siege); of Egypt (foundation of Alexandria, campaign to the Siwa Oasis, the shrine of ZEUS AMMON and the welcome of ALEXANDER by the priests as the son of god); and of Mesopotamia.

331 ANTIPATER suppressed a Spart. uprising at the b. of Megalopolis. Sparta joined the Corin. League. After the crossing of the rivers Euphrates and Tigris

1 Oct. 331, the b. of Gaugamela ('oblique battle order', as at the Granicus and at Issus). Flight of DARIUS; proclamation of ALEXANDER as king of Asia; entrance into Babylon and Susa. Seizure of the Pers. gold treasures (50,000 talents).

330 Persepolis burned in revenge for the destruction of the Acropolis in 480; Pasargadae and Ecbatana occupied. With the **end of the Pan-Hellenic campaign,** the Greeks were dismissed.

The Empire of Alexander

After murdering DARIUS, the satrap BESSUS assumed the royal title; ALEXANDER simultaneously proclaimed himself legal successor of the Achaemenids (adopting Pers. royal dress). Thereupon opposition to ALEXANDER grew in Macedonia: PHILOTAS was executed, his father PARMENION murdered. The satrapies of Aria, Drangiana and Arachosia were conquered.

329 Subjugation of Eastern Iran. BESSUS captured and executed. Advance across the Jaxartes.

328 Warfare in Sogdiana; marriage of ALEXANDER to ROXANE, daughter of the Sogdian prince (beginnings of a policy of reconciliation). **Introduction of Pers. court ceremonial** (*proskynesis* = prostration) opposed by Gk and Maced. retinue: execution of the historian CALLISTHENES, a nephew of ARISTOTLE, after the 'Conspiracy of the Pages' (327). ALEXANDER killed CLITUS, the friend of his youth, in a fit of anger.

327–325 **Ind. campaign** to reach the southern and eastern limits of the inhabited world (*ecumene*): **the idea of world domination.**

326 Vict. over PORUS and his war-elephants at the b. of the Hydaspes. PORUS became a vassal of ALEXANDER. A mutiny of the soldiers at the Hyphasis forced ALEXANDER's return. Construction of a fleet and a journey s. down the Indus. Return march of the army under ALEXANDER and CRATERUS through Gedrosia and Carmania to Persepolis; return journey of the fleet under NEARCHUS along the coasts of the Ind. Ocean and the Pers. Gulf to the mouths of the rivers Euphrates and Tigris.

324 **Plan to fuse Macedonians and Persians** into a new class of masters (this policy was the basis for ALEXANDER's further plans: conquest of the w. and fusion of all peoples through resettlement). Multiple marriage ceremony between Macedonians and Iran. women at Susa. ALEXANDER mar. Pers. princesses. Amnesty for polit. exiles in Greece. After the mutiny of the discharged veterans at Opis, **the empire was reorganized at Babylon.** Persians and Macedonians received equal rights (*homonoia* = harmony; *koinonoia* = community); Persians were accepted into the army. The 3 parts of the Empire were brought together under ALEXANDER in personal union: as Pers. king in Asia, hegemon of the Corin. League in Greece and king of Macedonia.

Milit. and civilian powers were separated in the satrapies, but a single financial admin. for the entire Empire was retained. **A unified currency was est.** (Attican coin measure). Instead of an Eastern monarchical economy (storage of gold), a world economy. Gold and silver currency did not exist side by side: silver was the basis of the imp. currency. This provided the necessary precondition for the establishment of a vast econ. area. Gk became the universal language (*coine*). Expeditions for econ. planning: research into the causes of the flooding of the Nile, journey of NEARCHUS and ONESICRITUS from the Indus delta to the mouths of the Euphrates and Tigris. c. 70 cities were founded to serve not only as garrisons, but also as centres for the expansion of Gk civilization. While preparing for further campaigns against Carthage and in the Western Mediterranean, ALEXANDER d. of fever

13 Jun. 323 in Babylon (aged 33 yrs). 'The name of ALEXANDER stands for the end of an epoch of world history and the beginning of a new one' (J. G. DROYSEN).

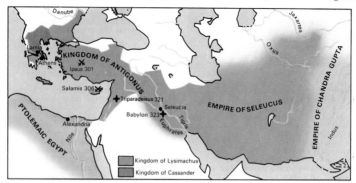

The Diadochi Kingdoms, 303 B.C.

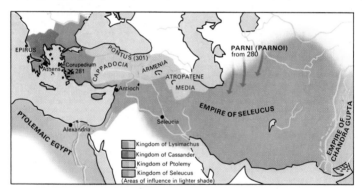

The Diadochi Kingdoms after 301 B.C.

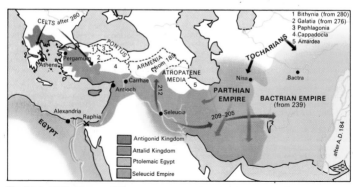

The Diadochi Kingdoms, c. 180 B.C.

The Wars of the Diadochi (323–280)

After the death of ALEXANDER THE GREAT, the struggle for his throne began between his successors (the Diadochi).

323 **Transfer of royal authority** to the Maced. magnates (regency for the minor son and half-brother of ALEXANDER). **Division of the realms of power:** PERDICCAS became regent, ANTIPATER took charge of Macedonia and Greece, ANTIGONUS of Phrygia and Lycia, PTOLEMY of Egypt and LYSIMACHUS· of Thrace.

In the following yrs (to 281) the struggle for power proceeded among the successors (the Wars of the Diadochi). Some attempted to preserve the unity of the Empire. After the murder of PERDICCAS during an attack on Egypt in

321, the redistribution of offices at Triparadeisus occurred: ANTIPATER became regent, ANTIGONUS and CASSANDER imp. generals.

316 murder of ALEXANDER's mother OLYMPIA by CASSANDER, who became master of Macedonia (ROXANE and her son murdered 310).

316 EUMENES, who had been appointed by ANTIPATER's successor POLYPERCHON as imp. general, d. in the struggle with ANTIGONUS, the 'one-eyed'. CASSANDER, PTOLEMY, LYSIMACHUS and SELEUCUS, governor of Babylon, allied against ANTIGONUS, who sought undivided power, in the

315–301 3rd War of the Diadochi. After PTOLEMY's interference in Greece, Athens was seized by DEMETRIUS POLIORCETES ('the Conqueror of Cities'), son of ANTIGONUS.

306 Naval vict. of DEMETRIUS over PTOLEMY at Salamis. Consequence: **the royal dignity for Antigonus and Demetrius,** later also for PTOLEMY, SELEUCUS, LYSIMACHUS and CASSANDER. **Dissolution of the Empire.**

301 Decisive b. at Ipsus. Vict. of SELEUCUS and LYSIMACHUS over ANTIGONUS, the last representative of cen. power (81 yrs old). Establishment of 4 kdms: Thrace and Asia Minor under LYSIMACHUS, Macedonia under CASSANDER, Egypt under PTOLEMY, the Pers. heartlands under SELEUCUS.

During the following yrs (295–285) – and after an adventurous life of piracy – ANTIGONUS' son DEMETRIUS obtained Athens, and after CASSANDER's death Macedonia also. LYSIMACHUS, SELEUCUS and PTOLEMY formed an alliance against DEMETRIUS and drove him out of Macedonia. He was taken prisoner by SELEUCUS and d. 283.

281 b. of Corupedium. LYSIMACHUS (75 yrs old) was defeated by SELEUCUS and his son.

End of the Wars of the Diadochi. Establishment of 3 great monarchies: Macedonia under the Antigonids; **Asia Minor** under the Seleucids; **Egypt** under the Ptolemies.

The Hellen. States

Phase 1: 304–220 Balance of the great powers. Expansion and world-wide acceptance of Gk civilization.

Phase 2: 220–30 Decline of the Hellen. states. The policies of all Hellen. states were inter-connected. Orient. states and ctrs. appeared. Interference by the Romans. Subjection and exploitation of the eastern territories by Rome (p. 85).

Egypt

304–30 Rule of the Ptolemies, est. by ALEXANDER's historian and general PTOLEMY I, after whom all subsequent rulers were named. The Museum of Alexandria was founded (PTOLEMY II). The successors fought with the Seleucids over the possession of Syria and Palestine (long-distance trade-routes); but in the long run only Egypt could be held. Confusion over the succession to the throne and Rome's growing infl. led on

8 Mar. 30 to the **fall of Alexandria.** Egypt became a Rom. province (p. 93).

The State: Alexandria ('Hub of the World') was the focal point of a strongly centralized state. The land (owned by the king) was administered by an official bureaucracy after the ancient Egypt. model. The king's income came from state monopolies (mines, grain, oil, breweries, buildings), export (papyrus, glass), tax-farming and the forced labour of the inhabitants.

Macedonia

279–168 Rule of the Antigonids, est. by ANTIGONUS GONATAS, son of DEMETRIUS, after the vict. over the Galatians at Lysimachaea (277, p. 69).

215 Alliance of Macedonia with Carthage under PHILIP V (221–179), leading to

215–205 the 1st Maced. War (p. 81), concluded by the Peace of Phoenice (re-establishment of the *status quo ante*).

202 Alliance with ANTIOCHUS III against Egypt. Urged by Pergamum, Athens and Rhodes, Rome intervened in the

200–197 2nd Maced. War. With the defeat imposed at Cynoscephalae, all non-Maced. territories were surrendered.

196 The autonomy of all Gk cities proclaimed by ꞏFLAMININUS at the Isthmian Games (p. 85).

179–168 PERSEUS. Consolidation of his power; conflict with EUMENES II OF PERGAMUM, who draws Rome into war against Macedonia.

171–168 3rd Maced. War. Defeat of PERSEUS at Pydna by the Romans under AEMILIUS PAULLUS (168). Demise of the Antigonid monarchy. Partition of Macedonia into 4 independent territories. Persecution of the enemies of Rome in Greece (execution and deportation of 1,000 hostages from Achaea, POLYBIUS among them).

148 Following an uprising, the sep. Maced. states were eliminated and the **Rom. province of Macedonia est.** (p. 85).

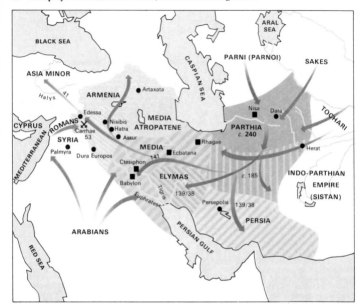

The Parthian Kingdom

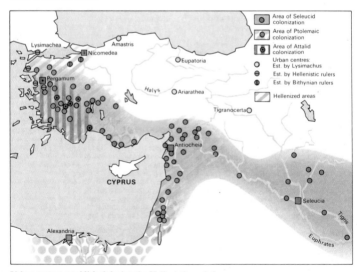

Urban centres established during the Hellenistic period

Greece

323–322 The Lamian War. Greece's attempt to maintain independence was defeated by ANTIPATER. Timocracy was introduced; suicide of DEMOSTHENES. Greece occupied by Maced. garrisons.

266–261 The Chremonidean War. Athen. attempt at liberation misfired; but, following negotiations, the occupying troops were withdrawn (262). Athens became free and, though politically unimportant, was recognized **as cap. of Gk civilization** (philosophical academies).

The newly founded **leagues** were polit. innovations, taking the place of the old city-states:

1. Aetolian League. It reached its greatest extension after the repulsion of the Gauls at Thermopylae and Delphi (279), but was weakened by the 'War of the Allies' (220–217), when Macedonia intervened because of Aetolian piracy in the Aegean Sea.

2. Achaean League (c. 280: Sicyon, Corinth, Argos, Aegina), formed to oppose the Aetolian League and Sparta, where king CLEOMENES III attempted soc. reform (*ephors* abolished, the *perioeci* made full citizens, helots freed).

222 Defeat of Sparta by the Achaean League and Macedonia at Sellasta (elimination of the monarchy).

The struggles between the leagues and the capable diplomacy of Rome brought about the polit. decline of Greece. When the Achaean League rose against the Romans it was defeated at the Isthmus.

146 Dissolution of the Achaean League and **destruction of Corinth.** Autonomy for Sparta, Athens and Delphi.

145 Incorporation of the defeated Gk cities into the province of Macedonia.

Mesopotamia, Persia, Asia Minor

304–64 Rule of the Seleucids, founded by SELEUCUS I NICATOR. No cohesive territ. unity: establishment of independently ruled units in Asia Minor and in the E. made feasible by the loose (federalist) admin.; retention of the Pers. organization into satrapies, but under Gk–Maced. governors (*strategoi*). Cap. Seleucia (instead of Babylon); many other urban centres founded in Asia Minor and Syria. Coexistence of Greeks (adoption of the Attican currency and Gk administrative language), Macedonians (milit. settlements) and natives (Aramaic the administrative language together with Gk). In exchange for the delivery of 500 war-elephants for the war against ANTIGONUS and DEMETRIUS, SELEUCUS I left the Ind. provinces to CHANDRAGUPTA (p. 43). Under his successor ANTIOCHUS I SOTER (the 'Saviour'), parts of Asia Minor separated from the Seleucid state.

c. 280 Establishment of the kdm of Pontus on the Black Sea by MITHRIDATES. During the 2nd cent. gradual Hellenization. Having gone through the 3 Mithridatic Wars with Rome, Pontus was limited to the area around the Bosporus under PHARNACES, who was defeated by CAESAR in 47 at Zela.

279 Incursion of the Celts (= Galatians) into Asia Minor; they had been called by NICOMEDES, who – with their aid – founded the **kdm of Bithynia** which had its cap. at Nicomedia. Bithynia became Rom. by inheritance in 74.

275 The Galatians were pushed back by ANTIOCHUS I into that area of Asia Minor named Galatia after them.

263–133 The kdm of Pergamum founded by EUMENES I. 230 Vict. of his nephew ATTALOS I over the Galatians at Pergamum ('groups of Gauls').

Establishment of the Library. The monumental Altar to ZEUS at Pergamum (now in Berlin) was built under his successors EUMENES II and ATTALOS II. ATTALOS III bequeathed his kdm to the Romans in 133. The E. was lost during the reigns of ANTIOCHUS II THEUS ('God') and CALLINICUS (the 'Victor').

247–227 the kdm of the Parthians, est. by the invasion of the Scyth. tribe of the Parni (= Parthians) under ARSACES I: **a feudal state which tied itself to the traditions of the Achaemenids.** Under MITHRIADES I (171–138) – after 140 'King of Kings' – expansion of domination over all of Iran and Mesopotamia. His son PHRAATES II d. in the defensive struggle against the Sacas, whose aid against the Seleucids he had requested. Rest. of power by MITHRIADES II (124–87). Under his successors, domestic confusion and conflicts with the Romans.

53 b. of Carrhae. Vict. of the Parthians over the Romans; the result of the superiority of their mounted bowmen. Subs., conflicts continued with Rome over Armenia.

227 A.D. Ardashir of the House of Sasani defeated the Parthian king ARTABAN V.

239–130 The Greco-Bactrian kdm. Struggles along the northern border with the Yue-chi and Tochari, who had been displaced by the Huns.

223–187 Antiochus III the Great, most important of the Seleucid rulers; after initial successes in Syria, Palestine and the E. (where he obtained Ind. territories), fought with the Romans (192–188).

190 b. of Magnesia. Defeat of ANTIOCHUS. Loss of Asia Minor by the Peace of Apamea. Beginning of the dissolution of Seleucid rule. Gradual decay resulting from domestic conflicts, wars with the Parthians and struggles over the throne.

64 Termination of the Seleucid Empire by POMPEY (p. 91).

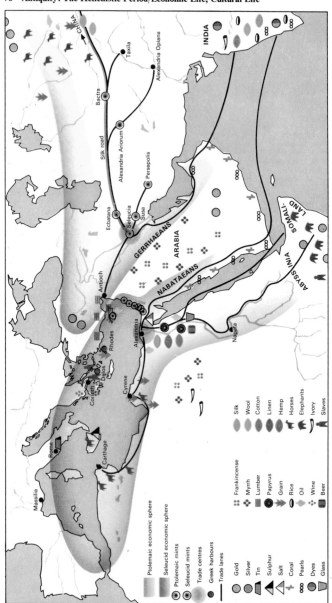

The economy of the Hellenistic period

The Diffusion of Gk Culture

The victs. of ALEXANDER THE GREAT and the establishment of the Diadochi kdms were the basis for the diffusion of Gk culture in the Orient.

The carriers of Gk culture were: merchants, artisans and mercenaries migrating from the mother country into the newly founded cities (a uniform 'metropolitan' urban civilization took the place of the previous polis-centred or nat. ctr.).

The State: the pillars of Diadochi rule were: (a) officialdom; (b) the financial admin.; (c) the mercenary army. The patriarchal absolute monarchy continued to exist; a small upper class of Macedonians and Greeks dominated the states developing on Asiatic soil, which were **large-size states based on nationality** (the land was the private property of the ruler: 'land obtained by the spear').

Characteristics of the dynasties:

1. Assembly of the army.
2. Legitimacy of the rulers based on their milit. and polit. achievements as individuals.
3. Dyn. relationships (marriage policy).
4. **Introduction of the ruler-cult in Egypt** and the Seleucid Empire.

The Museum of Alexandria, with its library of several 100,000 papyrus scrolls, was the **centre of ctr.** during the 3rd cent.; later on the library of Pergamum also became a cult. centre. Increasing specialization was the mark of Hellen. science. Important scientists: ERATOSTHENES OF CYRENE (280–200): measurement of the earth (its global shape), geography, historical chronology (1184 Trojan campaign, 844 LYCURGUS, 776 1st Olympiad).

Mathematics: Euclid (c. 300): textbook of geometry (*The Elements*). ARCHIMEDES OF SYRACUSE (280–212): discoveries in mathematics and physics (anticipation of integral calculus, determination of the specific weight of objects, engines hurling projectiles during the defence of Syracuse against the Romans).

Literature (sophisticated literature at court and in the metropolitan atmosphere for experts and 'connoisseurs'): CALLIMACHUS OF CYRENE, librarian of Alexandria (310–240): elegies, epigrams, court-poetry (*Lock of Berenice*), histories of customs and festivals (*Aitia*). THEOCRITUS OF SYRACUSE (c. 270): pastoral (bucolic) poetry and idylls. APOLLONIUS RHODIUS (295–215): the epic *Argonautica.*

Medicine: HEROPHILUS, the discoverer of the nerves and the brain as the cen. organ of the nervous system, and ERASISTRATUS OF CEOS, who occupied himself with the study of blood-circulation (theory of the pneuma), led to autopsies on human bodies during the 3rd cent.

Philosophy: Athens was the 'academy of the world'. New schools were est. in addition to the ancient Academy and the Peripatetic school: **Epicurus of Samos** (342–271): reticence towards polit. life ('live withdrawn'), lack of fear of death and of the gods, acceptance of pain, the fight of reason against the passions. **Zeno of Citium** (336–263); the founder of **Stoicism**: ethics at the centre of philosophy. The world (*ecumene*) is the fatherland of man (cosmopolitanism). All conflicts between men were to be eliminated. Beginning of the humanistic ideal in antiquity. The shaping of the rounded individual personality. POSIDONIUS OF APAMEA (130–50), founder of a school on Rhodes: fusion of Stoicism with mysticism and mantic historiography.

Astronomy: ARISTARCHUS OF SAMOS (320–250): heliocentric universe, axis-rotation of the earth, revolution of the earth about the sun. HIPPARCHUS OF NICAEA in Bithynia (190–120): catalogue of the stars, timing of eclipses, discovery and description of the precession of the equinoxes resulting from the ecliptic. In **astrology,** the fate of man was tied to the stars.

Philology: ARISTOPHANES OF BYZANTIUM (257–180): editions of the classics with introductions. CRATES OF MALLOS (c. 170) at Pergamum: allegorical explanation of HOMER. ARISTARCHUS OF SAMOTHRACE (217–145): commentaries. DIONYSIUS THRAX (170–90): elementary Gk grammar.

Economic life: fusion of Orient and Mediterranean into a world-wide trading area with international trade centres (Alexandria and Seleucia) and world-market prices. Trade with India, China, Arabia and the interior of Africa. From 200 price rises and social unrest continued.

Art: transfer of the centres of art to the periphery of the Gk world (Rhodes, Alexandria, Pergamum). **Realistic art** (the statue of DEMOSTHENES) and the new **idealism** of Pergamum art (the Pergamum Altar). Grandiose city-planning (modelled after HIPPODAMUS) with streets intersecting at right-angles and fortifications to withstand the new siege engines. The centre of the cities was the agora; then gymnasium, theatre, council hall, public halls and baths.

Sculpture: the Barberinian Satyr, the Dying Gaul, Nike of Samothrace, the Boxer. Development of court art:, busts of ALEXANDER and other rulers.

Architecture: monumental, pompous buildings (loss of a sense of proportion).

From the 2nd cent., intellectual reaction of the native pop. against Hellenization. Adherence to native ctr. and language. Orient. counterforces, an increase of power in the border states (Parthians, Indians) and a general econ. crisis were the causes of the decline of Hellen. civilization.

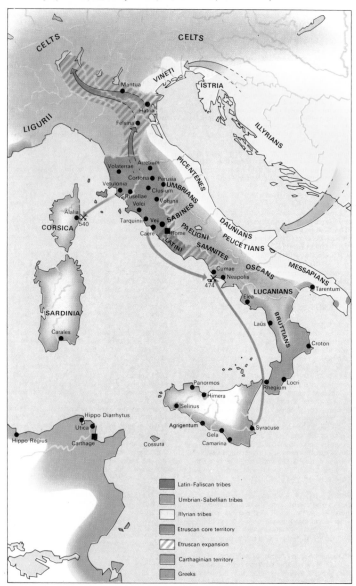

Ancient Italy

Italy in the Early Period

The Neolithic ctrs. of **Molfetta and Stentinello** and the **Remedello ctr.** of the early metal-working period were followed by the **Terra-mare ctr.** of the Bronze Age (*terra mara* = dark soil, of the settlements) – with its fortified villages of pile dwellings (Palafitte) in the N. – and the **Extraterremariculi ctr.** of Cen. and Lower Italy.

c. 1000 B.C. Beginning of the Iron Age: moving into Italy during the 'great migration', the Italic people brought with them the **Villanova ctr.:**

1. The **Latin–Faliscan group** in Latium, the Tiber valley and around Falerii ('cremating Italic people'; urns containing ashes, kept in holes in the ground: *pozzi*).
2. The **Umbrian–Sabellian** or **Oscan–Umbrian group** in Umbria, Campania, Southern Italy and the Sabine Hills ('interring Italic people': bodies buried in graves: *fosse*).
3. The **Illyr. tribes** of the Danube region who, influenced by their neighbours the Thracians, brought with them mounted warfare and the iron weapons of Inner Asia.

The designation **Italy** (from *vituli* = young bulls, sons of the bull-god) initially applied only to the south-western tip of the peninsula; later to the entire area up to the Alps.

From 900 immigration of the **Etruscans** (Tyrrhenoi, Tyrsenes, people of Rasenna), prob. from Asia Minor. Gradual subjugation of the area between the Arno and the Tiber (metal-rich Tuscany).

c. 600 Founding of a **'League of 12 Cities'** (modelled after the Ion. League of Cities).

6th cent. Expansion of power to the N. into the Po valley and the S. beyond Rome into Latium and Campania. Overland trade to Cen. and Northern Europe from Felsina (Bologna).

c. 540 Naval vict. of the Etruscans, in alliance with the Carthaginians, over the Greeks at Alalia. Naval supremacy of the Etruscans in the North-western Mediterranean was thereby secured (maritime trade).

5th cent. Decline of Etrus. power followed the expulsion of the Tarquinians from Rome and

474 the naval b. of Cumae (Cyme), which saw the Etruscans defeated by the fleet of Syracuse under HIERO (p. 57).

396 Conquest of Veii by the Romans and decay of Etrus. power in the Po valley as a result of Celt. incursions.

State and admin.: there was no coherent political organization; but the Etruscans held a dominant position in Italy because of the League of Cities. The cities were ruled by kings; later on, the nobility gained strong influence through noble officials who were elected. Their insignia were: the purple striped toga (*toga praetexta*), the ivory chair (*sella curulis*); also, they were accompanied by official guards carrying the axe tied in a bundle of rods (*fasces*) as the symbol of power over life and death.

Distinctive cult of the dead: the dead were laid in reinforced tombs, later under mounds (tumuli) in 'cities of the dead' accompanied by sacrificial celebrations and performances (gladiators). As the diviners of the will of the gods through the study of livers and intestines and the flight of birds, priests played an important role. A cult-associated lunar calendar governed the official actions of the kings. Under Gk infl., fresco painting and metalwork developed to high perfection. Original contributions: *canopi* (funerary urns with covers shaped like human heads), realistic busts (initially of clay). The Etruscans were of historical importance mainly as mediators of ctr. between Greece and Rome.

c. 750–550 Establishment of the Gk colonies in Lower Italy (Magna Graecia) and in Eastern Sicily.

c. 800 Establishment of Phoenician naval bases in the Western Mediterranean (Western Sicily and N. Africa) to secure and control maritime trade. Following the conquest of Tyre by the Assyrians, **Carthage became the protector of the Phoenician colonies** in the Western Mediterranean. Occupation of the Pityusae, Western Sicily and Sardinia. After the naval b. of Alalia, Tartessus in Southern Spain was dest. and the Straits of Gibraltar were blocked by the Carthaginians to monopolize the tin trade with Britain. The Balearic Islands, Corsica and Sardinia controlled the coasts of Southern Gaul, and Italy, Sicily, Malta and Pantelleria the passage into the Western Mediterranean.

c. 750 Foundation of Rome through the joining of the Latins ('*Roma quadrata*' on the Palatine) and the Sabines (Esquilin, Viminal and Quirinal) to form a single urban community under Etrus. infl. (the name of the city was derived from the Etrus. *gens ruma*). 21 Apr. 753 was later taken as the date of the founding, and the beginning of recorded time ('*ab urbe condita*'). Myths regarding the founding of Rome: raising of the twins ROMULUS and REMUS by the she-wolf, AENEAS, abduction of the Sabine women by the Latins under ROMULUS, and the agreement with TITUS TATIUS, the prince of the Sabines.

750–510 Legendary tradition of the **reign of 7 kings over Rome:** ROMULUS, NUMA POMPILIUS, TULLUS HOSTILIUS, ANCUS MARCIUS, TARQUINIUS PRISCUS, SERVIUS TULLIUS, TARQUINIUS SUPERBUS.

Under the Tarquinians, Rome took the place of Alba Longa as the dominant polit. power in Latium. Construction of Ostia and further extension of the salt-works at the mouth of the Tiber (Via Salaria).

The pop. consisted of peasants and landowners; in addition to them there were shepherds and artisans. The means of exchange were cattle (*pecus,* ' thus *pecunia* = money). Adoption of writing from the Greeks of Lower Italy (the Chalcidic alphabet was a forerunner of the Latin).

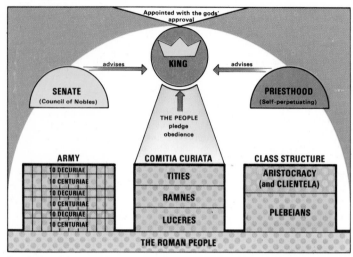

Appointed with the gods' approval

KING

advises ← → advises

SENATE (Council of Nobles)

PRIESTHOOD (Self-perpetuating)

THE PEOPLE pledge obedience

ARMY

| 10 DECURIAE |
| 10 CENTURIAE |
| 10 DECURIAE |
| 10 CENTURIAE |
| 10 DECURIAE |
| 10 CENTURIAE |

COMITIA CURIATA

TITIES

RAMNES

LUCERES

CLASS STRUCTURE

ARISTOCRACY (and CLIENTELA)

PLEBEIANS

THE ROMAN PEOPLE

Constitution of the monarchy

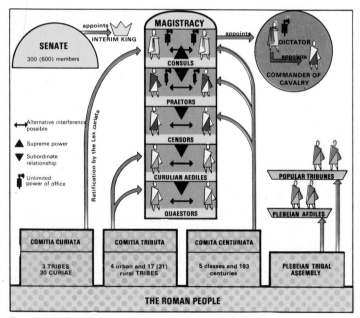

SENATE

300 (600) members

appoints → INTERIM KING

MAGISTRACY

appoints →

DICTATOR

COMMANDER OF CAVALRY

appoints

CONSULS

PRAETORS

CENSORS

CURULIAN AEDILES

QUAESTORS

Alternative interference possible

▲ Supreme power

▼ Subordinate relationship

Unlimited power of office

Ratification by the Lex curiata

POPULAR TRIBUNES

PLEBEIAN AEDILES

| COMITIA CURIATA | COMITIA TRIBUTA | COMITA CENTURIATA | |
| 3 TRIBES 30 CURIAE | 4 urban and 17 (31) rural TRIBES | 5 classes and 193 centuries | PLEBEIAN TRIBAL ASSEMBLY |

THE ROMAN PEOPLE

The constitution of the republic ('Senatus populusque Romanus')

The Constitution of the Monarchy and the Republic

The foundation of Rome was a conscious polit. act (*populus Romanus quirites,* or *quiritium*), to bring about a loosening of tribal ties and greater autonomy for the families. The place of the tribes (*gentes*) was taken by the people (*populus* = communal levy, cf. *magister populi* = master of the communal levy; *populus* later signified the totality of citizens = *cives*).

During the **monarchical period** the **king** (*rex*) was appointed with the approval of the gods; he was supreme milit. leader, priest and judge. The *imperium* (supreme power) and the *auspicium* (divination of the gods' will) were the bases of royal power. The king was assisted by the advisory Council of Elders (*senatus; senes* = the eldest) of the tribal leaders (*patres gentium*) and the priesthood. The assembly of the people was organized into 30 *curiae* (*curia* = *coviria* = community of men; *comitia curiata*): the citizens were arranged in 3 districts (= *tribus*: Tities, Ramnes, Luceres) of 10 *curiae* each. Each *tribus* supplied 100 mounted men (*celeres* = the 'towering') and 10 centuries of infantry each (= one *millennium*).

The **Servian army and constitutional reform** (end of monarchical period): the area and citizens of the state were divided into territ. administrative districts (*tribus*); 4 were urban, 17 (later 31) rural; they formed the basis for taxation and milit. levy. The tribal principle was thereby broken. In connection with the **tribus organization**, the *comitia centuriata* was est. as the basis for the army (timocracy: property and wealth, not blood relationship, as the determining factor). This assembly of the army (levy of the people carrying arms) became the most important popular assembly in the Republican era ('each constitution of the state is a constitution of the army'). The levy was called to the Field of Mars upon command of the consuls by the raising of the red banner of war on the Capitol. The army assembly of the patricians and plebeians was organized in **193 centuries** based on **5 levels of property** (*classes*): 18 centuries of mounted men, 80 centuries of heavily armed men (hoplites), 90 centuries of lightly armed men, 4 centuries of technicians and musicians, 1 century of the propertyless men (*capite censi*). Half the centuries consisted of citizens up to 46 yrs old (*juniores*), who made up the field army; the other citizens (up to 60 yrs old) remained for the protection of the city (*seniores*). Duties: determination of war and peace, election of the highest officials (consuls, praetors, censors), legislative decisions and criminal jurisdiction over the citizens. Voting took place according to class by roll-call and balloting. In the event of a tie the mounted centuries and the first class (18 + 80) carried the vote (privilege of property-owners from their contribution to the hoplite detachments). With the abolition of the monarchy, the top position in the state was occupied by the **'highest annual official'** (*praetor maximus*), the possessor of the '*imperium*'; later the **consuls. Senate, Magistracy** and **Popular Assembly,** though continuously in tense relationship, held each other in balance and formed the pillars of the Rom. Republic.

1. **The Senate** (300 members) consisted of the heads of clans (*patres*) and former consuls; later on plebeians (*conscripti*) were added. Duties: advising the magistrates (*senatus consultum*) – advice later became binding command – and affirmation of popular decisions (*auctoritas patrum*). Election of an interim king (*interrex*) to take charge of affairs for 5 days upon vacancy of the consulate.

2. **The Popular Assemblies:** *Comitia curiata, Comitia tributa, Comitia centuriata* (see above).

3. **The Magistracy** (officials): limitation of office to 1 yr and equality of co-office holders (annuality and collegiality) to prevent the despotism of individuals.
   (a) **Consuls** (*consules* = adviser): duties: conduct of war, finances and the judiciary. In times of emergency (war) the consul appointed a dictator (former designation: *magister populi*), who exercised unlimited power without accountability or colleagues for a maximum period of 6 months, and who himself appointed his own aide, the commander of cavalry (*magister equitum* = 'Master of the Horse'). Later other offices (*honor* = office) were instituted because of the increase in gvtl functions. Age limitations and the determination of terms in official positions were intended to prevent abuse of office.
   (b) **Praetors:** they were to adjudicate legal conflicts. At first there was the *Praetor urbanus* (*Collega minor* of the consuls), responsible for legal disputes between Rom. citizens from 366. After 247, disputes between Romans and aliens as well as between aliens were adjudicated by the *Praetor peregrinus*.
   (c) **Censors** (former consuls (*consulares*), they were excluded from official careers; elections of censors took place every 5 yrs): to guide morality and property investment.
   (d) **Curulian Aediles:** from 366 on, for police-supervision, market-supervision, festivals and the care of the temples.
   (e) **Quaestors:** from 447 on, in charge of public finance.

Dictator, consuls and praetors possessed unlimited official power (*magistratus cum imperio*). All other officials possessed only limited power (*magistratus cum potestate*). Official power was limited by subordination to the Law and the right to intercession (opposition of one official to the action of his colleague: *jus intercedendi*). Appeal: the *comitiae (provocatio).*

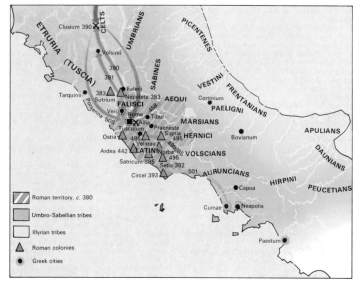

Rome and Central Italy to 380 B.C.

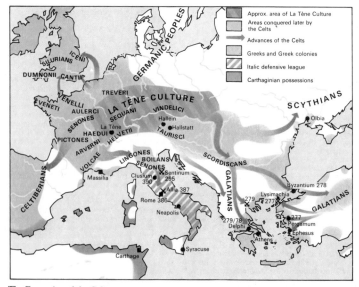

The Expansion of the Celts

Class Struggles

The gap between the patricians, with their polit. and relig. privileges, and the plebeians (*terrae filii* = sons of the earth, also fatherless) grew ever wider. The indebtedness of the plebeians, and the repeated violation of the patricians' pledge (*fides*) to improve the econ. and legal position of the plebeians, aggravated the situation.

494 Retreating to the sacred mt (*mons sacer*) or Aventine, and pledging mutual allegiance (*lex sacrata*), the **plebeians est. a milit. levy of their own.** Return of the people after concessions by the patricians: **creation of the Concilia plebis tributa** (assembly of the plebeians by tribes) chaired by the popular tribunes. The Popular Assembly was responsible for the election of the tribunes (at first 2, after 472, 4 (5) consistent with the urban districts (*lex publilia*); still later 10), and popular decisions (*plebiscitae*). From **287, (lex hortensia)** decisions of the Popular Assembly became binding on the entire pop. Duties and rights of the 'inviolable' (*sacrosancti*) **popular tribunes:** protection of the plebeians from arbitrary acts by the magistrates (*jus auxilii*), right of intercession regarding punishment or arrest of a citizen (*jus intercedendi*), power of veto over official acts of magistrates and decisions of the senate, except for war. As overseers of the Temple of the Trinity of Ceres, Liber and Libera, the **plebeian aediles** were aides of the popular tribunes. Dedicated in 493 on the Aventine Hill, the Temple was the centre of plebeian relig. life and contained a treasury and archives.

Reactions of the patricians: *c.* 485 exclusiveness of the clans. Continued conflict between the patricians, who utilized their rural *clientela*, and the plebeians, whose tribunes in turn threatened the patricians with court action before the plebeian assembly.

c. **450 The Laws of the Twelve Tables** (*leges duodecim tabularum*) effected reconciliation: a commission of 10 men was to codify the customary law (*decemviri legibus scribundis*). Contents: civil law, criminal law and trial procedure, public law and relig. law (strong infl. of Gk law: SOLON's code). Prohibition of marriage between patricians and plebeians (a prohibition voided by the *lex canuleia* of 445). The 12 bronze tables were displayed in the Forum. **The concept of the state prevailed over the concept of class.**

367–66 Licinio–Sextian Laws: (1) Easing of debts (interest paid deducted from amount due). (2) The size of property acquired from public lands fixed (500 *jugera* = 125 hectares). Abolition of consular power for milit. tribunes (practised from 445); plebeians admitted to the office of consul in their place. **A nobility of office holders** (*optimates, nobiles*), consisting of patricians and plebeians, developed. All offices opened to plebeian upper class (dictator 356, censor 351, praetor 337).

300 This development completed with admission to relig. offices (*lex ogulnia*); **end of class struggles;** settlement in the interest of the state.

Foreign Affairs

c. **510 Treaty between the Rom. Republic and Carthage** (1st public Rom. treaty): recognition of Carth. trade monopoly in the Western Mediterranean by Rome; Rom. allies not to be troubled by Carthage.

498–493 The Lat. war ended with the recognition of the autonomy of the Lat. cities by Rome. Rome was to have the supreme command during war. Trade and marriages. 486 the Hernici admitted. The Rom. offensive followed the struggles with the Aequi and Volsci, who advanced from the mts into the plains (legends of CORIOLANUS and CINCINNATUS).

406–396 10 yrs war with the Veii ended with the conquest and destruction of the city. Rom. advance to the N. was now possible; however, at this time the migration of 2 peoples began:

1. The Celts gradually migrated from their homes on the upper Rhine and the upper Danube to France, Spain, the Brit. Isles and southward along the Danube (La Tène period). Iron weapons secured a position of supremacy for them. The tribes were led by warlike aristocracies. The fact that only priests could offer sacrifices and decide legal questions was the basis of the priesthood's (the Druids) great infl.

c. 400 Incursion of the Celts into Italy and settlement in the valley of the Po. The first encounter with the Romans at **Clusium** (390) was followed by

387 the sack of Rome by the Gauls: beaten by the Celts led by their duke (= Brennus) at the Allia, the 'Hellenic' city of Rome was taken and burned. The capitol was besieged. Receiving ransom, the Celts withdrew with much booty (*Vae victis!* = 'Woe betide the defeated!') Consequences: loss of Rom. power through attacks by surrounding tribes.

From 380 reconstruction of the city. Erection of a strong wall around the Seven Hills (the Servian Wall).

358 Renewal of the treaty between Rome, the Latins and the Hernici in the face of the Celt. threat.

2. The Samnites advanced in 4 directions: Corfinium, Picenum, Apulia and to the western coast of Italy. Conquest of Capua, Cumae and Posidonia. Formation of a league.

354 Rom.–Samnitic alliance of defence against the Gauls and to keep their common neighbours in check (the Vosci, Aurunci and Campanians).

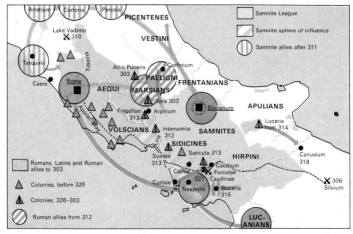

The Second Samnite War, 326–304 B.C.

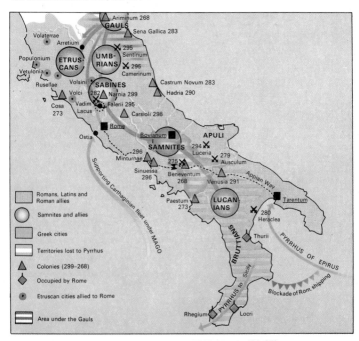

The Third Samnite War, 298–290 B.C.; **the war with Tarentum, 282–272** B.C.

348 2nd treaty between Rome and Carthage: closure of the western Mediterranean to Rom. and Lat. trade, but free trade with Sicily and Carthage. Freedom from Carth. interference for the Lat. cities subject to Rome.

345 Subjugation of the Aurunci. The Sidicini joined the Samnites. Because of a Rom. treaty with Capua (*Foedus aequum*).

343–341 the **1st Samnite War** broke out, ending in a compromise peace: the Samnites agreed to the joining of Capua to Rome, the Romans to the Sidici–Samnite union.

340–338 The Lat. War. A revolt of the Latins, who revived the ind. Lat. League; beaten down by the Romans and their Samnite allies (340 b. of Sinuessa), the Lat. League dissolved. The individual communities were tied to Rome by varying legal arrangements (see below). The bowsprits captured in the naval b. of 338 decorated the speaker's stand (= *rostra*) in the Forum Romanum.

338 Capua granted legal equality with Rome: army, coinage and self-admin.

329 Complete subjugation of the Vosci after the seizure of Privernum.

326–304 2nd Samnite War caused by Rom. aid to Naples, then under Samnite pressure, and the Rom. occupation of Fregellae (328), then fortified against the Samnites.

321 The Rom. army was surrounded in the **Caudine passes** ('Caudine Forks'); it was allowed to withdraw under humiliating circumstances (hostages, return march under a symbolic yoke of spears). Construction of the **Via Appia** as a supply-line for Capua and to aid in the war against the Samnites. Defeat of the Etruscans, allies of the Samnites since 311, at Lake Vadimo (310), and encirclement of the Samnites by the establishment of colonies (garrisons). Advance to Apulia and Samnium (seizure of Bovianum, the Samnite cap.).

304 Peace treaty: Campania annexed by Rome, the Samnite League remained intact, but Samnite expansion prevented.

306 3rd Rom. treaty with Carthage.

298–290 3rd Samnite War (coalition: Samnites, Etruscans, Celts, Sabines, Lucanians, Umbrians). Victs. of Rome over individual opponents. Occupation of Bovianum (298). Breakthrough of the Samnites to the N. and union with the Celts and Etruscans in Umbria.

295 Rom. vict. at Sentinum: peace with the Etruscans. Foundation of the Rom. colony Venusia (20,000 Rom. citizens) in Apulia (291).

290 Peace with the Samnites, who were obliged to do milit. service.

285–282 Struggles with the Celts. Conquest of the territory of the Gallic Sennones (Ager Gallicus, together with the colony Sena Gallica). **Rome's domination of Cen. Italy thereby secured.**

282–272 Rom. war with Tarentum. Tarentum's sphere of interest was encroached upon by Rom. assistance to Thurii (against the Lucanians), Locri and Rhegium. Open war followed when a Rom. fleet was attacked in the harbour of Tarentum, which it was not allowed to use by the terms of the treaty of 303. Tarentum allied with king PYRRHUS OF EPIRUS, who defeated the Romans at the head of 20,000 mercenaries, 3,000 Thessalian mounted men and 26 war-elephants

280 at the b. of Heraclea. The Bruttians, Lucians and Samnites joined him.

279 Vict. of Pyrrhus at Ausculum. Great losses (Pyrrhic victory). His peace offer, demanding the vacating of Lower Italy, was rejected by the Senate. War-alliance of Rome with Carthage, which sent an auxiliary fleet to Ostia.

278–275 Successful campaigns of PYRRHUS against the Carthaginians in Sicily; called by the Gk cities, he conquered all of it with the exception of Lilybaeum. His aim to create a kdm of Sicily and Lower Italy was thwarted by the opposition of the Gk cities and their surreptitious alliance with Carthage. PYRRHUS returned to Italy after great losses.

275 The Romans defeated Pyrrhus at Beneventum. He returned to Epirus.

272 Peace after the surrender of Tarentum: territ. concessions by Tarentum. The Gk cities of Lower Italy became allies of Rome. **Rom. domination of Lower Italy secured.**

State and Admin.
The milit. successes were sustained by the **organization of Rom. rule** in Cen. and Lower Italy. The communal Rom. state was preserved by the delegation of Rom. citizens to all colonies (city-state and Empire remained tied). The **Ital. Defensive Community** consisted of: (a) **Citizens of Rome** and Rom. territory, Rom. citizens in the colonies, and tribal groups which had been given Rom. citizenship; (b) communities **with the rights** – except for voting – **of Rom. citizens** (*civitates sine suffragio . . municipia*); (c). **the allies** (*socii, civitates foederatae*), whether autonomous or recognizing Rom. overlordship. The territory of Rome measured 130,000 sq. kms., and had 292,000 armed Rom. citizens. **Finances:** levies of war taxes (*tributum*) and indirect taxes (tolls = *portoria*). **Coinage:** at first unminted copper (*aes rude*) in bars and plates; later imprinted copper bars (*aes signatum*) with images or an inscription; after 300, heavy copper coins (*aes grave*) with a Janus-head on the face and a bowsprit on the reverse. Beginning of silver coinage.

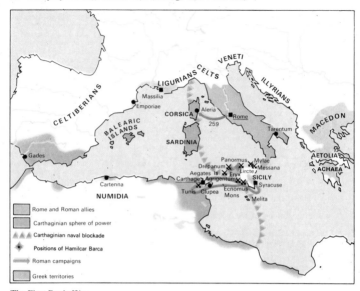

The First Punic War

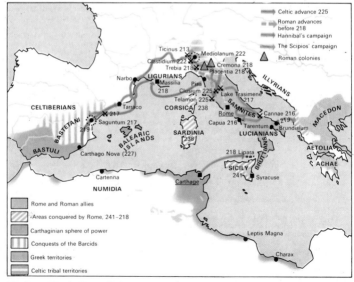

The Second Punic War to 216 B.C.

The 1st Punic War (264–241)

The 'Mamertines' (sons of Mars, Campanian mercenaries), defending Messana, appealed to Rome and Carthage for help against HIERO OF SYRACUSE. Following the landing of a Rom. army, Syracuse and Carthage formed an alliance; but after the defeat of their armies at Messana, HIERO allied himself with Rome. The Romans conquered Sicily as far as Agrigentum (261).

260 Naval b. of Mylae. Vict. of the Romans with newly constructed ships (modelled after a 5-oared Punic vessel they had found stranded). With the invention of the boarding bridge, land-war tactics were used in naval warfare.

256 Naval vict. of the Romans at Cape Ecnomus enabled them to land in Africa. Advance of the Rom. army to Carthage, which sued for peace, but then rejected the severe Rom. peace conditions.

255 b. of Tunis. Utilizing cavalry and elephants, the Carthaginians were victorious under the Spart. mercenary leader XANTHIPPUS. A Rom. fleet transporting the survivors was dest. by a storm. The Romans for the moment gave up naval warfare; however, they conquered Sicily, except for the Carthag. bases of Lilybaeum, Drepanum and Eryx. A newly built Rom. fleet was victorious at **Panormus** (250), but was dest. at **Drepanum** in 249. After yrs of wearying petty warfare with HAMILCAR BARCA, another Rom. fleet was financed by a forced loan from senate members (200 penteres).

241 Naval vict. of the Romans off the Aegates Islands. Peace treaty: Carthage gave up **Sicily (1st Rom. province,** 227) and paid a war indemnity of 3,200 talents over 10 yrs.

After revolts of mercenaries and Libyans against Carthage, the Sard. mercenaries appealed to Rome for aid. Rome declared war on Carthage and forced the cession of Sardinia (238, united with Corsica to become 2nd Rom. province, 227) and payment of a further 1,200 talents. The Tyrrhenian Sea became the *mare nostrum* of the Romans.

229–228 A Rom. fleet fought the Illyr. pirates. Elimination of piracy, payment of tributes by the Illyr. queen TEUTA. The Illyr. coast was under Rom. rule from 219. After an advance by the Celts,

222 vict. of the Romans at Clastidium and conquest of Mediolanum, cap. of the Celt. Insubres. Establishment of colonies (Placentia, Cremona, Mutina) and construction of the Via Flaminia.

From 237 reorientation of Carth. policies (the Barcids). Carthage conquered Spain to compensate for the loss of Sardinia and Sicily, obtaining the ore-rich south-eastern regions in 236 (Sierra Morena), which made possible the payment of the last instalment of war indemnities to Rome (231). Foundation of Carthago Nova (227).

226 The Ebro Treaty: HASDRUBAL, HAMILCAR'S son-in-law, promised not to cross the Ebro for unfriendly purposes. The Romans

recognized Carth. rule s. of the Ebro. After HASDRUBAL'S murder (221), HAMILCAR'S eldest son HANNIBAL became Carth. commander-in-chief.

219 Rom.–Carth. conflict over Saguntum, which was conquered by HANNIBAL despite Rom. intervention. Demand: surrender of Saguntum and extradition of HANNIBAL. Carthage refused, whereupon Rome declared war.

The 2nd Punic War (218–201)

HANNIBAL's surprise attack (crossing the Pyrenees and Alps with 50,000 men, 9,000 cavalry and 37 war-elephants) frustrated the Rom. war-plan (to attack Spain and, from Sicily, Africa). Costly battles in Upper Italy diminished the strength of HANNIBAL's army to 26,000 men. HANNIBAL's brother HASDRUBAL protected Spain with an army. Consul P. CORNELIUS SCIPIO sent his brother CN. CORNELIUS SCIPIO CALVUS to Spain; returning from the Rhône to Italy, he was defeated at the Ticinus in autumn 218. Consul TIBERIUS SEMPRONIUS LONGUS, coming from Sicily, joined with SCIPIO, and together they were defeated in

Dec. 218 at the b. of the Trebia. The Celts joined the Carthaginians. After HANNIBAL's crossing of the Apennines in

217, defeat of Consul C. FLAMINIUS at Lake Trasimene. **Quintus Fabius Maximus** *(cunctator* = procrastinator) **was appointed dictator.** Cautious, delaying conduct of the war (Fabian tactics). Under the next consuls on

2 Aug. 216, b. of Cannae, the worst Rom. defeat in history. The outflanking of the Rom. army by the Carthaginian cavalry led to the loss of almost 50,000 Romans out of an army of 86,000 men, among them the consul AEMILIUS PAULLUS. Capua, the Samnites, Lucanians and Bruttians seceded from Rome. Renewal of defensive Rom. strategy (strategy of attrition). HANNIBAL took up winter quarters in Campania; he had to abandon aggressive conduct of the war through insufficient support from Carthage.

215 Alliance of Hannibal with Philip V of Macedonia (1st Maced. War to 205), whose advance into Illyria failed.

Spain: after the first naval vict. of the brothers P. and CN. CORNELIUS SCIPIO at the mouth of the Ebro and the conquest of Saguntum, a vict. was won over HASDRUBAL (216), whose breakthrough into Italy was prevented. The Romans advanced to the river Guadalquivir and concluded an alliance against Carthage with SYPHAX, ruler of Western Numidia (212).

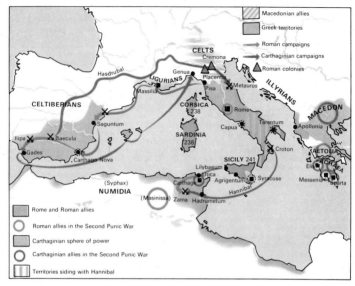

The Second Punic War to 202 B.C.

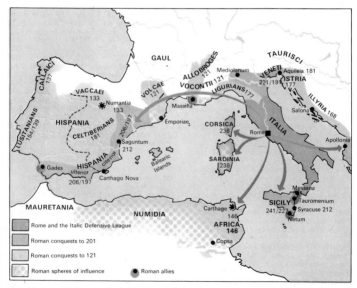

The Western Mediterranean in the 3rd and 2nd cents, B.C.

Sicily: after the death of HIERO OF SYRACUSE, his successor allied with Carthage (215). A 2-yr siege (ARCHIMEDES' engines of war used for defence) by a Rom. army under the consul MARCELLUS led

212 to the conquest and sack of Syracuse. Sicily was reconquered by the Romans and abandoned by the Carthaginians (210).

212 Seizure of Tarentum by Hannibal (secession of the Gk cities along the s. Ital. coast) and HANNIBAL's vict. at Capua.

212 Alliance of Rome with the Aetolian League to obtain relief in the struggle against PHILIP V OF MACEDONIA (later joined by Elis, Messena and Sparta, 211): conquered territories to fall to the league, booty to the Romans. ATTALUS I OF PERGAMON joined the alliance, 209.

211 Siege and conquest of Capua by the Romans made possible by the failure of HANNIBAL's diversionary attack on Rome ('*Hannibal ante portas*'). Capua became *ager publicus* (common land).

Spain: following on the defeat and death of the brothers SCIPIO, brought about by HASDRUBAL and the Numidian prince MASINISSA, the Romans retreated to the Ebro (211). Instead of a consul (*pro consule*) the Romans sent to Spain (210) 25-yr-old PUBLIUS CORNELIUS SCIPIO, who conquered Carthago Nova in 209. After the costly b. of Baecula (208), HASDRUBAL broke through into Italy. Rome was now forced to withdraw its troops from Greece. PHILIP V concluded peace with the Aetolian League (206).

207 b. of the Metaurus river (Sena Gallica). Adopting the Carth. tactics of outflanking and of using legions for independent operations, the Romans were victorious under M. LIVIUS SALINATOR and C. CLAUDIUS NERO. Death of HASDRUBAL.

After SCIPIO's victory over MAGO and MASINISSA at Ilipa (206), the Romans advanced to Southern Spain (seizure of Gades). Departure of the Carth. fleet under MAGO for the Balearic Islands, and from there to Genoa to win over the Ligurians and Gauls once more for the fight against Rome. **End of Carth. rule in Spain.** SCIPIO returned to Rome and was elected consul (205). Peace between Rome and PHILIP V (205).

204 Scipio's crossing to Africa (MASINISSA's defection from Carthage. Rom. victory at Tunis (203) and fruitless peace negotiations lead to HANNIBAL's recall from Italy. (203 death of MAGO in Upper Italy.)

202 Decisive b. of Zama. The Carth. army dest.; HANNIBAL fled to Hadrumetum and advised peace. **Peace treaty:** abandonment of Spain, surrender of Numidia to MASINISSA, payment of reparations to the amount of 10,000 talents over 50 yrs, surrender of warships, except for 10 triremes, prohibition of warfare outside Africa, warfare in Africa only with Rom. permission. The territory of Syracuse became part of the province of Sicilia. The Carth. defeat manifested the vict. of the Rom. citizen (willingness to sacrifice) over the Carth. trader.

SCIPIO received the honorary title AFRICANUS and a triumphal celebration. Subs., continual revolts took place in Spain. Before the first of these (191–189) Spain was divided into 2 provinces Hispania Citerior and Hispania Ulterior (197). The revolt of the Lusitanians, starting in 147 (led by VIRIATHUS until his murder in 139), and that of the Celt. Iberians was terminated by P. CORNELIUS SCIPIO AEMILIANUS after many Rom. defeats by the

133 seizure of Numantia. PUBLIUS CORNELIUS SCIPIO AEMILIANUS received the additional honorary title of NUMANTINUS.

Consequences of the Punic Wars: birth of an **aristocratic party** (the Optimates, led by famous families) and a popular party (Populares); terms of office of annually appointed officials were extended to enable them to carry out long-term milit. tasks. After expansion of Rom. power beyond Italy, provinces were est. in the subj. territories; these were the property of the Rom. people. In exchange for payment of a tax (*stipendium*), the land remained in the hands of the original owners. The **admin. of the provinces** was carried out by praetors as deputies of the Rom. people. The provinces were **exploited** by leasing the collection of taxes and duties to tax-farmers (= *publicani*), most of whom belonged to the **equestrian class** which rose to power during the 2nd cent. Rome became the leading centre of banking and capital. Through their relationship as '*clientela*', many states lost their autonomy (MASINISSA OF NUMIDIA, PRUSIAS OF BITHYNIA, etc.): they recognized the overlordship of Rome and suffered the supervision of their foreign policy.

Rome's intervention in the Eastern Mediterranean did not initially aim at the conquest of the Hellen. states. Rather it was based on polit. considerations: maintenance of the balance of power.

Econ. life: the utilization of slaves during the 2nd Punic War led to the development of a war industry; slavery was also introduced on the large estates (*latifundia*) during the 2nd cent. The wasting of the lands of Southern Italy during the wars led to the desolation of that area; the peasants moved to the city of Rome. End of the ancient Rom. agrarian and peasant state. *c.* 180 the Rom. silver dinar was coined (weight 4·55 gms.). Extension of Rom. long-distance trade throughout the Mediterranean.

Culture: under the infl. of the **Scipionic circle**, incl. PANAETIUS (Stoic ethics), POLYBIUS (writing of history), C. LAELIUS (rhetoric) and LUCILIUS (satire), the Gk ideal of civilization was adopted.

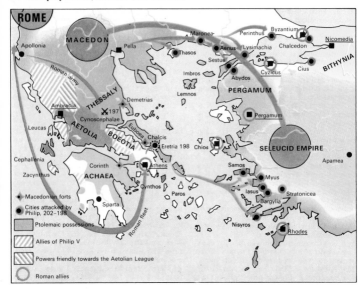

The Second Macedonian War, 200–197 B.C.

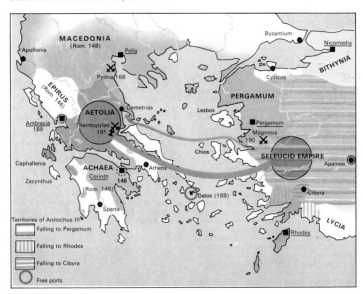

The war against Antiochus III, 192–188 B.C.

200–190 War with the Gauls in Upper Italy.
Rome suppressed the uprising of the Boii
and Insubres, who were supported by
scattered Carthaginians. The Via Aemilia
was built to extend the Via Flaminia to
Placentia (187). The colony of Aquileia was
founded as a trade metropolis for northern
Europe (181).

200–197 2nd Macedonian War. Appeals for
aid by Pergamum, Rhodes and Athens against
the expansionary effects of PHILIP V OF
MACEDONIA, who concluded an alliance
directed against Egypt with ANTIOCHUS III
OF SYRIA. A Rom. fleet protected the
Piraeus and threatened Eretria, which was
taken by the Romans (198). After the Rom.
breakthrough into Thessaly under T.
QUINCTIUS FLAMININUS they were, in

197, victorious at Cynoscephalae. Peace treaty:
PHILIP V surrendered hegemony in Greece;
payment of 1,000 talents as a war indemnity.
Surrender of the fleet, exc. for 6 ships.

**196 Declaration of independence for the Gk
states** by FLAMININUS at the Isthmian Games.
The Romans left Greece (194).

192–188 Rome's war with Antiochus III, who
had forced the Egyptians out of Syria and
Palestine, after re-establishment of Seleucid
rule in the E. (campaign in Bactria). Allied
with the Aetolian League, he wanted to
obtain 'the Ptolemaic possessions in the
Aegean and landed in Thessaly. After the
defeat of ANTIOCHUS at Thermopylae (191)

190 the b. of Magnesia on the Sipylus. Vict.
over ANTIOCHUS by the Romans under L.
CORNELIUS SCIPIO aided by his brother
SCIPIO AFRICANUS. The Aetolian League
was defeated in

189 by the seizure of Ambracia.

188 Peace of Apamea. ANTIOCHUS obliged to
pay 15,000 talents in 12 annual instalments
and to surrender all warships exc. 10. The
possessions in Asia Minor were given to
Rhodes and Pergamum, making them, as
buffer-states, factors balancing the power of
the Seleucid kdm. **Rome was mistress of the
Eastern Mediterranean.**

Rome and Carthage

HANNIBAL, elected to the highest office of
Carthage (Sufete, 196), fled (195) to ANTIOCHUS
III because of a Rom. extradition demand.
ANTIOCHUS rejected HANNIBAL'S plan to
transfer the war to Italy. After the Peace of
Apamea, HANNIBAL fled to king PRUSIAS OF
BITHYNIA; the Romans demanded his extradition. **Suicide of Hannibal (183).** His great
opponent, SCIPIO AFRICANUS, was accused of
high treason, and L. SCIPIO, who after the
defeat of ANTIOCHUS III had received in
'triumph' the honorary title of ASIATICUS, of
embezzlement. The leader of the anti-Scipionic
party, CATO, censor since 184, was engaged
in fighting corruption within the nobility.
SCIPIO AFRICANUS d. 183 in self-imposed exile.

171–168 3rd Macedonian War. PERSEUS, son
of PHILIP V, attempted to restore hegemony
over Greece and was denounced in Rome by
EUMENES OF PERGAMUM. Initial Rom.
failures and ambiguous position of Rhodes
and Pergamum.

22 Jun. 168 b. of Pydna, vict. of Rome under
L. AEMILIUS PAULLUS, son of the consul of
the same name who had d. at Cannae.
Peace followed the capture of PERSEUS at
Samothrace: elimination of the Maced. kdm
by partition into 4 autonomous territories.
1,000 hostages of the Achaean League
(among them the historian POLYBIUS) were
brought to Rome (p. 95). **Delos became a
free port** and competed with Rhodes (which
fell to Athens in 166). Because of the
enormous booty, the Rom. citizens were
excused payment of war contributions
(*tributum*). After an uprising, Macedonia
became a Rom. province (148; p. 67). As a
result of Rom. intervention after the b. of
Pydna, ANTIOCHUS IV had to leave Egypt.
An uprising of the Achaean League was
suppressed following

146 the destruction of Corinth. The territories
of the Achaean League came under Maced.
provincial admin. The Via Egnatia, from
Dyrrhachium to Thessalonice, was constructed.

149–146 The 3rd Punic War. Constant conflicts with MASINISSA, who was prodded by
Rome, drove Carthage into a war not
approved by Rome (150). Rome declared
war (CATO: '*Ceterum censeo Carthaginem
esse delendam*'). After the landing of 2 Rom.
armies, the Carthaginians capitulated, but
then refused to leave the city. They renewed
the struggle. Sent to Carthage, P. CORNELIUS
SCIPIO AEMILIANUS (147) accomplished

146 the seizure of Carthage, which was dest.
despite a plea by P. CORNELIUS SCIPIO.
The survivors were sold into slavery. The
Carth. territory became the Rom. province
of Africa. Triumph of SCIPIO AEMILIANUS
(honorary title: AFRICANUS MINOR).

136–132 1st Slave War. The Syrian EUNUS
brought the slaves of the Sicil. *latifundiae*
together and led them into the fight against
Rome (at times there were 200,000 slaves
in revolt). EUNUS assumed the royal dignity
in the Hellen. fashion. He was taken
prisoner after the capture of Enna and
Tauromenium; 20,000 slaves were crucified.

**133 Attalos III of Pergamum bequeathed his
kdm to the Romans;** it became the Rom.
province of Asia in 129.

The family: holding all-inclusive, unlimited and indivisible authority (*patria potestas*) over the wife (*mater familias*), children (*liberi*), slaves (*servi*), domestic animals, movable and immovable property, the father (*pater familias*) stood at the head of the family. Upon the father's death, the *patria potestas* ceased and the sons became masters of their lives and property. Domestic discipline was enforced by the father's authority (*disciplina, potestas; auctoritas*), which was based on his experience (*sapientia*), his mature judgement (*consilium*) and his probity (*probitas*). Prudence (*diligentia*), strictness (*severitas*) and self-control (*continentia, temperantia*) governed the dignified and noble conduct of his actions (*gravitas*). Diligence (*industria*) and consistency (*constantia*) enabled him to reach his aim. The younger generation was educated by the example of the older (*mos maiorum*). Modesty (*modestia*) and reverence (*reverentia*) characterized the relationship of the younger generation to the older, which demanded obedience (*obsequium*), respect (*verecundia*) and purity (*pudicitia, integritas morum*). This domestic discipline (*disciplina domestica*) was the basis of milit. discipline (*disciplina militaris*) and thus of Rom. power and greatness.

Citizenship: virtue (*virtus*), liberty of conscience and action (*libertas*), glory (*gloria*), reverence and piety (*pietas*), loyalty and reliability (*fides*) and a public position (*dignitas*) were the measure of the values of the Rom. citizen, who placed himself at the service of the community (*res publica*) and worked for the power and greatness of his fellow Romans (*maiestas populi Romani*). The welfare of the people was to him the supreme law (*salus populi suprema lex*). The life of the Roman, in which the state occupied the most important part, moved in 3 spheres: *res publica* (the state), and *res privata* (private matters); the latter always had to be subordinated to the state. This state was a state of laws, in which the law (*lex*) had taken the place of the king (*rex*). The singling out of the individual was permitted on 2 occasions:

1. The triumphal entry of a victorious commander.
2. The funeral of a nobleman.

There was no written constitution. The experiences of earlier generations (*mos maiorum*), which constituted the most important educational factor in Rome, were the foundations of public thought and action.

The Law: the greatest contribution of the Rom. people (acc. to HERDER 'the proud law-giver of the nations') was in the field of law. Added to the *jus civile* (the customary law, flowing from sources of civil law) was the *jus gentium* (the law of peoples). It was a modification of parts of the *jus civile* after the expansion of Rome beyond Italy; it could also be applied to non-Romans without changes. *Jus civile* and *jus gentium* were part of the *jus publicum* (= *jus populi*): the law determined by the people. It was distinct from the *jus privatum* (= *jus singulorum*), which applied to the legal relations between families, and later between

citizens (*cives*). During the later Imp. period, coercive gvtl measures were introduced and justified on the basis of the *jus publicum*. The praetor developed the *jus praetorianum*, later the *jus honorarium*, by virtue of his official position; it was recorded in the official edict containing the principles underlying his instructions to the judges (*juris dictio*) which the praetor published at the beginning of his term of office. The edict was valid for the term of office of the praetor; after examination, adoption by his successor (the *edictum perpetuum* developed at the end of the Republic).

Care of the Law was at first entrusted to the priests, since it was part of the divine order. After the establishment of the Law of the Twelve Tables it still remained in the hands of the priests; only after publication of the 'lament' and calendar by the scriptor CN. FLAVIUS, on the urging of the censor APPIUS CLAUDIUS CAECUS, could every citizen gain information about the laws then valid (consequence: admission of plebeians to priestly offices). Apart from the legal pronouncements (*lex*) and the recorded legal materials (*jus scriptum*), there were the *mores*, the unwritten customary law (*jus non scriptum*). Laws of the Republic were proposed by the magistracy and passed by decision of the Popular Assembly. At first **jurists began their activities** as counsellors. Later jurisprudence was made a science, reaching its highest point during the Imp. period through the formation of law schools (*sectae*): the Sabinians and the Proculians. On the basis of a privilege granted by the Emperor, important jurists were permitted to give legal opinions (*responsa prudentium*) which were binding on the judges. Imp. legislation was important; it completed development of the legal system. The laws were codified in the *Corpus Juris*. Adoption of Rom. Law by the Eur. peoples has maintained its importance to the present day.

Religion (from the Lat. *religio* = concern for the will of the gods, which is revealed in their instruction and direction (*fatum*); *negligentia* = neglect of the gods' will): The supreme divine trinity: 1. JUPITER (*Optimus Maximus*), formerly the 'Radiant Father of the Heavens', then the God of Rain and Wind, Storm and Thunder; 2. MARS, formerly the God of Agriculture, then the God of War and Master over Life and Death; 3. QUIRINUS (with the same functions as MARS). Later (from 506) the divine trinity of JUPITER, JUNO and MINERVA was revered. At the time of their cult a new epoch began: that of the Republic. Other important gods were: JANUS, the God of Beginnings (January), LIBER (DIONYSUS), the God of Fire, MERCURIUS (HERMES), the God of Trade; important goddesses: VESTA, the Goddess of the Hearth, and CERES (DEMETER), the Goddess of Fruitfulness; also, there were special deities dwelling in springs, groves and caves. The revelations and actions of impersonal deities (*numina*) were decisive in certain historical situations because they provided guidance (*prodigia*).

Religion (*contd*):

New gods were adopted through appeal to them (*evocatio*: appeal to the gods of another city to leave the site of their cult and move to Rome), and through the introduction of cults with the aid of the *interpretatio Romana*. Among these was the cult of CYBELE OF PHRYGIA (205), which was brought to Rome under the name *Magna Mater* ('Great Mother').

During the Imp. period: worship of the Emperor, who represented the state, and a proliferation of mystery cults (e.g. ATTIS, MITHRAS). Rom. religion was state religion (supervision by the magistrates; exercise of the ritual by priests as representatives of the state). Separation of public cults (*sacra publica pro populo Romano*) and private cults (*sacra privata*) of the families (*gentes*), exercised by the *pater familias*. Deities of private life: PENATES (protector of supplies), GENIUS (potency of the male), LARES (protector of field and home), *Di parentes* (ancestors), *Di manes* (deities of the dead).

Collegia of priests: *Pontifices* under the *pontifex maximus*, *vestales* and *augures*, who divine the gods' will by observing the flight of birds, also *haruspices* (study of entrails, esp. livers). The *duumviri* cared for the books of the Sybillines; a *flamen* was responsible for each deity.

Art: The foundations of Rom. art were:

1. Gk art, which came to Rome by 2 routes: (a) by way of Italy and Sicily (Magna Graecia), and (b) via the Etruscans (the first shrines and images of gods were 'Tuscan'). The Romans also learned the Eastern concept of nature through the Etruscans; they imitated it, but subordinated it to their own laws.

2. The ancient Italic ctrs. (Terramare and Villanova ctrs.) and the Rom. character. The Rom. feeling for form was expressed in:

1. Symmetry and axiality (i.e. the stress on the main axis), which was already present in the Terremare settlements; these settlements were prob. laid out in accordance with the principles of land surveyance. Later this technique returned in the Rom. camps with their intersecting main roads (*cardo* and *decumanus*).

2. The shaping of space (the wall no longer is an end in itself, but the container of space). The Gk 'corporal style' (the temple one great sculpture in the round) became the Rom. 'spatial style' (façade and interior space the main elements of artistic form).

The creative achievement of Rom. art.

Architecture: unlike Gk architecture, which centred on the temple, monumental Rom. architecture grew out of practical needs (equality of sec. and relig. architecture). **New technique:** moulding techniques and mortar were used; bricks, arch- and vault-construction. Among the most important structures were those devised by engineers (waterworks and aqueducts, such as the Pont du Gard in southern France); the multi-storeyed Rom.

house (a result of housing shortages) which featured decorative façades (balconies and columned halls); palaces (deriving from the Italic villa) in which the architectonic plan was linked to highly developed horticultural art. The Imp. Forums, with their temples (foundation = a podium with a stairway to the front, accentuating the entrance-side) and columned halls, stand out because of their monumentality and compositional coherence. The incorporation of a multiplicity of rooms into one architectural unit was made possible by systematic planning (Imp. Thermes with cross-vaults, barrel-vaults, domes and partial domes). The Basilica, a hall-like structure with several aisles and heavy barrel-vaults, served as market and courtroom; during later antiquity it became the site of Christ. communal worship, even though it had a flat roof, apsis and raised centre-aisle. Apart from the longitudinal structures, there were the domed central-plan structures (Pantheon), deriving from the ancient Italic buildings and heralding the Christ. central-plan structures (Hagia Sophia at Constantinople).

Sculpture:

1. The portrait bust (portrayals of heads reflecting exactly the features of the face, contrasting to Gk idealization and hero-worship), based on the wax-portraits of ancestors (*imagines maiorum*) kept in the atrium of the Rom. house. Contact with Hellen. art led to greater sophistication, and later to strong illusionary effects. During later antiquity their orientation changed from the here to the hereafter.

2. The historical relief, shaped after illustrations carried in the triumphal processions and later kept in the temple or the homes of those honoured. The first representative example was the peace altar of AUGUSTUS (*ara pacis*), dedicated on 9 Jan. 9 B.C. The triumphal arches followed. High points: the columns of TRAJAN and MARCUS AURELIUS.

Decorative **wall painting** (Pompeii) eventually gave way to the mosaic art of later antiquity (Ravenna).

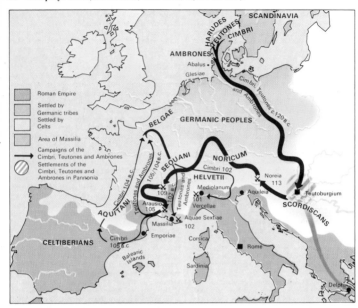

Campaigns of the Cimbri, Teutones and Ambrones

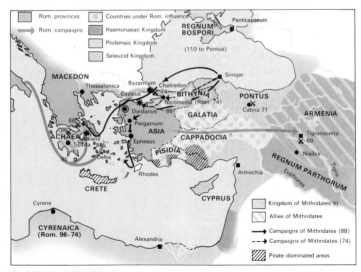

The Mithridatic War, 88–64

The Reform Movement of the Gracchi (133–121)

133 As Popular Tribune TIBERIUS SEMPRONIUS GRACCHUS attempted the settlement of proletarians by the allocation of land from the public lands (*ager publicus*); property acquired from public lands was therefore limited to 1,000 *jugera* (250 hectares) and the royal treasure of Pergamum was distributed to the new settlers. His colleague M. OCTAVIUS, who opposed the measure, was illegally removed from office by the *comitia tributa*. While attempting to secure his own illegal re-election, TIBERIUS GRACCHUS was slain.

123 The plans were taken up again by his younger brother C. SEMPRONIUS GRACCHUS: **The land-reform law was renewed** (*lex agraria*) and certain judgeships were given to equestrians (*lex iudicaria*) to gain their support. He failed because of a proposal to give full citizenship to the Latins and citizenship to all Italic allies (opposition from the senatorial party and the lower classes). The Aventine was occupied by GRACCHUS and his supporters and the Senate declared an emergency. His supporters slain, GRACCHUS had himself killed by a slave (121).

111–105 The Jugurthine War. After the partition of the Numidian kdm by a commission of the Senate, JUGURTHA became sole ruler as a result of his attack on his co-ruler ADHERBAL and his seizure of Cirta (112). The war (bribe of the Romans by JUGURTHA and Rom. failures) was ended by the vict. of MARIUS (106) and the surrender of JUGURTHA to SULLA (105). Part of Numidia became a Rom. province.

113–101 War against the Cimbri and Teutones, who, coming from Jutland with the Ambrones, defeated the Romans at

113 the b. of Noreia (in Carinthia). Two addit. Rom. armies were defeated in Gaul, one at Arausio (105): panic in Rome (the '2nd Celtic Storm'). Elected consul, MARIUS carried out an **army reform:** formation of a professional army of proletarians with pension rights after 16 yrs' service; his sponsorship of the reform created personal ties of the army to him as commander. Reorganization of the army by division of the legion (*c.* 6,000 men) into 10 cohorts of 6 centuries or 3 maniples each. The allies supplied the cavalry. Vict. of MARIUS over the Teutones at

102 b. of Aquae Sextae: and over the Cimbri at the

101 b. of Vercellae.

100 A programme of land-settlement initiated by the Popular Tribune L. APULEIUS aided by MARIUS, who had been elected Consul for the 6th time, failed because of resistance from the Optimates. The revolt was subdued by the senators and the equestrians.

91 Proposals of the Tribune M. LIVIUS DRUSUS: the renewal of the Gracchian agrarian laws, the allotment of judgeships to equestrians and the citizenship for the Italic allies. DRUSUS was murdered, leading to the

91–89 War of the Allies. The allies est. a new state (cap. Corfinium = Italia) and elected an Italic senate (500 members). A concession by Rome ended the civil war: the allies were granted citizenship (89: *lex plautia papiria*).

88–84 1st Mithridatic War (beginning of the civil wars). Attack by MITHRIDATES VI OF PONTUS against Rom. territory in the E.; appeal to the Greeks to rise against Rome.

88 'The Ephesian Vespers': murder of 80,000 Romans in Asia Minor. SULLA, having been charged with the conduct of the war by the Senate, was deprived of his command by the people, who gave it to MARIUS. SULLA conquered Rome and re-established the rule of the Senate (plebiscites valid only with approval of the Senate). After SULLA's departure for Asia, MARIUS and his supporters returned to Rome. Reign of terror over the Optimates by CINNA and MARIUS, who d. during his 7th consulship (86). After seizing Athens, SULLA defeated the troops of MITHRIDATES (Chaeronea 86, Orchomenus 85) and forced him into the

84 Peace of Dardanus: surrender of the conquered territories and the fleet, payment of 3,000 talents. The **2nd Mithridatic War** (83–81) under the Propraetor L. LICINIUS MURENA enforced the fulfilment of the peace conditions. SULLA returned to Rome in 83 and dest. the Marians and their allies, the Samnites and Lucans, in the

82 b. of the Colline Gate (SULLA's sobriquet: FELIX = the lucky one); thereupon, conquest of the provinces of Sicily and Africa by POMPEY, who received a triumph and the honorary title MAGNUS ('the Great').

82–79 Dictatorship of Sulla: publication of proscription lists: 90 senators and 2,600 equestrians killed. **Restoration of senatorial rule:** memberships in the standing courts were restricted to senators (no equestrians). The Senate was increased to 600 members; every quaestor entered it. Consuls and praetors went to the provinces after their terms of office expired (*pro consule, pro praetore*). The office of the Tribune was weakened: legislative initiative of the Popular Assembly was possible only with the approval of the Senate; the Popular Tribune could hold no other official positions.

79 SULLA voluntarily gave up the dictatorship and d. 1 yr later.

Distribution of the provinces to Caesar, Pompey and Crassus

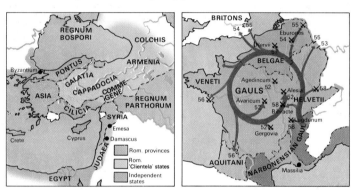

Reorganization of the East   **Caesar's conquest of Gaul**

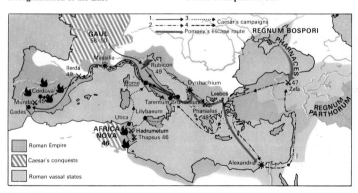

The civil war

77–71 POMPEY's struggle in Spain against the remaining Marians under SERTORIUS. Subjugation and reorganization of Spain.

74–64 3rd Mithridatic War. After initial successes of L. LICINIUS LUCULLUS, mutiny of the army; LUCULLUS recalled by the Senate (68).

73–71 Slave uprising under Spartacus, who was killed fighting M. LICINIUS CRASSUS in Apulia. Remnants of the army of slaves were beaten by POMPEY and taken prisoner.

70 Consulate of Pompey and Crassus: The Sullan laws were abolished, the powers of the tribunes restored; judgeships were filled in equal proportions by senators, equestrians and ordinary citizens; plebiscites were given the force of law.

67 Utilizing extraordinary powers (*imperium extraordinarium*), POMPEY ended the campaign against the pirates in the Mediterranean and was given

66 the command against MITHRIDATES, whom he defeated at the Euphrates. After the subjugation of Pontus

64 the E. was reorganized under Pompey: Pontus, Syria and Cilicia became Rom. provinces; Armenia, Cappadocia, Galatia, Colchis and Judea became Rom. *clientelae.*

63–62 'The Conspiracy of Catiline' discovered and suppressed by CICERO, who had been elected Consul as the '*homo novus*' (*pater patriae* = father of the fatherland). CATILINE and 3,000 supporters d. at Pistoria (62). Following his return from the E. POMPEY discharged his army and celebrated his triumph. The Senate did not approve POMPEY's reorganization of the E. and the distribution of land to his veterans; as a result, in

60 the 1st Triumvirate of Pompey, Crassus and Caesar was est. (private agreement of mutual support, without legal sanction).

59 Caesar's consulate: execution of POMPEY's demands, fixation of taxes for provincial pop. CAESAR received the provinces of Cisalpine Gaul, Illyricum and Gallia Narbonensis for 5 yrs.

56 Conference of Luca: renewal of the Triumvirate, followed by

55 the consulate of Pompey and Crassus. Partition of the provinces: CAESAR received Gaul for an additional 5 yrs, POMPEY, Spain, and CRASSUS, Syria.

53 CRASSUS' defeat and death fighting the Parthians at **Carrhae.**

58–51 Caesar's conquest of Gaul: vict. over the Helvetii at Bibracte and over ARIOVISTUS in Alsace at Mühlhausen (58); the Belgic tribes were subj., esp. the Nervii (57); campaign against the tribes of Brittany and vict. over the Aquitanians (56). The Germ. tribes of the Tencteri and Usipetes were pushed back. 1st crossing of the Rhine and crossing to Britain (55). 2nd crossing to Britain and struggles with the army of Britain under CASSIVELLAUNUS. Uprising of the Eburones under AMBIORIX and of the Nervii and Treviri (54); suppression of the revolt and 2nd crossing of the Rhine (53);

revolt of the Gauls under VERCINGETORIX, conquest of Cenabum, Avaricum and Lutetia Parisiorum, but Gergovia was not taken. Siege and surrender of Alesia (52); the subjugation of Gaul completed (51).

52 Because of the anarchy prevailing in Rome (gang warfare), POMPEY, who sided with the Senate, was elected Consul without colleagues (*sine collega*) to restore order. After the Senate rejected CAESAR's proposition that the armies be discharged simultaneously, it demanded the dissolution of CAESAR's army and his resignation from his position. The Senate, on

7 Jan. 49, issued an **'ultimate' decision** (*Senatus consultum ultimum*): POMPEY was charged with defending the Republic against CAESAR.

49–46 Civil war with POMPEY. CAESAR crossed the Rubicon and conquered Rome and Italy. POMPEY and part of the Senate fled to Greece. CAESAR conquered Spain (vict. at Ilerda) and crossed to Epirus.

9 Aug. 48 Defeat of Pompey at Pharsalus. 20,000 of POMPEY's supporters surrendered, and he fled to Egypt, where he was murdered.

48–47 The Alexandrian War. CAESAR was encircled at Alexandria (burning of the great library); later he was victorious at the Nile and made CLEOPATRA queen.

47 Caesar's vict. at Zela over PHARNACES OF PONTUS (*veni, vidi, vici* = 'I came, I saw, I conquered'). He returned to Italy, then to Africa again.

46 Caesar's vict. at Thapsus over POMPEY's supporters (CATO's suicide at Utica). CAESAR celebrated his triumphs in Rome and was appointed dictator for 10 yrs and *praefectus moribus* (censor for customs and morality).

Reorganization of the state: census of citizens; recipients of free grain reduced to 150,000; municipal reform for Italy (*lex Julia municipalis*).

45 Caesar's vict. at Munda in Spain over the sons of POMPEY. CAESAR was made dictator for life (*dictator perpetuus*) and *imperator*, consul for 10 yrs, supreme commander of the army, *Pontifex Maximus* and holder of tribunal power. He had the right to nominate and appoint officials. Land distribution to the soldiers, care of the provinces, enlargement of the Senate to 900 members, reform of the calendar. Construction of the Basilica Julia and enlargement of the Forum Julium.

15 Feb. 44 ANTONIUS (MARK ANTONY) offered CAESAR the royal diadem; but CAESAR rejected it.

15 Mar. 44 (the Ides of March) Caesar murdered after a senatorial conspiracy led by C. CASSIUS and M. JUNIUS BRUTUS.

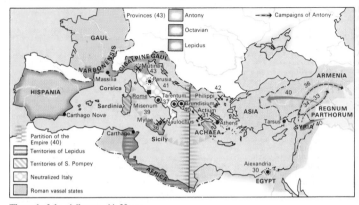

The end of the civil wars, 44–30 B.C.

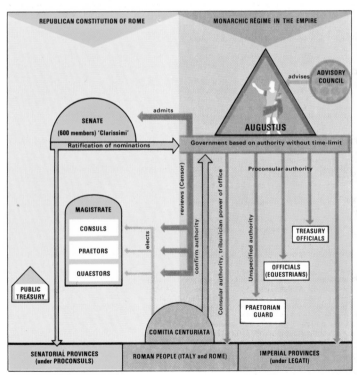

The constitution of the Principate

The Conclusion of the Civil Wars

With the death of CAESAR the Senate assumed power over the state. It executed CAESAR's orders and granted amnesty to his murderers. Although CAESAR's grand-nephew C. OCTAVIUS (OCTAVIAN) had been adopted by him and made his heir, ANTONY obtained the inheritance for himself. After the funeral and the publication of CAESAR's testament, the murderers had to leave Rome. The dictatorship was abolished.

44–43 The Mutinensian War. M. BRUTUS went to the province of Macedonia, CASSIUS to Syria, and DEC. BRUTUS to Gaul, where he was besieged by ANTONY at Mutina. OCTAVIAN, leading his private army, received pro-praetorian power and defeated ANTONY in the b. of Mutina (the Consuls MIRTIUS and PANSA d. in battle). OCTAVIAN received the Consulate for 43 B.C. Special tribunals were appointed to deal with the murderers of CAESAR.

1 Nov. 43 2nd Triumvirate (Antony, Lepidus and Octavian), sanctioned by the public law (lex titia: Triumviri rei publicae constituendae = 3 men to reorder the state) and limited to 5 yrs. The provinces of Sicilia and Africa went to OCTAVIAN, Cisalpine Gaul to ANTONY, Gallia Narbonensis and Spain to LEPIDUS. Reign of terror in Rome through proscriptions (130 senators, 2,000 equestrians, CICERO among them).

42 Twin b. of Philippi. CASSIUS and, 20 days later, M. BRUTUS were beaten by ANTONY. ANTONY went E. (Athens, Syria, Egypt). After the Perusian (Perugia) War, caused by OCTAVIAN's ruthless conduct in settling his veterans, and a struggle with the Consul L. ANTONIUS, ANTONY's brother, the mediation of MAECENAS in

40 led to the **agreement of Brundisium. Partition of the Empire:** ANTONY received the E., OCTAVIAN the W., LEPIDUS Africa; Italy was neutralized.

39 Pact of Misenum: S. POMPEY received Sicily, Sardinia, Corsica and Achaea in return for grain shipments to Rome.

38 Renewal of the Triumvirate for 5 yrs.

37 Pact of Tarentum. ANTONY gave his fleet to OCTAVIAN for the struggle against S. POMPEY.

36 VISPANIUS AGRIPPA's victs. over S. POMPEY at Mylae and Naulochus. LEPIDUS was pushed aside by his election as Pontifex Maximus. After separation from OCTAVIAN's sister OCTAVIA in

36 marriage of Antony with Cleopatra VII. ANTONY campaigned fruitlessly against the Parthians, but was able to occupy Armenia (34). He attempted to establish a Hellen.–Orient. sultanate (gifts of Rom. territories to CLEOPATRA, co-rule of CAESARION). Publication of his will (32), which had been deposited with the vestals by OCTAVIAN, and beginning of the

32–30 Ptolemaic War, which was decided by the

Sep. 31 b. of Actium: naval vict. of AGRIPPA over the fleet of CLEOPATRA, surrender of 19 legions without a fight.

3 Aug. 30 Seizure of Alexandria (suicide of ANTONY and CLEOPATRA). **Egypt became a Rom. province.**

After the reorganization of the E., a triumph in Rome, and the settlement of 120,000 veterans, the extraordinary powers (Potestas omnium rerum) of OCTAVIAN were gradually reduced during his 6th Consulate.

13 Jan. 27 Rest. of the Republic through OCTAVIAN's resignation from power before the Senate.

16 Jan. 27 The Senate bestowed the **honorary title 'Augustus'** on OCTAVIAN.

The Principate

(Princeps = first among equals.) It is based on the consensus universorum (= general consensus) and represents a compromise between monarchical and republican forms. Power was delegated by the Senate and the people. Characteristics of the Principate: authoritarian power (auctoritas) and reverence for traditional forms (mores maiorum).

AUGUSTUS received the Consulate for the community of Rome (27–23); for the Empire he received an undefined Imperium (dominant power): supreme command over the army, foreign policy, the right to conclude int. agreements; he also received an Imperium pro consulare for the imp. provinces, which were administered by legates (legati Augusti pro praetore provinciae).

1 Jul. 23 After giving up the Consulate, AUGUSTUS **was granted tribunal power** for life without being a popular tribune (tribunicia potestas); the intercession of popular tribunes against measures of AUGUSTUS was therefore impossible.

22 AUGUSTUS refused to assume the Consulate and the duties connected therewith, but he did take charge of certain areas: the supply of grain (cura annonae), and the road system (cura viarum).

19 AUGUSTUS was given consular power for life (Imperium consulare) and the supervision of morality for 5 yrs (cura morum): this meant that he received the power of these offices without holding them.

From 12 B.C. **Augustus was Pontifex Maximus;** in 2 B.C. the title pater patriae was bestowed on him.

The Senate administered the pacified provinces (senatorial provinces) and the treasure of the state (Aerarium populi Romanum); however, the fiscal admin. was carried out by the Princeps. The equestrian order became an aristocracy of service (command over the imp. bodyguard – the Praetorian Guard – the prefects and officials); friends (amici Caesaris) advised the Princeps.

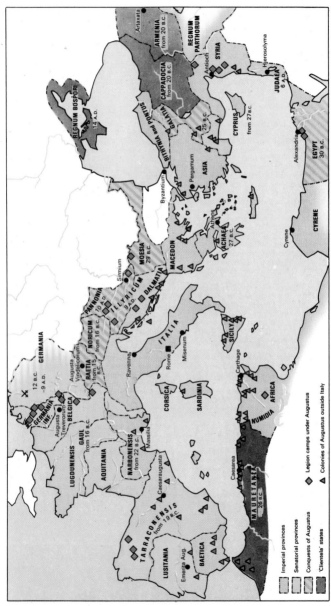

The Empire of Augustus

Augustus and his Successors

7–25 Reorganization of the provinces of Gaul and Spain by AUGUSTUS. Galatia, inherited from king AMYNTAS, became a Rom. province.

0 A peaceful understanding was reached with the Parthian king PHRAATES IV, who returned the legion standards taken from CRASSUS and ANTONY; Rome renounced further expansion.

8 Legislation governing morals: prohibition of marriage between senators and freedmen, punishment for the breaking of marriage vows. Granted tribunal power, AGRIPPA became co-regent for 5 yrs.

7 Sec. celebration of the City of Rome ('Carmen seculare' of HORACE), and proclamation of world peace (pax Augusta).

6–13 AUGUSTUS in Gaul. Reorganization of the province: Aquitania, Lugdunensis, Belgica.

5 Advance of TIBERIUS and DRUSUS, the Emperor's stepsons, to the Upper Danube: the provinces of Raetia and Noricum est.

3–9 Subjugation of the Pannonians by AGRIPPA (d. 12) and TIBERIUS. The Middle Danube reached. After securing the Euphrates and Danube frontiers, advance in 4 campaigns to the Elbe:

2–9 The Germ. Wars of Drusus: subjugation of the Batavians, Frisians and Chauci. After struggles with the Quadi and Marcomanni, DRUSUS reached the Elbe and d. there.

0 Jan. 9 Dedication of the peace altar on the Field of Mars (Ara pacis Augustae).

–6 1st command of TIBERIUS in Germany; he advances to the Elbe.

B.C. After receiving tribunal power, TIBERIUS quarrelled with AUGUSTUS, and instead of reorganizing Armenia, went as a private individual into voluntary exile to Rhodes (5 B.C.), but returned in 2 B.C.

Succession to Augustus: owing to the fact that those chosen to succeed him had d. one after the other, AUGUSTUS secured the succession by the adoption of TIBERIUS (26 Jun. 4 B.C.) – TIBERIUS JULIUS CAESAR.

A.D. 4–6 2nd command of Tiberius in Germany: pact with the Cherusci, subjugation of the Langobards, establishment of a prov. admin., construction of roads and safeguarding of the newly won territories by legion camps. The war against the Marcomanni had to be interrupted because of the revolt of the Pannonians (6–9); the revolt ended with victory over the Dalmatians. Pannonia became a Rom. province (10). The Danube frontier was secured.

b. of the Teutoburger Forest. The Cherusci under ARMINIUS dest. 3 legions commanded by VARUS. The province of Germania was abandoned; but the Rhine frontier was held.

8 Aug. 14 Death of Augustus at Nola (aged 76 yrs). Deification (consecratio) of the departed Princeps (Divus Augustus). A record of AUGUSTUS' reign, composed by himself (res gestae), was displayed on 2 bronze plates attached to pillars in front of the Mausoleum Augusti (the Field of Mars).

(A copy in Gk and Lat. was found in the Roma Temple at Ancyra (Monumentum Ancyranum, Ankara).)

Literature: Livius Andronicus (c. 284–c. 204), 'inventor of the art of translation', est. Lat. literature (translation of the Odyssey = Odusia and Gk tragedies). GNAEUS NAEVIUS (c. 270–c. 201) wrote Lat. comedies and the Rom. national praetexta (historical dramas). He also composed the Bellum punicum, an epic of the 1st Punic War (235). The comedies of **Titus Maccius Plautus** (c. 254–184) had a popular, somewhat obscene and burlesque quality. ENNIUS (239–169) composed an epic on Rom. history in hexameters (the Annals). The founder of Rom. historiography was FABIUS PICTOR, whose Annals (= annual record of events) appeared in Gk c. 200. LUCILIUS (180–102), a member of the circle of the Scipios, wrote satires; his contemporary, P. TERENTIUS AFER (TERENCE), wrote comedies, which were without the bluntness of PLAUTUS. **Cato** left a history of Rome and Italy (the Origins) and the earliest agricultural handbook. **Polybius**, brought from Greece as a hostage to Rome (168), composed his Universal History (pragmatic writing of history). **M. Terentius Varro**, CAESAR's librarian and Rome's greatest scholar, wrote a history of culture; he also wrote about the Lat. language and agriculture.

Cicero (106–43) composed courtroom and public addresses, rhetorical and philosophical tracts (De re publica = On the State; De legibus = On the Laws, etc.) and many letters to acquaintances, to his brother, and to his publisher T. POMPONIUS ATTICUS (109–32).

Cornelius Nepos (100–27) wrote biographies; **G. Sallustius Crispus** (SALLUST) (86–35) the Conspiracy of Catiline and the Jugurthine War. T. LUCRETIUS CARUS incorp. Epicurean philosophy into a didactic poem: De rerum natura (On Nature). The Neoterics introduced Hellen.–Alexandrian poetry: **C. Valerius Catullus** (87–54), epigrams and love-poetry; **Quintus Horatius Flaccus** (HORACE) (85–8), epodes; **P. Vergilius Maro** (VIRGIL) (70–19), Bucolica (pastoral poetry).

Caesar (100–44) wrote commentaries on the campaigns in Gaul (Bellum gallicum) and the civil war (Bellum civile). Literature was promoted as part of the process of cult. renewal by AUGUSTUS, his friend MAECENAS, ASINIUS POLLIO and MESSALLA. VIRGIL composed the Georgics and Aeneid, and justified the rise of the Rom. people. His profound humanism was shared by HORACE: satires, odes (Carmina), epistles (letters on art).

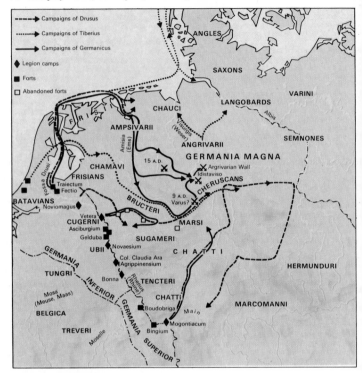

The Romans in Germany

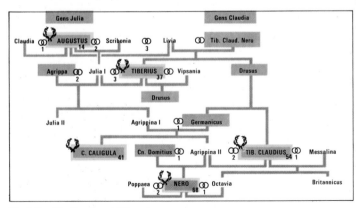

The Julian-Claudian Imperial Dynasty

The Julian–Claudian Dynasty (to A.D. 68)

14–37 Tiberius. The power to elect officials transferred from the people to the Senate. Mutiny of the Legions in Pannonia and along the Rhine was suppressed by GERMANICUS. He undertook a

14–16 campaign against the Germ. tribes, discontinued because of excessive costs. The Germ. tribes then fought between themselves.

17 The provinces of Cappadocia and Commagene est.

22–31 Impact of the selfish Praetorian Prefect SEJANUS, who moved the guard to a camp on the outskirts of Rome. His accusations led to major public trials, executions and suicides. Embittered, TIBERIUS retired to Capri (27).

31 Fall and execution of SEJANUS as a conspirator; but additional trials followed.

37 Death of Tiberius at Misenum.

37–41 Caligula ('Soldier's boot') = **Gaius Caesar Germanicus.** He abolished the trials presided over by the Emperor and restored to the people the right to elect the magistracy. **The Principate of Augustus was changed into a Hellen.–Orient. divine monarchy (Caesar and God):** introduction of Hellen. court-ceremonial and veneration of the Emperor as divine (CALIGULA thought of himself as ALEXANDER, CAESAR and God). Ostentatious campaigns in Germania and Britain.

41 Murder of CALIGULA by the Prefect of the Praetorians, CASSIUS CHAEREA.

41–54 Claudius. Return to the traditions of AUGUSTUS (administrative order), but extension of court-officialdom by imp. freedmen (NARCISSUS). Great infl. of women.

43 Conquest of southern Britain.

46 Establishment of the province of Thrace.

54 Murder of CLAUDIUS by AGRIPPINA, whose son NERO ascended the throne.

54–68 Nero Claudius Caesar. Guided by the philosopher SENECA and BURRUS, Prefect of the Praetorian Guard, NERO's early years were happy ones for Rome.

58–63 Reconquest of Armenia by CORBULO and compromise peace with the Parthians.

60–61 C. SUETONIUS PAULLINUS suppressed an uprising in Britain.

With the murders of BRITANNICUS, his mother AGRIPPINA, his wife OCTAVIA, and BURRUS, the reintroduction of trials presided over by the Emperor (62), and the burning of Rome, NERO's reign became utterly arbitrary (**'Caesar madness'**).

After the failure of PISO's conspiracy (65), which cost SENECA his life, revolt of C. JULIUS VINDEX, governor of Gaul, joined by S. SULPICIUS GALBA in *Hispania citerior* and M. SALVIUS OTHO in *Lusitania.*

68 Suicide of NERO.

68–69 The Year of the 4 Emperors: GALBA, VITELLIUS (commander of the legions on the Rhine), OTHO and VESPASIAN.

The Flavian Dynasty (69–96)

69–79 T. Flavius Vespasianus. After VESPASIAN's accession to the throne, the revolts of the Batavians on the Rhine and the Jews in Palestine (in revolt from 66) were put down.

70 Conquest of Jerusalem (the arch of TITUS at Rome). Securing of the frontiers.

74 Subjugation of the Neckar region: *Agri decumates.*
Increase of the membership of the Senate to 1,000 owing to the inclusion of the plebeian municipal nobility of Italy, to which VESPASIAN belonged. Spain received the Lat. Law. Frugality in the economy of the state. Erection of the Amphitheatrum Flavium (Colosseum).

79 The eruption of Vesuvius during the reign of VESPASIAN's son **Titus,** burying Pompeii, Stabiae and Herculaneum. G. PLINIUS SECUNDUS (PLINY THE ELDER), the early scholar of natural science, d. in the disaster.

81–96 Domitian. The conquest of Britain, initiated again in 78, was completed with the establishment of defences in Scotland (84).

83 Campaign against the Chatti. Construction of the *limes* begun. Severe struggles against the Dacians, who were loc. on the Lower Danube and had been united under their king DECEBALUS (85–9). The Emperor's initially benevolent rule deteriorated into despotism (claim of the title *Dominus et Deus*), leading to a palace conspiracy and eventually

96 to the murder of DOMITIAN.

Literature: A. TIBULLUS (55–19) and S. PROPERTIUS (50–15) were, after **P. Ovidius Naso (OVID)** (43 B.C.–A.D. 17), the creators of the Augustan elegy (autobiographical in character). OVID also composed the *Amores, Metamorphoses,* mythological poems and the *Ars amatoria* (*On the Art of Love*).
Titus Livius (LIVY) (59 B.C.–A.D. 17) was the great historian who, proud of Italy's unity and full of patriotism, wrote the history of Rome in 142 vols. (*Ab urbe condita = From the Beginning of the City*), interpreting its course as the consequence of *virtus Romana* (Rom. virtue) and divine providence. **L. Annaeus Seneca** (4 B.C.–A.D. 65), tutor of NERO – influenced by stoicism (dialogues and tragedies) – and PETRONIUS (*Satiricon, Trimalchio's Feast*) followed during the Julian–Claudian period. It was under the reign of DOMITIAN that the satirist D. JUNIUS JUVENALIS (JUVENAL) (58?–140?) and M. VALERIUS MARTIALIS (MARTIAL), the master of the epigram, came to renown. The greatest historian of the period was **Cornelius Tacitus** (55?–117?). An effective story-teller and an analytical psychologist, he placed great personalities at the centre of his works (modelled after SALLUST): *Histories, Annals, Germania.* **G. Suetonius Tranquillus** (70–146) wrote biographies (*De viris illustribus*). **L. Apuleius** was the author of *Metamorphoses* (*The Golden Ass,* which contains the folk-tale 'Cupid and Psyche').

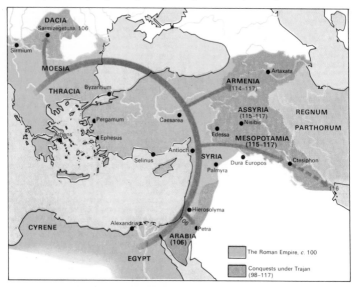

Trajan's conquests in the east

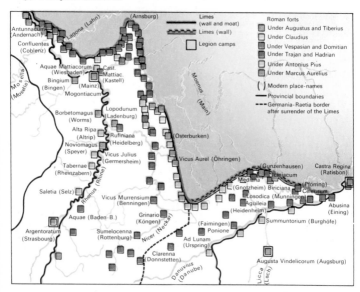

The Limes of Germania Superior and Raetia

The Adopted Emperors (96–192)

Subsequent emperors ascended the throne by adoption. **The dyn. principle was changed to adoptive emperorship (choice of those most fit to rule).**

96–8 M. Cocceius Nerva. Appointed Princeps by the Senate, he adopted the Spaniard

98–117 Trajan after the mutiny of the Praetorian Guard (97). TRAJAN was the first emperor to have a provincial origin. The Senate gave him the title *Optimus* in 114. He subj. the Dacians in several campaigns (101–2, 105), establishing the province of Dacia; the kdm of the Nabataeans in Northern Arabia (106); the province of Arabia; and, after a victorious war against the Parthians and the conquest of Armenia and Mesopotamia, the provinces of Armenia, Assyria and Mesopotamia: **greatest extent of the Rom. Empire.**

117–38 Hadrian, governor of Syria from 116, concluded peace with the Parthians, giving up the conquered territories. Rest. of the Euphrates frontier; at the same time fortifications (*limes*) were built to secure the frontiers in England (Hadrian's Wall), and along the Rhine, Danube and Euphrates. After extension of chancery bureaucracy, HADRIAN undertook extensive journeys to supervise the admin. of the Empire (the 'travelling' emperor; 121–5, 126–9). The reconstruction of Jerusalem as the colony Aelia Capitolina led

132–5 to the revolt of the Jews under Bar Kochba, ending with the conquest of Jerusalem by HADRIAN.

138 Death of HADRIAN and burial in the monumental circular tomb (Mausoleum Hadriani, Castel Sant'Angelo).

138–61 Antoninus Pius continued the peace policies of his predecessors. The *limes* fortifications were extended, the army strengthened by native auxiliaries. In Britain the frontier was extended to the Firth of Forth (the Antonine Wall).

161–80 Marcus Aurelius, 'the philosopher on the Imp. Throne', at first ruled jointly with his brother (by adoption) L. VERUS (to 169): **the Dual Principate.**

162–5 War against the Parthians, who occupied Armenia, Cappadocia and Syria. The war ended with the Rom. victory at Dura Europos (163) and the occupation of Mesopotamia. Because of the plague, which spread from E. to W. over the entire Empire, peace was concluded. Following the crossing of the Danube by Marcomanni, Quadi and Sarmatians

167–75 the 1st Marcomanni War began. An offensive by MARCUS AURELIUS (171) to secure the Danubian frontier eventually brought peace: the Quadi and Marcomanni evacuated a strip of territory along the left bank of the Danube. During the campaign MARCUS AURELIUS composed his major work, the *Meditations*, written in Gk.

176 Erection of a triumphal column (the Marcus Column), with scenes of the Marcomanni War. **Commodus became co-ruler:** **the adoptive principle abandoned in favour of dyn. inheritance.**

178–80 2nd Marcomanni War. The Romans est. the legion camp Castra Regina (Regensburg, 179). But after the death of MARCUS AURELIUS at Vindobona (Vienna) the Romans were forced to give up their offensive policies as a result of the disadvantageous peace treaty. This decision was made by

180–92 Commodus, who thought of himself as the reincarnation of HERCULES and MITHRAS ('Caesarean delusion'). After an unsuccessful conspiracy (182), brigand wars in Italy (186) and uprisings in Africa and Britain, COMMODUS fell victim to a palace insurrection.

193 2nd 4-emperor year: DIDIUS JULIANUS (Rome), P. NIGER (Syria), CLODIUS ALBINUS (Britain) and SEPTIMIUS SEVERUS (Pannonia).

The Severi (193–235)

193–211 Septimius Severus defeated his imp. rivals and attempted to legitimize his rule by fictitious adoption (son of the divine MARCUS AURELIUS). After a fruitless Parthian war (197–9), he stayed for a time in the eastern provinces. He preferred Syria (preference for Palmyra) and Africa (increasing importance of Carthage). Owing to the settling of the families, the frontier army turned into a **militia.** Severus disregarded the powers of the Senate, abolished tax-farming and eliminated the prerogatives of Rome and Italy.

208–11 Severus' Brit. campaign. He was accompanied by JULIA DOMNA ('the mother of the camp') and his sons CARACALLA (2nd co-ruler after 198) and GETA (3rd co-ruler after 209). Death in Eboracum (York).

211–17 CARACALLA; he had his co-ruler GETA and most of the latter's supporters murdered in 212.

212 Constitutio Antoniana: all free inhabitants of the provinces received full Rom. citizenship – **Unity of the Empire.** After struggles along the Rhine (Alamanni) and Euphrates (Parthians), the Emperor was murdered. A brief reign by MACRINUS was followed by the proclamation of CARACALLA's nephew, ELAGABALUS OF EMESA, the priest of the Syr. Sun-god, as Emperor by the army.

218–22 Elagabalus ruled under the fateful infl. of his grandmother JULIA MAESA. **Introduction of the Syr. cult of Baal at Rome.** After the murder of ELAGABAL and his mother SOAEMIA by the guard, his cousin ascended the throne.

222–35 Severus Alexander ruled under the infl. of his mother JULIA MAMMAEA, who was regent. The army under C. JULIUS VERUS MAXIMUS mutinied at Mainz after indecisive struggles with the Parthians (231) and incursions by the Marcomanni (232). The Emperor and his mother were slain.

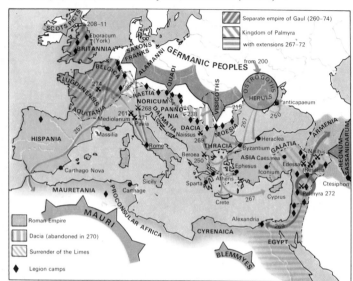

The Roman Empire in the 3rd cent.

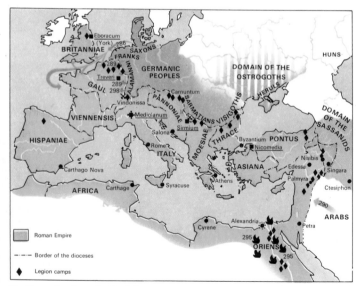

The Roman Empire under Diocletian

Threats from Abroad

The 'crisis of the Ancient World' began as a result of the attacks by the mounted peoples living on the borders of the Empire (Germans, Sarmatians, Persians, Berbers, Moors). The lack of '*clientela*' states resulted in the surrender of provinces and the establishment of separate states. The Neo-Pers. **Empire of the Sassanids** subs. became the Rom. Empire's strongest and most dangerous enemy.

227–41 Ardashir I thought of himself as the successor of the Achaemenids. Revival of the teachings of ZARATHUSTRA (ZOROASTER), which became the state religion; but along with it spread the syncretic, gnostic teachings of MANI (217–77). During the 3rd and 4th cents. constant struggles with the Romans in Mesopotamia, Syria and Armenia, which was partitioned in 384. From the end of the 4th cent. struggles with the 'Hephtalites' (White Huns). The constant tensions between the centralizing monarchy (chancery bureaucracy) and the feudal nobility, which did not permit a determined foreign policy, led to the relig.-socialistic reforms of the Mazdak (high-priest) under KAWADH I (488–531), which were directed against the nobility: demand of communal property and marriage. Suppression of the Mazdak's followers and **reform of the state under Khosru I** (531–79): tax reform after the Rom. example (establishment of a nobility of officials, survey of the lands). Subs. the state maintained itself against Eastern Rome and defeated the Hephtalites. Expansion under KHOSRU II PARVIZ (590–628) up to Egypt (614). (Removal of the relic of the Cross from Jerusalem.)

628 Peace with the E. Rom. Emperor HERACLIUS (return of the relic of the Cross, p. 139).

637 Termination of the Sassanid kdm by the Arabs (p. 139).

The Soldier Emperors (235–305)

These were proven generals, but also men of the provinces, who, proclaimed by the army – the decisive element of power – were almost all murdered after brief reigns.

235–8 Maximinus Thrace defeated the Alamanni. Incursion of the Persians into Mesopotamia (237).

238–44 Gordian III, with the aid of Goth. auxiliary troops in the b. of Resaina (242), defeated the Persians under SHAPUR I (241–72), who had invaded Mesopotamia; he forced them to evacuate Mesopotamia.

244–9 M. Julius Philippus, son of an Arabian sheik, was able to celebrate the 1st millennium of Rome's founding.

249–51 Decius (of Illyr. origin) attempted to revitalize Rome and its religion. His measures brought about the first general persecution of Christians (p. 107). He d. fighting the Goths.

From 250 the plague spread from Ethiopia.

251–3 Trebonius Gallus concluded peace with the Goths.

253–60 Valerian assumed the defence of the E. and appointed his son GALLIENUS as co-ruler

in the w. The frontiers of the Empire were threatened: attacks by the Goths, Quadi and Sarmatians (254), and by the Parthians (256). The Franks and Alamanni crossed the Upper Ger.–Raetian *limes*; Mauret. tribes pressed on the frontier in northern Africa. VALERIAN was taken prisoner by SHAPUR I at Edessa (260) and d. captive.

260–68 Gallienus carried out a **reform of the army:** he est. a reserve army, and a mounted army for quick dispatch to troubled border regions.

268–70 Claudius II defeated the Alamanni (268) and the Goths in the b. of Naissus (269).

270–75 Aurelian defeated the Alamanni at Pavia (271), subj. the **Palmyran state of Empress Zenobia** (272) and the separate empire of Gaul (274), which had been est. in 260 ('30 Tyrants'): rest. of Imp. unity.

274 Assumption of the title 'Lord and God' (*Dominus et Deus*) and introduction of the sun cult of Emesa (*Sol invictus*) which, tied to the cult of the Emperor, was made a state-wide cult. **Tacitus** (275–6) was succeeded by

276–82 Probus, who secured the Rhine and Danube frontiers.

283–4 Carus defeated the Persians, but he and his sons Carinus and Numerian were murdered.

284–305 Diocletian carried out comprehensive Imp. reforms to ease the burden of Imp. admin. by decentralization (293). DIOCLETIAN and his co-ruler MAXIMIAN (286) adopted their Prefects of the Guard, GALERIUS and CONSTANTIUS CHLORUS, and appointed them as successors (*Caesares*): **introduction of Tetrarchy.** DIOCLETIAN received the E. (Nicomedia), MAXIMIAN, Italy and Africa (Milan), CONSTANTIUS, Spain, Gaul and Britain (Trier and York), and GALERIUS, Illyricum, Macedonia and Greece (Sirmium). After a 20-yr reign the Augusti were to resign in favour of the two Caesares, who again would appoint Caesares as aids (*apparitores*).

297 Organization of the Empire into 12 administrative districts (dioceses) – governed by diocesan supervisors (*vicari*) – and 101 provinces. The Empire became an absolute monarchy = **Dominate** (Divine Emperor with Imp. vestments and crown council). The citizens became subjects (*subjecti*) and were at the disposal of the ruler; peasants were tied to the soil (*coloni*) and corporations of artisans were forced to supply the army.

301 Price controls introduced because of inflation. Uprisings in the interior were suppressed, the Imp. frontiers secured and Rom. rule in the E. extended.

305 Abdication of Diocletian and Maximian.

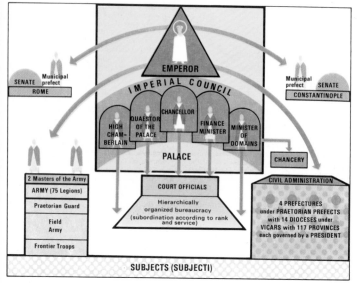

The constitution of Diocletian and Constantine

The Roman Empire in the 4th cent.

Constantine the Great

After the termination of the first tetrarchy the new Augusti, GALERIUS and CONSTANTIUS, appointed SEVERUS and MAXIMINUS DAIA as Caesars; however, the tetrarchic system failed because of the dyn. ambitions of the individual rulers (CONSTANTIUS' son, CONSTANTINE, at York; MAXIMIAN's son, MAXENTIUS, at Rome), which led to conflicts.

308 Imp. conference at Carnuntum: LICINIUS appointed Augustus of the w.; DIOCLETIAN, however, rejected the title of Augustus.

312 Defeat of MAXENTIUS by CONSTANTINE at the Milvian bridge, making CONSTANTINE ruler of the w.

313 LICINIUS defeated MAXIMINUS DAIA at Adrianople.

324-37 Constantine the Great.

324 Constantine's victories over Licinius at Adrianople and Chrysopolis: **Constantine was sole ruler** (*totius orbis imperator*).

11 May 330 Byzantium, renamed Constantinople, was made the Christian cap. (the 2nd Rome) in conscious contrast to 'heathen' Rome.

Consummation of the absolute state through the extension of DIOCLETIAN's imp. reforms. Strict court ceremonial to emphasize the divine nature of the Emperor (gilded robe, diadem, *proskynesis*). Commanded by the 'masters of the army' (*magistri militum*), the milit. was subject to the Emperor; so were the Prefects of the 4 parts of the Empire, the Crown Council (*Sacrum consistorium*), and the Prefect (*Praefectus urbi*) of Rome and Constantinople.

1. The army, increased to 75 legions (900,000 men), consisted of the field army (*comitatenses*), the army of the frontier (*limitanei*) and the guard (*candidati*). Neighbours (*foederati*) assumed the protection of the frontiers.

2. Organization of the Empire into 4 prefectures: Oriens (Constantinople), Illyricum (Sirmium), Italia (Milano), Gaul (Trier); there were 14 dioceses and 117 provinces.

3. The Crown Council consisted of the following ministers (*comites*): 'Supervisor of offices' = chancellor (*magister officiorum*), 'supervisor of the sacred palace' (*quaestor sacri palatii*), chief chamberlain (*praepositus sacri cubiculi*), minister of finance (*comes sacrarum largitionum*) and treasurer (*comes rerum privatarum*). The chancery and the court officials were subject to the Crown Council. Two commanders of the palace guard (mounted and foot) assumed the protection of the Emperor.

4. The senates of Rome and Constantinople became city councils.

The separation of milit. and civil power was crucial (abandonment of Rome's 1,000-yr-old tradition). Hered. ties of people to their occupations. Introduction of head and real-estate taxes.

337 Constantine the Great d. after receiving baptism on his deathbed. After conflicts over the inheritance and the death of his brothers, CONSTANTIUS II emerged as sole ruler.

The Successors of Constantine

337-61 Constantius II. Arianism was made binding on the entire Church.

357 b. of Argentoratum (Strasbourg): rest. of the Rhine frontier. During the struggle against the Persians in the E., CONSTANTIUS' nephew and successor JULIAN (361-3) d. The last member of CONSTANTINE's dynasty, he was called APOSTATA because of his preference for non-Christ. religions and cults. The war was brought to an end by JOVIAN (363-4): Rome lost Armenia.

364-75 Valentinian I, chosen as Emperor by the court, elevated his brother VALENS to Augustus and co-ruler in the E. (Oriens with Constantinople), where he waged war against the Goths. VALENTINIAN defeated the Alamanni. Rest. of the Rhine frontier and Hadrian's Wall in Britain.

c. 375 Destruction of the Ostro. kdm in southern Russia by the Huns. Death of ERMANERICH. **Beginning of the Barbarian migrations.** VALENTINIAN I was succeeded by

375-8 Valens, and – until 383 – by Gratian. The Visigoths rose after having been allowed to settle within the Empire in 376. VALENS was defeated and d. in the

378 b. of Adrianople (Hadrianopolis).

379 Theodosius I was named co-emperor in the E. by Gratian. Settlement of the Ostrogoths in Pannonia, and of the Visigoths in Macedonia.

380 The Edict of Thessalonia prohibited Arianism in the E. Athanasianism became the state religion (Catholicism).

382 Renewal of settlement and peace arrangements with the Visigoths (p. 115).

384 Treaty (peace and friendship) between THEODOSIUS and SHAPUR III (384-8): Armenia was partitioned. GRATIAN d. during the struggle against the usurper MAGNUS MAXIMUS. GRATIAN's brother VALENTINIAN II took refuge with THEODOSIUS. THEODOSIUS temporarily recognized MAGNUS MAXIMUS, then

388 defeated him at Aquileia.

391 Christianity became the state religion (prohibition of all heathen cults).

392 VALENTINIAN II was murdered by ARBOGAST, the Frank. army commander of THEODOSIUS. EUGENIUS was appointed Emperor in the w. (392-4). Reintroduction of heathen cults.

394 Defeat and death of EUGENIUS on the Frigidus at Aquileia.

394-5 Theodosius the Great was sole ruler. After his death, the Empire was partitioned between his sons. ARCADIUS received the E., HONORIUS the w.: **end of imp. unity.** Establishment of an E. Rom. empire which followed its own course, and a w. Rom. empire (with the cap. at Ravenna after 404) which, though threatened by Germans and Huns and ruled by weak emperors, continued to exist for another 80 yrs.

476 With the deposition of Romulus Augustulus by Odoacer the W. Rom. Empire ceased to exist.

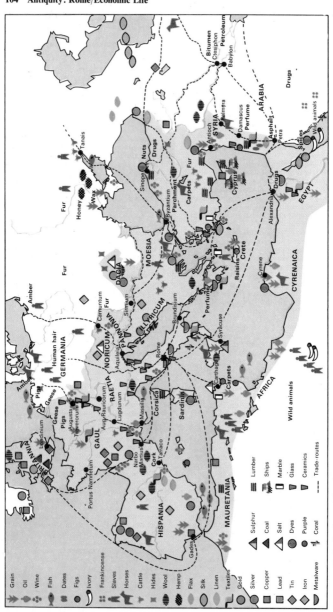

Economic life in the Roman Empire

Econ. Life in the Rom. Empire

Currency: from the time of CAESAR, **gold coinage** was used as well as the ancient republican silver currency (1 aureus = 15 silver denars). A **double currency**, remaining stable to the end of the 2nd cent. despite evidence of decay, was thereby est.; the aureus became the principal medium of exchange in business, esp. in non-Rom. countries. An inflation of the denar set in at the beginning of the 4th cent. owing to the progressive deterioration of the currency which set in from the early 3rd cent. (prices tripled); the silver currency of antiquity was thus eliminated. Following DIOCLETIAN's attempts to stabilize the silver currency (1 aureus = 20 pieces of silver [argentei]) CONSTANTINE formalized the gold currency: 1 piece of gold (*solidus*) = 24 silver denars (*siliquae*).

Econ. areas: during the 1st cent. large econ. regions developed in the Rom. Empire: Italy with Sardinia, Corsica and the southern Alp. area; Gaul, Britain, Ireland, Scotland and Western Germania; Africa (from Morocco to Tripolis); the Alp. and Balk. areas; Greece, Asia Minor, Crete, Cyrenaica, Southern Russia and the area of the Black Sea; Palestine, Syria and Mesopotamia; Egypt and Nubia. Still subordinate to Italy during the 1st cent., these large areas became increasingly autonomous during the 2nd. As a consequence of the competition of the provinces, Italy experienced a lowering of land values and gradual desolation. During the 3rd cent. the **large econ. regions became completely autonomous,** depriving Italy of its markets.

Trade: Peace in the Empire during AUGUSTUS' reign (**pax Augusta**), benefiting the entire Medit. civilization, was the basis of commercial activity. Rome, as the Imp. residence and cap. of the Empire, became the centre of an excellent network of roads. To secure the polit. and strat. unity of the Empire it was the state which built the connecting links for land and sea travel (construction of postal and relay stations). Lighthouses along the coasts, and harbour and docking facilities were also constructed. Canals extended the natural river connections in the interior. The state therefore became the guardian of the econ. cohesion of the Medit. world.

From the beginning of the Imp. period an extension of **long-distance trade** which included Ireland, Scotland, Germania, northern and south-eastern Europe was noticeable. Rom. Africa was connected with cen. and western Africa, Egypt with eastern Africa and Ethiopia. Caravans brought long-distance trade to the Orient: southern India, China, Siberia and Ceylon. Long-distance trade was no longer in the hands of men belonging to specific trades, but rather in those of **non-specialized long-distance traders** (*pragmatheutes*), who were assisted by offices, bookkeepers and agents. Palmyra became one of the most important centres of long-distance trade in the E. Relying on its wealth it attempted to establish an independent state (p. 101). A precondition for the functioning of long-distance trade was protection and aid by the state. **Local trade** continued, except for interruptions by brigands and invading tribes which began in the 3rd cent.

Artisanship: larger shops gradually took the place of the one-man shop, esp. on private and public estates. The state erected **public workshops** (*fabricae* = artisan enterprises) to satisfy the needs of army, navy and bureaucracy since independent artisanship regressed increasingly in the cities during the 2nd cent. Artisans, who at first voluntarily joined in **corporations,** were forced to supply the state during the 3rd cent. Later on, state-enforced ties to occupations evolved, a development completed by DIOCLETIAN's establishment of **coercive corporations** for artisans (297): a **regulated economy** to secure the supplies for the army.

Agriculture: the uniform agrarian techniques which developed during the Imp. period (plants, machinery, fertilizer) were soon adopted by the non-Rom. village ctrs of Eurasia and Africa. The large-scale supplies offered by these areas soon constituted serious competition for Rom. agriculture. Although the rate of growth of large cities increased during the 2nd cent. (Carthage, Milan, Lyon), differences in the way of life between city and countryside increasingly disappeared. The **villa** of the landowning upper class became an important focal-point of ctr. The extent of slavery lessened, as did that of the free peasantry, which was unable to protect itself adequately against armed brigands and others. Free peasants surrendered their land to large landowners, who in turn provided protection for them on their fortified estates and against arbitrary actions by tax officials. **Free peasants became coloni** who, though personally free, were tied to the soil by DIOCLETIAN's measures. From the 3rd cent. part of the urban proletariat also migrated to the countryside to obtain as *coloni* the livelihood the city did not provide for them. Because of the reduction of trade, **barter economy** was resumed (barter of goods, payment in kind). With the end of the Imp. period the emphasis in econ. life shifted from the cities, where wealth decreased and anarchy often prevailed, to the countryside. This development was connected with increasing **decentralization,** which under DIOCLETIAN and CONSTANTINE was extended also into the sphere of politics (introduction of the tetrarchy, responsibilities divided according to areas; CONSTANTINE's creation of 4 prefectures).

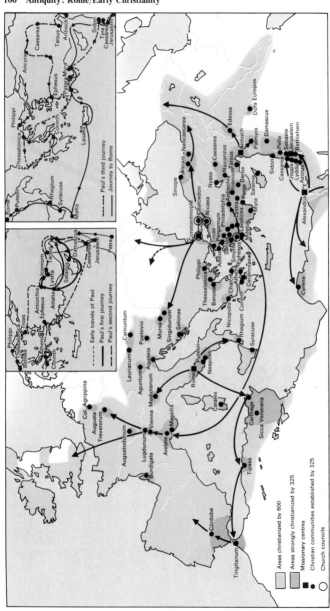

The diffusion of Christianity (insets: the journeys of Paul)

Paul's third journey
Journey to Rome

Early travels of Paul
Paul's first journey
Paul's second journey

Areas christianized by 600
Areas strongly christianized by 325
Missionary centres
Christian communities established by 325
Church councils

The Diffusion of Christianity

The first community (Baptism and the Eucharist) 50 days after the resurrection of Jesus (Pentecost). The Jew.–Christ. community was at first led by St James the Greater (executed 44), then by St James the Less (crucified 62). The first martyr of the Christ. community was Stephen.

Saul, sent by the High Council to Damascus to fight the Christ. community, was converted on the way. Fruitlessly pursuing miss. activity in Arabia, he returned to Tarsus, from where he was brought to Antioch by Barnabas.

45–8 1st miss. journey of Paul and Barnabas: conversion of gentiles; circumcision and Jew. dietary laws were no longer observed by them.

48 Council of the Apostles at Jerusalem: recognition of the leading position of the Jerusalem church, organization of regional miss. activity (Peter and the original apostles assumed the miss. activity among the Jews, Paul and Barnabas among the gentiles), recognition of Paul's teachings (independence from Jew. law and proclamation of the *Gratia Dei* (= the Grace of God)).

49–52 2nd miss. journey of Paul with longer stays at Corinth (1st and 2nd Letters to the Thessalonians).

54–8 3rd miss. journey of Paul to Ephesus (letters to the Galatians, Corinthians (1st and 2nd) and Romans), and to Corinth. Delivering the offertory in Jerusalem, Paul was arrested and kept prisoner at Caesarea (58–60). From there he appealed to the judgement of the Emperor and began the

60–61 Journey to Rome (letters to the Philippians, Ephesians and Colossians).

64 Beheading of Paul on the road to Ostia and crucifixion of Peter on the Mons Vaticanus. Christianity spread from **Antioch** to Syria and Edessa, from **Ephesus** to Asia Minor and Gaul, from **Alexandria** to the s. and se. of the Rom. empire, from **Rome** to Italy and Africa and from there to Spain. **Constantinople** became the centre for the christianization of the Balkans (Goths and Slavs).

During the 2nd cent. **Christianity experienced internal crises** over:

Gnosticism: the attempt to alter Christ. teaching into a mystic cosmology with redemptory principles.

Marcionism: the fusion of Pauline and dualistic Iran. concepts (establishment of a separate church).

Montanism: asceticism and renewal of early Christ. ecstasy with proclamation of additional revelations.

The Consolidation of Christianity

The crisis caused by Gnosticism was overcome by the establishment of the **early Cath. Church** formation of synods and agreement on certain fixed norms): the rules of the faith (*regula fidei*) as professed at the time of Baptism, the Canon of sacred literature *c.* 180 (inclusion of the O.T.), the development of the monarchistic episcopate (through the theory apostolic appointment and succession).

Joining of communities in groups. The democratic principle of leadership was eliminated by a **hierarchical constitution:** bishops and priests (*clerus*) stood apart from laymen. The Church became the hierarchically organized, visible instrument of salvation (Cyprian). The **conflict between the Rom. state and the Christ. Church** was caused by the Christ. insistence on the difference between the kdms of God and the world, the Christ. refusal to make sacrifices to the Emperor, and the claim to divine position by later emperors. After the early and limited persecutions under Nero (64), Domitian (81–96) and Trajan (98–117), in

249–51 the 1st general persecution of Christians under Decius (rest. of Ancient Rome) was initiated: few were executed, but many left the faith (*lapsi*).

257–8 Persecution under Valerian (death of Cyprian of Carthage, Primate of Africa from 250).

260 Edict of Toleration by Gallienus and 40 yrs of peace.

303–11 Persecution under Diocletian, ended by the

311 Edicts of Toleration of Galerius and Licinius. After the conversion of Constantine

313 the Milan Edict of Toleration: complete relig. freedom and equality for Christianity, return of Church property, elimination of the cults of the state.

The **Christ. apologetics** of the first half of the 2nd cent. (Justin the Martyr) were followed by the great **Fathers of the Church** Irenaeus, Hippolytus, Cyprian, Clement of Alexandria and Origen (Logos-Christology: connection of Gk thought with the eastern concept of the *logos*). The **Monarchianists** were the opponents of Logos-Christology (pluralistic monotheism): 1. Adoptionism: Christ is man; 2. Modalistic monarchianism: Christ is a mode of God.

318–81 The Arian controversy. Arius, Presbyter of Alexandria, taught that Christ was created – therefore not eternal – and different from the Father. Later teaching: similarity (Homoiousianism).

325 Council of Nicaea. Cal. by Constantine the Great, it formulated the creed after the teaching of Athanasius: the Son is equal to the Father (Homoousianism = likeness of God).

381 The 2nd Ecumenical Council of Constantinople confirmed the Nicene Creed.

Mediators of Gk theology in the W.:

1. **Jerome** (*c.* 345–420), translated the Bible into Lat. (the *Vulgata*).

2. **Ambrose** (*c.* 340–97), Bishop of Milan, wrote instructions as to Christ. duties modelled after Cicero: *De officiis ministrorum.*

3. **Augustine** (354–430), after his conversion (386) Bishop of Hippo Regius (395): the *Confessions, De civitate Dei (The City of God).*

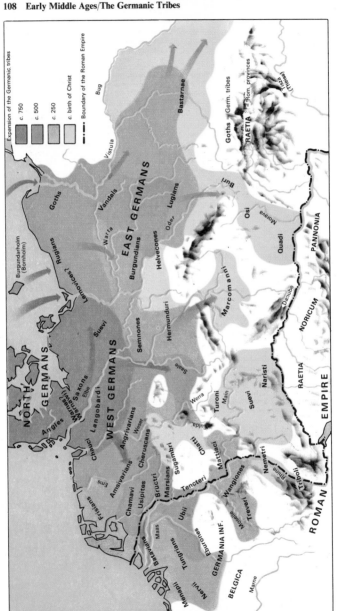

Areas of settlement and origin of the Germanic tribes in Central Europe

The Germ. tribes. Belonging to the Indo-Eur. family of languages, they developed towards the end of the Neolithic ctr. of Western Europe, incl. the Funnel-necked beaker ctr. and the Cord-impressed ware or Battle-axe ctr. They inhabited Southern Scandinavia, Denmark and Schleswig. The designation 'German' was first used by PLINY THE ELDER (d. A.D. 79) in his *Naturalis Historia*, by TACITUS in his *Germania* (A.D. 98), and in PTOLEMY's *World Geography*. Three groups are differentiated:

1. The **N. Germ. tribes** were those living in Scandinavia.
2. The **E. Germ. tribes**, related to the N. Germ. tribes, had migrated from Scandinavia into the region E. of the Elbe (Vandals, Burgundians, Goths, Rugians and others).
3. The **W. Germ. tribes** (Rhine, Weser, N. Sea and Elbe Germans) were divided by PLINY into 3 sub-groupings (not ethnic units, but groupings by cults): the **Ingaevones** (on the coast of the N. Sea), the **Istvaeones** (along the Rhine), and the **Herminones** (in the interior); they claimed their descent from the 3 sons of MANNUS. These groups included: Cheruscans, Ubii, Batavians, Chatti, Franks (consolidated into one tribe by the joining of the Usipetes, Tencteri, Sugambri and Buctri), Chauci, Frisians, Saxons, Suevi, Semnoni, Hermunduri, Langobardi, Marcomanni, Quadi and others.

Settlement and economy: settlements were on single estates or in small villages. The rectangular houses of post construction built during the Iron Age united the hearth, the hearth corner and the stable under a gable roof. At first there was **farming** (wheat, barley, oats, rye, flax, millet, vegetables) and the raising of all known **domestic animals**, later Rom. **viticulture** and **fruit crops** were introduced. Settlement was by **clan** (identity of clan and village community): distribution of the ploughable land in ploughstrips to members of the clan with the obligation to till it. Community use of the commons (forest, grazing land, waters and other uses). Fenced-in property was privileged property (house and homestead), sacred as the seat of domestic gods and the burial-site of the ancestors.

Trade was carried on between the Germans and the Medit. area from the Bronze Age.

Society: there were 3 classes. 1. The **nobility** consisted of families deriving their ancestry from the gods. 2. The **Freemen**, capable of bearing arms and possessing polit. rights, made up the mass of the population. 3. The **Semi-free class** consisted of freedmen (*liberti*) and lites (*laeti, lassi*). The latter were subj. members of related tribes. The un-free (slaves) were prisoners of war, those born un-free or deprived of their freedom through inability to pay off their obligations (gambling debts).

The Germ. tribe, separated from its neighbours by wide strips of non-cultivated land, was organized in districts (*gau*), which again were subdivided into 'centuries'. The **clan** was the most important unit; its members were tied together by common ancestry. The clan provided peace, protection and justice for its members. The rest. of a member's honour was, among other things, sacred duty of the clan (feud, vendetta, and later, payments of money (*wergilt*)); it was not the duty of the individual.

Army: all men capable of bearing arms, organized acc. to clan, formed the fighting troops; they fought in wedge formation.

Law: there were no written statutes, but an unwritten common law based on a rational order and passed on by oral tradition.

Constitution: supreme authority rested in a general assembly (*Thing, Ding*), which met at regular intervals (**assembly of the army**). The princes made proposals which were accepted or rejected by the people. Voting took place (unanimous) on matters of war and peace and personal freedom; as a court, the **general assembly** decided in matters of violations of cults, treason, war-crimes and dishonourable conduct. Offenders were expelled from the community ('loss of peace'); capital punishment could be decreed and the method of execution chosen by the assembly. The E. Ger. tribes were led by **kings** (who had relig., milit. and judicial functions). Tribes without kings (the W. Germans, who only adopted monarchy later) chose dukes from the nobility during times of war: ability, not descent, was the determining factor. Kings, dukes and nobles had the right to a **following** (*gefolgschaft*), which consisted at first of young warriors in milit. training, and, later, of proven warriors who pledged an oath of fidelity binding them to serve till death.

Religion: beside the gods of fertility, NJÖRDR (identical with NERTHUS, the mother goddess), FREYR, and FREYJA, there were the Aesir. Usually 3 gods were prominent: **Wotan** (ODIN), the companion of the dead and master of magic, later God of War (his ecstatic cult indicates an eastern origin (horseback riding)); **Thor** (DONAR), the protector of the farmers against the giants, and **Tiwaz** (ZIU, TYR), the God of War, who in the N. competed with WOTAN. The gods were honoured during **cult festivals** which were celebrated by the tribes in specified areas at certain periods or after victorious wars: sacrificial animals were slaughtered and sacred meals with singing and dancing were shared. The areas in which cult festivals took place were **sacred groves**, mts and places near sacred trees, springs and stones. There were also **temples** with idols of wood or metal; as a result of later alien influence came images of gods as well. The will of the gods was divined by means of **oracles**. Polit. and relig. functions were performed by the same person; there was no priesthood.

The expansion of the Slavs

The Slavs (Slovene from *slovo* = the word), a major branch of the Indo-Eur. family of peoples, **originally lived** in the Pripet Marches. The area settled by Slavs later included parts of Poland, White Russia and the Ukraine. During the early cents. the history of the Slavs was connected with that of the Germans (Goths), Huns, Alani and Turkomans, with whom the Slavs often entered into mutually fruitful relationships (= symbiosis). PLINY THE ELDER, TACITUS and the geographer PTOLEMY cal. them **Venedi** or **Veneti**; the Germans called them **Wenden**; from the 6th cent. Byz. writers (PROCOPIUS and JORDANES) spoke of the *Sklavenoi*, placing them along the Lower Danube, but also in the eastern Alps. From 600, Slav. peoples (Abodrites, Sorbs, Veneti and Pomerani) settled E. of the Elbe in the areas vacated by Germ. tribes. As with the Czechs, their historical record becomes verifiable only in the Carol. period (805, construction by CHARLEMAGNE of the *limes sorbicus* = line of the easternmost Frank. trade settlements).

Groupings of Slav. tribes: the E. Slavs (Russians later subdivided into Ukrainians, White and Great Russians), W. Slavs (Poles, Pomerani, Abodrites, Sorbs, Czechs and Slovaks), and s. Slavs (Slovenes, Serbs, Croats and Bulgars). The unity of the Slav. world was disrupted by Ger. colonization in the Danubian area and the Eastern Alps after the dest. of the Avar kdm, and by the migration of the Magyars to the Hung. plain c. 900 (owing to pressure from the E. by the Patznaks): separation of the w. Slavs in the N. from the s. Slavs.

Society: originally the Slavs lived in clans (reverence of ancestors), consisting of large familial communities. Several of these familial communities made up larger soc. units led by elders. These again made up the tribe with its milit. organization (the century as the basic unit of the levy, then the millennium) and its common relig. cult. The leaders of the familial communities gradually developed into an aristocratic upper class. The particularism of the tribes prevented the establishment of any great-power status for the Slavs. Titles of rulers used in later times were borrowed from other languages: *kunedzi* (prince) was Germ. (king); *korlji* (Czech *Kral*) was derived from the name of CHARLEMAGNE; the title of Tsar from the Rom. Caesar.

Econ. life: the Slavs occupied themselves with farming, hunting, fishing, the raising of domestic animals and bee-culture in the extended areas of their settlement. There were also – predominantly living in the towns – artisans (specialists): carpenters, weavers, potters, tanners and furriers. Active trading developed along the rivers. Raw materials (honey, wax, furs) were exchanged for textiles, weapons, utensils, jewellery, gold and silver. The Jews, Germans and Greeks at first monopolized trade; the Slavs themselves did so later. The trading centres of the E. Slavs became towns.

Religion: historical sources speak of names and images of gods, of the temples of the w. Slavs (the temple of ARKONA on the island of Rügen, the shrine of the god TRIGLAW at Stettin and that of SVARICIC at Rethra), of tree cults and oracles. The use of amulets and symbols indicates contacts with the Iranians and Turkomans. The E. Slavs knew the God of Thunder and Lightning, PERUN. The supreme deity of the ancient Slavs was SVAROG, an early God of the Heavens and Thunder. The Slavs of the Havel area worshipped DAZBAG (God of the Sun) and JAROVIT (God of Spring). Within the familial communities the fertility gods ROD and ROZANICY were worshipped. All tribes worshipped nature.

The christianization of the Slavs began with the advance of Rom. and Byz. civilization into Eastern and Cen. Europe: during the 6th cent. miss. activity from Aquileia among the Croats; during the 8th cent. from Salzburg among the Slovenes. Miss. activity among the Wends, the Czechs (from Regensburg), the Abodrites and Elbe Slavs (from Verden at the Aller) was initiated during the reign of CHARLEMAGNE. The Slavs joined the Eastern Church c. 850. The Apostles of the Slavs, CYRIL and METHODIUS, conducted miss. activity within the Greater Moravian Kdm from 863; they later joined Rome.

864–5 Conversion of the Bulgars (1st autocephalous Eastern Church).

866 Christianization of a group of the Rus.

948 Establishment of the bpcs of Havelberg, Brandenburg and Oldenburg.

966 Baptism of duke MIEZKO OF POLAND.

968 Establishment of the archbpc of Magdeburg with the suffragan bpcs of Meissen, Merseburg and Zeitz (moved to Naumburg in 1032) by OTTO I (intended to bring about the conversion of the Elbe Slavs).

973 Establishment of the bpc of Prague.

983 Suppression of Christ. miss. activity during the rebellion of the Slavs (Havelberg, Brandenburg).

988 Baptism of the Varan. prince VLADIMIR.

1000 Establishment of the archbpc of Gnesen.

1001 Establishment of the archbpc of Gran (Esztergom). With the establishment of this archbpc, the Pol. and Hung. churches were freed of Ger. infl.

All Slav. states attempted to establish autonomous churches (autocephalous bpc or patriarchate). The Slav. language, based on a Maced. dialect, became the language of the Slav. churches and the written language of the Balk. and E. Slavs. With their acceptance into the community of Christ. peoples, the Slavs reached a higher cult. level; the new common faith of the developing Slav. states also contributed to the fusion of heterogeneous ethnic and cult. elements. Despite their split into Rom. Cath. (w. Slavs) and Gk Orth. (E. Slavs) states, both groups were part of Eur. civilization by virtue of their Christianity.

The Huns

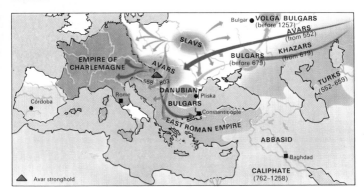

Bulgars and Avars

Khazars, Patzinaks, and Hungarians (Magyars)

The Mounted Peoples of Northern Eurasia

Stretching from Eastern Europe (Poland) to Eastern Asia (Yellow Sea), the **steppes** were the home of the mounted nomadic peoples, whose **econ. base** was the common ownership of cattle. Common interests (such as protection from the forces of nature and hostile tribes) rather than blood-ties or property bound the families together. With the *pater familias* at the centre, they formed communities of interest, which again formed tribes, and the tribes 'hordes'. Possessing a common ctr. and concept of life, all mounted nomadic peoples were **characterized** by aspirations to dominate others, organizational talent, broad planning and the formation of world empires on a federalistic basis. Every conquered enemy became a friend (no racial prejudice) once he identified with the interests of the Horde.

Religion: the wide horizon of the steppes directed the eyes of the people 'who spanned the bow' to the skies, which brought the rain, sustaining the herds. This was the seat of the **omniscient Heavenly Father. Shamans** est. contact with the gods through sacrifices and – in ecstatic states – through guiding the souls of the departed into the hereafter. This shamanistic religion repeatedly checked the major religions (Judaism, Christianity, Islam and Buddhism) which were advancing into the steppes, or continued to co-exist with them.

Society: consisting of free warriors with equal rights, the Horde was led by the **prince**, who became '**Kagan**' in the nomadic empire. The occupation of the blacksmith, the producer of weapons, was the basis of their rise to power for many of these princes. The blacksmith had contact with the gods, who taught him his art; often he was chosen by the god (**black-smith monarchy**). The idea of the monarchy often fused with the concept of God; thus GENGHIS ('the one sent by fate') became after his death 'the mighty one of the heavens'.

The conception of empire: the sky was the only factor making orientation within the limitless expanses of the steppes possible. The universe rotated around the Polar star, 'the axis of the world', under which the Mongol. world rulers resided ('navel' of the world; identification of the 'world' and the ethnic centre of the people). This world concept provided the nomads with their task: subjugation and pacification of the peoples of the '4 corners' (= the 4 directions of the sky). All rulers failed in this task as soon as their peoples were led out of the steppes and encountered the urban civilization of the w.

The Huns advanced westward into the southern Rus. steppe after they had been forced out of China and the 2nd empire of the Huns in Turkestan and Dzungaria (36/35 B.C.) had been dest. by the Chinese.

375 Destruction of the Ostro. kdm in Southern Russia. The Germ. and Germ.–Sarmantian peoples were subjugated.

441–53 After the elimination of his brother BLEDA, ATTILA became sole ruler and advanced into the E. Rom. Empire (which had to recognize him as an equal partner) and towards the w.

451 After **the b. of Catalaunian Fields (Châlons),** ATTILA retreated to the centre of his Empire (the plains of the Tisza in Hungary) and d. there without having introduced polit. order comparable to that of the w. among the Huns (bureaucrats, nobles, officers). The Germans, under ARDERIC, king of the Gepids, dest. the kdm of the Huns.

The Bulgars: remnants of the Hunᶜ retreated into the steppes of Southern Russia, where, mixing with the Ugrians, they est. a Bulg. state, which reached its greatest power under KUVRAT (d. 679). After the destruction of this state by the Khazars, one group est. a Danube–Bulg. state, and another a Volga–Bulg. state, which were eliminated by the Mongols (13th cent.); the remainder subjected themselves to Khazar rule.

The Avars, reinforced by Huns and Bulgars, migrated into the plains of the Tisza after their eastern Asiatic state had been dest. by Turkoman tribes (552). Together with the Antes and Sklavenoi **Slav.–Avar community was est.** (p. 111). After flowering under KAGAN BAJAN (565–602), the state succumbed to the attacks of CHARLEMAGNE between 791 and 796.

The Khazars were a semi-nomadic people (working of the soil and trade) who est. a kdm N. of the Caucasus. Entertaining close relationships with Byzantium, their state received its income from tariffs and maintained a standing army. It collapsed because of attacks by the Varangians.

965 Seizure of Sarkel at the mouth of the Don – the westernmost boundary fortification – by **Svatoslav of Kiev.**

969 Itil, the cap. at the mouth of the Volga, was taken.

The Patzinaks advanced into the Balkans after the 10th cent., until in 1091 they were decisively defeated by ALEXIUS COMNENUS at Leburnion (p. 175).

The Cumans est. a state in Southern Russia which existed 1154–1222. They maintained cordial relations with Kiev. The state was dest. by the Mongols.

The Magyars advanced to the w. during the 9th cent. Unlike the Huns and Avars, they occupied not only the steppe areas (*deserta Avarorum*) of the s., but the entire region of the Carpathians. After the destruction of the kdm of the Khazars, they lost contact with the nomadic life of the steppes and est. new ties in the w. (acceptance of Western civilization and religion; p. 169).

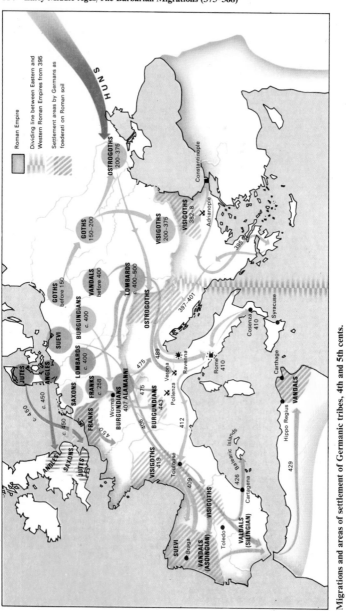

Migrations and areas of settlement of Germanic tribes, 4th and 5th cents.

The Barbarian Migrations (375–568)

The early movements: between 230 and 200 B.C. the Bastarnae and Skiri moved (to the Black Sea), to be followed later by the Cimbri, Teutones and Ambrones (p. 89). CAESAR defeated the Suevi, who had invaded Gaul under ARIOVISTUS (58). The advances of the Romans under AUGUSTUS were negated by the defeat of VARUS (A.D. 9); but the Rhine–Danube frontier was held. Later (74) the area between the Danube and the Upper Rhine (*agri decumates*) was added and secured by the *limes*. The early struggles with the Marcomanni (166–180) were followed by incursions of the Chatti (171), the Alamanni (from 213), the Goths (236) and the Franks (from 257). After the surrender of the Upper Rhenish-Raetian *limes* frontier (260), the Alamanni began to advance along the frontier of the Rhine; after the surrender of Dacia (270), the Goths attacked along the Danube frontier. During the 4th cent. Germans were settled as **foederati** along the frontiers; they received annual payments (*annonae foederatae*) and assumed the protection of the frontiers. **Ger. settlements on Rom. soil** were est. during the 5th cent.

The **E. Germans** were most prominently represented in the **'Barbarian migrations'** between 375 (incursion of the Huns) and 568 (settlement of the Langobardi in Italy).

Causes: the tribes were forced to migrate by climatic changes and increases in pop. which led to a land shortage. A desire for war and adventure was not the least of their motives.

The advance of the Huns gave the **impetus** (p. 113); they dest. ERMANERICH's kdm of the Ostrogoths on the Black Sea (375).

Consequences: the western part of the Rom. Empire was eliminated. It was replaced by Germ. kdms. The Germans were converted to the Arian form of Christianity by the Goth WULFILA (*c.* 310–80), who translated the Bible into Gothic (*Codex Argenteus* at Upsala). The area E. of the Elbe, vacated by the Germans, was settled by Slavs.

The Visigoths were admitted into the Empire by the Emperor VALENS (376). After an uprising, caused by shortages of supplies, they defeated the Romans in

378 at the b. of Adrianople. THEODOSIUS settled them again in Thrace and Moesia (382). Under the leadership of ALARICH, who assumed the royal title, the Visigoths sought new habitats. After a campaign of pillage through the Balkans and the Peloponnesus, ALARICH was named *magister militum Illyricum* (= master of the army of Illyrian). He then undertook

401–3 an attack on Italy. Beaten back by STILICHO at Pollenza (402) and Verona (403), the Visigoths laid siege to Rome after STILICHO's death (408). Retreat of the Goths after payment of an enormous indemnity. Futile siege of HONORIUS at Ravenna.

410 Conquest and pillage of Rome. ALARICH d. in Southern Italy (Cosenza) before the planned crossing to Africa.

410–15 ATHAULF, successor and brother-in-law of ALARICH, mar. GALLA PLACIDIA. the captured step-sister of HONORIUS. After his death his brother WALLIA founded the **Tolosanian kdm of the Visigoths** (Tolosa = Toulouse).

Pushed aside by the Visigoths, **the Vandals** left their habitats and settled in Slovakia and Transylvania. With the Quadi, Suevi and Alani they crossed the Rhine frontier (406), which had been deprived of its legions by STILICHO; they moved to Gaul and reached Spain (409), where they were settled as *foederati*. Under GEISERICH (428–77) they crossed to Africa (429) and est. the Vandal kdm.

The Burgundians migrated into the Rhine–Main area *c.* 400 and est. a kdm along the mid-course of the Rhine under GUNDAHAR (= Gunther; acc. to legend the cap. was at Worms). It was dest. by Hunnish auxiliary troops called in by the w. Rom. commander AETIUS (436).

443 Settlement of the Burgundians on the Saône and the Rhône to protect the Alp. passes; the Burgundians est. a kdm.

The Ostrogoths. At about the birth of Christ the Goths settled at the mouth of the Vistula; during the 2nd cent. they migrated to the SE. and split into Visigoths and Ostrogoths. The Ostro. kdm along the Black Sea was dest. by the Huns. After ATTILA's death (p. 113) the Ostrogoths settled in Pannonia. Under THEODERIC of the royal house of Amals, who, a hostage, had been raised at the E. Rom. court, they plundered the Balkan peninsula. After his appointment as *magister militum* and *patricius* of Italy (488), he moved there with the Goths and defeated ODOACER in 3 battles. ODOACER had been proclaimed 'king of the army' by a force of Germ. mercenaries. He had conquered Sicily and Dalmatia and dest. the Danubian kdm of the Rugians. After the surrender of Ravenna (3-yr siege: 'Battle of the Ravens'), ODOACER was murdered by THEODERIC. Establishment of the Ostro. kdm.

Jutes, Angles and **Saxons** (p. 129); **Franks** (p. 121); **Langobards** (p. 119).

The N. Germans did not leave their areas of settlement in Scandinavia and Jutland. The fusion and union of several Germ. tribes and splinter groups led to the formation of the following tribal associations in the area between the Elbe and the Rhine which, however, did not represent uniform bloodlines: **Alamanni, Saxons, Franks** (Salians, Ripuarians, Moselle and Main Franks, Chatti), and later, **Thuringians** and **Bavarians**.

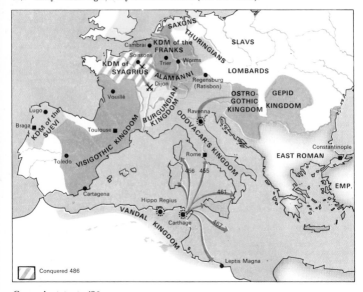

Germanic states to 486

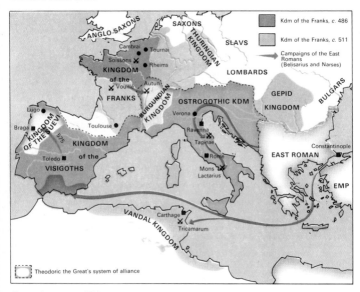

Germanic states, c. 526

The **Germans** were admitted into the Rom. Emp. as *foederati* and settled on *coloni*-estates. The lands allotted to them were loc. in regions settled by Romans; therefore, a fusion of Germ. and Rom. elements soon took place. However, the Germans shortly freed themselves from their obligations as *foederati* and est. sovereign monarchies based on principles anticipating international law. Rom. civilization was not dest. by the Germans. The establishment of the Germ. states had been prepared by the decentralization of the Rom. Empire under DIOCLETIAN (break-up of public power).

The kdms of the E. Germans did not last: they lost contact with the regions of their origin, and the small number of conquerors could not be replenished. Added to this was the relig. contrast: the Arian conquerors est. nat. churches under royal leadership; the subj. pop. was Rom. Cath.

The Vandal Kdm in Africa (429–534)

After the conquest of Hippo Regius (AUGUSTINE, one of the 'fathers of the Church', d. during the siege, 430), the Vandals settled in the area of Tunis and were recognized by Rome as *foederati* (435). After the conquest of Carthage (439) the Romans recognized the conquered territory as a sovereign state (442): **establishment of the 1st Germ. state on W. Rom. territory.** Rom. landowners lost everything out (in the taking of land the *jus hospitalis* was not observed). GEISERICH regulated the right of royal succession on the basis of seniority, doing away with Germ. dyn. right based on blood relationship: the eldest became successor to the throne. The fleet of the Vandals dominated the Western Mediterranean, putting Rome, which depended on grain imports from Africa, under pressure. The conquest of the Rom. province in Africa was recognized by the Emperor ZENO (474).

455 Seizure of Rome by the Vandals. Art treasures were *not* destroyed (vandalism), but systematic plunder took place.

The kdm was weakened after GEISERICH's death as a result of struggles between nobility and king and relig. conflicts (persecution of Catholics).

534–5 Destruction of the Vandal kdm by BELISARIUS (p. 139).

The Tolosanian Visi. Kdm (419–507)

The Visigoths were allotted two thirds of the land of Aquitania as tax-free property (cap. Tolosa = Toulouse); the king and army in turn assumed the role of protection; the king ruled as imp. governor. The pinnacle of Visi. power was reached under

466–84 Eurich, founder of Visi. power in Spain. The most ancient Germ. code of law, written in Lat., was composed at his direction (*Codex Euricianus*, 470). His successor

484–507 ALARICH II d. fighting the Franks under CLOVIS at Vouillé (p. 121).

The Visi. Kdm in Spain (507–711)

The new kdm was weakened through struggles between the king and the nobility.

551 Cal. into the country, the Byzantines conquered the s.

568–86 LEOWGILD, who made Toledo the cap., pushed the Byzantines back and conquered the kdm of the Suevi (575), who had moved into the area *c.* 409.

586–601 REKHARED I became a Catholic. Allying itself with the upper Germ. nobility, the Church gained great infl. The Church councils of Toledo were simultaneously assemblies of the kdm at which decisions of the king were made binding: offenders punishable by excommunication.

633 Introduction of elective monarchy.

649–72 REKISWINTH created a legal code binding on Goths and Romans (*Lex Visigothorum, c.* 654).

711 Vict. of the Arabs over the Visigoths under RODERIC (p. 135).

The Kdm of the Burgundians (443–534)

Settled under AETIUS along Lake Geneva, the Burgundians extended their kdm along the Rhône and Saône. It blossomed

between 480 and 516 under GUNDOBAD, who had Burg. law codified (*Lex Burgundium*; 516). After several futile attempts, the Franks were, following THEODERIC's death, able

534 to conquer the Burg. kdm after their vict. at Autun.

The Ostro. Kdm in Italy (493–553)

493–526 Theoderic the Great segregated Romans and Goths (prohibition of intermarriage). The Goths received a third of the available landed property because of their service as warriors. Civil admin. and economy remained in Rom. hands. Relig. differences also prevented Goth.–Rom. understanding.

THEODERIC's **polit. aim** was a system of alliances of Germ. states directed against Byzantium, to be strengthened by dyn. marriages. The failure of this policy (counteracted by the Frank, CLOVIS), worries about the succession to the throne, and tensions between the Arian Goths and the Cath. Romans clouded the king's last years. BOETHIUS, who wrote his *De consolatione philosophiae* in prison, and his father-in-law, SYMMACHUS, were executed because of their opposition to the Senate.

526 Death of THEODERIC at Ravenna.

535–53 the Goth. War of Justinian. WITIGES, elevated to the throne by the Goths (536–40), was taken prisoner by BELISARIUS after the siege of Ravenna.

542–52 TOTILA regained Italy proceeding from Verona (exc. for Ravenna); he resisted BELISARIUS from 544 to 549, but then d. fighting NARSES at Tadinae. His successor TEJA d. a few months later on the Mons Lactarius.

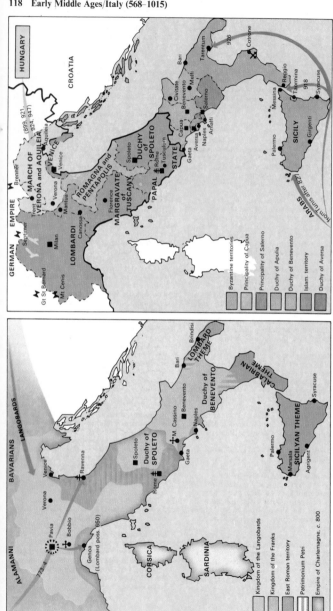

The Kingdom of the Langobards in Italy

Italy in the 9th and 10th cents.

The Lang. Kdm in Italy (568–774)
The Langobards moved from their original
home in Scandinavia to the Lower Elbe, and
from there to Moravia, and est. their first kdm
in the Danubian region (Pannonia). After the
destruction of the Gepid kdm by the Langobards and the Avars under King ALBOIN, the
Langobards, joined by some Gepids, invaded
Italy and established a second kdm (568).
Pavia was conquered (572). The Langobards
settled esp. in the plains of the Po, but also in
northern Tuscany, in Umbria, Spoleto and
Benevento. After the completion of the conquest c. 650, there existed, apart from the kdm
(Pavia), the following practically autonomous
duchies: Trent, Friuli, Spoleto, Tuscany,
Benevento. The Byzantines retained the
Exarchate of Ravenna, Istria, the environs of
Rome and Naples, the southern tips of Italy,
and Sicily. Consequences: Italy fragmented
into a Lang. (later Frank., then imp.) region
and a Byz. (later Norm. and partly papal)
region. Rule by dukes was eliminated after the
rest. of the monarchy (584). Since the Romans
were deprived of their polit. rights and Rom.
admin. was abolished, the Lang. kdm became
a purely Germ. state. Under
584–90 AUTHARI, who mar. THEUDELINDE,
daughter of the Bav. duke, cordial polit.
relations with Bavaria were initiated.
Domination by the Frank. kdm (payment
of tributes).
590–615 AGILULF concluded peace with the
Franks and an armistice with the Byzantines.
636–52 ROTHARI had the Lang. common law
codified: *Edictus Rothari* (643). His successors became Catholics. The people gradually
converted to Catholicism after 600. The
pinnacle of power was reached
661–71 under Grimwald I by union with the
duchy of Benevento. Victorious struggles
with the Franks, Byzantines, Avars and
Slavs. After GRIMWALD's death, conflicts
over the succession to the throne arose
(power of the aristocracy).
712–44 LIUTPRAND attempted the unification
of Italy through the subjugation of the
dukes of Spoleto and Benevento and attacks
on Ravenna and Rome.
751 Seizure of Ravenna by AISTULF (749–56):
termination of the Exarchate of Ravenna
and thereby of Byz. rule in Cen. Italy.
756–74 DESIDERIUS, duke of Tuscany, king.
773–4 Conquest of the Lang. kdm (seizure of
Pavia) by CHARLEMAGNE (p. 123). DESI-
DERIUS forced to abdicate. The Lang. kdm
merged with that of the Franks; the duchy
of Benevento, however, remained autonomous.

Italy under the Carolingians (774–887)
In addition to the duchy of Benevento, new
'Lang.' domains were est. at Naples, Salerno
and Capua. The Arabs intervened in the
politics of Lower Italy (827); first incursions
of the Hungarians into the plains of the Po.
The Margraves of Friuli, Tuscany and Spoleto,
growing stronger in the frontier territories,
became increasingly independent.

The Nat. Ital. Kings (888–962)
After the death of CHARLES III (p. 125),
Margrave BERENGAR OF FRIULI was crowned
king of Italy; however, he was initially
forced aside by WIDO (891–4) and LAMBERT
(892–8), the dukes of Spoleto, who, thinking
themselves heirs to the Lang. kdm, forced
the popes to crown them as emperors.
894 ARNULF OF CARINTHIA was recog. as king
and crowned Emperor (896); however, he
returned to Bavaria. After the death of
LAMBERT in
900, LOUIS OF PROVENCE was crowned king at
Pavia; he was crowned Emperor at Rome
as LOUIS III (901). After his subjugation and
blinding by BERENGAR at Verona (905),
LOUIS returned to Provence, where he d. 928.
915 BERENGAR crowned Emperor. His defeat
by the Hungarians at the Brenta (899) was
followed by their continual pillaging forays.
BERENGAR had to pay tributes to them.
Attacks by the Arabs on Reggio, Oria and
Tarentum.
922–6 King RUDOLF II OF JURAN BURGUNDY
was summoned to Italy and removed
BERENGAR, who was murdered (924). After
the death of his father-in-law, BURCHARD
OF SWABIA, he left the rule of Italy to
926–47 HUGH OF VIENNE (Provence), who was
able to assert himself over EBERHARD OF
BAVARIA, chosen by the opposition party.
After HUGH's death his son LOTHAR became
king (crowned 931 as co-regent and mar. to
ADELAIDE, daughter of RUDOLF II OF JURAN
BURGUNDY). After his death in
950 BERENGAR II OF IVREA was crowned.
LOTHAR's widow was kept captive by him.
951 Otto the Great, whom ADELAIDE had cal-
to her aid, gained dominance over Upper
Italy. He made BERENGAR a vassal king; but
BERENGAR and his son ADALBERT quarrelled
with the papal state. Pope JOHN XII appealed
to OTTO THE GREAT for help; the 2nd Ital.
campaign (961–5) strengthened the latter's
rule in Upper Italy. BERENGAR was taken captive; ADALBERT d. in exile. After their coronation, the Ger. kings thought of themselves
also as rulers of the Lang. kdm (Imp. Italy),
which belonged to the Christ. Imperium.
After the death of OTTO III, the notables of
Lombardy chose as king
1002–15 ARDUIN OF IVREA; but he was defeated
by HENRY II. Subs. 2 parties emerged in
Italy: the Ghibellines (after the Staufen
castle, Waiblingen), who were followers of
the Ger. rulers; and the Guelphs (Welfen,
the papal party), who opposed the Ger.
rulers.

Tribal settlement of the Franks, 260

Franks as foederati in N. Brabant, 358

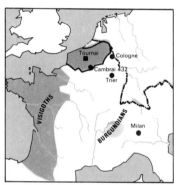

Territory of the Franks, *c.* 460

Kingdom of the Franks and Kingdom of Syagrius, *c.* 480

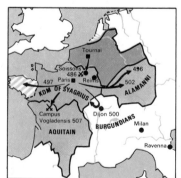

Kingdom of Clovis

The kingdoms under the sons of Clovis

The Frank. Kdm under the Merovingians

The Franks (Salians, Ripuarians) expanded slowly from the frontier of the Rhine to the sw.; however, they remained in touch with their original home. During the 5th cent. they reached the Somme. The numerous regional kings under whom they lived were eliminated by force and the polit. unity of the entire tribe was achieved

482–511 by Clovis, who removed what remained of w. Rom. rule by his victory in

486 over the Rom. Dux Syagrius. CLOVIS obtained the land between the Somme and the Loire.

c. 496 Victory over the Alamanni; their remnants were protected by THEODERIC THE GREAT. CLOVIS's Cath. Burg. wife CLOTILDA is said to have inspired CLOVIS to convert to Christianity as the battle progressed. He was baptized by Bishop REMIGUS at Reims on Christmas Day 497 or 498. Consequence: in contrast to the system of THEODERIC (sep. existence of Goths and Romans), CLOVIS and his successors succeeded in establishing a homogeneous body politic by the fusion of Galloromans and Franks.

c. 500 Victory over the Burgundians at Dijon. The Burg. king GUNDOBAD was able to maintain his position with Visi. help.

507 b. of Vouillé (Vouglé): CLOVIS conquered the Visi. kdm as far as the Pyrenees with the aid of the Burgundians (p. 117). Because of THEODERIC's intervention, he did not reach the Mediterranean (Septimania remained Visigothic). After CLOVIS's death in Paris the kdm was divided between his sons.

531 Conquest of the Thur. kdm (King ERMINFRIED) with the aid of the Saxons.

532–4 Subjugation of the Burg. kdm (b. of Autun, p. 117) by CLOTHAR I, CHILDEBERT I and CLOVIS's nephew THEUDEBERT I (534–48).

535–7 To assure Frank. neutrality, the Ostrogoths surrendered to them what remained of Alamannia and Provence (incl. the mouth of the Rhône: access to the Mediterranean).

539 THEUDEBERT's vict. over the Ostrogoths and Byzantines; but he was unable to conquer Upper Italy. Bavaria became a dependency of the Frank. kdm.

558–61 CLOTHAR I united the Frank. kdm; however, after his death the kdm was again partitioned: beginning of internal conflicts (the kings and local aristocracy were at odds). These struggles resulted in the **division of the kdm into 3 parts:** Austrasia (Champagne, the areas of the Maas and Moselle) with the cap. at Reims; Neustria (the Romanic w. between the Scheldt and the Loire) with Paris the cap., and Burgundy (the area of the Loire and the Rhône) with the cap. at Orleans.

613–29 Clothar II united the entire kdm after the aristocracy of Burgundy and Neustria under the leadership of Bishop ARNULF OF METZ (614–29) and PEPIN THE ELDER (d. 640), had come over to his side; even so, he had to pay for this assistance by issuing the

614 Edictum Chlotarii: the king committed himself henceforth to choose the royal officials (counts) from the property-owners of the county (elimination of an officialdom dependent on the ruler and surrender of public authority to the landowning aristocracy). The heartlands, Austrasia, Neustria and Burgundy, received a measure of autonomy under the authority of a *major-domo* who headed the royal household; he was also chief of the king's retainers and thereby senior to the entire aristocracy.

629–39 DAGOBERT I once again united the entire kdm. After his death, renewed partitions: the Merov. state decayed. The elevation and reign of the palace majors began.

The Rise of the Carolingians

679–714 PEPIN II OF HERISTAL became *major-domo* of Austrasia and after the

687 vict. at Tertry over the *major-domo* of Neustria–Burgundy he ruled the entire kdm as chancellor. Consequences: **preservation of the unity of the kdm;** shifting of polit. power to the Moselle, Maas and Lower Rhine.

689 Vict. over **Radbod** and the Frisians. Joining of Western Frisia to the Frank. kdm. To convert the Frisians the bpc of Utrecht and the monastery of Echternach were est. (c. 690, WILLIBRORD). Alamannia could not be tied to the kdm (709–12). After Aquitania (672), the Bavarians, Thuringians, Alamanni and Bretons also became almost independent.

714–41 Charles Martel, illegitimate son of PEPIN II, struggled for the position of *major-domo* and restored the kdm after conflicts with Neustria and Aquitania. Subjugation of the Alamanni and Thuringians; struggles against the Saxons. Bavaria became dependent. In the

732 b. of Tours and Poitiers (defensive success of the infantry), CHARLES MARTEL defeated the Arabs under ABD AR-RAHMAN (p. 135). He ruled from 737 without a Merov. king, and before he d. in

741 divided the kdm between his sons, who had been raised in the monastery of St-Denis: CARLOMAN received the E. (Austrasia, Swabia, Thuringia); PEPIN the w. (Neustria, Burgundy, Provence); Aquitania and Bavaria came under joint rule. Several campaigns led to the subj. of the Aquitanians, Bavarians, Saxons and Swabians.

743 Removal of the last Merov. 'shadow' king (CHILDERICH III). After CARLOMAN's entry into a monastery, PEPIN became sole ruler of the Frank. kdm (p. 123).

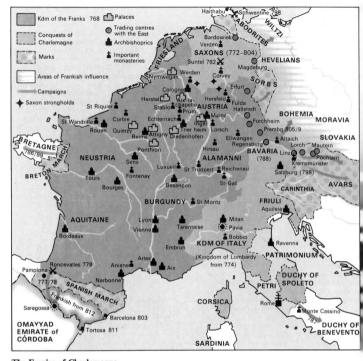

The Empire of Charlemagne

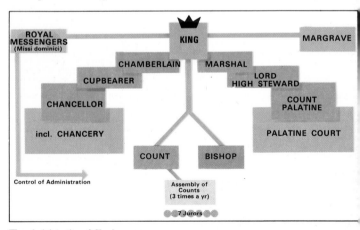

The administration of Charlemagne

he Carolingians (751–814)

51–68 Pepin. Pope ZACHARY (741–52) agreed to the dethronement of the last Merov. king, who was sent to a monastery.

51 PEPIN was elevated to the throne by 'all the Franks' at Soissons and anointed 1st king of the Franks by BONIFACE, the Papal Legate.

4 Agreements of Ponthion and Quierzy: Pope STEPHEN II (752–7) asked for PEPIN's aid against the Lang. king AISTULF (p. 119); he placed Rome under the protection of the Frank. king and anointed PEPIN once more at St-Denis. PEPIN and his sons received the title *Patricius Romanorum* (Protector of the Romans). Two successful campaigns of PEPIN (754, 756) forced AISTULF to return the conquered territories (the Exarchate of Ravenna, Pentapolis), which were then given to the Pope (the Donation of PEPIN). These areas together with Rome became the Papal States (p. 140). Subj. of Saracenic Narbonne (759).

0–68 The duchy of Aquitania was annexed after successful campaigns.

8 Pepin partitioned his **kdm** between his sons CHARLES and CARLOMAN; the latter however **d.** before the outbreak of open conflict (771).

arlemagne (768–814)

2–804 The Saxon Wars began with the conquest of the Eresburg and the destruction of the Irminsul (sacred wood). Mass baptism of the nobility. WIDUKIND and the free peasants were opposed to the nobility, who favoured union with the king of the Franks. Crushing of WIDUKIND's rebellion (779–80). The destruction of a Frank. army at the Süntel mts (782) led to

2 the massacre of Verden at the Aller: execution of 4,500 rebellious Saxons (the number is questioned), delivered into CHARLES's hands by the Saxon nobility. Renewed revolt and advance of CHARLES to the Elbe (783–5).

5 Peace between WIDUKIND and CHARLES and the baptism of WIDUKIND at the Imp. palace at Attigny. After renewed revolts of peasants over the clerical 'tithe', Saxons were deported to Frank. territory and Franks were settled in Saxon territory. Permanent subj. of the Saxons after a final campaign (804). Reconciliation of Franks and Saxons by the *lex Saxonum* (Saxon Law, 802); although it was based on Frank. law (the *lex Ripuaria*), it also took the ancient Saxon common law into account. Christianization proceeded from the bpcs of Bremen, Verden, Minden, Münster, Paderborn and Osnabrück, which were subject to the archbpcs of Mainz and Cologne, controlled by CHARLES. LOUIS THE PIOUS est. Hildesheim and Halberstadt. Corvey on the Weser, est. by an order from Corbie in northern France (822), was to become the most important Saxon monastery.

3–4 Conquest of the Lang. kdm. After the conquest of Pavia (p. 119), CHARLES called himself 'King of the Franks and Lango-

bards'; he reaffirmed the Donation of PEPIN and placed the Papal States under Frank. protection (domination).

789–812 Several wars with the Slavs made the Liutici, Sorbs and Czechs tributaries. Frontier marks were est., but no miss. activity was undertaken among the Slavs.

788 Duke THASSILO of BAVARIA was removed (banishment into a monastery): **elimination of the last tribal duchy.**

791–6 After attacks on Friuli and Austria, the Avars were subj. in 3 campaigns: destruction of the Avars' stronghold (882 last mention of the 'ring'). Miss. activity among the s. Slavs, who had been subj. by the Avars, emanating from Aquileia and the archbpc of Salzburg (798). The campaigns against the Saxons, Slavs and Avars incorp. the area from the mouth of the Oder to the Adriatic Sea into the Empire of CHARLEMAGNE. After the defeat of a Frank. army in the valley of Roncevalles (778; death of Count ROLAND, *The Song of Roland*) and the Arab incursion into Narbonne (793)

795 the Sp. Mark was est.

23–4 Dec. 800 Pope LEO III (795–816) **crowned Charlemagne Emperor.** The Imp. title: '*Romanorum gubernans imperium*'.

812 Treaty of Aix-la-Chapelle. The E. Rom. Emperor MICHAEL I recog. CHARLES as Emperor in exchange for the surrender of Istria, Venetia and Dalmatia (the 'dual-emperor problem'). Following the Byz. example, CHARLES's son LOUIS placed the crown on his own head (without papal participation; *a Deo coronatus*).

28 Jan. 814 CHARLEMAGNE **d.** at Aix-la-Chapelle and was entombed in the Dome.

The Carol. Empire

The royal gvt was based on the **royal court**, the **palace court**, and the **chancery** under the **chancellor** (an educated cleric), who was also *Kapellan* (chaplain) for spiritual matters. The office of the *major-domo* disappeared; the chamberlain was at the head of the royal household; there were also the seneschal, the cupbearer and the marshal. Besides the count, no longer a royal official, there was now the **sovereign lord who enjoyed immunity** but did not have judicial privileges. The secular caretakers of the spiritual lords were the **bailiffs.** Royal messengers (*missi dominici*, a spiritual and a secular lord), equipped with special powers, served to control the counts, the clergy and the admin. The frontier marks were composed of several counties and often also contained the territories of tributary tribes; the Empire also contained sub. kdms (e.g. Aquitania). Three meetings of the entire realm were held each year (mandatory attendance). In special cases, judgement was rendered by from 7 to 12 jurors.

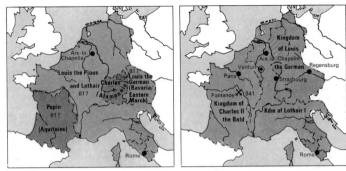

The Carolingian Empire, 829

The Treaty of Verdun, 843

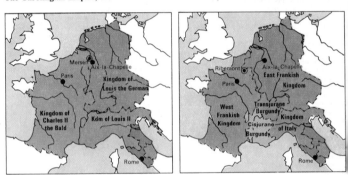

The Treaty of Mersen, 870

The Treaty of Ribemont, 880

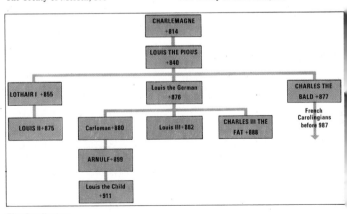

The Carolingians

The Carol. Empire (814–43)

814–40 Louis the Pious reigned strongly, infl. by his spiritual advisers.

816 Coronation of Louis by Pope Stephen IV (816–17) at Reims: bestowal of the imp. dignity by the Pope.

817 Ordinatio imperii: the order of imp. succession conveyed the imp. dignity upon the oldest son Lothair; the younger sons received parts of the Empire (Pepin: Aquitania; Louis the German: Bavaria). Addit. fragmentation of the state was not to take place. Lothair became co-emperor. Louis the Pious violated this order when he est. an additional state for Charles the Bald (Alamannia, 829), the son of his second wife Judith.

830 Revolt of the sons Pepin, Louis and Lothair. Serving as regent in Italy Lothair had himself crowned by Pope Pascal I (817–24); by the **Constitutio Romana** (824) he received imp. powers in the Papal States (control of the courts, oath of allegiance by newly elected popes before their consecration).

833 2nd revolt of the sons after Louis the Pious took Aquitania from Pepin. On the 'Field of Lies' at Kolmar Louis's army went over to his sons. The Emperor was removed from the throne, but restored to it again by Louis the German and Pepin, who sought to curtail Lothair's power.

838 After Pepin's death Charles the Bald received Aquitania.

840 Civil war between Louis the German and Charles the Bald on the one side, and Lothair on the other.

841 Lothair defeated in the **b. of Fontenoy** (nr Auxerre). Louis and Charles affirmed their alliance in

842 in the **Oath of Strasbourg** (the most ancient documents of the Old High Ger. and Old Fr. languages). Partition of the Empire in

843 by the **Treaty of Verdun** into Middle, Eastern and Western kdms. Emperor Lothair I received the Middle Kdm ('the bowling alley'), which stretched from the North Sea across Burgundy to the Gulf of Gaeta and included the imp. cities of Aix-la-Chapelle and Rome. Louis the German received the e. Frank. Kdm and Charles II the Bald the w. Frank. Kdm. Theoretically and nominally, imp. unity was preserved.

The Middle Kdm (843–75)

843–55 Lothair I. After his death the kdm was partitioned among his sons: Louis II (d. 875) received Italy and the Imp. crown; Lothair II (d. 869), the area from the North Sea to the sources of the Maas and Moselle (*Lothari regnum* = Lothringen = Lorraine); Charles (d. 863), Burgundy and Provence. After Charles's death, the brothers divided up his land.

870 Treaty of Mersen: upon the death of Lothair II, Louis the German inherited the eastern half of Lorraine, including Aix-la-Chapelle. After the death of Louis II,

Charles II the Bald obtained Italy and was crowned Emperor by Pope John VIII (872–82).

The E. Frank. Kdm (843–911)

843–76 Louis the German. Attacks by the Normans (p. 131; 845, destruction of Hamburg) and the Hungarians (862, p. 113). After his death, Bavaria and the southeastern marks went to Carloman (d. 880); Franconia, Thuringia and Saxony to Louis III (d. 882); Alamannia (Swabia) to Charles III the Fat (d. 888).

876 b. of Andernach: attempting to seize the eastern half of Lorraine after the death of Louis the German, Charles II the Bald was defeated by Louis III.

880 Treaty of Ribemont: Louis III received the western half of Lorraine from the grandchildren of Charles the Bald. Except for minor changes, the western boundary of the Middle Kdm remained the Franco-Ger. border throughout the Middle Ages.

881–7 Emperor Charles III the Fat gained Italy by force, was crowned Emperor by Pope John VIII, and became sole ruler after the death of his brothers. He won control over the w. Frank. Kdm (exc. for Lower Burgundy).

887 Diet of Tribur: Charles III forced to abdicate.

887–99 Arnulf of Carinthia, the son of Carloman, was elected king by all the Ger. tribes. The concept of the complete empire was not abandoned: the oath of fealty of the pretender to the throne in the w. Frank. Kdm. Coronation of the Emperor by Pope Formosus (896).

900–11 The e. Frank. Kdm was torn apart by internal feuds during the reign of Louis the Child. Constant incursions by the Hungarians (p. 169). The failure of cen. royal authority to stem the attacks of intruding enemies (Hungarians, Normans) led to **tribal duchies being est.:** Saxony, Thuringia, Bavaria, Swabia, Lorraine and Franconia.

The W. Frank. Kdm (843–87)

843–77 Charles II the Bald was crowned Emperor in 875. Because of the early deaths of his son Louis the Stammerer (877–9) and Louis's 2 sons, the kdm was dissolved.

877 Lower Burgundy (Cisjurane) became an autonomous kdm under Boso of Vienne.

888 Upper Burgundy (Transjurane) became an autonomous kdm under the Guelph Rudolf I (888–912). The sons of both rulers became kings in Italy (p. 119).
After the removal of Charles III from the throne, Odo, Count of Paris (888–98), was chosen as the first anti-king. Although the Carolingians ruled nominally for another 100 yrs, real power rested in the hands of the Robertians, the successors of Odo. Large territ. states crystallized in what was then France as they had in Germany: Isle-de-France, Champagne, Aquitaine, Gascogny, Toulouse, Gothia, Catalonia, Brittany, Normandy and Flanders.

The state and the constitution: the **king** stood at the head of the Frank. state; his power rested on the charismatic qualities ('sacred royalty') of his heritage, the econ. power derived from his landed properties (royal territories, royal estates, eccles. dependencies) and the royal retainers. The king ruled through the **royal ban** (ban = *imperium* = authority), the milit. **army ban** in foreign affairs and the **judicial ban** in domestic affairs. Succession to the throne was governed by the **dyn. principle:** elevation to the kingship from that family which represented the principle of 'sacred royalty' (electoral and hered. principles). The **nobility** gradually placed itself between the king and the people and became the antagonist of the king. The **people** (free peasant-warriors entitled to polit. rights) acted jointly with the king at the annual **Field of Mars** celebration; however, after the b. of Tours and Poitiers, the peasants, who fought on foot, became militarily and politically expendable. The assembly of the army was retained in Austrasia, but it was replaced by the assembly of notables in Burgundy and Neustria.

Admin.: the centre was the **royal court** (*palatium*). The **major-domo** headed the royal household; the **Count Palatine** was the judge of the court (*comes palatii*). The **chancery** with the scribes (*notarii*) was under the direction of counsellors 'in personal attendance' drawn from the laity (*referendarii*). Appointed by the king, **counts** (*comes*), who later became feudal lords, officiated in the cities (*civitates*) and in the administrative districts, which extended outward from the core of the Frank. kdm ('county admin.'). The count had authority over the milit. levy, the admin. and the judicial system. **Dukes** (*dux*) were appointed by the king for larger territories along the frontiers and for the territories of the Alamanni, Thuringians and Bavarians.

The Church: a nat. church of the Franks came into being under CLOVIS. The king, who became head of this nat. church because of the sacred character of his kingship, issued eccles. laws (*capitularia ecclesiastica*), appointed bps, and exerted strong infl. over eccles. synods of the realm. The relationship of CHARLES MARTEL to the Church was conditioned by the interests of the state: distribution of eccles. estates as fiefs to his vassals, appointment of trustworthy laymen as bps and abbots, support of miss. activity in the eastern territories to strengthen Frank. infl. Under CARLOMAN and PEPIN, the sons of CHARLES MARTEL, **Boniface** reorganized the Church in the Frank. realm: eccles. estates were put in order, disciplining of the clergy and establishment of new bpcs (Reims, Sens, Rouen). The Frank. bps recognized the authority of Rome and subordinated themselves to the Pope (747).

Trade: trade with the Orient, which had still been carried on under the Merovingians, was stopped by the incursions of the Arabs. The money economy disappeared simultaneously. The area between the Rhine and the Loire became the new focus of trade. In addition to the Jews and Syrians, the Frisians were active as traders (trade with England and Scandinavia, trade centre at Doorstad).

Agriculture: because of the decline of trade and crafts and the shortage of money, agriculture, large estates and a barter economy gained in importance. A new agrarian system developed in the area between the Seine and the Loire (extension to the N. and E.): the **'hide system'** (*Hufensystem*, cohesion of house yard and arable land of the possessor of a 'hide of land' with rights to the use of the common forest and meadow), in conjunction with the division of the arable land into strips, the community-owned march, and the 3-field system, replaced the ancient field-grazing economy with its predominant animal husbandry (p. 117). Consequences: the cultivation of grains became the main task of agriculture; pop. increase.

The large holdings (former Rom. public lands, forests not privately owned) were in the hand of the king, who gave parts of them to eccles. and sec. notables (*potentes*). The dispersal of locations was characteristic of these large holdings: surrounding the lord's estate (*Salhof*) and land, the dependent estates could either be close by or widely dispersed. On these large holdings (in part owned by churches and monasteries) Rom. techniques of agriculture continued to be practised (the cultivation of fruits, wine and vegetables; stone construction); their self-sufficiency was made possible by the existence of workshops (*gynaeceas*; smithy, mill, etc.).

The manorial system developed out of the fusion of the estate economy of late antiquity headed by the Rom. estate owner with his dominance over his *coloni* (obligation to raise taxes and milit. levies), with the Germ. system of property ownership: the house of the lord was beyond the public domain; he enjoyed personal jurisdiction over individuals ('*Munt*' – the free, the unfree, and his retinue of warriors – as well as things ('*Gewere*') – houses, peasant-estates, parishes. Manor received **immunity** (Lat. *immunitas* = exemption from specific public obligations) similar to that enjoyed by the Emperor's treasury, the Church and selected private estates of the senatoria aristocracy during late antiquity. Extended Frank. immunity consisted of the prohibition of the *introitus*, the *exactiones* and the *districtio* (free entrance, exactions and coercive power) of the counts. The gradual development of **judicial privileges** (tied to immunity) – not only over minors and the unfree, but also over free copy-holders and peasants, who had placed themselves under the personal 'protection' of the lord (representation in court and army and assumption of public obligations by the lord) – led to the jurisdictional authority of the lord, which made the free peasants and copy-holders serfs. This process was accelerated by the intensive use of corvées and their forced labour.

The town: not only did the town lose its polit. privileges; it also lost its position as econ. and pop. centre. The town was still seat of the bp and centre of the diocese; and in the s. still

he residence of the count (whose administra-
ive district is the N. was the county). The
oyal residences of the Merovingians were still
ocated in the towns; the palaces of the
Carolingians were located in the country.

Church, Ctr., Government

The Church: after the break between Rome and
Byzantium over the 'iconoclastic dispute' (p.
39), the Papacy tied itself to the ruling house
of the Franks (protection from the Langobards). The new Carol. dyn. was thereby
legitimized and the Papacy protected from
attacks by the Langobards. At PEPIN's coronation the sacred character of kingship was not
bestowed by dyn. right (heathen reverence for
dynasties tracing their descent from the gods),
but by anointment (relig. authority: *Dei
gratia* = by God's grace).
CHARLEMAGNE's conception of imp. dignity
was not based on the tradition of the Caesars,
but on the Germ. conception of the royal
priest taken in conjunction with the August.
conception of the *Civitas Dei* (City of God).
Imp. dignity was conveyed by the Pope as
translator imperii (based on the papal conception of the vacancy of the imp. throne at
Byzantium). As protector of the Church,
appointed by God, CHARLEMAGNE demanded
for himself the supreme position within and
authority over the Church (theocracy: the
state Church). Protection of the Church was
the obligation of his royal office, imposed on
him by God. Synods of the realm were held
under CHARLEMAGNE's supervision; king and
popular assembly dealt with church matters:
compensation for confiscated eccles. estates
through the tithe, securing the econ. self-
sufficiency of individual churches, establishment of metropolitan church-units (12 Fr., 5
Ital. and 4 Ger. archbpcs), establishment of
parishes (independent parishes in the country),
raising the educational level of the clergy (*vita
canonica*: community life of the clergy),
standardization of the liturgy, supervision of
the moral conduct of the laity. CHARLEMAGNE
also intervened in doctrinal disputes of the
Church (adoptianism, iconoclasm, the '*filio-
que*'-controversy). Bps were appointed by the
ruler.

Ctr. (the 'Carol. Renaissance'): summoned
from England, Ireland, Spain, Lombardy and
Italy by CHARLEMAGNE, the 'scholars of the
Court' formed the intellectual centre which
was to carry out the cult. mission of the age.
Alcuin (*c.* 730–804) came from York to head
the palace school (781, abbot of St-Denis from
796). **Paulus Diaconus** (*c.* 720–95), the historian
of the Langobards, PETRUS OF PISA, PAULINUS
of AQUILEIA, and THEODULF, bp of Orléans,
worked alongside him. Among the Frank.
laymen was **Einhard** (*c.* 770–840), the bio-
grapher of CHARLEMAGNE (*Vita Caroli*). The
palace school (*schola palatina*) became the
model for the cathedral and cloister schools
which were est. throughout the realm. Instructed by CHARLEMAGNE, the monastic
communities, hitherto anti-intellectual, ascetic
and eremitic, est. institutions of learning,

furthered the sciences, and became the trans-
mitters of the lit. traditions of classical and
Christ. antiquity. Ctr. was conveyed through
the *Artes liberales* (studies worthy of a free
man, in contrast to the *Artes mechanicae*: the
arts of the artisan): grammar, rhetoric, dialectics (the *trivium*); arithmetic, geometry,
astronomy, music (the *quadrivium*). (For art,
see p. 156.)

Gvt: the gvt provided for the elimination of
the pressing burden of the milit. levy on the
small peasants, the collection of the tribal laws,
and the enforcement of the law by means of
orders (*capitularia*). The popular court was
reformed by the institution of the jury system.
Only 3 genuine *ding* assemblies continued to
be held annually. They included the entire
jurisdictional community, and were presided
over by the count. The jurors (7) acknowledged
the *ding* assemblies and sat in judgement.

The Development of Feudalism

Preconditional for the development of feudalism was the existence of cavalry (the
armoured knight), which had come to the
foreground *c.* the mid 8th cent. The fief made
the knight economically independent and
enabled him to equip himself (horse, armour).
The late-Rom. *commendatio* (submission to
protection), under which one man placed
himself in the service of another as his **vassal**
(from the Celt. *gewas* = knight) fused with the
Germ. tradition of personal fellowship (*Gefolgschaft*), based on loyalty. Loyalty elevated the
service obligation of the knight to a matter of
honour. Mutual loyalty of lord and vassal and
the duty of obedience on the part of the vassal
(*hominium* = feudal service; *fidelitas* = oath of
fealty) determined the personal aspects of
feudalism; added to this was the material side:
the **fief**, the piece of land given as a loan by
the lord (*beneficium, feudum*), became a precondition for the vassal's service. Service and
loyalty were the legal justifications for the fief,
for which the vassal in turn assumed personal
obligation. Since vassalage and the granting of
a benefice were conceived of in terms of a
personal relationship, the fief, initially, was
returned at the time of the death of the lord
or the vassal; however, the fiefs soon became
hered. The capitulary of Kiersy (877) stipulated
that fiefs were to be bestowed upon qualified
heirs of the father. Feudal grants were not
limited to the class of mounted knights. To
strengthen the personal bond between king
and office-holders, the notables (*potentes*), too,
received their offices (duchies, counties), and
in addition to their allodials (*allod* = free
property), other domains as fiefs. Fiefs and
feudal offices at first became hered. *de facto*,
later *de jure*: a loosening of the ties of the
nobility to the rulers was the consequence.
The fiefs, at the disposal of the nobility
(purchase, sale, partition), developed into
infant territ. states.

England in the Roman period

The conquest of Jutes, Angles and Saxons

The Anglo-Saxon struggle against the Danes and Norwegians in the 9th cent.

England, *c*. 1066

Conquests of the Jutes, Angles, Saxons and Danes

The **Jutes, Angles** and **Saxons** landed in England c. 450; England had been abandoned by the Romans c. 400. They drove the Britons to Wales (legend of King ARTHUR), Cornwall, Scotland and Brittany (Aremorica) and est. 7 states: Kent (Jutes); Northumbria, Mercia, East Anglia (Angles); Essex, Sussex, Wessex (Saxons). Northumbria's domination during the 7th cent. was followed by that of Mercia expanding to Cornwall and Wales in the 8th.

793 Pillage of the monastery of Lindisfarne (p. 131) by the Normans: beginning of the 'Viking Age'.

802–39 King EGBERT OF WESSEX, who had grown up at the court of CHARLEMAGNE, attained dominance over the Anglo-Saxon states. During his reign the incursions of the vikings (Danes) multiplied.

866 They began their systematic conquest from London and the Isle of Thanet in the mouth of the Thames. N. of the Thames, England became a land settled by Danes (Danelaw), governed by them from '5 burgs' (East Anglia and the '5 burgs' 870–917, Northumbria 876–926).

England (871–1066)

871–99 After severe struggles (establishment of burgs and building of a fleet), **Alfred the Great,** king of Wessex, defeated the Danes at

878 Edington. After seizing London (885), he forced a partition of the land along the line London–Chester. The importance of ALFRED THE GREAT rests in his activity as law-giver (collection and ordering of laws) and translator of historical and ethical writings (BEDE, BOETHIUS, OROSIUS). The Dan. states were subj. to his successors EDWARD THE ELDER (899–924) and ETHELSTAN (924–39).

937 ETHELSTAN defeated the allied Danes (from Dublin), Scots and Welsh at Brunanburh (location unknown), and est. diplomatic ties with Germany and France. He est. an admin. and chancery without the office of *major-domo*, which had been so dangerous for the Frank. state.

959–75 Edgar, ruler of all England, had himself crowned and anointed as 1st king by St DUNSTAN, Archbishop of Canterbury, in accordance with a ritual designed after a W. Frank. model (973). Influenced by concepts from Gorze and Cluny (p. 141), a reform of the Church set in.

978–1016 ETHELRED THE UNREADY attempted in vain to prevent Dan. incursions by levying heavy tributes on his subjects in form of the Danegeld. The Danes conquered all England (1013).

1016–35 King Canute the Great was elected king by the English and made England the centre of his North Sea empire (p. 163). He mar. ETHELRED's widow and became a Christian. Land distribution to his retinue, but no general confiscation. Except for a bodyguard, the army was discharged and sent home. Overall unity of the state was no longer aimed for (new duchies were est. to which relatives – but also Englishmen – were appointed as dukes). After his death, CANUTE's sons ruled until 1042.

1042–66 EDWARD THE CONFESSOR, son of ETHELRED, came into conflict with the Anglo-Saxon nat. party under earl GODWIN OF ESSEX because of the establishment of a cen. admin. staffed with Normans. After EDWARD's death, GODWIN's son HAROLD was elected king. He defeated the Norwegians at Stamfordbridge (p. 163); but was defeated by duke WILLIAM OF NORMANDY, who had landed with an army in England, on

14 Oct. 1066 at the b. of Hastings (death of HAROLD).

State and Constitution

The Anglo-Saxon people divided into 'notables' (*thegns* = swords, Thanes), free warriors (*ceorls* = Kerle) and the unfree. Admin. and judicial authority over the villages were in the hands of the Thanes and the 4 'best'. A new division of the state took place during the 10th cent. by the **establishment of territ. centuries;** however, larger territ. units remained intact. Later on shires developed (counties with burgs as centres), proceeding from Wessex and gradually covered the entire country. The large **earldoms** (earls), often growing out of the mediatization of independent lesser princes and the joining of several counties under one hand, constituted a threat to the monarchy; this was overcome by the appointment of dependent royal officials. The **sheriff** (*shiregerêfa* = graf (count) of the shire), the royal official controlling the earl, gradually gained infl. over the centuries by travelling the circuit of the local courts ('turn' of the sheriff).

Christianization

Three churches existed in England c. 660: the Old Briton Church in Wales, the Iro-Scotch in Ireland and Scotland (a monastic church with severe asceticism), and the Anglo-Saxon, which was in close contact with Rome. The conversion of the Anglo-Saxons was carried out by abbot AUGUSTINE, the first archbp of Canterbury (p. 140), who had been sent by Pope GREGORY THE GREAT. THEODORE OF TARSUS, archbishop of Canterbury (669–90), organized the Anglo-Saxon Church (Metropolitan centres at York and Canterbury). During the 7th cent. the Iro-Scotch church was incorp., the Old Briton Church from the 8th cent. on. BEDE (*Beda Venerabilis* = the Venerable BEDE, 673–735) was the great historian of the Anglo-Saxons (*Historia ecclesiastica gentis Anglorum*). The anon. author of *Beowulf* was a member of the clergy.

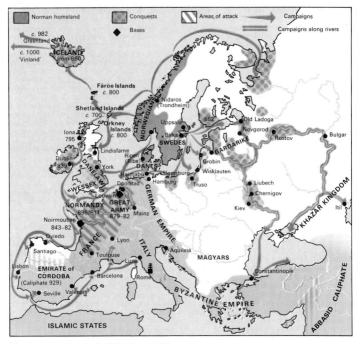

Legend:
- Norman homeland
- Conquests
- Areas of attack
- Campaigns
- Bases
- Campaigns along rivers

c. 982 Greenland
c. 1000 'Vinland' from 860
ICELAND
Fāroe Islands c. 800
Shetland Islands c. 700
Iona 795
Orkney Islands c. 800
Nidaros (Trondheim)
Uppsala
862
Old Ladoga
Novgorod
Rostov
Bulgar
Dublin 839
Lindisfarne
York
WESSEX
DANELAW
Haithabu
Ripen (Ribe)
Birka
Grobin
Wiskiauten
GARDARIKE
DANES
Doorstad
Hemsburg
Hamburg
Truso
Liubech
Chernigov
Kiev
KHAZAR KINGDOM
Itil
NORMANDY 896/911
Louvain
Mainz
GREAT ARMY 879-82
GERMAN EMPIRE
Noirmoutier 843-82
Oviedo
FRANCE
Lyon
Toulouse
Luna
Aquileia
Rome
MAGYARS
Constantinople
Santiago
Lisbon
EMIRATE of CORDOBA (Caliphate 929)
Seville
Barcelona
Valencia
ITALY
BYZANTINE EMPIRE
ABBASID CALIPHATE
ISLAMIC STATES
NORWEGIANS
SWEDES

Norman campaigns in the 8th, 9th and 10th cents.

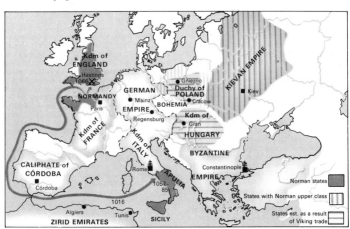

Kdm of ENGLAND
Hastings 1066
NORMANDY
Paris
Kdm of FRANCE
GERMAN EMPIRE
Mainz
Regensburg
Gniezno
Duchy of POLAND
Cracow
BOHEMIA
Kdm of HUNGARY
Gran
KIEVAN EMPIRE
Kiev
CALIPHATE of CÓRDOBA
Córdoba
Kdm of ITALY
Rome
APULIA 1057-85
BYZANTINE EMPIRE
Constantinople
1016
Algiers
Tunis
ZIRID EMIRATES
SICILY

Legend:
- Norman states
- States with Norman upper class
- States est. as a result of Viking trade

States established in Europe by the Normans

Danes, Swedes and Norwegians are **Normans** (= North men) or **vikings**; in Russia they are called **Varangians.** The expansion of the Norsemen was caused by overpopulation, enjoyment of fighting, a lust for glory and adventure, and dissatisfaction with the polit. situation at home (the establishment of royal domains prompted the freedom-loving, warlike nobles to migrate). The technological basis for expansion was the keeled long-boat (Gokstad, Oseberg), with reinforced bottom for the keel and mast instead of the ancient oared vessel (Nydam, Kvalsund).

The Early Period

c. 500 the Danes inhabited the Dan. islands, Schonen, later Jutland.

c. 600 the kings of Svear extended their dominance from Uppsala to all of Sweden and (after 650), with the inhabitants of Gotland, controlled the Baltic area (Finland, Courland, E. Prussia): during the 8th cent. the Baltic Sea was a Swed. *mare nostrum* closed to Fris. trade. Norway consisted of splinter kdms and peasant republics.

790–840 Plunder and raids along the coasts – esp. of Celt. territories: Lindisfarne (793); Jarrow, Monkwearmouth (794); Rechru, Skye, Iona (795). From 799 on pillage of the Fris. coast, prompting CHARLEMAGNE to est. a coastguard. Characteristic of these early viking raids were the attack during the spring and the return home during the autumn.

After 840 (death of LOUIS THE PIOUS) these campaigns became the undertakings of enormous armies which occupied fortified camps at the mouths of rivers and wintered there.

1. The Dan. vikings (the **great army**) annually plundered the Frank. cities nr rivers; they undertook campaigns of plunder in Asturia and Portugal (844), in the Balearic Islands, in Provence and Tuscany (859–62) and, after their return, subj. Northumbria and E. Anglia in England (Danelaw = the territory subject to Dan. law). Only ALFRED THE GREAT (p. 129), king of Wessex, by creating a fleet, succeeded in maintaining himself against them. Later campaigns were carried out under the leadership of Dan. kings. England was united to Denmark under CANUTE THE GREAT (p. 163).

2. The Nor. vikings occupied the Orkneys and Shetlands during the 8th cent.; later the Faroes, the Hebrides and Ireland. After the unification of Norway (872) under HAROLD FAIRHAIR (c. 860–933), many Norwegians left home and (from 874) settled in Iceland (discovered 860),. The era of conquest was ended with the establishment of the **Law and the Ding** (930). Greenland was discovered in 982, America (Vinland) c. 1000 (p. 225).

3. The Swed. vikings undertook campaigns into the E. Eur. area. Summoned by Slav. and Fin. tribes, they entered the area of Novgorod under RURIK (p. 133). c. 1000 Christianization and settlement of the vikings.

Establishment of States (9th–12th cents.)

Normandy:

896 Dan. vikings settled at the mouth of the Seine.

911 Agreement of St-Clair-sur-Epte between the Seine vikings under ROLLO and the Frank. king CHARLES THE SIMPLE (898–923): ROLLO received the land as a fief and in exchange assumed its defence. After his baptism (912), he became duke and vassal of the king; the fief became a duchy.

Lower Italy:

1059 The Normans acknowledged the Pope's feudal authority at the Synod of Melfi. ROBERT GUISCARD became duke (*Dux Apuliae et Calabriae*). The Normans put an end to Byz. rule in Lower Italy, and also to that of the Arabs in Sicily: conquests of Messina (1061) and Palermo (1072).

1130 Roger II (1105–54) united Sicily, Calabria and Apulia (*Rex Siciliae, Calabriae and Apuliae*) into a kdm and made Palermo its cap. Conquests of Amalfi (1137), Naples (1139) and Gaeta.

1186 Henry VI mar. the Norm. heiress CONSTANCE, daughter of ROGER II, and inherited the Norm. kdm (1194).

England: see p. 129.

Russia: warlike merchants, the Swed. vikings est. areas of domination (*Gardarike*) in the region of Lake Ladoga between 800 and 850 by erecting fortified residences in the midst of the Slav. tribes. Those in the N. were united by RURIK into the state of Novgorod (p. 133).

The Norm. states were founded by a class of war-loving lords which was absorbed in short order by the native pops. that it had subj.

Trade: dominated by Jews (Mediterranean and Orient) and Frisians (in Europe) during the 8th and 9th cents., trade was taken over by the far-flung trading network of the vikings. Goods were exchanged by rivers and seas (ships were dragged overland to cover short distances between rivers). Because it controlled the Rus. trade-lanes (the Dnieper to Byzantium, the Volga to the Arabian world), the emphasis of world trade shifted to Sweden (Birka); after 900 it shifted to Haithabu, which had been founded to control shipments and shorten distances between the SE. and W. More important than the trade with Greece was that with the Arabs (silver from Western Turkestan and Afghanistan: find of 40,000 Arab. silver coins on Gotland). The vikings supplied furs, slaves (from the Baltic, Slav. and Fin. territories) and jewellery made from precious metals. Viking trade ceased c. 1050. Silver mined in the Harz mts replaced the stream of silver from Arabia (exhaustion of the silver mines in the eastern part of the Caliphate). The Slavs took over trade in the Baltic.

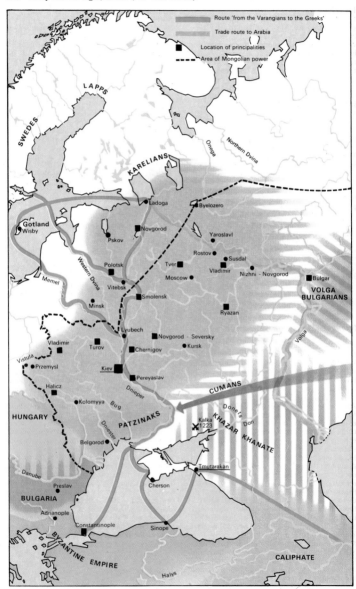

Route 'from the Varangians to the Greeks'

Trade route to Arabia

■ Location of principalities

- - - Area of Mongolian power

LAPPS

SWEDES

KARELIANS

Onega

Northern Dvina

● Ladoga

● Byelozero

Gotland
Wisby

● Novgorod

● Pskov

Yaroslavl ●

Rostov ●

Susdal ●

Western Dvina

Polotsk ■

Tver ■

Vladimir ■

Nizhni - Novgorod ●

● Bulgar

Moscow ●

Memel

Vitebsk ●

Smolensk ■

VOLGA
BULGARIANS

● Minsk

Ryazan ■

Lyubech ■

Novgorod - Seversky ■

Volga

Vladimir ■

Turov ■

Chernigov ■

● Kursk

Vistula

● Przemysl

Kiev ■

Pereyaslav ■

Dnieper

CUMANS

Halicz ●

● Kolomyya

Bug

PATZINAKS

Donets

Don

Kalka
1223 ✗

KHAZAR
KHANATE

HUNGARY

Dniester

● Belgorod

Danube

Tmutarakan ●

● Preslav

Cherson ●

BULGARIA

● Adrianople

Constantinople ●

● Sinope

CALIPHATE

BYZANTINE EMPIRE

Halys

The Kievan Empire, c. 1000

The Age of the Varangians

The Rus. state was est. after the Swed. Varangians (RURIK) had been invited into the land by Slav. and Fin. tribes and had est. footholds among the Slavs. RURIK united Northern Russia from Novgorod. Two of RURIK's retainers,

858 ASKOLD and DIR, made their way to Kiev along the route 'from the Varangians to the Greeks'. Their 1st assault on Constantinople was repulsed in 860.

882 Oleg the Wise (879–912) united N. (Novgorod) and S. (Kiev); Kiev became cap. of the Rus. state, soon imperilled by nomadic incursions into the south-eastern steppe regions.

The State of Kiev (Kievan Rus)

944 After a futile attack on Constantinople, IGOR (912–45) concluded a trade agreement with Byzantium and opened the state to Christ. infl.

957 Baptism of his widow OLGA.

961(?)–72 Sviatoslav controlled the int. trade routes. He dest. the Khazar state and the kdm of the Danubian Bulgarians and thereby caused difficulties with Byzantium; on his return (972), SVIATOSLAV was slain by the Patzinaks who were allied with Byzantium. His successors, the Ruriks, ruled over the Rus. principalities. One of them

978–1015 VLADIMIR I THE SAINT ('Bright Sun') became sole ruler with the aid of the Varangians (980). After his baptism (988) and marriage to the Byz. princess ANNA, sister of BASILEUS II, Kiev became the centre of relig. life (seat of the Metropolitan).

1019–54 Yaroslav the Wise succeeded VLADIMIR after prolonged fratricidal wars (support of the Varangians). Fighting against the Poles, he seized the castles of CZERWIEN; however, cooperating with Emperor HENRY III (p. 147), he supported CASIMIR I in the rest. of Piast rule (1039). He defeated the Patzinaks in 1036. His naval attack on Constantinople in 1043 failed.

After the elimination of their co-rulers, VLADIMIR and YAROSLAV THE WISE created a united Rus. state in which, during the 10th cent., the Varan. upper class was absorbed by the Slav. majority. After attacks against the state of the Volga Bulgars (965 and 985) – a state made wealthy by the trade between N. and E. Russia – relations between the two states improved. Kiev became the art. and intellectual centre of Russia. Under YAROSLAV THE WISE, the 1st compilation of Rus. law – a combination of Byz. laws and Slav. traditions – was made (vengeance curbed by a system of punitive measures).

The Principalities

After 1054 Russia dissolved into principalities. Redistribution of power after every death of a Kievan prince (principle of seniority) weakened the state. Even a general meeting of reconciliation held by the princes at Liubech in 1097 (redistribution of power), and strong rulers like VLADIMIR MONOMACHUS (1113–25) and MSTISLAV THE GREAT (1125–32) could not halt the decay. Conflicts and rivalries, cleverly exploited by Byzantium, dominated the fate of the Rurik dynasty. After the establishment of the Lat. empire (1204), the Rus. Black Sea trade was lost to Venice.

The 12th and 13th cents. also saw the beginning of the econ. and cult. decline of Kiev. The principalities disintegrated, with the exception of Greater Novgorod and Pskov. Nevertheless, the Upper Volga basin was colonized and a state, composed of village communities and having an absolutist form of gvt, was est. The country disintegrated into territorially ruled parcels.

The state of the Ruriks: the state was headed by the prince, who did not rule absolutely, but was the supreme judge. His main task was the defence of city and country. He was assisted by the council of the Boyars (landowning nobility) and the urban assemblies (combination of monarchic, aristocratic and democratic elements).

Achievement of the Kievan states: the fusion of Slavs and Varangians through Byz. Christianity and ctr.

Mongolian Rule

1223 The Mongols, also cal. Tartars, were victorious in the b. of the River Kalka, but the vict. was inconsequential because of GENGHIS KHAN's death in 1227.

From 1245 rule of the Mongols over all Russia. Karakorum became the residence of the Great Khan UGUDEI (p. 179). His subordinate BATU est. the rule of the 'Golden Horde' at Sarai (1251), which separated from the cen. gvt of the state in 1260.

Admin.: counting and registration of the tax-paying pop. Taxes were collected by 'counters' (private 'tax-farmers'). Levies of Rus. recruits and deportation of workers. The rule of the Rus. princes was not changed, but representatives of the Khan (Baskads) were present at the courts. The princes had to recognize the overlordship of the Khan (by paying homage to him) and obtain a letter of recognition (*jarlyk*). The Rus. Church continued to occupy a privileged position since the Mongols practised relig. tolerance: priests were free from taxation and Church properties were not confiscated; in exchange the Church readily submitted to the rule of force.

Consequences of Mongolian rule: destruction of the personal dignity of man (prostration and kissing of the hem of the ruler's robe); low social position of women. Cruel punishments (torture, maiming). Cessation of contacts with the w. and isolation of Orth. Russia.

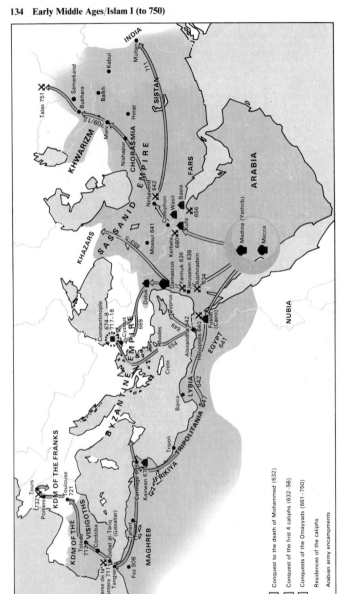

The expansion of Islam to 750

Conquest to the death of Mohammed (632)

Conquest of the first 4 caliphs (632–56)

Conquests of the Omayyads (661–750)

Residences of the caliphs

Arabian army encampments

The teachings of Islam (= 'submission to the will of God') were proclaimed by MOHAMMED after he experienced his calling (610): the impending judgement of the world (reward and punishment for one's actions) and the teachings of ALLAH, the creator and judge, who determines the fate of man. The **5 main obligations of the Muslim** are the confession of faith ('There is no God but ALLAH, and MOHAMMED is his prophet'), the obligatory prayer (5 times daily), charitable gifts (tax), the fast in the month of Ramadhan and the pilgrimage to Mecca. The **3 fundamentals of the faith** are the **Koran** (God's word, 114 suras), collected and put into written form by OTHMAN (see below), the **Sunna** (= the traditions of the habits and sayings of the prophet), and the **ijma** (= the accord of the faithful). A split between Sunnites and the Shia took place under ALI (see below; the Sunna was disputed). The Shi'ites considered ALI to be the legitimate successor of the prophet (the legitimist party); they were opposed by the Kharijites, who believed that any one of the faithful could be chosen as leader of the community.

The Prophet
c. 570–632 Mohammed. After his proclamation he was forced to leave Mecca:
15 Jun. 622 The 'Hegira' (= flight to Medina, the 'city of the prophet'; beginning of the Isl. calendar).
Nov. 630 Return of MOHAMMED to Mecca. He purified the city and eliminated idol-worship in the Kaaba, the ancient Arab. shrine. The new teaching prevailed in Arabia.
632 Death of MOHAMMED at Medina.

The Elected Caliphs (632–61)
632–4 The Caliph (= successor) ABU BAKR subj. the disobedient Arab tribes and advanced to Syria and Persia.
634–44 Omar, 'the ruler of the faithful', transformed the nat. Arabian state into a theocratic world-empire and est. a milit. admin.: the commander of the Arab. troops of occupation simultaneously became the civil governor representing the Caliph, relig. leader and sec. judge. OMAR conquered Syria and Palestine (Damascus 635, Jerusalem 638), Persia (seizure of Ctesiphon 636, b. of Nehavend 642); his commander AMR IBN AL-AS conquered Egypt (Alexandria was abandoned by the Byzantines in 642).
644–56 The Omayyad OTHMAN was chosen caliph and continued the policy of conquest: advance of the Arabs to Barca (642–5). The governor of Damascus, MO'AWIYA, fought against Byzantium. After a Byz. fleet threatened Alexandria, an Arabian fleet was constructed. The Arabs became a sea-power. OTHMAN favoured the Omayyads and was murdered by opponents.
656–61 ALI, a cousin and son-in-law of the prophet, moved the cap. to Kufa after struggles with MOHAMMED's widow A'ISHA (1st Civil War) and vict. in the 'camel-battle' of Basra: **Medina became politically**

unimportant. MO'AWIYA wanted to avenge the death of his cousin OTHMAN. ALI was murdered after the indecisive b. of Siffin (657) and the arbitration of Adhroh (658). (The result of the arbitration had been unsatisfactory and part of his adherents had left ALI: **Kharijites.**)

The Omayyad Dynasty (661–750)
661–80 MO'AWIYA compensated the incompetent sons of ALI for their loss of power. Damascus became the cap. Rest. of the admin., systems of finance and taxation. Attacks on Byzantium (after 667) failed. Kabul, Bukhara and Samarkand were conquered in the E.
680–83 YAZID I defeated ALI's son HUSAYN and his adherents at **Kerbela** (10 Oct. 680 = **relig. holiday of the Shi'ites**); Kerbela became the site of pilgrimages.
685–705 ABDULMALIK restored the unity of the Empire after suppressing the rebellions of the Shi'ites and Kharijites and eliminating the rival caliph at Mecca. Securing of domination over N. Africa (conquest of Carthage 698). **Introduction of Arabian currency.**
705–15 The zenith of Omayyad power was reached under **Walid I:** conquest of Transoxania, the Indus region (711) and Spain: TARIQ crossed the Straits of Gibraltar (= Jebel al-Tariq) and dest. the Visi. army under RODERIC (p. 117).
718 Fruitless siege of Constantinople.
732 The defeat of Tours and Poitiers prevented the further advance of the Arabs in the w. The soc. and econ. crises caused by the equal taxation of converted non-Arabs, together with uprisings of the Shi'ites and Kharijites, and conflicts between the Omayyads and the Abbasids, led to the downfall of the Omayyad Dynasty.
750 MARWAN II was decisively defeated in the b. of the Zab (a tributary of the Tigris). Only ABDURRAHMAN escaped the bloodbath that befell the Omayyads; he est. the **Emirate of the Omayyads at Córdoba** in Spain (756).

State, Society
The Arab world-power fused people of the most varied origins and religions. Despite these differences, **a coherent Arab ctr.** quickly developed: religion (Islam) and language (Arabic) soon predominated everywhere since translation of the Koran was prohibited. Subj. peoples were neither converted by persuasion, nor were they forced to accept Islam; rather, they were obliged to pay taxes. Later on difficulties arose between the caste of warriors (who paid no taxes) and the subjects who had converted to Islam. Equality demanded by the non-Arabian segment of the pop. had to be granted.

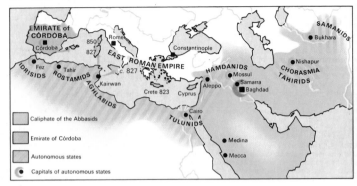

The expansion of Islam in the 8th, 9th and 10th cents.

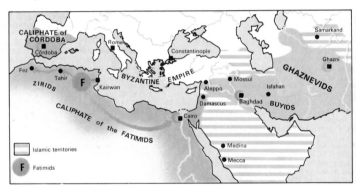

Autonomous Islamic states, c. 1000

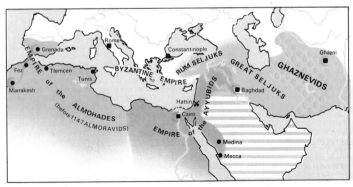

Autonomous Islamic states, c. 1180

The Abbasid Dynasty (750–1258)
The 1st caliph of the dynasty, ABU'L-ABBAS, d. 754. He was succeeded

754–75 by al-Mansur (= the Victorious), the real founder of the Abbasid Dynasty, who created the power base for the new state with the aid of Pers. auxiliary troops (762 establishment of the cap. at Baghdad). The Arabs lost their predominant position; **leadership passed to the Persians:** introduction of Pers. court-ceremonial, gvt of the state by viziers, reorganization of the admin. after the Pers. and Byz. models. The caliph, surrounded by his court, became inaccessible to the public. The greatest flowering of the caliphate was attained under

786–809 Harun al-Rashid (famous for the role he plays in the *Thousand and One Nights*). Despite victorious struggles against Byzantium, the dissolution of the Empire began: the Idrisid Dynasty in Morocco (788) and the Aghlabids in Kairwan (801) gained their independence. The Empire faced decay after HARUN AL-RASHID's death because of conflicts among his sons.

Internal conflicts, Shi'ite uprisings, the rise of autonomous dynasties (the Tahirids in Khorasan) led to the **loss of polit. power by the Caliph** during the 9th cent.; he confined himself to the role of spiritual head of all the faithful, while the gvt of the state fell into the hands of the **Amir al-Umara** ('Great Emir' after 936). The princes of the ind. dynasties soon claimed the title for themselves.

940–1256 The Abbasid Dynasty was politically unimportant.

1256 Incursion of the Mongols into Persia.
1258 Conquest and destruction of Baghdad by the Mongols (p. 179).

Internal Development
In spite of great successes in foreign affairs (domination of the Mediterranean into the 11th cent. and conquest of India), **distinct trends** in matters of religion (sects), domestic politics and ethnic relations developed from the 9th cent. on (separate states under the despotic rule of unrelated dynasties). Decisive infl. on all states was exerted by the **intrusion of Turk. peoples** from the 8th cent.; they formed the **palace guard** at every Isl. court during the 9th cent. Their leaders became governors and exercised effective power. The Ghaznevids of Afghanistan were the 1st Turk. dynasty (962–1186). Islam suffered losses during the *Reconquista* of Spain (p. 187) and the retaking of Sicily.

Culture: the Arabs fused the Orient. and Hellen. intellectual legacies in the centres of Isl. civilization (Baghdad, Damascus, Cairo, Mecca, Samarkand) and made the result the basis of an Isl. science which reached its apogee during the 9th and 10th cents. and influenced the Christ. w., reaching Europe esp. by way of Spain.

Autonomous Isl. States
Spain experienced a period of great flowering under the **Omayyad Dynasty** (755–1031). The most important ruler was ABD AR-RAHMAN III (912–61), who restored the cen. power of the Emirate during the struggle with the aristocracy and claimed the Caliphate (929). After the rest. of Arabian rule over all of Spain by AL-MANSUR, conflicts over the succession to the throne soon set in (1008–31) and led to the establishment of Andalusia as a separate state (period of the Reys de Teija, 1031–86). The Berber Almoravids were summoned to combat the Christ. offensive initiated by King ALPHONSO VII OF CASTILLE (1086–1147, p. 187); the Almoravids were succeeded by the Almohades (1150–1250). The last remnant of Moorish power, the Emirate of Granada, was eliminated by the Castil. conquest (p. 187).

North Africa: 3 smaller dynasties were founded *c.* 800: the Rostamids of Tahir, the Idrisids of Fez (808–930) and the Aghlabids of Kairouan (801–909). They all succumbed to the **Fatimids,** who, as descendants of the prophet's daughter FATIMA and her husband ALI, claimed authority over all the faithful (909–72) and quickly conquered Egypt (969). The Zirids (972–1167) at first ruled as governors in the Fatimid admin. in Ifrikiya; but they soon became independent (1041). During the 11th cent. N. Africa and Spain came under the rule of the Almoravids (1061–1163), whose power was dest. by the Almohades (1147–1269) under ABD AL-MURMIN, the most important Moslem ruler of N. Africa. The state of the Almohades was dest. by Christ. and Arabian attacks.

Egypt: the dynasties of the Tulunids (868–905) and the Ikhshidids (935–69) were succeeded by the **Fatimids** (969–1171), who refused to recognize the authority of the Abbasid Caliphs (anti-Caliphs). Their power gave way to the Ayyubid Dynasty (1171–1250), whose founder, the Kurd SALHAD-DIN (SALADIN) defeated HITTIN, the king of Jerusalem (1187). Subs. the Turk. Mameluke palace guard, repulsing the Mongol attack on Egypt (1260), gained infl. in

The East: Northern Mesopotamia was ruled by the Ramdanids of Mosul and Aleppo (890–1003); the Samanids (819–999), at first governors in the Tahirid admin. of Transozania, ruled there independently from 875 (development of Pers. nat. literature). The largest state was formed by the Buyids (932–1055). During this period a sense of Iran. polit. identity developed. Nominally only the highest bureaucrats (AMIR AL-UMARA), the Buyids resided after 945 at Baghdad and were in effect the real power. Polit. leadership of the Isl. world was subs. exercised by the Turks; the Seljuk Empire became the most important state.

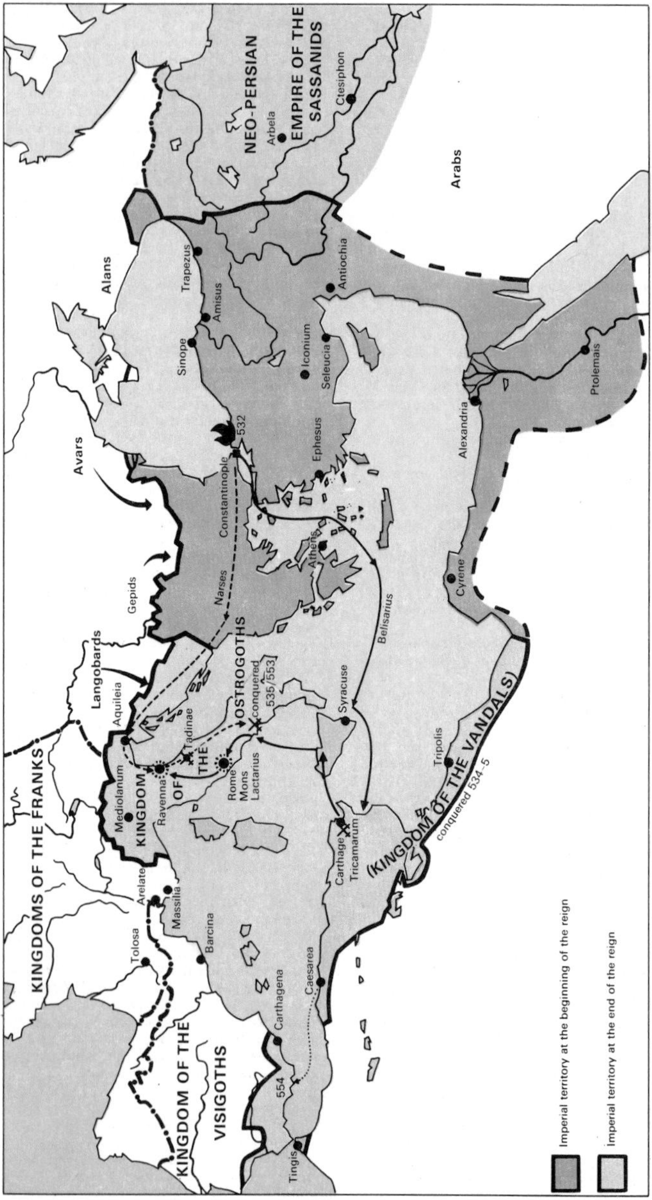

EMPIRE OF THE SASSANIDS

NEO-PERSIAN

Arbela

Ctesiphon

Arabs

Alans

Trapezus

Avars

Amisus

Sinope

Antiochia

Iconium

Seleucia

Ephesus

532

Constantinople

Alexandria

Ptolemais

Cyrene

Narses

Gepids

Athens

Belisarius

Langobards

Aquileia

OSTROGOTHS

Mediolanum

Ravenna

THE

KINGDOM   Conquered 536/553

Rome   Mons Lactarius

Syracuse

KINGDOMS OF THE FRANKS

OF

Tadinae

Carthage   Tricamarum

Tripolis

(KINGDOM OF THE VANDALS)

conquered 534–5

Arelate

Tolosa

Massilia

Barcina

Caesarea

KINGDOM OF THE VISIGOTHS

Carthagena

554

Tingis

Imperial territory at the beginning of the reign

Imperial territory at the end of the reign

Justinian's Empire

The Early Byz. Period

Rom. law and admin., Gk language and civilization, and Christ. faith and morality were the **foundations of the Byz. Empire**. The most important factor of power was the Church; from 479 the Emperor received his crown from the Church. Dogmatic conflict within the Church (Christology = the relationship of CHRIST to humanity) weakened the Empire. The conflict was terminated in

431 by the 2nd Ecumenical Council of Ephesus: the teachings of NESTORIUS (stress on the human nature of CHRIST) were rejected; the teachings of CYRIL OF ALEXANDRIA (stress on the divine nature of CHRIST) were recognized.

451 4th Ecumenical Council of Chalcedon: the Monophysite doctrine was condemned as heresy; the teaching of the dual nature (*duae naturae, una persona*), formulated by Pope LEO I in accordance with AUGUSTINE'S interpretation, was declared binding.

The infl. of the Germans at court during the first half of the 5th cent. was eliminated by Emperor LEO I THE GREAT (457–74) with the aid of the Isaurians, who came from Asia Minor and took the place of the Germans as they moved to the w.

476 ODOACER (ODOVACAR) was recognized as Rom. *patricius* in Italy.

527–65 Justinian, mar. to THEODORA (d. 548), ended the war with the Persians by agreeing to an 'eternal peace', which enabled him to regain the western part of the Empire: N. Africa 535, Italy 553, Southern Spain 554 through BELISARIUS and NARSES. Excessive econ. and financial drain resulted in heavy indebtedness of the state. After suppressing the Nika insurrection of the circus parties (532), the Emperor secured autocratic power **(Caesaropapismus).**

528–35 Codification of the Rom. Law (*Corpus juris civilis*): the *Institutes* (text), the *Digest* or *Pandects* (writings of classical jurists), the *Codex Justinianus* (collection of imp. constitutions), and the *Novellae* (the constitutions issued by JUSTINIAN after 534).

568 Italy was lost to the Langobards.

582–602 Maurice: after incursions into the Balkans by Avars and Slavs, MAURICE est. exarchates to fortify the Empire: Ravenna, Carthage. The exarch had milit. and civil power, increasing his overall authority. MAURICE took Armenia in 591.

Development of the Middle Byz. Empire

610–41 Heraclius (title: *Basileus* instead of *Imperator*). Gk became the official language. HERACLIUS completed the work of MAURICE by devising a new **constitution**. He divided Asia Minor into milit. districts (*themes*) headed by *strategoi* who wielded milit. and civil authority. A peasant militia was created (*stratioti*) by the settlement of soldiers. Every *stratiot* was obliged to do milit. service; he was given hered. possession of property which was to sustain him and provide him with the means to equip himself.

628 After the twofold attack of the Avars and

Slavs and the Persians on Constantinople (626), the Persians were defeated and the Sassanid Empire collapsed. Because of constant attacks by the Arabs, which followed those of the Persians, the Balkan peninsula had to be surrendered to the Slavs who, however, under CONSTANS II POGONATUS (641–68) acknowledged Byz. overlordship. The attacks of the Arabs on Constantinople (674–8) were repulsed.

717–802 The Syr. (Isaurian) Dynasty. The state weakened by the **iconoclastic dispute,** caused by the infl. of Eastern sects hostile to images, the Jews and Islam. Supported by Pope GREGORY III, the advocates of icons, seeing them as symbols and aids to meditation, resisted the iconoclasts with determination.

740 Vict. over the Arabs at Akroinon. The subsequent campaigns of CONSTANTINE V (741–75) turned the Byzantines' struggle for existence into a border war. The expansion of the Arabs was redirected towards the w.: N. Africa and Spain.

751 The fall of Ravenna (collapse of Byz. rule in Italy) and the

800 coronation of CHARLEMAGNE, which could not be prevented by the Empress IRENE, made the **ties between the Papacy and the Franks possible.**

812 MICHAEL I conceded the title of Basileus to CHARLEMAGNE.

820–67 The Amoric (Phryg.) Dynasty. Occupation of Crete by the Arabs. Renewed flowering (after the termination of the iconoclastic dispute) took place.

842–67 under Michael III. Miss. activity among the Slav. peoples: CONSTANTINE and METHODIUS went to Moravia. Khan BORIS OF BULGARIA (852–89) had himself christened (865): the sovereign powers of the Byz. patriarch were recognized (870).

863 Vict. over the Emir of Melitene (beginning of Byz. offensive policies in Asia).

867 The Patriarch PHOTIUS separated the Orth. Church from Rome.

The Army, the constitution, and econ. life: organization into *themes* increased the milit. striking power. The army consisted of the *themes* – supplied by milit. levies – and the guard regiments (Tagmata) which were stationed at Constantinople; the navy consisted of fleets drawn from the *themes* and the imp. fleet of the cap. Division of the cen. admin. into *logotheses* under the direction of Logothetes (the most important Logothete: the Dromos, the chief of gvtl policy). The **process of feudalization,** brought about by the formation of an aristocracy composed of members of the *themes* and by the increase of monastic properties, turned free peasants and *stratiots* into serfs of large landowners, no longer subject to control by cen. authority. Byzantium again had to hire mercenaries. Control of the state over the urban economy was preserved through the guild organization. Conflicts between the bureaucratic nobility of the cap. and the milit. nobility of the provinces. Intrigues at court.

The Rise of the Papacy

After the Church fathers IRENAEUS and TERTULLIAN had endorsed Rome as the apostolic city, CLIXTUS I (217–22) proclaimed the **exceptional position of the Rom. Bp** (Mat. 16: 18) against the opposition of TERTULLIAN and ORIGEN, and thereby became the creator of the **concept of the Papacy**. The Church father CYPRIAN defended the primacy of PETER in terms of the honour due to him, but he was convinced of the **legal equality of all bps.**

325 The 4 patriarchates of Jerusalem, Antioch, Alexandria and Rome (the only patriarchate in the w.) were placed on a level of 'spiritual equality' by the Council of Nicea.

c. **375** After DAMASUS I (366–84) asserted the **teaching authority of the Rom. Bp** on the basis of the legacy of PETER (use of the term 'Apostolic Chair'), the evolution from Rom. Bp to Pope (*Papa*) began and THEODOSIUS THE GREAT acknowledged the Bp of Rome as guardian of the true faith and supreme authority. SIRICIUS (384–99) composed papal letters (*decretalia constituta*), borrowing from imp. decrees in form, which testified to the **identity of Pope and Peter.**

440–61 Leo I, the 'secret w. Rom. Emperor', was the first authentic pope and the **founder of Rom. Primacy.**

445 The Edict of VALENTIAN III: confirmation of the primacy of the Rom. Bp over the Occident (Italy, Spain, N. Africa and Southern Gaul). As successors of PETER, who had been given special powers by CHRIST, the bps of Rome were the vicars of CHRIST (*vicarii Christi*), and therefore held the supreme judgeship (Mat. 16: 18), the highest administrative position in the Church (John 21: 25–7) and the supreme teaching authority (Luke 22: 32).

451 Protest of LEO I against the declaration of the Council of Chalcedon regarding the equality of the bps of Rome and Byzantium. The successors of LEO continued to press the claims for increased power.

492–6 Gelasius I, in a letter to the Emperor ANASTASIUS I, asserted **'the doctrine of the 2 powers':** responsibility of the bps before God for the sec. rulers and subordination of the sec. rulers to the priests as dispensers of the sacraments (as Church members, the rulers were subject to Church discipline).

498–514 SYMMACHUS. During his pontificate it was stipulated that the Pope could not be judged by any man (*Constitutum Silvestri*). Subs. the popes became politically dependent on the Ostrogoths, then on the Langobards.

590–640 Gregory I the Great, the first monastic pope, called himself '*Servus Servorum Dei*' ('servant of the servants of God'; later this became the official title). He simplified AUGUSTINE's doctrine into a 'Vulgar' Catholicism and, by centralizing the admin. of the papal properties (patrimonies = *latifundiae* of the Rom. Church), became **founder of the worldly power of the Papacy in Italy**, and thereby gradually the sec. ruler of the city of Rome (assumption of polit. and administrative functions). Alienation from Byz. civilization and orientation towards the Germ. peoples, whose importance was recognized by him (ties to Rome): Visigoths, Sueves and Langobards became Cath. **The Anglo-Saxons were converted** by the monk AUGUSTINE, sent to King ETHELBERT OF KENT in 596 (establishment of the archbpc of Canterbury). The Anglo-Saxons placed themselves under papal jurisdiction.

664 The Synod of Whitby granted the Pope the following rights in England: the establishment of bpcs and the naming of bps. The Celt. rite was quashed in favour of that of Rome. Rome renewed its claims to primacy over the E.

680–81 The 6th Ecumenical Council of Constantinople condemned the monotheletic doctrine, proclaimed by Emperor HERACLIUS I (2 natures of Christ, but only 1 will) with the approval of Pope HONORIUS I (625–38); HONORIUS was now condemned as a promoter of heresy: **repudiation of Rome's claim to infallible teaching authority.**

722 After his ordination, BONIFACE made a vow of obedience to Pope GREGORY II and left for Germany to undertake miss. activity there. He was made archbp in 732. Prompted by him, a general synod of the Franks placed itself under the Pope's authority.

752–7 STEPHEN II turned away from Eastern Rome and **est. ties with the Frank. kdm** (p. 123): foundation of the Papal State ('Donation of Pepin') (p. 123). The Pope now claimed independent rule over the land, which claim he supported with a forged document, the **'Donation of Constantine'** (*Donatio Constantini*); this document based Rome's independence from the E. on CONSTANTINE THE GREAT's supposed gift of the city of Rome and the western part of the Empire to the Pope.

800 LEO III (795–816) crowned CHARLEMAGNE Emperor (p. 123).

847–52 Produced in the diocese of Reims, the pseudo-Isidoric decretals (forged papal canons) were intended to strengthen the position of the bps vis-à-vis the Metropolitans, synods and sec. powers; the independence of the Church was to be attained by the Pope as guarantor of its freedom. The supremacy of the Pope on earth was therefore proclaimed (*Papa caput totius orbis*).

858–67 NICOLAS I. Because of the waning of Carol. imp. power, the Pope, as the representative of the Church's claims to power appealed to the pseudo-Isidoric decretals with the intention of replacing the system of nat. churches by a cen. Rom. admin.

867 Renewed schism with the Eastern Church because of the trial of PHOTIUS, Patriarch of Constantinople.

The Expansion of Monasticism

Monasticism developed in the Middle East esp. in Egypt and Syria. Purpose: to preserve an austere form of Christianity by pursuing ascetic and eremitic ideals. ANTONIUS left for the loneliness of the desert *c.* 300 (life of the anchorite or eremite). PACHOMIUS (292–346) est. the 1st monastery (cenobitism or monast. life). Aim of monastic life: to achieve perfection through the most severe asceticism. From the 4th cent. on monasticism spread from Egypt throughout the Near East. BASILEIUS THE GREAT, Metropolitan of Caesarea in Cappadocia in 370, created an obligatory rule for Gk monasticism. After 451, the Council of Chalcedon, the bps assumed the supervision of the monasteries in their dioceses; monast. vows binding for life.

From 370 expansion of Western monasticism under the infl. of the '*vita Antonii*' (Lat. trans. of EUAGRIUS OF ANTIOCH).

480–543 Benedict of Nursia (Norcia, E. of Spoleto). He est. the first monastery of Monte Cassino in Campagna *c.* 529 and, with the '*regula Benedicti*', created Western monasticism. The Bened. rule combined Rom. discipline with ancient monast. traditions: *stabilitas loci* (remaining in the monastery), in clear distinction to the itinerant ascetics; *conversio morum* (poverty and chastity), *oboedientia* (obedience to the abbot). Emphasis on manual labour (*ora et labora* = pray and work) and rejection of exaggerated asceticism. Tasks of the monastery: hospitality, care of the poor, establishment of a monast. school. **Monasteries became cult. centres** (collection and preservation of classical literature, the writing of history; also the raising of animals, agriculture and viticulture). Supported by GREGORY THE GREAT and CHARLEMAGNE, the Bened. rule became that predominant in the Occident; from

743 it was generally accepted in the Frank. kdm.

816–17 First monast. reform led by BENEDICT OF ANIANE: strict observance of the Bened. rule.

10th/11th cents. 2nd reform movement. The Clun. movement grew out of the opposition to the secularization of monast. life which resulted from the temporal powers of eccles. princes and the intervention of sec. princes who demanded eccles. privileges for themselves; it spread outward from the monasteries of Cluny (founded 910) and Gorze. Demands: reform of monast. life, monasteries to be brought under the protection of the Papacy (not under the rule of the episcopate), severe monast. discipline and obedience to the abbot. Led by the Abbot of Cluny, some 200 monasteries joined in a congregation (Order). Addit. reform movements were initiated by the **Camaldolese** (founded 1012 by ROMUALD OF RAVENNA), the **Carthusians** (founded 1084 by BRUNO OF COLOGNE), and the **monastery of Hirsau** in 1069. They concentrated on the care of souls.

1098 The Cistercians est. by Abbot ROBERT OF MOLESME (d. 1100). Strong infl. of St BERNARD, who entered Cîteaux in 1112 and became 1st Abbot of Clairvaux in 1115 (*Clara vallis*).

1119 '*Charta caritatis*': perfection of the Bened. rule by STEPHEN HARDING, 3rd Abbot of Clairvaux. The Cist. Order was reorganized as a result of the est. of other communities. The 'General Chapter' of the abbots, which met annually, formed the highest authority. The monasteries were supervised by the mother house, which was watched in turn by the 4 most senior 'daughter' communities (La Ferté, Pontigny, Clairvaux, Morimond). Characteristics of the Cistercians: severe asceticism, simplicity (monastery churches without towers), mystical piety, econ. activity. Colonization of the Ger. E.

1120 Establishment of the **Premonstratensian Order** at Prémontré by NORBERT OF XANTEN, who became archbp of Magdeburg in 1126. Members were not monastics, but *canons regular* (priests dedicated to charitable foundations, living under a rule (*regula*)). Activity: the care of souls and miss. activity, esp. E. of the Elbe.

Mendicant Orders: their ideal was the *Imitatio Christi* – to live the life of JESUS. Unlike the old aristocratic orders loc. in the country, these orders, operating in the cities, developed into homeless, centrally led, obedient and disciplined auxiliary organizations of the Papacy. It was the Order which a monk entered, not the monastery; this was no more than his quarters.

Francis of Assisi's attempt at reform – to diffuse all Christianity with the original Christ. spirit – resulted in the establishment of the **Franciscans** or **Minorites** (*Ordo fratrum minorum* = O.F.M.) after hindrance from the Curia.

1223 HONORIUS III confirmed FRANCIS's Order. Tasks: to awaken popular piety and scientific work; absolute poverty demanded.

1216 Establishment of the **Domin. Order** (*Ordo fratrum praedicatorum* = O.P.) by DOMINICUS OF CALERUEGA (1170–1221). This Order was intended to combat heresy (first against the Albigensians) and to restore them to hierarchical authority through miss. activity. Main task: itinerant preaching; from 1231 it was the **Order of the Inquisition.**

The **Clares** formed the feminine branch (2nd Order) of the mendicants. The 'laymen' formed the '3rd Order' (Tertiarians); they were controlled by the 1st Order. The **Carm. Order** developed out of Eremite communities on Mt Carmel in Palestine (1156). The **Augustinian Eremites** were est. in Italy in 1256.

Central Europe at the time of the Saxon emperors

After the E. Frank. Carol. family became extinct, the notables of the kdm. assembled at Forchheim, chose

911–18 Conrad I of Franconia as king. He vainly attempted to assert the royal prerogatives against the dukes. Lorraine joined the Western Kdm.

The Saxon Emperors (919–1024)

919–36 Henry I was elevated to the royal throne by the Franks and Saxons. **Struggling against the dukes** he subj.

921 ARNULF OF BAVARIA, who had been est. as anti-king.

925 Lorraine reverted to the overlordship of the Eastern Kdm. Duke GISELBERT later mar. HENRY's daughter GERBERGA.

926 After the death of BURKHARD II OF SWABIA, the Frank. Count HERMANN was made Duke of Swabia.

928–9 In the **struggle against the Slavs,** the Hevellers (Brennaburg on the Havel) and Sorbs (both Wendish peoples) were subjugated. An uprising of the Liutici and Abrodites was defeated at Lenzen. **To hold back the Magyars,** HENRY obtained an armistice (for 9 yrs), and used the time to construct garrisons and create an army of armoured knights. With this army he

933 defeated the Magyars at Riade.

936–73 Otto I, the Great, son of HENRY and designated by him as his successor, was elevated to the throne by the secular notables at Aix-la-Chapelle and – after acclamation by the people – was anointed and crowned by the archbps. At the coronation feast he was attended by the dukes: EBERHARD OF FRANCONIA was Lord High Steward, GISELBERT OF LORRAINE was Chamberlain, HERMANN OF SWABIA was Cup-bearer, ARNULF OF BAVARIA was Marshal.

936–7 Organization of the marches under HERMANN BILLUNG and the margrave GERO (securing of the Eastern Frontier).

938 OTTO's half-brother THANKMAR was killed in battle. EBERHARD OF BAVARIA was obliged to abandon claims to eccles. power.

939 The revolt of the dukes EBERHARD OF FRANCONIA and GISELBERT OF LORRAINE and OTTO's brother HENRY was put down at the b. of Andernach by HERMANN OF SWABIA. EBERHARD was killed in battle, GISELBERT drowned in the Rhine. Pardoned, HENRY once more vainly conspired and then submitted definitively (941). Granting of duchies to OTTO's relatives: Franconia was confiscated; CONRAD THE RED received Lorraine (944); HENRY Bavaria (947); LIUDOLF Swabia (950).

950 Subjugation of Duke BOLESLAV OF BOHEMIA.

951–2 Summoned to her aid by ADELAIDE OF BURGUNDY, OTTO journeyed to Pavia (1st Ital. campaign) and declared himself king of the Franks and Langobards without formal election or coronation; he mar. ADELAIDE. BERENGAR was given Italy as a fief, but he had to surrender Istria, Friuli and Verona to Bavaria.

953–4 A revolt of Liudolf and Conrad the Red was overcome after the incursion of the Magyars had been dealt with: Swabia went to BURKHARD III, Lorraine to OTTO's brother BRUNO, archbp of Cologne.

10 Aug. 955 Otto's vict. over the Magyars on the Lechfield. In Oct., vict. over the Slavs on the Recknitz.

The establishment of the bpcs of Schleswig, Oldenburg, Havelberg, Brandenburg (948), Meissen, Merseburg and Zeitz (later Naumburg) – all subject to the Archdiocese of Magdeburg – led to successful **miss. activity among the Slavs;** Prague (973) and Olmütz (975) became subject to Mainz.

961–5 2nd Ital. campaign of OTTO.

2 Feb. 962 Otto crowned Emperor at Rome.

966–72 3rd Ital. campaign: the Lang. princes of Lower Italy paid homage to OTTO. Indecisive struggles against Byz. Calabria; in exchange for the vacation of Byz. territories, Byzantium acknowledged OTTO's imp. dignity.

973–83 Otto II, mar. to THEOPHANO, niece of the E. Rom. emperor, undertook campaigns against HARALD BLUETOOTH in Denmark (974) and against Bohemia.

976 The Bavarian HENRY THE QUARRELSOME was deprived of his duchy: Carinthia became an ind. duchy; the northern part (p. 144) and the E. march went to BERCHTOLD and LUITPOLD of the Babenberg family.

980–83 Ital. campaign, made necessary by attacks of the Fatimid Arabs on the Lang. principalities and tensions with Byzantium.

982 Vict. of the Arabs at Cotrone in Calabria.

983 Great uprising of the Slavs: loss of the E. Elbian territories.

983–1002 Otto III, until 995 under the regency of his mother THEOPHANO and his grandmother ADELAIDE, undertook a campaign in Italy in 996; made his cousin BRUNO Pope – GREGORY V (996–9) – and was crowned Emperor.

999 GERBERT OF AURILLAC became Pope SYLVESTER II.

1000 Establishment of the archbpc of Gnesen as an independent eccles. territory, and proclamation of King BOLESLAV CHROBRY of Poland as 'brother and aide in the Empire'.

1001 Establishment of the archbpc of Gran for Hungary.

1002–24 Henry II. 1003–18 Fruitless wars with BOLESLAV CHROBRY; 1004 conquest of Bohemia; but under the **Peace of Bautzen** BOLESLAV retained Lusatia and the territory of Milzen as imp. fiefs (p. 167).

1007 Establishment of the bpc of Bamberg: miss. activity among the Slavs of the Main.

3 Ital. campaigns: HENRY was crowned king at Padua (1004) and Emperor at Rome (1014). His campaigns prevented further expansion of Byzantium in Lower Italy (1021–2).

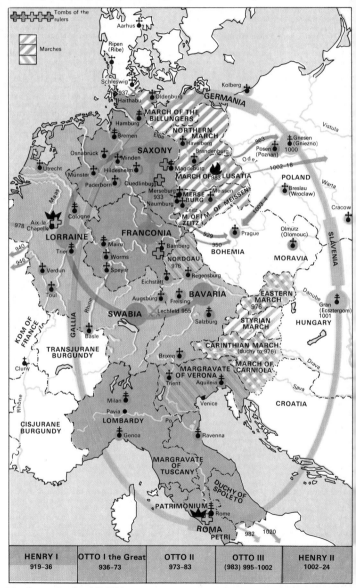

| Tombs of the rulers | |
| Marches | |

Aarhus

Ripen (Ribe)

Schleswig
937
Haithabu · Oldenburg · Kolberg
GERMANIA

Hamburg
MARCH OF THE BILLUNGERS
Bremen · **NORTHERN MARCH**
Havelberg

Osnabrück · Minden **SAXONY** · Brandenburg
Utrecht · Münster · Hildesheim · Magdeburg · **MARCH OF**
LUSATIA
Paderborn · Quedlinburg

Vistula

963 ‡ Gnesen (Gniezno)
Posen (Poznan) 1000
1002–18
Odr

POLAND
Breslau (Wroclaw)

Warta

Cracow

1002–4

Cologne · Merseburg · **MERSE-BURG** · Meissen **M. OF MEISSEN**
933 · Naumburg · Zeitz
978 · Aix-la- · **M. OF ZEITZ**
Chapelle · 929 · Prague
LORRAINE · 950 · **BOHEMIA**
940 · Trier · **FRANCONIA** · Mainz · Bamberg
946 · Worms · **NORDGAU**
Verdun · Speyer · 976
· Eichstätt · Regensburg
Toul · Augsburg · Freising · **BAVARIA**
· Lechfeld 955
SWABIA · Salzburg

Olmütz (Olomouc)

MORAVIA

SLAVENIA

Danube
EASTERN MARCH
976 · Gran (Ecsztergom) 1001
STYRIAN MARCH · **HUNGARY**

KDM OF FRANCE · **GALLIA** · Rhine · Basle
TRANSJURANE BURGUNDY

Cluny
Rhône
CISJURANE BURGUNDY

Brixen
CARINTHIAN MARCH (duchy to 976)
MARGRAVATE OF VERONA · Trient · **MARCH OF CARNIOLA**
· Aquileia

Drava

Sava
CROATIA

Milan · Venice
Pavia · Po
LOMBARDY · Genoa · Ravenna

MARGRAVATE OF TUSCANY

DUCHY OF SPOLETO

PATRIMONIUM · Rome
ROMA
PETRI · 982 · 1020

| HENRY I 919–36 | OTTO I the Great 936–73 | OTTO II 973–83 | OTTO III (983) 995–1002 | HENRY II 1002–24 |

The German Empire, 919–1024

State and Politics

The indivisible realm (Reich; Regnum Francorum; from the end of the 11th cent. also Regnum Teutonicum) was headed by the king (Rex, Rex Francorum), who conducted himself acc. to Frank. law. After the imp. coronation at Rome, he called himself 'Imperator Augustus' (from 982 'Imperator Romanorum Augustus'); up to the time of his coronation as Emperor, the elected king carried the title 'Rex Romanorum' (from HENRY III on). The election was the key to the throne (election of the candidate and formal elevation to the royal dignity; later divided into 2 steps: election and Kür = the bestowal of an honour). The king was elected by the 'great men' (i.e. 'notables') of the realm. The Designation (nomination by the predecessor with the approval of the notables) was governed by dyn. principles (selection from the royal clan), and the duty of the notables was to follow the king. The coronation at Aix-la-Chapelle included the following ceremonies: election and homage by the secular grandees upon the 1st formal occupation of the throne, the lords' approach to the king's hand, the oath of fealty, the eccles. blessing (incl. the presentation of the insignia, the sacred lance, the crown and the sword of the realm), the anointment, the coronation and the 2nd occupation of the throne (formal seating in the throne-chair of CHARLEMAGNE). The ceremony was concluded by the royal banquet.

The king was commander-in-chief of the army and ultimate justice of the peace. His power rested in his personal landholdings and the royal domains; in his authority over the nat. church (the regalia and spolia = eccles. spoils); the Regalia (the sovereign rights of the king: the hunting, mining, 'salt', market, safe passage, and 'Jew.' privileges, the right of coinage and tolls; and (not least) in his sacred dignity and the loyalty of his retainers.

The new tribal duchies (Saxony, Bavaria, Swabia and Lorraine) were created during the period of Carol. decay in the 9th cent. Lorraine, inhabited by Rhenish Franks, was the remnant of LOTHAIR's realm (Regnum Lothari). The Franks ('the people of the Reich') and the Thuringians did not establish separate duchies. Struggling against the Slavs, CONRAD I still depended on the support of the bps; HENRY I, however, declined anointment and coronation after his election and intended to be a popular ruler, cooperating with the dukes. Recognized at first only by the Franks and Saxons, he gradually eliminated the opposition of the s. ger. tribes. His death forestalled his journey to Rome and coronation as Emperor.

Otto I: failing in the attempt to establish a patriarchal monarchy, the king turned to the only institution which stood above tribal differences: the Church.

Ottonian church policy: the eccles. domain, which was part of the royal domain, was increased, and the sec. power of the bps was boosted. The bps of the realm, who, as occupants of the highest offices of the realm, became the pillars of royal power, was est. In exchange for generous royal grants and complete immunity

(supreme judicial authority was exercised by an eccles. official who was not a member of the nobility), the episcopate was obliged to render milit. and financial contributions (servitium regis: two thirds of the royal army and expenses). The Church became the defender of the unity of the realm. Celibacy of the eccles. princes prevented the hered. passing on of offices and fiefs and thus the pursuit of dyn. interests.

Policy in the W.: conflicts with France centred on the possession of the duchy of Lorraine, which was wealthy, highly developed culturally and densely populated.

942 After the campaign of OTTO I (940), LOUIS IV of France was forced to abandon his claims to Lorraine.

946 A 2nd campaign in France provided OTTO I with the power to arbitrate.

978 King LOTHAIR of France used his attack on OTTO II at Aix-la-Chapelle to attempt to regain Lorraine.

980 OTTO II led a retaliation campaign into the vicinity of Paris; peace was concluded at Margut on the Chiers: conclusion of the struggles over Lorraine.

Burgundy: following the conclusion of a treaty of friendship between HENRY I and RUDOLF II of Burgundy (935), OTTO I protected CONRAD III, son of the deceased RUDOLF II, who had been raised at the Saxon court, from the attack of King HUGO OF PROVENCE AND ITALY (946).

1006 The contract of succession between the childless RUDOLF III of Burgundy and HENRY II, designating the latter heir, prepared the ground for the incorporation of Burgundy into the Empire under the Emperor CONRAD II (p. 147).

Imp. and Ital. policies: these grew out of Carol. tradition. OTTO I considered himself to be legal successor to the Frank. Imperium; he was, however, unable to restore it completely. With the imp. dignity went the overlordship over the Patrimonium Petri and the protectorate over the Church. The ind. Ital. policy of the s. Ger. princes was terminated. The possession of Upper Italy – economically prosperous – constituted a considerable increase in power. The Carol. tradition explains OTTO's coronation at Aix-la-Chapelle (unlike his father), his policies towards France and Burgundy and his Ital. policy, OTTO I seeing himself as the legitimate successor of the Frank. emperors. (Towards the end of his reign he spent nearly 10 yrs in Italy.) Otto III attempted the 'Renovatio Imperii Romanorum' (= rest. of the Rom. Empire): Rome was to become the imp. cap., from which the Empire (=Imperium: Germania, Roma, Gallia, Slavenia) was to be ruled (997).

1001 Assumption of the title 'Servus apostolorum' (= servant of the apostles) to enable him to gain infl. over Poland and Hungary, which had been placed under the authority of the Holy See.

Policy in the E.: this grew out of the task of the Res Publica Christiana: to spread the faith and subjugate the heathens (barbarians). No colonization as yet during the 9th and 10th cents.

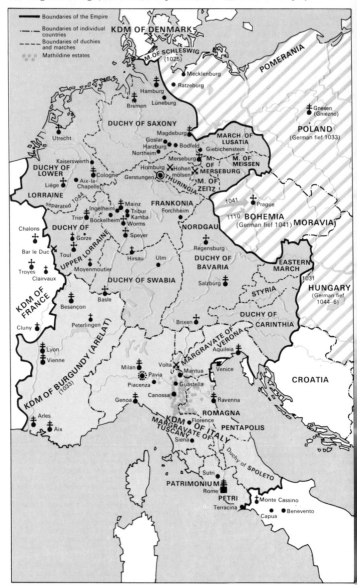

The German Empire under the Frankish (Salian) emperors, 1024–5

The Frank. or Salian Emperors (1024–1125)

024–39 Conrad II, great-grandson of Duke CONRAD THE RED, was elected at Kamba across Oppenheim on Franconian soil (dyn. principle) and crowned at Mainz. He granted hered. rights to his vassals and made their fiefs inalienable (1037). He surrendered the March of Schleswig to CANUTE THE GREAT (1025), and the area between Fisha and Leitha to the Hungarians; however, MIESZKO II (p. 167) had to give up Lusatia and the area of Milzen (1031).

033 The kdm of Burgundy was joined to the Ger. Empire. The connection with imp. Italy was secured by the control of the important western passes through the Alps. The 'Imperium' was made up of the '*Trias*': Germany/Italy/Burgundy.

026–7 1st Ital. campaign of CONRAD. Coronation with the 'crown of iron' at Milan.

027 Imp. coronation at Rome.

037–8 2nd Ital. campaign: struggling against ARIBERT OF MILAN, who was supported by the rising bourgeoisie, a Ger. emperor was defeated for the first time by the Lombard cities. ARIBERT presented to the militia of Milan (*Carroccio*) the carriage with the Imp. banners, symbol of the freedom of the cities.

039–56 Henry III, mar. to AGNES OF POITOU, strove for a reform of the Church. After the subj. of BRETISLAV OF BOHEMIA (1041) and the vict. over Hungary (1044), Bohemia and Hungary became Ger. fiefs.

046 The Synods of Sutri and Rome: HENRY III removed 3 popes and eliminated the infl. of the aristocratic factions of Rome in the election of the popes.

047 Imp. coronation of Henry III.

After the partition of Lorraine (1044) continuous fighting went on between the Emperor and Duke GOTTFRIED THE BEARDED, who had been enfeoffed with only Upper Lorraine. GOTTFRIED secretly mar. BEATRICE OF TUSCANY (1054) and est. a powerful territ. state. By granting privileges to the cities, HENRY III curtailed the powers of the margrave. BEATRICE and her daughter MATHILDA were placed under arrest and brought to Germany.

045 Elevation of ADALBERT to the archbpc of Bremen. The attempt to make Bremen the Patriarchate of the N. failed.

056–1106 Henry IV. The power of the princes increased during the regencies of his mother AGNES OF POITOU (until 1062), of Archbishop ANNO OF COLOGNE (until 1063), and of Archbishop ADALBERT OF BREMEN (until 1065). After HENRY's assumption of power, ADALBERT was removed from his position by the princes (1066). In the struggle with the princes HENRY IV relied on the lower nobility, the *ministeriales* and the citizens of the imp. cities, which were striving to grow. His unscrupulous conduct in rounding out his possessions in the area of the Harz mts led to the uprising of the Saxons, their attack on HENRY at Harzburg, the destruction of the castles (1073), and the peace of Gerstungen. The Saxons submitted themselves to HENRY definitively after 1075 his **vict. at Homburg on the Unstrut.**

The Reform Papacy (1046–1075)

The purely relig. reform movement of Cluny (p. 141) grew during the 11th cent. into demands for **comprehensive Church reform.** The efforts of the reformers were directed against simony (purchase of eccles. offices and dignities) and clerical marriage (celibacy). The *Pax Dei* movement ('Peace of God') in France strengthened the reform party.

1040 Proclamation of the Pax Dei by the clergy: protection of priests, peasants, travellers and women. *Treuga Dei* (*trève* = armistice): no fighting from Wednesday evening to Monday morning and on all holy days (i.e. fighting only on 90 days of the yr).

1046 Synod of Sutri: the Emperor invited Pope CLEMENS II (1046–7) to purge the Church of the evils of simony and clerical marriage. Appointed by the Emperor, Bishop BRUNO OF TOUL became

1049–54 Pope Leo IX. He directed his efforts to the support of the reform movement. Adherents were called to Rome: HUMBERT OF SILVE-CANDIDA, PETRUS DAMIANI, FREDERICK OF LORRAINE, HUGO CANDIDUS and HILDEBRAND; efforts to enforce the *primatus Petri* ('primacy of St Peter'; collection of legal documents outlining the position of the Rom. Church (*libertas ecclesiae. Romanae*)).

1054 Schism of the Lat. and Gk Churches (p. 175).

1057 Cardinal HUMBERT composed the *Libri tres adversus simoniacos*, the 3rd book of which denied rights to laymen in the Church.

1059 The electoral decree of Pope Nicholas II (1058–61): the cardinal-bps were to elect the Pope. The infl. of the Rom. nobility and the Ger. Emperor was excluded. Lay investiture was prohibited. The Papacy was strengthened by alliance with the Normans of Lower Italy (1059 enfeoffment of ROBERT GUISCARD with Apulia, Calabria and Capua), with the Countess MATHILDA of TUSCANY, and with the *Pataria* of Milan, a revolutionary soc. and eccles. movement.

1073–85 Gregory VII (Hildebrand). The **dictatus Papae** expressed the concept of a Papacy constituted along monarchistic and centralized lines: as the supreme and absolute ruler of the universal Church the Pope was allowed to remove not only bps, but kings, who, as representatives of God, were representatives of the Church. The 'right order of the world' and the 'freedom of the Church' were the ends of the struggle. The sacral character of the monarchy (king = *Vicarius Dei*) was no longer accepted (royal office divorced from spiritual realm).

The Investiture Struggle

1074 Lenten Synod: clerical marriage prohibited (decrees governing celibacy).

1075 Lenten Synod: the **prohibition of lay investiture** initiated the struggle with the Ger. monarchy. **Commencement of the investiture struggle.** GREGORY VII threatened HENRY IV with excommunication.

Jan. 1076 Synod of Worms: HENRY IV and the Ger. bps declared the Pope deposed.

1076 Lenten Synod: **deposition and excommunication of the Ger. king** by GREGORY VII (punitive papal command); subjects freed from the obligation of their oath of fealty.

Oct. 1076 Assembly of the princes at Tribur (Trebur): in the presence of papal legates the princes decided to depose the king unless the excommunication was lifted.

25–8 Jan. 1077 Canossa. HENRY's demonstration of penance forced the Pope to lift the excommunication; HENRY had to recognize the Pope as arbiter in his struggle with the princes. The humiliation of the king lessened the prestige of sec. authority. The princes did not wait for papal arbitration and elected RUDOLF OF SWABIA king: free election with disregard of dyn. right. The subsequent civil war (1077–80) ended with the death of RUDOLF (b. of Hohenmölsen, 1080).

1080 2nd excommunication of HENRY by GREGORY. Election of Archbishop WIBERT OF RAVENNA as Anti-Pope. Victory of the Lombards over the army of MATHILDA. After the conquest of Rome (1083) during the 1st Ital. campaign

1084 Imp. coronation of Henry IV by the Anti-Pope CLEMENS III.

Resisting from the Castel Sant'Angelo, GREGORY was relieved by the Normans under ROBERT GUISCARD. HENRY IV was forced to leave Rome. After the Norm. sack of the city, GREGORY also had to leave. He d. on 25 May 1085 at Salerno. The attempt to establish the unity of the Church and the sec. world under the leadership of the Papacy (subordination of the monarchy to the Papacy) had failed; the concept of the divine nature of the monarchy had not yet been shaken.

1085 Proclamation of the 'peace of God' by HENRY IV at Mainz.

1088–99 The conciliatory attitude of URBAN II saved the work of GREGORY VII. The prohibition of lay investiture was renewed at the Synod of Clermont (1095) and the swearing of oaths of fealty by ecclesiasticals to sec. lords was outlawed.

1090–97 2nd Ital. campaign of HENRY IV. URBAN's policies led to the establishment of a Lombard League, the defection of the Emperor's son CONRAD, and the alliance between the Guelphs and Tuscany. After the confirmation of his Bav. possessions by the Emperor, GUELPH lifted the blockade of the Alp. passes. After the proclamation of a general pacification (*Landfrieden*), his son

1104 HENRY (V) defected and placed himself at the head of a conspiracy of the princes

which obtained approval from the Pope Motivation: HENRY's fear of losing the right to succession because of the Emperor' conflicts with the Church and the Emperor' favouring of the lesser nobility and *minis teriales* over the upper nobility.

1106 HENRY IV was forced to abdicate; h died at Liège before the matter was definitel decided.

1106–25 Henry V. He granted Saxony t LOTHAIR OF SUPPLINBURG. The sovereignt of the Empire over Bohemia was restore (1110).

1110–11 1st Ital. campaign.

1111 Treaty of Sutry between PASCAL II (1099 1118) and HENRY V: the king renounced th right to investiture; the Church gave up th imp. estates it had held since the time c CHARLEMAGNE. The treaty could not b enforced because of the resistance of the bp and prelates. Taken prisoner, the Pop confirmed the king's rights to investiture i the peace of Ponte Mammolo. Followin struggles between HENRY and the princes (esp. LOTHAIR OF SUPPLINBURG), and a 2n Ital. campaign, which resulted in the confiscation of MATHILDA's estates,

23 Sep. 1122 the Concordat of Worms wa concluded by HENRY V and CALIXTUS I (1119–24). It was based on the distinctio made by Fr. theologians (IVO OF CHARTRES between the *temporalia* (sec. estates given a fiefs) and the *spiritualia* (eccles. dignity). Th king gave up the right to investiture wit 'ring and staff'. Canonical elections i Germany were to take place in the presenc of the king or his deputy; investiture by th sceptre was to precede consecration; in Ital and Burgundy it followed consecration b 6 months.

Consequences: loosening of dependence on th Emperor led to the disappearance of th Ottonian Imp. Church; the bps were trans formed from imp. officials into imp. vassals the princes of Germany and the cities c Upper Italy were strengthened.

France: since only few of the Fr. bpcs wer subject to the crown, the question of investitur was not vital for the Fr. king. A conflict lik that in Germany did not therefore develop In a treaty with PASCAL II, PHILIP I surrendere the right to investiture with 'ring and staff' he was to give the *temporalia* in fief in exchang for an oath of fealty by the bp.

England: the refusal by Archbishop ANSELM OF CANTERBURY to swear the oath of fealt led to his exile by HENRY I (1100–35) and th Eng. investiture struggle. 1107 'free election of the bps at the court of the king followed b the latter's confirmation; by means of document the king then conferred the *tem poralia* upon the elected before he was conse crated; the elected was obliged to rende homage to the king in exchange. The kin acknowledged the right of appeal to Rome.

Poland: Archbishop HENRY KIETLICZ o GNESEN (Gniezno; 1199–1219) assured eccles liberty through canonical election of bps i most duchies.

Universal Rule of the Papacy (12th/13th cents.)

Despite the schism of ANACLETUS II (1130–38), and the unrest created by the demands of ARNOLD OF BRESCIA for a return of the worldly Church to apostolic poverty, the Papacy reached its pinnacle through the work of BERNARD OF CLAIRVAUX (deepening of piety) during the 12th and 13th cents. (the predominance of the Ger. Church was broken). The Papacy was supported by France. In the struggle over the leadership of occidental Christianity (imp. or curial world domination) FREDERICK I (p. 165), encountering the claims of

159–81 Alexander III, had to acknowledge them.

1179 The **3rd Ecumenical Lateran Council** concluded that a two-thirds majority of cardinals was mandatory for the election of a pope.

1198–1216 Innocent III thought of himself not only as successor of St PETER, but also as deputy of CHRIST or GOD (*Vicarius Christi*), from whom the worldly rulers received their realms as fiefs. Limitation of episcopal power, centralization of power by means of papal legates. Sicily, England and Portugal became feudal dependencies. Intervention in the internal affairs of Germany (p. 173), France (p. 159) and Norway (p. 163). Legates were sent to Serbia and Bulgaria. Establishment of a Lat. Church in the Lat. Emp. (1204).

215 4th Ecumenical Lateran Council: decisions regarding episcopal inquisition; prohibition of the establishment of new Orders. GREGORY IX (1227–41) and INNOCENT IV (1243–57) continued the quest for universal rule (p. 173). The completion of the universal Papal Church was attained by the

c. 1140 Decretum Gratiani (the compilation of the Canon Law): Canon Law became autonomous. With later additions it formed the **Corpus Juris Canonici.**

The Inquisition

Up to the 12th cent. heresy was punished by the Church by excommunication and monast. imprisonment. Following the establishment of the episcopal Inquisition (1215), the papal Inquisition was created by GREGORY IX (1231). The death penalty for heretics was simultaneously introduced in Germany and France.

The Sects

The entanglement of the Church with the world after its liberation from the ties to the world (*libertas ecclesiae*) led to the **establishment of sects** which denied the Church's rights to rule and possess properties and which demanded apostolic poverty. The **Cathari sect** developed out of the Bogomils of Bulgaria (radical dualistic doctrine, severe asceticism, imitation of the apostles' lives) and the movement of migrating heretics (heresy = special opinion). Establishment of episcopal churches. Following the **Council of the Heretics of St Felix de Caraman 1167,** the radical dualistic doctrine of NICETAS OF BYZANTIUM prevailed. The most important sect was the **Albigensians** (city of Albi) in s. France. The **Waldensian** sect, founded by the merchant **Peter Waldes** of Lyon (the ideal of poverty: evangelical perfection), spread rapidly. In addition to the Fr. Waldensians (*pauperes spiritu*), a 2nd group developed in Upper Italy (*pauperes Lombardi*). Fusing with the 'humiliates' (the humble ones), it made itself independent in 1210. Preaching in the vernacular (translation of the Bible into Provençal). The literal interpretation of the 'Sermon on the Mount' led to the denial of oaths, condemnation of the death penalty, rejection of a hierarchical Church, denial of the existence of purgatory and the relevance of indulgences, and the renunciation of the adoration of saints. The Cath. Church fought the sects through the newly founded Orders (p. 141), the 'crusades' and the Inquisition.

1209–29 The Albig. Wars (p. 159).

Philosophy

Scholasticism (*scholasticus* = belonging to the school) refers to the science and theology of the Middle Ages which, using a logical method, reconsidered the preceding traditionalistic theology, developed the dialectical method, and aimed at gaining a deeper understanding of the faith.

Early scholasticism: proceeding from faith, **Anselm of Canterbury** (1033–1109) strove to comprehend its essence (*credo ut intelligam* = I believe, so that I may comprehend); he became the founder of the 'theory of satisfaction' (*Cur Deus homo*) and established ontological proof of the existence of God. **Peter Abelard** (1079–1142) became the creator of the dialectical method (*sic et non* = yes and no). The **controversy over universals** was the major philosophical problem of the time: realism asserted the existence of general concepts (*universalia*), nominalism asserted that they were abstractions of the mind. PETER LOMBARD composed the medieval dogmatic text 'Sententiarum libri IV'.

High scholasticism: ARISTOTLE's works, made known by Jew. and Arab philosophers (esp. AVERROËS (IBN RUSHD, 1126–98)), were the basis of the systems of thought of the scholastics who belonged to the two mendicant orders (*summae*):

ALEXANDER OF HALES (d. 1245): *Summa Universae Theologiae,* ALBERTUS MAGNUS (1193–1280): *Commentaries on Aristotle,* and **Thomas Aquinas** (1225–74): *Summa contra Gentiles* (Against the Heathens), *Summa Theologica* (The Main Work), *De Regemine Principum* (Concerning Political Philosophy). Nature and the supernatural (reason and revelation) were united in a great harmonious system. In contrast with the intellectualism of AQUINAS, which was marked by a certain didactic quality, **Duns Scotus** (d. 1308) asserted the conceptions of AUGUSTINE (voluntarism, the principle of order).

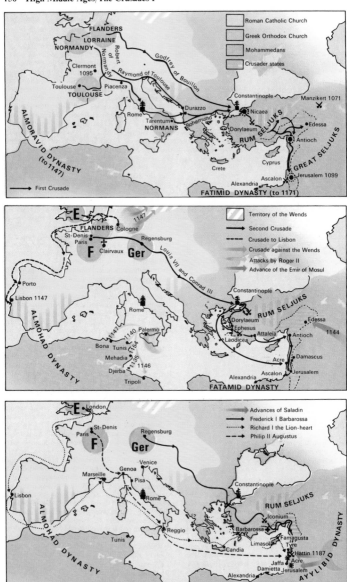

The First, Second and Third Crusades

Roman Catholic Church
Greek Orthodox Church
Mohammedans
Crusader states

FLANDERS
LORRAINE
NORMANDY
Robert of Normandy
Godfrey of Bouillon
Clermont 1095
Toulouse
TOULOUSE
Piacenza
Raymond of Toulouse
Rome
Durazzo
Tarentum
Bohemund
NORMANS
Constantinople
Nicaea
Dorylaeum
Manzikert 1071
RUM SELJUKS
Edessa
Antioch
Crete
Cyprus
GREAT SELJUKS
Alexandria
Ascalon
Jerusalem 1099
FATIMID DYNASTY (to 1171)
ALMORAVID DYNASTY (to 1147)

→ First Crusade

Territory of the Wends
→ Second Crusade
--- Crusade to Lisbon
⇒ Crusade against the Wends
⇒ Attacks by Roger II
⇒ Advance of the Emir of Mosul

E
FLANDERS
Cologne
1147
St-Denis
Paris
Clairvaux
F
Ger
Regensburg
Louis VII and Conrad III
Porto
Lisbon 1147
ALMOHAD DYNASTY
Rome
1147
Palermo
1140
Bona
Tunis
1154
Mehadia
1135
Djerba
1146
Tripoli
Constantinople
RUM SELJUKS
Dorylaeum
Ephesus
Laodicea
Attaleia
Antioch
1144
Edessa
Damascus
Acre
Alexandria
Ascalon
Jerusalem
FATAMID DYNASTY

➤ Advances of Saladin
→ Frederick I Barbarossa
···· Richard I the Lion-heart
--- Philip II Augustus

E
London
Paris
St-Denis
F
Regensburg
Ger
Venice
Marseille
Genoa
Pisa
Lisbon
Rome
ALMOHAD DYNASTY
Reggio
Tunis
Constantinople
RUM SELJUKS
Iconium
Barbarossa
Famagusta
Limasol
Tyre
Candia
Hattin 1187
Jaffa
Acre
Damietta
Jerusalem
Alexandria
AYYUBID DYNASTY

1st–3rd Crusades: Causes

A consequence of the regeneration of the Church and intensified internal religiosity, the crusader movement was evoked by the advance of the Seljuk Turks, who, under ALP ARSLAN, successor to TUGHRIL BEG (crowned Caliph at Baghdad in 1055), had taken Jerusalem and Syria from the Fatimid caliphs of Egypt and decisively defeated the Byz. army in the b. of Manzikert (1071, p. 175).

1074 Gregory VII planned to come to the aid of the Christians of the Orient at the head of an army of occidental knights (as *Dux* and *Pontifex*). In addition to the liberation of the Holy Sepulchre and the territories conquered by the Seljuks, it was his aim to reunite the Gk and Rom. Churches. After the establishment of the Sultanate of Rum (or Iconium) in Asia Minor

1095 ALEXIUS COMNENUS sent legates with a request for help to Pope URBAN II, who was attending at the Synod of Piacenza.

26 Nov. 1095 Synod of Clermont: URBAN II convinced the knights and princes of the w. by his famous and enthusiastically received sermon to join in the Crusade (*Deus lo volt* = God wills it). Jerusalem became the password, the white cross the symbol.

Two intellectual currents met and gave impetus and force to the crusader movement:

1. The conception of the pilgrimage to the Holy Land: pilgrimages, carried out without arms since the days of antiquity as meritorious journeys, had increased during the 11th cent. because of the deepening of Christ. piety; however, they had encountered increased resistance and hostility from the Seljuks.

2. The concept of a Holy War against the heathen as necessary and justified became very strong, esp. since Jerusalem was not the only objective of the crusaders of the w.; they were also to fight against Islam and the Wends.

1096 The first unorganized campaign of adventurers led by the hermit PETER OF AMIENS, who inspired the masses by his crusading sermons, disintegrated under the attacks of Bulgars and Seljuks.

1096–9 The 1st Crusade (without the excommunicated rulers HENRY I and PHILIP I of France) was under the leadership of ROBERT OF NORMANDY (the Northern French), GODFREY OF BOUILLON, BALDWIN OF FLANDERS, ROBERT II OF FLANDERS (Lorrainians and Flemish), RAYMOND OF TOULOUSE (the s. French), BOHEMUND OF TARENTUM and his nephew TANCRED (Normans). ADHEMAR, the Bishop of Puy, was the papal legate. After the successful siege of Nicaea and the vict. over the Sultan of Rum at Dorylaeum, a 7-month siege aided by treason led to the fall of Antioch. A relief army under KETBOGA, Emir of Mosul, was dispersed by a successful sortie of the besieged crusaders (the holy lance was found).

15 Jul. 1099 After 5 weeks of siege, **Jerusalem was stormed.** Christ. feudal states with ind. vassals were est. after the Fr. model.

The **kdm of Jerusalem** was est. by GODFREY OF BOUILLON, the 'Protector of the Holy Sepulchre'. He was succeeded by his brother BALDWIN (1100–18), who assumed the title of king. Internal weakness and difficulties over the succession to the throne led to the disintegration of the kdm in 1187. The principality of Antioch and the earldoms of Edessa and Tripolis became smaller vassal states. Antioch and Jerusalem became the seats of patriarchs. The crusader states were weakened by the constant struggles between the Nor. princes of Antioch and the Byzantines as well as by those of the Christ. states between themselves. Conflicts between the different pop. groups compounded matters. The Christ. cause was greatly aided by divisions of the enemy (Seljuks v. Fatimids). The crusader castles form lasting monuments to the time.

1144 The conquest of Edessa by IMADEDDIN ZENKIS, the emir of Mosul, led to

1147–9 the 2nd Crusade under the leadership of the Hohenstaufen CONRAD III and the Fr. king LOUIS VII, who took the cross under the spiritual infl. of BERNARD OF CLAIRVAUX. Cooperation between the Ger. and Fr. armies was fatally affected by the alliance of LOUIS VII and ROGER II OF SICILY (anti-Byz. power struggle) and the counter-alliance of MICHAEL COMNENUS and his brother-in-law CONRAD III. After defeats at Dorylaeum and Laodicea, CONRAD and LOUIS, who joined forces at Jerusalem (1148), undertook fruitless campaigns against Damascus and Ascalon.

1187 Conquest of Jerusalem by the sultan SALADIN, who had earlier defeated the Christians in the b. of Hattin.

1189–92 3rd Crusade. Filled with genuine crusading enthusiasm and acting in accordance with his conception of the universal functions of the Emperor, FREDERICK I BARBAROSSA placed himself at the head of an undertaking involving the entire w.; but after the brilliant vict. of Iconium, he drowned on 10 Jun. 1190 in the river Saleph. His son, Duke FREDERICK OF SWABIA, led part of the army before Acre, where he d. in 1191. RICHARD I THE LIONHEART of England and PHILIP II AUGUSTUS of France took Acre in 1191. RICHARD concluded an armistice with SALADIN: the coastal strip between Tyre and Jaffa was ceded to the Christians; pilgrimages to Jerusalem were to be allowed. RICHARD granted Cyprus, which he had conquered in 1191, as a fief to GUY OF LUSIGNAN.

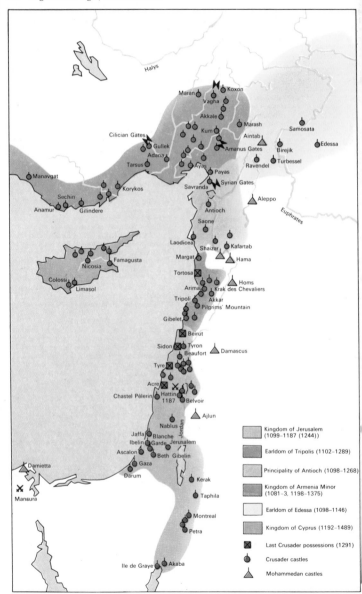

The Crusader States

Kingdom of Jerusalem (1099–1187 (1244))

Earldom of Tripolis (1102–1289)

Principality of Antioch (1098–1268)

Kingdom of Armenia Minor (1081–3, 1198–1375)

Earldom of Edessa (1098–1146)

Kingdom of Cyprus (1192–1489)

Last Crusader possessions (1291)

Crusader castles

Mohammedan castles

Halys

Maran Koxon Vagha Akkale Marash Samosata

Cilician Gates Kum Aintab Birejik Edessa

Gullek Amanus Gates Ravendel Turbessel

Adana Ayas Payas

Tarsus Savranda Syrian Gates

Manavgat Korykos

Sechin Gilindere

Anamur

Aleppo

Euphrates

Antioch

Saone

Laodicea Kafartab

Margat Shaizar Hama

Famagusta

Nicosia Tortosa

Colossi Arima Krak des Chevaliers

Limasol Tripoli Akkar Homs

Pilgrims' Mountain

Gibelet

Beirut

Sidon Tyron

Beaufort

Tyre Damascus

Acre

Chastel Pèlerin Hattin 1187 Belvoir

Ajlun

Nablus Jordan

Jaffa Blanche

Ibelin Garde Jerusalem

Ascalon Beth Gibelin

Gaza

Darum Kerak

Damietta Taphila

Mansura Montreal

Petra

Ile de Graye Akaba

4th–7th Crusades

1197 Although the well-prepared crusade of Emperor HENRY VI aimed at winning the Holy Land, it also aimed at attaining the ancient goal of Norm. policy in the E.: the conquest of the Byz. Empire. Because of the sudden death of the Emperor, only a small coastal strip near Antioch was taken.

1202–4 4th Crusade. Pope INNOCENT III (1198–1216) cal. the nobility of Europe to a new crusade, with Egypt as the objective. A large proportion of the Fr. nobility followed the call (Margrave BONIFACE OF MONTFERRAT, BALDWIN of FLANDERS, and others). The crusaders had to conquer Zara in Dalmatia for Venice so that it would assure their transportation. Following a plea by the Byz. Prince ALEXIUS and considering Venet. trading interests in the Levant, the Doge ENRICO DANDOLO directed the crusader army to Constantinople, which was taken (p. 175). Union of the Gk and Rom. Churches failed. Driven out for a short while, the crusaders (the 'Latins') conquered the city a second time. After merciless plundering the **Lat. Empire** was est. (map, p, 206). Proceeding from Nicaea with the aid of Genoa, MICHAEL PALAIOLOGOS, the head of the Gk imp. party, eliminated it in 1261 (p.207).

1212 The 'Children's Crusade'. Corrupt merchants transported thousands of boys and girls from Marseille to Alexandria, where they were sold into slavery.

1228–9 5th Crusade. Excommunicated by the Pope, Emperor FREDERICK II led a campaign to Acre and obtained Jerusalem, Bethlehem, and Nazareth from Sultan ELKAMIL OF EGYPT by treaty.

1244 Conquest of Jerusalem by the Moslems: definitive loss of the city to Christianity.

1248–54 6th Crusade. St LOUIS, king LOUIS IX of France, intended to destroy Egypt, the strongest Islam power. He took Damietta (1249), but was defeated at Mansura and taken prisoner with his entire army. He was released against a heavy ransom, fortified Acre, and returned to France (1254).

1270 7th Crusade. LOUIS IX journeyed to Tunis, where he succumbed to the plague together with a large part of his army.

1291 Acre, the last Christ. bulwark, was conquered by the Mamelukes. Tyre, Beirut and Sidon were abandoned by the Christians. The Lusignan dynasty continued to rule Cyprus until 1489; Rhodes was controlled by the Knights of St John until 1523.

Consequences of the Crusades

The Crusades failed because the nat. interests of the states involved could not be squared with the universal idea which had inspired them. Byzantium sought help from the W. to defend its threatened frontiers. The commercial interests of Venice and the polit. ambitions of the Normans made these states constant enemies of Byzantium; without their co-operation (transport and security of supplies), milit. operations were impossible.

Results: the seaports of Upper Italy and the cities of Southern France fl. because of the trade with the E. The money economy quickened and a wealthy middle class developed; the standard of living rose. (Great demand for Eastern goods). Though torn politically, France gained in nat. consciousness (*gesta Dei per Francos*). The W. became more conscious of its ctr. because of the contacts and contrast with the superior Byz. and Arab civilizations; the cult. level of the W. rose. The Papacy experienced the pinnacle of its power; it was, however, precisely this expansion of power which for wide sectors of the pop. undermined any feeling of reverence for the Holy See. The terrible catastrophe of the 2nd Crusade damaged the reputation of the Papacy; BERNARD OF CLAIRVAUX appeared to many to be a false prophet, and sec. anti-clerical intellectual currents spread. The Crusades can only be viewed and understood in the context of the attacks against Islam everywhere (in the Pyrenees; conquest of Lisbon, 1147; N. Africa) and against the non-Christ. peoples of the E. (the fruitless crusade against the Wends, called for by BERNARD OF CLAIRVAUX).

The milit.-relig. Orders of Knights: combining the ascetic with the chivalric ideal (the vows of the monk: poverty, chastity, obedience; the tasks of the knight: protection of the oppressed), they were est. at the time of the Crusades.

1. The Knights of St John. Originating in the fraternity of the hospital of St John in Jerusalem, they were approved by Pope PASCAL II in 1113 and transformed into an Order in 1120 by RAYMOND DU PUY. Purposes: care of the sick and milit. service. Apparel: black coat with a white cross; red coat in times of war. The order was transferred to Cyprus in 1291; from there, in 1309, to Rhodes; and thence, in 1530, to Malta (until 1798, 'Maltese').

2. The Knights Templars. The order was est. by HUGH DE PAYENS who joined with several Fr. knights to secure the conquest of the Holy Land and to protect pilgrims (1120). Apparel: white coat with red cross. CLEMENS V dissolved the order at the Council of Vienne in 1312.

3. The Teutonic Knights. Founded in 1190 before Acre as a fraternity to serve the sick, it became a chivalric milit. order in 1198. Apparel: white coat with black cross. After temporary settlement in Transylvania, from where the knights were removed by ANDREAS II OF HUNGARY (1225), they settled in Prussia (HERMANN OF SALZA). Seats of the grand master: Acre, Venice (after 1291) and the Marienburg (after 1309, p. 199).

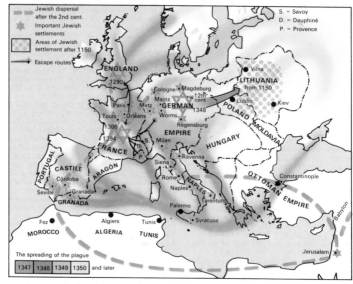

Expulsions of the Jews in Europe; the progression of the Black Death

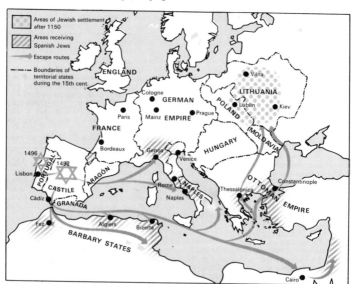

The expulsion of the Jews from Spain

The End of the Jew. Nat. State

After the abortive revolt of BAR KOCHBA (p. 99), the Jews were prohibited from entering Jerusalem (the Rom. colony Aelia Capitolina) under penalty of death. The Jew. **nat. state** thus ended with the loss of its polit. and nat. centre. For the relig. community of the Jews, **life in the Diaspora** now began; its intellectual focal point was to be the **synagogue** (place of the communal assembly).

Mesopotamia: many of those driven out turned to Babylon, where they achieved econ. prosperity among the Parthians. Persecutions by the caste of magician-priests took place under the Sassanids, but the situation of the Jews improved under the rule of the Arabs (p. 135). The Jew. religion ('religion of the Book') – like the Isl. – asserted a strict monotheism.
c. 500 Completion of the Babylonian Talmud, which consisted of the *Mishna* (the teachings) and the *Gemara* (dialogues concerning the *Mishna*). From Babylon the Jews migrated to Afghanistan, Persia, India, Armenia and into the region of the Caucasus.

The Jews in the Rom. Empire

The Jews – like all other inhabitants of the Empire – were granted citizenship under CARACALLA (212). They settled in every region of the Empire (esp. in Asia Minor, the Balkans, N. Africa and Spain). The development of **hatred for the Jews** was traced by Rom. writers to their relig. separatism; Jehovah's claims to exclusiveness, their image-free worship and the ritual laws of purity. The **Jew. decrees** of the Christ. emperors CONSTANTINE, THEODOSIUS (417, 423) and JUSTINIAN degraded the Jews to lesser citizenship. The Christ. state church pursued the same aims (councils from the 4th to the 7th cents.).

The Jews during the Middle Ages

Gregory the Great (590–604), who est. the direction of papal Jew. policy for the Middle Ages, rejected coerced baptism and endeavoured to win the Jews over by favours. The Jews were considered defenceless foreigners, and had to place themselves under the personal protection of the king (*Königsmunt* = special protection of individual persons), first practised by LOUIS THE PIOUS (814–40). Subs. the Ger. kings also granted privileges. The Church's prohibition of usury forced the Jews to deal in money (the Jew as creditor, the Christian as debtor). This and the pogroms taking place during the time of the 1st Crusade made protective laws for the Jews as non-Christians (not as merchants and inhabitants of the city) necessary.
1103 The general pacification of Mainz under HENRY IV: in addition to clerics, women and merchants, the Jews were singled out as 'pacified'. Because they were not allowed to bear arms, the Jews came to need protection. Rendered unable to use arms (the mark of the free man) they were therefore unfree.
1096–1215 The first great persecutions of the Jews took place during the age of the Crusades. The **major accusations** concerned

blasphemous treatment of the host and ritual murder.
1236 Under FREDERICK II the Jews were designated as 'servants of the chamber' (**servi camerae nostrae**). The concept of the 'bondage of the Jews' – conceived by the Church in spiritual terms – was given a juristic interpretation under the infl. of Rom. law: *Servitus camerae* (personal and econ. dependence on the Emperor).
1215 4th Lateran Council: prohibition to hold offices and decree governing the apparel of Jews.

Expulsions: the Jews were expelled from France in 1306, definitively in 1394 (exceptions: Provence, Dauphiné and Avignon); from England in 1209. The advance of the plague (the **Black Death**, 1347–54), affected the Jew. communities as badly as all others in Europe. This disaster, combined with pogroms (350 Jew. communities were destroyed in Germany), gave further incentive for the Jew. migration to the E. that had begun during the Crusades. Yiddish was the language in the areas of Jew. settlement; the Jews wore the special Jew. dress of the Middle Ages. Pursued by the Cath. Church of Spain from 1391, the struggle led to their expulsion under the Grand Inquisitor TORQUEMADA (1492). The Jews were expelled from Portugal in 1496.

The Jews during the 16th, 17th and 18th Cents.

Humanism and reformation: because of his knowledge of Hebrew, REUCHLIN became the spokesman of the Jews (struggle with the Dominicans and the baptized Jew, PFEFFERKORN, who demanded the burning of the Talmud). The 'synagogue' was for REUCHLIN no longer the vanquished inferior, but the sister of '*ecclesia*'. In the *Augenspiegel* (1511) he attempted to restore the original meaning of the Rom. law (the Jews are subjects of the empire) and of the Canon law (the Jews are the 'next of kin'). The Reformation did not improve the lot of the Jews. LUTHER's defence of the Jews ('That our Lord Jesus Christ was a born Jew', 1523) was followed – after his hope for their conversion had not been fulfilled – by his polemic 'Of the Jews and their Calumnies' (1542).

The Jew. policies of the **absolutist state** (17th/18th cents.) were guided by the principles of mercantilism: the establishment of a favourable balance of trade. After 1648 the financial needs of the Ger. princes for the maintenance of standing armies and the execution of foreign policy made the opening of new sources of money necessary (monopolies, manufactures, taxation, lotteries, etc.). The court relied on the Jew. court agent. Court Jews formed a lesser aristocracy and were distinguished from the other Jews living from trade in second-hand goods, peddling, money-changing and pawning by 'general privileges', wealth and influence.

Art: Carol. art developed under the infl. of Byzantium (encounter with easternized late antiquity): the **palace chapel of Aix-la-Chapelle** (the cen. building) with its effective arrangement of the entrance hall, the raised centre part of which was flanked by 2 towers. The Rom. basilica became the model for monastery and episcopal churches; however, it was further developed by the **'tower profile'** and emphasis on the w. façade (to repel demons). In addition to extant **book decorations** and miniature sculptures (ivory reliefs), a few remnants of palace architecture and wall-painting have been preserved. **There was no sculpture in the round.**

The **Romanesque style** (term coined by the romantic writer DE GERVILLE in analogy with the term 'Romance languages', 1818) was the first monumental architectural style of the Christ. w.; it followed imp. Carol. art in time. The **basilica** was the greatest accomplishment of church architecture; in addition to the E. side, which had already been stressed in Carol. times (transept, apses), it further developed the w. side (façades, twin naves). The horizontal lines were broken by means of towers over the intersection of nave and transepts, over the w. entrance, and along the sides of the nave (multiple towers). The proportionality of its relation to vertical lines made the massive **Romanesque structure**, with its characteristic alternation of rounded (cylindrical) and rectangular (cubic) forms, into a unit. Introduced *c.* 1100, the **vault** gave unity to the room and integrated wall and ceiling. **Sculpturing** raised figures from flat surfaces and created free-standing figures. These sculptures of archaic severity harmonized with the structure **(structure-related sculpture)**. High points are found in the Tympanon reliefs (representation of the Last Judgement) and the figures adorning the portals. **Wall-painting** (without allowances to create the illusion of space and 3-dimensional bodies) illustrated scenes from the Old and New Testaments and the lives of the saints. The severe style of the early Romanesque period in **Germany** (Ottonian art: the Dome of Magdeburg, St Cyriacus at Gernrode) was followed by the mature and large vaulted structures (the Domes of Speyer, Mainz, and Worms). Regional schools in **France**: Normandy (twin-towered w. façade: St-Étienne in Caen), Burgundy (choir with ambulatory and radiating chapels), Provence (imitation of antique forms: St-Trophime in Arles).

The **Gothic style** with its technical innovations (pointed arches, flying buttresses, cross-ribs) developed in the Isle-de-France, the French crown lands, Picardy, Champagne, and spread all over Europe. The **Goth. cathedral** was the greatest achievement of this universal style of relig. architecture: a longitudinal, multi-naved structure with transepts and a choir surrounded by the ambulatory and radiating chapels (the focal point of the ritual). The **arrangement of the foundation** was the determining factor. By shifting the weight of the vault by means of ribs and clustered pillars to the buttresses which

were on the outside of the structure, the high walls of the cen. nave could be broken up into skeleton-like weightbearing portions and free 'filling' areas (glass walls). The verticalism of the new style led to the elimination of the horizontal wall stripe between the arcades and windows of the 3-naved basilicas (the emporia disappeared).

The Early Gothic in **France** (St-Denis, consecration of the choir in 1144; Sens (begun 1142)) continued into the High Gothic (Chartres, begun 1194; Reims, begun 1211; Amiens, begun 1220; Beauvais, begun 1272, height of the choir 48 m.). The Late Gothic (Linear Gothic) merely modified the great models.

The cathedrals of **England** (abbeys, in France episcopal churches) stressed the longitudinal axis; the space arrangement also is a distinguishing feature (choir, transepts, Mary Chapel: the Chapel of Our Lady). 'Early English' (York, Salisbury, Lincoln) was followed by the 'decorated style', which was marked by longitudinal choirs for the monastics and the adoption of Fr. tracery windows (Exeter, Wells). The 'Eng. chapter room', the consecrated area of the 'Perpendicular style' (King's College Chapel, Cambridge), developed during the 15th cent.

The Gothic was introduced into **Germany** by the Liebfrauenkirche (Church of Our Lady) in Trier (the cen. structure) and the Elizabeth Church in Marburg (*Hallenkirche* = hall churches). The domes of Strasbourg and Cologne led to the High Gothic style. *Backstein* Gothic (brick Gothic) developed in the N. (Cist. style, at Chorin, Doberan, *et al.*). The space arrangement of the hall church became important (Wiesenkirche at Soest, Marienkirche at Danzig) in the N. of Germany and in Scandinavia. The Late Gothic style was marked by the attempt to achieve colourful effects by alternating light and shadow (Lorenzkirche at Nuremberg). The Gothic spread to the Netherlands (wooden barrel-vaults), the Iberian peninsula and Italy.

The masons working on a particular structure were organized in 'cottages' (**Bauhütten),** and formed 'working-communities' (*Hüttenordnung* = precepts of the cottage) which passed on to succeeding generations technical details, principles of proportion, and methods of work as 'secrets of the cottage' (*Hüttengeheimnis*) and which also created 'cottage sculpture' (*Hüttenplastik*, cathedral sculpture).

Goth. sculpture, striving for internalization and humanization, was closely integrated with architectural style (Senlis, Chartres). It was characterized by idealism (the creation of human beauty after classical models in France) and naturalism with a noticeable striving for intellectualization (representation of the suffering CHRIST and MARY as mother: Madonna). Wall-painting receded (it was practised henceforth only in sec. structures). The **staining of glass,** enlivening the large windows of the cathedrals and filling the internal space with colourful light, became important (Chartres: 146 windows with 1,359 scenes). Beginning of tablet painting.

The State during the High Middle Ages: while the power of the king in France (p. 159) and England (p. 161) was strengthened by the loyalty of individual vassals, the oath of fealty and the remission to the crown of fiefs with expired feudal tenure, the power of the Ger. king was weakened by feudal laws (CONRAD II, 1037; LOTHAIR III, 1136) which granted the vassal hered. and inalienable rights to his property, provided for **mandatory enfeoffment** (vacated secular fiefs had to be granted to other vassals within a year, and there was, therefore, no expansion of the crown domain). and the increase in allodial properties (fiefs granted by the king often became private property because of the absence of a feudal register). Increasing centralization in England and France contrasted with feudal particularism in Germany, which not even the reorganization of the **milit. hierarchy** (stipulation of the order of ranks in the feudal hierarchy) could impede. It stipulated that the king had the 1st rank, the eccles. princes the 2nd, the sec. princes the 3rd, the free lords the 4th, those with judicial prerogatives and the *ministeriales* the 5th, their men the 6th, and all other nobles the 7th rank (acc. to the *Sachsenspiegel* and the *Schwabenspiegel*).

The nobility: the power of the great hered. feudal lords (the **'High Nobility'**), who hailed from the old Germ. noble families, the officialdom of the Frank. kings and the vassals of the crown, was based on the association of the count's dignity with his power to rule. In addition to the ancient counties – now hered. fiefs no longer conforming to the territ. boundaries of the tribal regions because of changes due to inheritance, partitions and conquests – new allodial and seigniorial counties were est. around castles, basing their power on immunity and judicial prerogatives; their rulers strove to extend those powers, as did the bpcs. and monasteries. Alongside the high nobility there was the **lesser nobility**: in England and France the **ligesse** (*homines ligii*), in Germany the **ministeriales**. Originally unfree, the *ministeriales* (subordinate officials of the king and vassals of the large territ. lords and crown vassals) became free by development of their own law, by the entry of free men into their ranks, by conscientious exercise and conduct of their offices and by service at court and in the military (no manual labour). A class of professional warriors became a blood nobility (during the Staufer period), generating a mutual ideal of life: **knighthood**; this was due to the heredity of fiefs and their acknowledged position as representatives of knighthood. Eur. nobility crystallized into upper and lower nobility: **Herren** and **Ritter** in Germany, lords and gentry in England, barons and *chevaliers* in France, and *grandes* and *hidalgos* in Spain.

Knighthood: BONIZO OF SUTRI's *Liber de Vita Christiana* provided a code for the Christ. knight (*miles Christianus, c.* 1090), which enjoined the knights to be loyal to their lords, to decline plunder, to sacrifice their lives for the lord, to fight for the welfare of the '*res publica*', to wage war against heretics, to protect the poor, widows and orphans, and to honour their oath of fealty. Together with the cardinal virtues of chivalry, bravery, justice, prudence and continence (models: ALEXANDER THE GREAT, CHARLEMAGNE), these tasks of the knight were continuously celebrated in the **lyrics** of chivalric court ctr., creating an idealized image of society through art. Courtship was the basis of chivalric poetry. Man's mission as chivalric action was expressed in the epic (the tournament, the court festivities, and the *àventiure*); lyrical poetry expressed the knight's homage to his lady. An insoluble conflict developed between the demands of the ideal and reality. The poets (the Troubadors of Provence, the *Trouvéres* of Northern France, and the Ger. *Minnesänger*) were men of lesser nobility, the audience consisted of lords and married women.

In **France**, **Chrétien de Troyes** composed his great courtly romances between 1160 and 1190 (*Romans courtois*): *Erec, Clieges, Lancelot, Yvain, Perceval* (incomplete treatment of the Grail theme); WILLIAM IX OF POITIERS (1071–1127) was the first troubador.

The high point of Ger. **Minnesang** was reached under REINMAR VON HAGENAU, HEINRICH VON MORUNGEN (between 1190 and 1200), and **Walther von der Vogelweide** (*c.* 1190–1230). The principal authors of courtly epic were HEINRICH VON VELDEKE (*Servatius, c.* 1170; *Eneit, c.* 1190), **Hartmann von Aue** (*Gregorius, Armer Heinrich*, 1190–1200; *Iwein, c.* 1205), **Wolfram von Eschenbach** (*Parcival, c.* 1210), **Gottfried von Strasbourg** (*Tristan, c.* 1210).

The *Niebelungenlied* was created *c.* 1200, the *Klage* ('lament') *c.* 1220, *Kudrun, c.* 1240. The heroic epics fall into the second half of the 13th cent.: *Hugdietrich, Wolfdietrich, Rabenschlacht, Rosengarten, Laurin, et al.*

The Law: EIKE VON REPKOW recorded the common law, incl. landowning and feudal laws, in the **Sachsenspiegel** (between 1220 and 1230). The incomplete *Deutschenspiegel* (High Ger. translation of the *Sachsenspiegel*) was continued in the **Schwabenspiegel** *c.* 1275. *c.* 1088 **Bologna** became the centre of the teaching of Rom. Law. Establishment of a school of law. The reintroduction of Rom. Law began during the 13th cent., esp. in England, France and Germany (p. 185).

In **Germany** the decrees governing the *peace of the land* were important. Based on the 'peace of God' concept, they were esp. directed against feuding, which could never be stopped completely (the 'king's peace' of HENRY IV, FREDERICK I BARBAROSSA and FREDERICK II). The decrees governing the 'peace of the land' or 'king's peace' also served as criminal law (the first, still incomplete, criminal legislation).

France under the Capetians

The Rise of the Capetians

987–96 Hugh Capet (from *cappa*: cape), the son of HUGH THE GREAT, was elected and crowned king under the infl. of Archbishop ADALBERT OF REIMS, the leader of the pro-Ger. party and with the assistance of the Empress THEOPHANO. His successors ROBERT THE PIOUS (996–1031), HENRY I (1031–60) and PHILIP I (1060–1108) carried the title *Rex Francorum* (king of the Franks), but were only shadow kings. The rise of the Capetians began with

1108–37 LOUIS VI THE FAT, who subj. unruly vassals of the crown domain. He regulated the process of investiture and, as co-regent of PHILIP I, est. the connection between the Fr. monarchy and the Papacy (protection against Germany). His advisor Abbot SUGER OF ST DENIS (1122–51) est. a cen. admin. and – through his friend BERNARD OF CLAIRVAUX – relations between the king and the new monast. orders. A feeling of **Fr. nat. consciousness** developed as a result of the crusades (the French thought of themselves as the 'chosen tools of God' = *Gesta Dei per Francos*) and

1124 the attack by the Emperor HENRY V (p. 148), the ally of his father-in-law, HENRY I of England. Dedication of the *auri flamma* and the golden royal banner.

1137–80 LOUIS VII (mar. to ELEONOR OF POITOU, heiress of Aquitaine) participated in the 2nd Crusade (p. 151). Abbot SUGER took the place of the king during his absence and introduced a direct tax to cover the expenses of the crusade. After her divorce from LOUIS VII (1152), ELEONOR mar. HENRY, Duke of Normandy and Count of Anjou, Maine and Touraine, bringing him Aquitaine (Poitou, Guyenne and Gascogny). HENRY became king of England (HENRY II) in 1154.

1180–1223 Philip II Augustus terminated the conflict with the Angevin state ruled by JOHN I (p. 161).

1202 A trial initiated against him by PHILIP II declared JOHN I 'without land', having been deprived of his fiefs. PHILIP II conquered the territory N. of the Loire. Capitulation of Rouen (1204).

1212 Alliance with FREDERICK I OF HOHENSTAUFEN against JOHN I, the Guelph emperor OTTO IV and the dukes of Flanders.

1214 b. of Bouvines: PHILIP II defeated his enemies. 5 yrs' peace with JOHN I at Chinon: the Eng. territories N. of the Loire remained in the hands of PHILIP II (a third of France was crown land).

1209–29 The Albigensian Wars in Southern France (p. 149): after the murder of the papal legate, PETER OF CASTELNAU, by a page of Count RAYMOND OF TOULOUSE, Pope INNOCENT III called for the Crusade. The crusader army under SIMON DE MONTFORT, Earl of Leicester, conquered Provence (1209–18). Seizure and burning of Béziers (1209). Victory of SIMON OF MONTFORT over RAYMOND VI and his brother-in-law PETER OF ARAGON at Muret (1213). SIMON d. in b. in 1218; RAYMOND reconquered his land.

1223–6 LOUIS VIII. France became hered. territory (coronation site; Reims). He took Poitou and Saintonge from the English (1224), conquered Avignon (1226) and Languedoc.

1226–70 Louis IX (St Louis).

1229 The treaty of Paris terminated the Albigensian Wars. RAYMOND VII OF TOULOUSE ceded the area of Albigeois loc. between the Tarn and the Agout, northern Kiersy and the Duchy of Narbonne to the crown. His daughter JOANNA inherited the remaining possessions after his death (1249). She mar. the 3rd son of LOUIS VIII, ALPHONSE OF POITIERS. Her possessions fell to the crown in 1271: the territory of the crown, which had been landlocked until 1202, now stretched to the Mediterranean. After his return from the Crusade (p. 153) LOUIS IX suppressed an uprising of the barons which had been supported by England, and defeated HENRY III (p. 161).

1259 Peace of Paris: HENRY III had to abandon Normandy, Maine, Anjou and Poitou, and recognize the Fr. king's overlordship of the Duchy of Guyenne (Aquitaine). After the death of the Emperor FREDERICK II (1250), LOUIS IX became the most powerful ruler in the w. ('arbiter').

State and Constitution

The power of the Fr. king was based on the domains of the crown. Following a period of feudal disintegration, large territ. states with a structured officialdom and functioning admins. developed during the 11th cent. This concentration benefited the monarchy, which gradually est. strong cen. power ('concentric concentration'). By further shaping the feudal law, the king placed himself at the top of the feudal pyramid. This was made possible by the feudalization of the land, the reversion of expired fiefs to the crown, and the vassals' obligation of loyalty to their lords (*homines ligii, ligesse*) so long as it did not conflict with their duty of allegiance to the king (*Rex: Dominus ligius ante omnes*). The cen. admin. was strengthened by the establishment of a **'parlement'** (highest court) and the development of officialdom. The **taille** (tax payment in exchange for existing service obligations) was the first step in the development of direct taxation. A budget was planned. For financial and milit. reasons the cities were granted communal privileges and thus strengthened.

England and France, 11th–13th cents.

1066–87 William the Conqueror was crowned king at Westminster after the **b. of Hastings** (1066), and subs. conquered all England (by 1071). Following several uprisings, the Anglo-Saxon nobility was deprived of its possessions.

1086 The Domesday Book ('doomsday': a record from which there was no appeal), a survey from all the properties of ·the realm recorded acc. to their annual yields.

1086 The Salisbury Oath: the oath of fealty of subordinate vassals was conditional on their liege obligation to the king (cf. p. 159). The king was at the head of the feudal pyramid, counselled by the *curia regis* (council of lords).

1087–1100 WILLIAM II (RUFUS). WILLIAM I's eldest son ROBERT (Curthose) inherited the Duchy of Normandy. After WILLIAM's death his younger brother

1100–35 HENRY I had himself crowned king. He defeated ROBERT at Tinchebray (1106) and reunited Normandy and England.

1107 The Concordat of Westminster terminated the investiture struggle (p. 148). The king forced the nobility to

1127 recognize his daughter MATHILDA (widow of the Emperor HENRY V (p. 148)) as heiress to the throne. She mar. Count GODFREY OF ANJOU (1128), who was nick-named 'Plantagenet' ('sprig of broom' – after his helmet decoration).

HENRY I est. an **exchequer** (*scaccarium*), to which the sheriffs (p. 129) of the shires had to account for their income (rents and feudal income) on 'pipe-rolls' (pipe-shaped rolls of annual accounts, after 1130/31) at Easter and Michaelmas (29 Sep.). The tribute paid to the vikings (Danegeld) became a general tax.

1135–54 STEPHEN OF BLOIS. After MATHILDA's landing in England (1139) a period of anarchy ensued (civil wars), which strengthened the position of the nobility and Church.

1154–1399 The House of Anjou–Plantagenet.

1154–89 Recognized by STEPHEN as heir to the throne (1153), **Henry II** became king. Together with England, his fiefs held from the Fr. crown (Normandy and Brittany from his mother; Anjou, Maine and Touraine from his father; Aquitaine from his wife ELEONOR (p. 159)) formed the Angevin realm. Rest. of royal prerogatives by

1164 the Constitutions of Clarendon: judgement of criminal ecclesiastics by eccles. courts, their punishment by secular courts, limitations on eccles. appeals to Rome. The chancellor (1155) of HENRY II, THOMAS À BECKET, Archbishop of Canterbury (1162), resisted and was murdered (1170). Penance of HENRY II at his grave (1174).

1171 Initiation of the conquest of Ireland.

1173–4 Revolt of HENRY's sons. HENRY's accomplishments: extension of the **king's court** (*curia regis*): after HENRY III *bancum regis* (king's bench), and establishment of a permanent court at Westminster (1178) of a permanent court with 5 assessors which was marked by

orderly processes of investigation and proof. Jurymen were chosen by the people. Gradual development of Eng. common law. The **exchequer** became a judicial body. The **sheriff** remained a royal official.

1189–99 RICHARD I THE LION-HEART, returning from the Crusade (p. 151), suppressed the revolt of his brother JOHN ('THE LANDLESS'). After RICHARD's death at the gates of the castle of Chaluz

1199–1216 JOHN I ascended the throne; he lost the territories in France, exc. Guyenne (p. 159), and, clashing with INNOCENT III (p. 149), was excommunicated (1209). He submitted because of the impending invasion of England by PHILIP II AUGUSTUS of France (recognition of STEPHEN LANGTON as Archbishop of Canterbury) and received England as a fief from the Pope (1213). After the suppression of the Lusignans (a Poitou dynasty)

1214 JOHN's allies were defeated in the **b. of Bouvines** (p. 159). After the peace of Chinon (loss of all territories N. of the Loire) the barons rose. At Runnymede near Windsor JOHN was forced to grant on

15 Jun. 1215 the Magna Carta libertatum: the king was forced to observe the 'ancient law' and to certify the privileges of the barons (their right to resist abuses of feudal privileges). Sep. demands and clauses concerning existing feudal law were added to the important general principles (preservation of the rights of the Church, respect for laws, etc.). The Magna Carta became the 'Bible of the Constitution'.

1216–72 HENRY III. The increase of eccles. power, unscrupulous taxation by the *curia*, the summoning of favourites ('*poitevins*') from s. France to the court to fill the highest offices of state, and the large burden of taxation caused by HENRY's ambition to obtain the Sicil. and Ger. crowns led to the

1258–65 Uprising of the Barons. Under pressure from SIMON DE MONTFORT, the 3rd son of the victor of the Albigensian War (p. 159), HENRY III was forced to grant

1259 the Provisions of Oxford: 15 barons were to counsel the king and control the admin. HENRY III allied himself with LOUIS IX (1259 Peace of Paris, p. 159) and the Pope, who freed him from his oath to follow the 'Provisions' (1261). After LOUIS IX had, as arbiter, declared the 'Provisions' void (Mise of Amiens, 1264), SIMON DE MONTFORT, as leader of the knights and burgesses, defeated the king

1264 in the b. of Lewes: establishment of a Great Council and calling of a parliament made up of 2 knights from each shire and 2 burgesses from each borough. EDWARD, son of HENRY III, defeated SIMON DE MONTFORT

1265 in the b. of Evesham (SIMON d. in the battle).

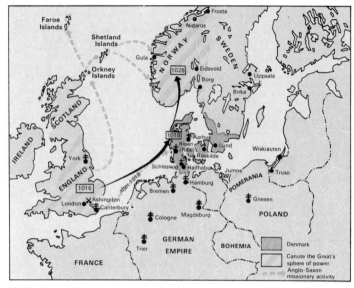

The North Sea Kingdom of Canute the Great in the 11th cent.

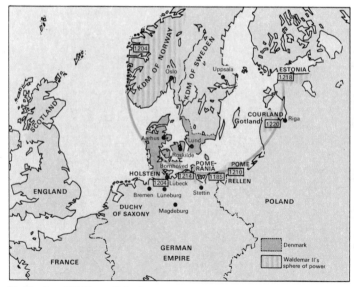

The Kingdom of Waldemar II the Conqueror

The first substantial kdms in Scandinavia were est. c. 900. Their kings converted to Christianity to elevate and strengthen their positions.

Denmark (935–1286)

. 935–45 King GORM THE OLD. Advancing from Jutland, he conquered the Swed. viking kdm of Haithabu (Schleswig). The bpcs of Ripen, Aarhus and Schleswig were est. (948) under his son HAROLD 'BLUETOOTH' (baptized c. 960). After his defeat by OTTO II (974), HAROLD was expelled by his son

85–1014 SVEN 'FORKED BEARD', who christianized Denmark and led a Dan. army against the Anglo-Saxons (994). His son

016–35 Canute the Great was recognized as king at London after his defeat of EDMUND (p. 129). After the death of his brother HAROLD he became king of Denmark (1019). Norway was subj. (1028). Anglo-Saxon priests carried on miss. activity and built up the Church.

104 Establishment of the archbpc of Lund. During the 11th and 12th cents. Denmark was often feudally dependent on Germany and weakened by struggles over the succession.

157–82 WALDEMAR I THE GREAT. Denmark's rise to major-power status began. With the aid of ABSOLON, Bishop of Roskilde, he subj. the provinces (building of castles); with HENRY THE LION

160–64 he campaigned against the Wends. Conquest of Rügen (1168). Rise of Church and nobility at the expense of the peasants.

182–1202 CANUTE IV, mar. to GERTRUDE, daughter of HENRY THE LION, refused to swear the oath of fealty to the Emperor and conquered Pomerania (1184). Homage by BOGISLAV OF POMERANIA (1185). His brother WALDEMAR, Duke of Schleswig, conquered Holstein with Lübeck and Hamburg (1201).

202–41 Waldemar II, the Conqueror. He conquered Lauenburg and Norway, Pomerelles, Estonia and Courland. FREDERICK granted him sovereignty over the land E. of the Elbe. During his captivity by Count HENRY OF SCHWERIN (1223–5) the conquests of Denmark were lost.

227 b. of Bornhöved: WALDEMAR II was defeated by the N. Ger. princes and the city of Lübeck. Consequences: acceleration of Ger.–Baltic trade, collapse of Dan. predominance. WALDEMAR abandoned further plans of conquest.

259–86 His grandchild, ERIK V GLIPPING, was obliged by the Dan. Magna Carta (1282) to convoke the assembly of the *Danehof* (consisting of prelates, barons and court-officials) annually, to work on legislation: limitation of royal power and the autonomous provincial assemblies (*Dings*).

Norway (c. 900–1280)

. 900 HAROLD FAIRHAIR of the Ynglingian dynasty est. a major kdm. Christianity was introduced – in part by forced conversions – under OLAF TRYGGVESSÖN (995–1000) and St OLAF (1016–28).

1035–47 After the expulsion of SVEN, the son of CANUTE THE GREAT, MAGNUS THE GOOD became king. His uncle HAROLD HARDRADA

1047–66 was killed at Stamfordbridge in the attempt to wrest England from HAROLD (p. 129). His successors est. bpcs. The development of the cities was promoted.

1130–1240 Civil wars over succession questions.

1152 Establishment of the archbpc of Nidaros (Drontheim).

1164 Diet of Bergen: the bps demanded the right to elect the king.

1184–1202 Sverrir led the anti-eccles. party of the 'birchlegs', overcoming the eccles. Baglar (curved-staff) party and forcing the bps to crown him despite the *interdictum* by INNOCENT III. Establishment of a strong hered. monarchy. His grandson

1217–63 HAAKON HAAKONSON was killed on the Isle of Man in the struggle over the Hebrides.

1261 Conquest of Greenland, 1262–4 Iceland.

1263–80 MAGNUS LAGABOETIR (Improver of the Laws) sold the Hebrides to Scotland (1266) and terminated the struggle with the Church (1277); the Church received jurisdiction over its affairs and was allowed to fill eccles. offices freely.

Sweden (995–1290)

995–1022 Olaf Skutkonung of the Upsala dynasty was baptized in 1008. After the death of his sons, the royal house of the Stenkils succeeded, leading to continual struggles between the Christ. Gautes (Goths) and the heathen Svear Upplands (Swedes) which only ended c. 1125 with the extinction of the Stenkils.

1130–56 SWERKER THE ELDER, the first king of the Swerker dynasty, ascended the throne. The Cist. Order was called. The Upsvear removed SWERKER THE YOUNGER from the throne and acclaimed ERIK KNUTSSON king (1208).

1164 Establishment of the archbpc of Upsala. Lasting more than half a cent., the struggle for the throne between the dynasties of SWERKER and ERIK did not end until both were extinct (1222, 1250).

1250–66 Jarl Birger of the Folkunger dynasty gained power. Friendly relations with Norway and Denmark. Conquest of s. Finland. Trading privileges for the Ger. Hanseatic League. Establishment of cities. Extensive legislation for the entire realm.

1275–90 MAGNUS LADULAS (= barncastle: protection of the peasants from the nobility). A nobility was formed from the families of peasants with large land-holdings. A hered. class of knights was est. by

1279 the Statute of Alsnö: those fighting on horseback were freed from their tax obligations.

The Empire of the Hohenstaufen, 1125–1254

1125–37 Rivalling the Hohenstaufen FREDERICK II OF SWABIA, LOTHAIR OF SUPPLINBURG was elected king. The ruling families in the territories along the eastern frontier were favoured (p. 171). The Guelphs of Saxony were strengthened by the marriage of HENRY THE PROUD to LOTHAIR's daughter GERTRUDE. Imp. coronation at Rome by INNOCENT II (1133). With his death, LOTHAIR's allodial estates and the duchy of Saxony fell to HENRY THE PROUD.

The Empire of the Hohenstaufen
1137–52 CONRAD III. Investing of ALBRECHT THE BEAR with Saxony, the Margrave LEOPOLD IV of Austria, of the Babenberg family, with Bavaria. By the
1142 Peace of Frankfurt, HENRY THE LION received Saxony and ALBRECHT THE BEAR the N. March in compensation; the Margrave HENRY II ('JASOMIRGOTT' = 'may God will it') of Austria got Bavaria. Unfortunate conclusion of the 2nd Crusade (p. 151) and reconciliation of CONRAD with HENRY THE LION, who forced the Abrodites to pay tribute in the crusade against the Wends (1147, p. 171).
1152–90 Frederick I Barbarossa brought about a compromise between the Guelphs and Hohenstaufen. Investing of his uncle GUELPH IV with the margravate of Tuscany and the duchy of Spoleto, his cousin HENRY THE LION with the duchy of Bavaria. To compensate HENRY II ('JASOMIRGOTT') Austria was made a duchy.

The Ital. Policy of Frederick I
1153 Treaty of Constance: FREDERICK I promised Pope EUGENE III his assistance against the Romans (the Rom. commune and ARNOLD OF BRESCIA) and Normans; the Pope promised Imp. coronation.
1154–55 1st Ital. campaign. FREDERICK I extradited ARNOLD OF BRESCIA and was crowned Emperor by Pope HADRIAN IV (1154–9; 1155). Because the promised attack against the Normans did not take place, the Pope reached an understanding with WILLIAM I OF SICILY (1154–66) in the peace of Benevento (1156): investiture of WILLIAM with Sicily, Apulia and Capua.
Oct. 1157 Diet of Besançon: clash of the papal legate Cardinal ROLAND BANDINELLI and chancellor RAINALD VON DASSEL (1156–67, 1159 Archbishop of Cologne) after the legate called the Imp. crown a 'beneficium' (feudum: investiture with, or bonum factum: benefit).
1158–62 2nd Ital. campaign. At the
Nov. 1158 Diet of the Roncalian Fields, FREDERICK demanded the return of the Imp. estates and rights (regalia) which had been violated by the now autonomous city-states and that Imp. privileges be safeguarded by Imp. officials.
1159 Papal election: ALEXANDER III (1159–81) and VICTOR IV (1159–64). The latter was recognized by the Emperor at the Synod of Pavia (1160). The w. was divided into 2

camps (until 1177). The meeting of LOUIS VII of France and FREDERICK I at St-Jean-de-Losne did not resolve the schism.
1163–4 3rd Ital. campaign: formation of the Veronese League of cities.
1165 At the Diet of Würzburg, RAINALD VON DASSEL demanded an oath denying recognition to ALEXANDER III.
1166–8 4th Ital. campaign: vict. of RAINALD VON DASSEL at Tusculum. The spread of contagious disease (death of RAINALD) forced the army to retreat. Formation of the Lombard League, which united with the Veronese League (the league fortress at Alessandria).
1174–8 5th Ital. campaign: futile siege of Alessandria; HENRY THE LION's refusal to perform his milit. obligation (meeting at Chiavenna). After the abortive attempt at a separate peace with the Lombard League and the
1176 defeat of Legnano, FREDERICK I concluded the preliminary peace of Anagni with Pope ALEXANDER III; then the
1177 Peace of Venice: armistice with the Lombard League and Sicily. Usufruct of the Mathildine estates until final disposition. Reconciliation with the Pope.
1183 Peace of Constance with the Lombard League: recognition of the Lombard League. Investiture of elected officials by the Emperor. Surrender to the cities of the regalia within their walls.
1178–80 Trial of Henry the Lion: indictment of the duke before the Imp. court by the Saxon nobles because of his breaches of the peace of the land. Because of his failure to appear he was placed under Imp. ban and, in a 2nd feudal judicial proceeding, lost his Imp. fiefs (the duchies of Bavaria and Saxony). Saxony fell to BERNHARD, Count of Anhalt, Bavaria to OTTO OF WITTELSBACH. Styria became an autonomous duchy. The Archbishop of Cologne received the ducal dignity for Westphalia and a part of Engern (Diet of Gelnhausen). After warfare within the Empire (1180–81), HENRY submitted (1181) and was granted the hered. estates of Brunswick and Lüneburg (exile to England). His vassals Mecklenburg and Pomerania became immediate vassals of the Emperor, Lübeck an Imp. city.
1184–6 6th Ital. campaign: alliance of FREDERICK I with Milan. Coronation of HENRY VI as king of Italy at Milan and his marriage to CONSTANCE OF SICILY. Pope URBAN III (1185–7) subs. allied himself with the N. Ger. princes opposed to the Emperor.
1187 Alliance of FREDERICK I and PHILIP II AUGUSTUS of France at Toul (p. 159): Beginning of the ties between Hohenstaufen and Capetians against the Guelphs and Anjous. At the
1188 Diet of Worms FREDERICK I took the cross (p. 151).
Foundations of Frederick's power: the Staufen estates, the Imp. estates, Transjurane Burgundy (he mar. its heiress BEATRICE, 1156). Coronation as king of Burgundy at Arles (1178).

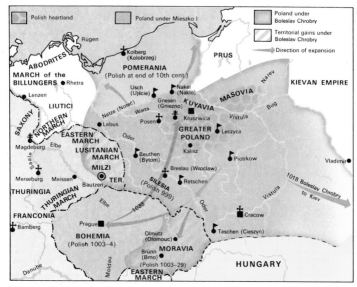

Poland in the 10th and 11th cents.

Subordinate Polish principalities and German eastward colonization, 12th and 13th cents.

Poland to 1320

Pol. tribal territories were consolidated into an ind. Pol. state at an early date (*poleni* = inhabitants of the fields); it came into contact and conflict with Ger. eastern policy.

960–92 Miezko I of the Piast Dynasty. After his marriage to the Czech princess DUBRAVKA he converted to Christianity (966). Poland thus became a Christ. state with its own bpc (Posen = Poznan). After the incursions of Wichmann (963, 967), a defeated vassal of OTTO I, a conciliatory peace was concluded. MIEZKO became a 'friend of the Emperor' (a relationship of personal loyalty, no feudal dependence). He paid homage to OTTO III in 985, but placed his land under the protection of the Pope. Under his son

992–1025 Boleslav I Chrobry (= the Brave) a friendly relationship with the Empire developed (the universalist conception of the Christ. empire by OTTO III). His daughter REGINLINDIS mar. Margrave HERMANN I of Meissen (Misnia). Poland's predominance over the w. Slavs was secured by the conquest of Cracow and the subjugation of the w. Slav. tribes.

1000 Establishment of the archbpc of Gniezno (Gnesen) as autonomous Pol. eccles. province with the bpcs of Wroclaw (Breslau), Cracow and Kolobrzeg (Kolberg). As a pilgrim to the grave of Bishop ADALBERT OF PRAGUE (at Gniezno), OTTO III took part in the ceremony of his canonization.

1002 Boleslav I Chrobry abandoned the universalist concept of a Christ. empire and initiated a pro-Pol. policy directed against Bohemia and the Empire.

1003–18 Conflicts with the Empire. The plan for a unified w. Slav. state conflicted with the conceptions of Ger. eastern policy. War broke out over the Lutitian lands, Lusatia (Lausitz), the March of Meissen (Misnia) and Bohemia.

1013 Boleslav Chrobry acknowledged the feudal overlordship of the Ger. king.

1018 Peace of Bautzen (Budziszyn): BOLESLAV received Lusatia and the territory of Milzen as Imp. fiefs (p. 143).

1024 After the occupation of Kiev during the struggles over the Rus. throne BOLESLAV had himself crowned king.

1025–34 Mieszko II. Mar. since 1018 to a granddaughter of OTTO II, he had to give up the royal crown and acknowledge his feudal dependence to the Ger. king (in consequence of his opposition to CONRAD II (1033)). Loss of Pomerania, Lusatia and large areas between the Vistula and the Bug.

1037–58 Casimir I. Heathen uprisings and incursions by the Bohemians (p. 169), who transported the remains of St ADALBERT to Prague and annexed Silesia (1038). After his expulsion CASIMIR returned to his country with Ger. help. The reconstruction of the Church (Ger. clergy) and the state (shift of power from Great Poland to Little Poland) was carried out from Cracow, the new cap. Return of Silesia by HENRY III (1054).

By 1138 the duchy of Poland was completely centralized and ruled by representatives of the duke (castellans), who were in complete command. Immunities for the Church, and later also for nobles, i.e. for formerly ducal officials and retainers, were granted under the infl. of Ger. law. The nobility consisted of the **magnates** and the **szlachta**, the lesser knightly nobility.

1058–79 Boleslav II. Because of the coalition directed against him (HENRY IV, Bohemia, Russia) BOLESLAV sided with GREGORY VII in the struggle between Empire and Papacy. He was crowned king in 1076, but soon driven from the throne by the eccles. and sec. nobility.

1079–1102 Vladislav Hermann.

1102–6 Zbigniev.

1106–38 Boleslav III. Renewed expansion of power as a result of the subjugation of Pomerania (1121) and the areas between the Oder and the Elbe (miss. activity of Bishop OTTO OF BAMBERG, 1124/5, 1128). 1135 acknowledgement of the feudal overlordship of the Ger. king and investiture with Western Pomerania.

1138 Introduction of the 'Seniorate': as supreme ruler, the eldest of the Piasts was to be in possession of Little Poland which had its cap. and coronation site at Cracow; the other members of the dynasty were to rule as dukes in Silesia, Mazovia, Kuyavia, Greater Poland and Eastern Little Poland with Sandomierz. The hoped-for strengthening of unity did not materialize; rather, the next cent. and a half witnessed continual struggles; the state consisted of territ. states. The concept of Pol. unity remained alive in the coherent organization of the Church and the traditions of the great noble dynasties.

1146 Vladislav, the eldest son of BOLESLAV III, was driven out by his brothers with the aid of the nobility. He fled to his brother-in-law CONRAD III.

1180 Assembly of the Pol. dukes and bps at Leczyca (Lentschiza). The 'seniorate' was abolished and the privileges of the clergy were confirmed. Pol. unity was not attained; the Piast principalities co-existed. However, the possession of Cracow remained the precondition for the rest. of the unity of the Pol. state.

1241 Mongol invasion. The Mongols drew back despite their vict. in the **b. of Liegnitz.**

1295 Przemysl II, the duke of Great Poland, attempted to restore unity by his coronation at Gniezno. But he was murdered in 1296.

1300–5 Wenceslas II of Bohemia became king with the aid of the Church and the Ger. inhabitants of the cities. After the extinction of the Przemyslids (1306) and the defeat of the rulers of the principalities,

1320 Vladislav Lokietek was crowned king in Cracow. Rest. of the unity of the Pol. state, without, however, the duchy of Silesia, which fell to Bohemia (p. 201).

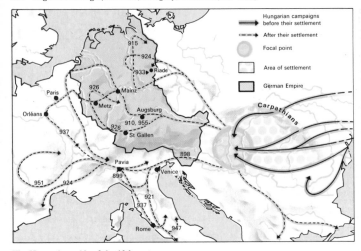

The Hungarian raids of the 10th cents.

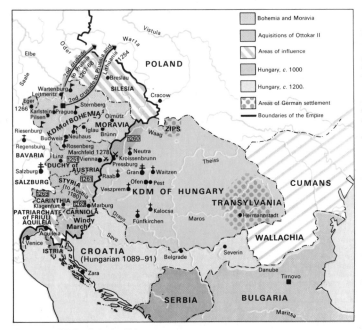

Hungary and Bohemia in the 13th cent.

Moravia (830–906)

After the immigration of the Slavs (c. 600), the Frank. merchant **Samo** freed the w. Slav tribes from Avar domination (after 626) and the infl. of the E. Frankish kdm (631 b. of Wogastisburg). With Samo's death the state fell apart and became a tributary of CHARLEMAGNE (805). Following the establishment of the **Moravian state** by MOYMIR (830–46) his nephew **Rastislav** (846–70) terminated subservience to the E. Frank. state by turning to Byzantium. An independent eccles. organization with a distinct liturgical and lit. language was created by the Slav. apostles CONSTANTINE and METHODIUS with papal approval; its independence was lost after the death of METHODIUS (885), who had been named archbp by Rome. Several fruitless campaigns of LOUIS THE GERMAN were followed by the great uprising under RASTISLAV. His nephew

870–94 Sviatopluk, who captured his uncle and surrendered him to the E. Frank. king, terminated the revolt after another 4 yrs of war by negotiating the

874 peace of Forchheim: SVIATOPLUK lost Lower Pannonia, but was able to continue his expansionist policy and acquire the Sudeten lands, Slovakia, Bohemia, Western Hungary and Silesia.

880 Transfer of Greater Moravia to St PETER and his vicar at Rome.

906 Destruction of Moravia by the Hungarians.

Hungary under the Arpads (896–1301)

Seven Magyar tribes (nomads of the steppes) took possession of the plains of the Theiss and Middle Danube under the leadership of ARPAD (896–907). Between 899 and 955 they campaigned in the w.: in the E. Frank. kdm, Italy, France, Lorraine, Burgundy, Spain and Byzantium. After their defeat at Augsburg (955) ARPAD's grandson GEZA (972–97) strengthened princely power and promoted the christianization and settlement of the Hungarians.

997–1038 St Stephen I est. Christ. royal sovereignty. The presence of Ger. knights at court and the enfeoffment of Benedictines with lands made Hungary into a Christ. state.

1001 Establishment of the archbpc of Gran and coronation of Stephen with a crown sent by SYLVESTER II. The king was assisted by a council of ecclesiastics and counts of the 'comitatus' (a constitutional order based on counties). Subs. the country was weakened by struggles over the dyn. succession, heathen uprisings and incursions from abroad.

1077–95 LADISLAS I united Croatia in personal union with Hungary. His successor COLOMAN I became king of Croatia.

1173–96 Bela III accomplished the annexation of Dalmatia, Croatia and Bisnia (p. 175) by conflicts with Byzantium. Cult. contacts with France were est. and the Cistercians and Premonstratensians were invited to the country. Transylvania was settled by Saxons who had been summoned to the country;

they were granted local autonomy (1224).

1205–35 Andreas II.

1222 ANDREAS issued the **'Golden Bull':** the high nobility and clergy were granted protection against confiscation of their estates, taxation, arrest; they were given unrestricted power over the estates of the lower nobility, which no longer supported the crown. Uncompensated milit. obligation applied only to service within the area of the country. The nat. assembly received the right to voice grievances and to resist the king (resistance clause).

1241 Collapse of Hungary under the Mongolian assault after the defeat at the Sajo river. Conflicts with OTTOKAR II of Bohemia followed. The Arpad Dynasty became extinct with ANDREAS III (1290–1301).

Bohemia

Tribal particularism was overcome during the 9th cent. by the Przemyslid Dynasty, which resided in the vicinity of Prague. The establishment of a strong and autonomous state was made possible by the effectiveness of the cavalry of the prince – an élite corps of professional warriors financed by the ruler – and by the transformation of castles serving as temporary shelters into permanent strongholds. After the murder of WENCESLAS, later proclaimed a nat. saint, Bohemia was incorp. into the Empire under its own dynasty during the 10th cent.

973 Establishment of the bpc of Prague under the jurisdiction of Mainz. Struggles between Bohemia and Poland were followed by the cession of

1054 Silesia to Poland. Moravia remained tied to Bohemia.

1061–92 VRATISLAV was elevated to the royal dignity by HENRY IV (1086). Following struggles over the succession, the strengthening of the nobility through the 'seniorate' and the introduction of primogeniture (1158)

1140–73 Vladislav II became hered. king. With the beginning of the Ger. movement towards the E. (1170 for Ger. merchants) cities were est. and a bourgeoisie developed alongside the native nobility and the clergy.

1198–1230 Przemysl Ottokar I. He was granted privileges by the Ger. rulers and the popes.

1253–78 Przemysl Ottokar II. Pinnacle of Boh. power. He supported the Teutonic Knights (the settlement on the Pregel river was named Königsberg in his honour 1225); he obtained Austria (1251); after the vict. of Kroissenbrunn over the Hungarians he obtained Styria (1261), parts of Slovakia (1260), Carinthia and Carniola. In

1273 he was defeated by RUDOLF OF HABSBURG in the election to the royal throne. He fell in the

1278 b. of Marchfeld. WENCESLAS II was given Bohemia and Moravia. After the death of WENCESLAS III (1306), Bohemia and Moravia were made Imp. estates (p. 195).

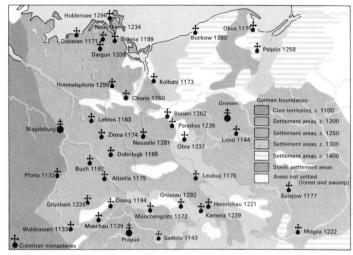

The German movement to the east, 12th and 13th cents.

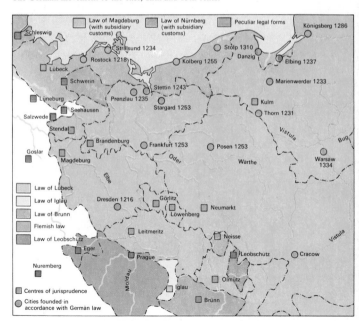

Urban legal practices in eastern Central Europe

The Ger. Movement to the E.

1125–37 Emperor LOTHAIR (of Supplinburg) gave renewed impetus to the movement to the E. Miss. urge and power-polit. factors prompted the Emperor to make the territ. princes executors of his eastern policy:

1110 the dynasty of Schauenburg (ADOLF VON SCHAUENBURG) in the county of Holstein;

1123 the Wettin Dynasty (KONRAD VON WETTIN) in the March of Misnia (Meissen), 1136 in the March of Lusatia (Lausitz);

1134 the Ascanians (ALBRECHT THE BEAR, Count of Ballenstedt, after 1150 Margrave of Brandenburg) in the N. March (Altmark);

1139–95 HENRY THE LION subj. the Abrodite prince PRIBISLAV (1167), and made the dukes of Pomerania feudal vassals; however, he lost the eastern territories in

1178–80 territ. and feudal litigation (p. 165).

Beginning in the 11th cent., the **wave of colonization** led to the settlement of areas desolated by war in France, and the addition of new arable land through the clearing of forests and irrigation in Germany. It was made possible by the **3-field system** developed in Northern France (alternation of winter crop, summer crop and fallow). Compared with the 2-field system, this method, with its predominance of grain production (construction of barns), resulted in increased productivity. **Improvement of agricultural techniques:** improvement of plough and harrow (now made of iron); development of the scythe to its present form; increased use of the threshing flail; processing of grains by means of watermills (from the 12th cent. by means of windmills). The horse replaced the ox as the draught animal.

The intensification of agriculture brought about the offering of a richer diet and the birth-rate rose. Still quite small during the 9th cent., the pop. of the E. Frank. kdm grew to such an extent during the 12th cent. as to match that of France. *Hufen* villages took the place of the smaller older villages; the number and size of the cities increased, leading to an increase in the prices of agricultural goods. Ger. territ. princes and the Slav. princes of Pomerania, Poland, Silesia, Bohemia, Moravia and Mecklenburg, as well as the native nobility and clergy, invited Ger. peasants and town dwellers to settle in the country. The eastern boundary of the Empire (Elbe, Saale, Bohemian Forest) was crossed. Monks and nuns migrated to the E.: among them August. canons, Premonstratensians, Cistercians, Teutonic Knights, Knights of St John, and Sp. Knights of Calatrava.

Settlement proceeded:

1. In uniformly planned **large villages** with equal property in squares or strips for all settlers (Frank. *Hufe* = 24 hectares or Flemish *Hufe* = 16,8 hectares as units of measurement) arranged by professional locators who were rewarded for their work by being given the henceforth hered. position of *Schulze* (village mayor). Establishment of distinct parishes with *Widmur* (1–4 *Hufen*). Because they had left their homes and endured privations during the process of settlement, the settlers received an improved soc. position: their estates could be bequeathed as hered. possessions, though usually the heirs had to make a payment of relief which – after the first 'free years' – was paid in the form of money or grain (the law of entail). The 3-field system replaced extensive and unplanned field and grass cultivation (alternation of tilled and fallow land for grazing, thus mainly animal husbandry). This led to an increase in arable land, and to a considerable increase in yields.

2. In **cities,** planned by Slav. territ. princes (judicial autonomy, the right to erect fortifications and autonomous municipal admin.), whose streets were arranged in a regular grid pattern with the market-place in the centre ('cen. market scheme'). The cities were loc. in the heart of the Slav. provinces. Governed by overseers (*Vogt*), they became econ., cult. and relig. centres and bases of long-distance trade. 'Ger.' law was given a privileged position (Magdeburg law and 'daughter' laws, Lübeck law, and s. Ger. laws).

3. In already est. Slav. agricultural and urban settlements, where the settlers either lived in accordance with their own law, or extended the Ger. law to cover the non-Ger. settlers.

4. In accordance with Ger. law, but by Slav. settlers, as in the eastern areas of Poland, in Lithuania, in the Ukraine and in White Russia, where only the Ger. legal norms were adopted and often modified (Lemberg, Kiev, etc.).

After 1250 beginning of 'daughter' colonization in the E.

1253–78 King OTTOKAR OF BOHEMIA est. more than 60 Ger. cities in his kdm.

14th cent. End of the movement to the E. The human resources for colonization were exhausted; the agrarian pop. migrated to the cities ('desolation': small villages disappeared).

Consequences: the movement to the E. brought about a peaceful cult. permeation of the country: following the recommendation of BERNARD OF CLAIRVAUX, the Slav. pop. was not subj. or exterminated. A living and econ. community of Slavs and Germans; but Germanization of wide areas between the Elbe, the Saale and the Oder. Pop. and food production grew 5-fold. The roomy and seaworthy *Koggen* enabled the Germans to take over trade (1158 2nd founding of Lübeck), which up to the 12th cent. had been in the hands of the Slavs and Scandinavians (Haithabu/Schleswig). Introduction of Western const., econ. and legal forms (Urban law and *Burgfreiheit* = i.e. freedom from interference by the castle).

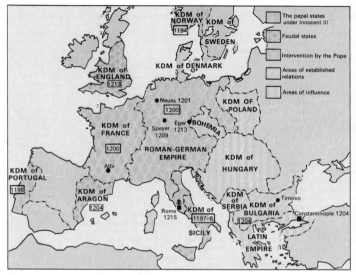

The world dominance of Innocent III

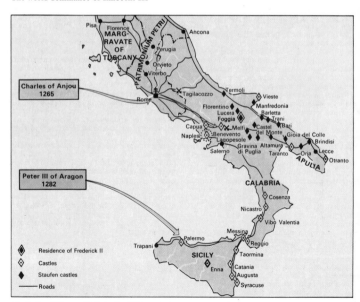

Central and Lower Italy in the 13th cent.

The Empire of the Hohenstaufen

1190–97 Henry VI had 2 enemies: HENRY THE LION and TANCRED OF LECCE, the half-brother of WILLIAM II OF SICILY, who had been chosen king by a Norm. faction.

1191 1st Ital. campaign: Imp. coronation by Pope CELESTINE (1191–8). The siege of Naples was discontinued (epidemic) and the army returned to Germany. The Pope invested TANCRED with Sicily.

1192–4 The opposition of the Ger. princes collapsed after the capture of RICHARD THE LION-HEART during his return from the Crusades. RICHARD swore the oath of fealty and paid an enormous ransom. HENRY THE LION reconciled himself with the Emperor (1194).

1194–5 2nd Ital. campaign: coronation of HENRY VI as king of Sicily at Palermo (1194) and **'unio regni ad imperium'** (personal union of Sicily and the Ger. empire). HENRY VI (32 yrs old) d. before the realization of his plan to create a hered. empire. His widow CONSTANCE assumed the regency for FREDERICK II. After her death (1198), Pope INNOCENT III (p. 149), who enforced **'recuperations'** (seizures) of Imp. estates (duchy of Spoleto, the marches of Ancona and Tuscany), became guardian of FREDERICK II. The monarchy was weakened by the struggles between PHILIP OF SWABIA (1198–1208) and OTTO IV (1198–1218) over the succession. The *ministeriales* of the Empire and the bourgeoisie were debased by the princes.

1201 With the treaty of Neuss, OTTO IV surrendered his Imp. privileges in the 'recuperated' areas, and with the

1209 treaty of Speyer he gave up the privileges secured by the Condordat of Worms. After the rest. of the Imp. privileges in Italy, OTTO was crowned Emperor at Rome, but then excommunicated because of his campaign in Lower Italy.

1210–50 Frederick II promised the Pope not to join Sicily to the Empire.

1213 The Golden Bull of Eger: confirmation of OTTO's concessions (1201, 1209).

1214 b. of Bouvines: PHILIP II AUGUSTUS (p. 159) defeated the Anglo-Guelph opposition led by OTTO IV. FREDERICK II won the support of the eccles. princes for the election of his son HENRY (VII) to the kingship by the

1220 Confoederatio cum principus ecclesiasticis: surrender of important *regalia* (market, coinage, and customs privileges, granting of the right to fortifications and judicial autonomy) to the eccles. princes.

The North and the East

1214 By the treaty of Metz, FREDERICK II surrendered the Ger. territories E. of the Elbe to WALDEMAR II of Denmark (p. 163) in exchange for his help against the Guelphs.

1226 The Golden Bull of Rimini: the Teutonic Knights were instructed to conquer heathen Prussia (p. 199).

1227 b. of Bornhöved (p. 163).

Emperor and Pope

After his coronation in Rome as Emperor (1220), FREDERICK II came to an understanding with the Pope; in the Treaty of San Germano (1226) he agreed to lead a crusade, proceeding to do so in 1227. However, he had to turn back because of an epidemic and was therefore excommunicated by Pope GREGORY IX (1227–41).

1228–9 FREDERICK carried on the crusade despite his excommunication. After his return he concluded the

1230 Peace of Ceprano: FREDERICK II was granted absolution and the Pope received special eccles. privileges in Sicily. The Emperor was again excommunicated in 1239, and, at the 1st Council of Lyon, declared deposed and a heretic.

The Reorganization of Sicily (1221–31)

Elimination of feudal and urban anarchy. Establishment of a modern state: administrative offices (paid officials), legislation, state-monopolies, and a fiscal system (direct and indirect taxation). Codification of the Sicil. laws

1231 in the Constitutions of Melfi.

Germany

After assuming the gvt as Ger. king, HENRY VII (1228) attempted to strengthen Imp. power by allying himself with the *ministeriales* and the cities; however, at the court assembly of Worms he was forced to grant the

1231 Statutum in favorem principum, which gave the sec. princes the same rights of territ. sovereignty that had been granted to the eccles. princes. When FREDERICK II confirmed the *Statutum* (1232), HENRY VII revolted against him and allied himself with the Lombard cities. FREDERICK II journeyed to Germany and sent HENRY VII to imprisonment in Apulia (d. 1242).

1235 Great *Landfrieden* (pacification) of Mainz. Reconciliation with the Guelphs (OTTO THE CHILD, grandson of HENRY THE LION, became Duke of Brunswick-Lüneburg). Decision to wage war against the Lombard cities. Their levies were beaten in the

1237 b. of Cortenuova. HENRY RASPE, Count of Thuringia, and Count WILLIAM OF HOLLAND were elected anti-kings.

1250 Death of FREDERICK II in Apulia.

1250–54 CONRAD IV. He d. soon after the seizure of Naples (1253).

The Decline of the Hohenstaufen (1254–68)

The Curia transferred Sicily to CHARLES OF ANJOU, brother of LOUIS IX OF FRANCE (p. 159), who defeated MANFRED, regent of Sicily, in the

1266 b. of Benevento (MANFRED was killed in the battle). In the

1268 b. of Tagliacozzo, CHARLES OF ANJOU defeated CONRADIN, son of CONRAD IV; CONRADIN was executed at Naples.

1282 The Sicilian Vespers: all Frenchmen were driven out of Sicily (p. 187).

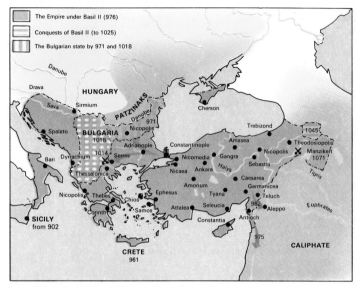

Byzantium in the 10th and 11th cents.

Byzantium in the 12th cent.

The Development of Byz. Power during the Middle Period (867–1025)

867–1056 The Macedonian Dynasty. A revival of Rom. Law took place under the emperors BASIL I (867–86) and LEON IV (886–912); legal texts: the 3 'Basilics'. **Pinnacle of Imp. power:** the Emperor as the chosen one of God. Complete bureaucratization of the state. Rest. of Byz. power in Italy through the conquest of Benevento (873) and Bari (876). The Arabs gained advantages during this time: conquest of Sicily (902) and takeover of Thessalonica (904).

907 Rus. attack on Byzantium. The attempts of the Bulgarian Tsar SYMEON (893–927) to conquer Byzantium failed. ROMANOS I LECAPENUS (920–44), the Byz. ruler, also defeated the Russians (941) and the Arabs (943).

963–9 as a general, **Nicephorus Phocas** regained Crete (961) and Aleppo (962); as Emperor, he regained Cyprus and Cilicia in campaigns against the Arabs.

969–76 John I Zimisces defeated the Russians in a '2-front war' (971), expelling them from the Balkans and making E. Bulgaria a Byz. province (971). Syria and Palestine were conquered. **The high point of the expansion of Byz. power** was reached during the reign of

976–1025 Basil II, 'the Slayer of the Bulgarians'. Because of the marriage of his sister to the Rus. grand-duke VLADIMIR (989) (who was baptized), the Orth. faith spread in Russia. The Rus. Church was placed under the authority of the Patriarch of Constantinople. After securing the conquests of his predecessors in Syria against the Fatimids, he overcame the w. Bulgarian state of SAMUEL in struggles which lasted decades (991–1014).

1014 Defeat of the Bulgarians in the Struma region: 14,000 prisoners were blinded. W. Bulgaria became a Byz. province (1018).

The Decline of the Middle Byz. Empire (1025–1204)

The **inexorable process of feudalization** undermined the fiscal and milit. foundations of the Empire (dissolution of the organization into *themes*). **Fiscal immunity** (complete freedom from taxation) was granted to large landowners, and tax collection was farmed out. The **pronoia system** was introduced (estates incl. all income were leased out for fixed periods as reward for services), as was the **charisticarius system** (transfer of monasteries and their estates as benefices to sec. administrators (*Charisticarii*) also through the power of the Emperor). Rise of a powerful **bureaucracy of officials** in the cap.

1045 The conquest of Armenia (last Byz. addition in the E.) was followed by

1054 The Schism between Eastern and Western Churches (the Great Schism) which resulted from the universalist claims made by both churches.

1059–78 The Dukas Dynasty: advance of the Normans, Patzinaks (p. 113) and Hun-

garians, and esp. the Seljuk Turks, who, after

1071 the vict. of Manzikert over the Emperor ROMANOS IV DIOGENES, est. the Sultanate of Iconium (Rum, 1080).

1081–1185 The Comneni Dynasty.

1081–1118 ALEXIUS I COMNENUS. Defensive struggles against the Normans under ROBERT GUISCARD, the Patzinaks, who advanced to Constantinople in 1090, and the Seljuks. 1092 initiation of an offensive policy.

1082 Because of their aid against the Normans, the Venetians received the right to trade in all parts of the Byz. Empire without paying customs duties (beginning of the Levantine power of Venice). A treaty with Pisa followed in 1111.

1096 Beginning of the transit of crusaders and the establishment of crusader states. ALEXIUS I obtained the recognition of Byz. sovereignty over Antioch (1108) and conquered western Asia Minor.

1118–43 John II dest. the Patzinaks (Berrhoe 1122), struggled with the Hungarians to gain control over Serbia, Dalmatia and Croatia (against Venice), and subordinated Little Armenia (Antioch 1138).

1143–80 MANUEL I attempted a **policy of restoration in Italy** which led to the econ. decline of Byzantium. Repulsion of the attacks of the Normans, led by ROGER OF SICILY, of the Serbs and the Hungarians.

1158 Feudal sovereignty over the Crusader states in Syria.

1159 Because of the renewed policy of intervention in Hungary, Croatia, Bosnia and Dalmatia came under Byz. infl.

1175 Alliance of Venice and the Nor. king WILLIAM II against Byzantium.

1176 Defeat at Myriocephalon by the Seljuks.

1185 Conquest of Thessalonica by the Normans.

1185–1204 The Angeli Dynasty. The Byz. Empire began its decline.

1187 Recognition of the 2nd Bulg. Empire (p. 205). Loss of Dalmatia, Croatia and Serbia.

1203 1st conquest of Constantinople by the Crusaders.

1204 2nd conquest of Constantinople by the Crusaders. Establishment of the Lat. Empire (p. 207).

The importance of Byzantium, bulwark of the w., lay in the defence against the Persians, Arabs and Turks. During this time the w. Eur. peoples were given the chance to develop their own nat. life. The great cult. achievement of Byzantium was the conversion of the Slavs, esp. of the Russians. Gk theology, eastern mysticism and monasticism influenced the w. Not least, however, Byzantium preserved the intellectual heritage of antiquity.

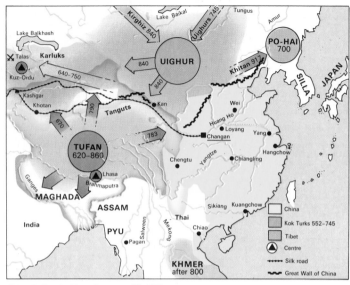

China during the Tang Dynasty, 618–907

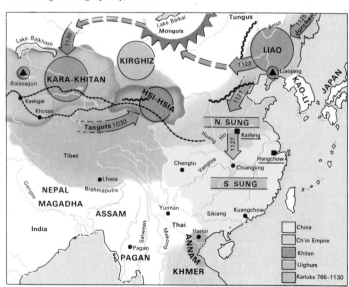

China during the Sung Dynasty, 960–1279

China under the Tang and Sung Dynasties

220–65 Period of the '3 kdms' (Wei, Wu, Shu). After temporary unification

317–589 separation of N. and s. China. While the N. was invaded by alien peoples (Huns, Turks), who est. 16 kdms with Chin. admin., the

222–589 the **'6 Dynasties'** continued the Chin. tradition in the s. LIANG WU-TI (502–50) promoted **Mahayana Buddhism**, which spread over China. Polit. predominance was assumed by the Turk.

420–588 Toba kdm (Wei Dynasty). Contemporaneous with its decline, General YANG CHIEN rose in power and reunited the entire Empire under

580–604 Emperor WENG **(Sui Dynasty).** YANG (to 618) chose his officials through

606 a written examination system (in use to the 20th cent.). The Imperial Canal linked the rivers Yangtze and Huang Ho. Milit. setbacks caused uprisings which led to the rise of the **Tang Dynasty (618–907).**

627–49 Under **T'ai Tsung, China reached the highest stage of its history:** establishment of autonomous milit. districts to secure the frontiers; the Eastern (Kök) Turks were annihilated; advance to Korea. 88 Asiatic peoples acknowledged Chin. sovereignty.

Culture: highest development of Chin. lyrical poetry by WANG WEI (699–759), LI PO (701–62), TU FU (712–70), PO CHÜ-I and HAN YÜ. The **Collection of Tang Poetry** includes 48,900 poems by 2,200 poets.

725 Establishment of the **Han-lin Academy** for the training of the highest officials. The **spread of Buddhism** influenced literature and art (painting, sculpture). Pilgrimages served to bring back stimuli from India.

During the 8th cent. early setbacks led to the decline of the Empire:

751 Defeat at the Talas by the Arabs; milit. uprisings supported by the Uighurs, Khitan Mongols, Tangut and Thai peoples.

790 Conquest of the w. by the **Tufan kdm,** which disintegrated during the 9th cent.; none the less, **persecutions of Buddhists** weakened the Empire **(844).** It was completely dissolved during

907–60 the Period of the 5 Dynasties. A renewal of the Empire was achieved, but only through the payment of tribute by the

960–1127 Northern Sung Dynasty, to the Khitan Mongols (Liao Dynasty) and to the Hsi-Hsia state. To retain control over the commanders,

1068–85 SHEN-TSUNG separated civilian admin. from the milit. and est. a militia. This did not, however, avert polit. catastrophe: the **Jurchen** tribes conquered Northern China and est. the Ch'in Empire (1125).

1127–1279 The Southern Sung Dynasty was, by paying tributes, able to retain its independence up to the time of the Mongol invasions (p. 211), but only with difficulty. In spite of polit. impotence a **2nd period of cult. and econ. flowering of China** (saltpetres, gunpowder, firecrackers, **printing, porcelain**).

Culture: flowering of **prose writing** (historical and geographical works, encyclopedias);

OU-YANG SIU and SU TUNG-PO were imp. essayists. Academies of painting were founded. **Sung philosophy** dogmatized Confucianism to the point of achieving state-wide moral standards and thereby est. a **cohesive Chin. civilization.** The 'scholastic' **Chu Hsi** (1131–1200) was the creator of the new Chin. language.

The Japanese Island Kdm

Waves of immigrants from Korea and the s. settled, formed clans and pushed the original inhabitants (Ainus) to the N. A religion of nature worship (*kamimomishi* = 'the way of the Gods') and an ancestor cult developed. The 'grandson of the Goddess of the Sun *Amaterasu*', who bore the title **Tenno** (Heavenly King), was considered the mythical founder and first **Mikado** ('High Portal') of the state.

660 B.C. Yamato: The Yamato kdm was actually est.

c. **120 B.C.** by **Jimmu-Tenno;** it was culturally dependent on China and politically dominated by Korea A.D. 363–662.

5th cent. A.D. Introduction of Chin. writing. The defenders of nat. Jap. Shintoism ('the Paths of God') were defeated in the struggle between the **Omi** and **Muraji** clans over the **introduction of Buddhism** (imported from China in 552 by KIMMI).

593–628 Empress SUIKO and Prince **Shotoku Taishi** promoted the 'Way of Buddha' by the erection of temples.

645–1192 The age of the bureaucratic state, modelled after China, was introduced

645 by the Taika reform (codified in the Taiho, 702): Imp. officials with hered. lands of their own took the place of the ancient constitution of the clans, strengthening the absolute Imp. power. First flowering in the

710–82 Nara Period. Chin. influence lessened following the fusion of Shintoism and Buddhism. Development of an aristocracy of officials (*kuge*) and warriors (*buke*) ran parallel with a court ctr. during the

794–1192 Heian Period (cap. Kyoto). Polit. dominance was achieved by the

967–1068 Fujiwara family. The struggle between the Taira and Minamoto families over the office and dignity of the supreme milit. commander was lost by the Taira

1185 in the b. of Dan-no-ura. Minamoto Yoritomo (to 1199) got the Tenno to name him hered. **Shogun** (victor over the barbarians) with a court at Kamakura.

1192–1333 The Kamakura Shogunate. While the Tenno (often a child or a monk) nominally remained the ruler and appointed officials, the actual governing was carried out by the Shogun and his vassals (cf. major-domo, p. 121). The dualistic administrative process was complicated by similar pressures at the court of Kamakura.

1219–1333 At the Kamakura court the **Hojo** family obtained the hered. dignity of the polit. regency **(Shikken).**

1274 and **1281** Mongol incursions were repulsed by armies of knights (Samurai, p. 211).

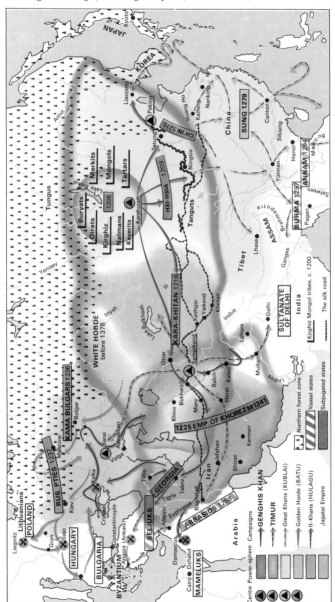

The Mongol Empires in the 13th–14th Cents.

he Mongol. Assault in the 13th Cent.

196 After eliminating his opponents, the tribal chief TEMUJIN ('Blacksmith', 1167–1227) was elevated to the position of GENGHIS KHAN and proclaimed 'supreme ruler'

206 at a Kurultai (imp. diet) of all Mongol., Turk. and Tartar peoples of the steppes (p. 113). The **Jasa** law made the milit. levies (*ulus*) into a nat. unit: the peoples were organized into *c.* 130 millennia and a guard led by hered. leaders, who always chose the **Great Khan** from the 'Golden Family' of the Temujin. *Biliks* (commands) secured domestic peace as thé country stood ready for the **conquest of the world**. Acknowledgement of a supreme God who could be revered in any suitable manner.

205–9 Subjugation of the Hsi-Hsia kdm, which served as the basis for an attack on China;

211–15 Devastation of the Ch'in Empire. The Mongols unleashed their milit. might (attacks from the flanks, encirclement, obstructed escape-routes, slaughters and massacres) in 2 carefully planned annual campaigns, and later utilized the technology of Chin. engineers (artillery, signal systems, the art of siege).

219–25 Attack on the **Empire of Khorezm**. 'Out of the saddle', 'the scourge of God' subj. a world-empire which stretched from Northern China to the Black Sea; but it could not be effectively governed by the thin layer of the Mongol. ruling class. The flowering ctrs. of Cen. Asia decayed; trade shifted from the Asiatic caravan routes to the Arabian sea lanes. The commander SUBUTAI by-passed the Caspian Sea and dest. a Rus. army in the b. of the Kalka.

227 **Death of Genghis Khan** and **partition of the Empire** between his 4 sons: JOTI, JAGATAI, TULUI and UGUDEI. Each received *ulus* (milit. levies), a *jurt* (grazing area) and *ingus* (a share in the tribute). **Karakorum** became the permanent cap.

229–41 The Great Khan **Ugudei** completed the subjugation of N. China (the Ch'in Empire to 1234) and Persia. On orders of the Kurultai

236–55 **Batu** (grandson of GENGHIS KHAN) conquered the w. with **Subutai**: destruction of the **Kama Bulgars** (1236); fall of Kiev (1240); invasion of Wallachia and Poland.

241 b. of **Liegnitz** (p. 167): the Ger.–Pol. army of knights was defeated.

241 b. of the **Sajo river** (p. 169): the Hung. army under BELA IV was also defeated. **Europe was saved** because of the sudden retreat of the Mongols, caused by the death of the Great Khan. BATU

251 **est. the rule of the Golden Horde** (the Kipchak Empire). Russia experienced exploitation, cult. decay and isolation from Europe and the Baltic (exc. Novgorod).

251–9 The Great Khan MONGKA dispatched two armies of half a million warriors each.

258 Concentric attack of **Kublai**, Great Khan (1260–94), on s. China (p. 211).

1251–65 HULAGU conquered Persia and est. the **Empire of the Il-Khans.**

1258 Baghdad, a city of a million inhabitants, dest.; elimination of the Abbasid Caliphate; conquest of Aleppo and Damascus. The Mongol. advance was broken by the superior bravery of the Mamelukes (mercenary slaves from the Black Sea region), who est. milit. rule over Egypt (to 1517) and inflicted

1260 **the defeat of Ain Jalut** upon the Mongols (Ain Jalut = the spring of Goliath). The Empire of the Il-Khans could not be extended beyond the Euphrates. It was islamized *c.* 1300, the conquerors fusing with the culturally superior native people.

1336 Dissolution of the Il-Khan Empire into subordinate dynasties.

The 2nd Mongol. Empire (Timur)

In 1360, appealing to the Koran, the heir presumptive of GENGHIS KHAN, **Timur** (the lame) or **Tamerlane** (1336–1405), proclaimed himself renewer of the Mongol. Empire. The Jasa law, however, remained in force. Recognized as Great Khan by the empires of Jagatai and Kipchak, TIMUR subj. the Ili area from **Samarkand** in 36 cruelly conducted campaigns, then

1370–80 the Khorezm country, and after 1380, Iran and the Empire of the Golden Horde with Sarai.

1398/9 Advance into India (Delhi, p. 211). The Ottomans had to submit to him after

1402 the b. of Angora (p. 209).

1405 Death of TIMUR before the beginning of a 'Holy War' against China. Family conflicts initiated the rapid decay of the Timurid Empire. The princes driven out returned.

Iran: last unification under

1452–69 ABU SAID, the Mogul sultan, who was, however, defeated by the Turkoman 'Horde of the White Sheep'. The native Safavid Dynasty shook off the alien rule.

1500–24 ISMAIL I, crowned 1502 at Tabriz, became first Shah of the Shi'ite **New Pers. Empire** (to 1722).

The Golden Horde (the Kipchak Khanate): the Tartars were not assimilated by the Rus.–Byz. civilization and were islamized only superficially.

Nogai Khan supported the Bulgarians against Byzantium in 1265 and allied himself with the Mamelukes against the Il-Khans. Under

1266–80 Mangu-Timur the state became independent (autonomous coinage). Already decaying internally, and constantly threatened by attacks from Muscovy (p. 203),

1378 the unification with the '**White Horde**' led to an increase in the power of the state, which was, however, lost as a result of the

1390–95 **attacks by Timur**. Dissolution into the sep. Khanates of the **Crimea** (1430–1783), **Khazan** (1445–1552), **Astrachan** (1466–1556). IVAN III liberated Moscow

1480 from Tartar rule.

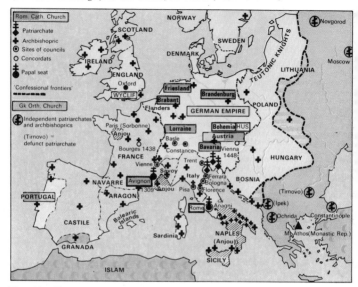

The schism (Rome/Avignon), 1378–1417

The universities up to the 15th cent.

Beginnings of the Universities

During the 12th cent. corporations of teachers and students were formed (*Universitas magisrorum et scholarium*) at monastery and cathedral schools. Grouped by nations (of itinerant students) and classified by academic degree (*Baccalaureus,* Licentiat, Magister – later doctor), these corporations were given administrative and judicial autonomy. Lectures in Lat.) and disputation were the method of instruction. **Salerno** (medicine) and **Montpellier** (law) were ancient universities. **Paris** students under the control of eccles. faculty nd the Law School of **Bologna** (sec. faculty under the control of the students) became the models. New universities were est.: (a) by migration from est. ones (Oxford, Palencia rom Paris; Padua, Siena from Bologna); (b) by imp. or papal foundations (later also by princes).

The End of Papal World Domination

The Staufers were defeated with Fr. help (p. 173). Even so,

294–1303 BONIFACE VIII demanded exemption of the Church from taxation and sec. sovereignty. Fr. jurists rejected any sort of limitation of 'the most Christ. king'. BONIFACE responded with the

302 Bull 'Unam Sanctam', which crassly spelled out the papal claims for supremacy. PHILIP IV (p. 191) planned a general council to deal with the 'simoniac and heretic'. His chancellor NOGARET confronted BONIFACE at Anagni.

303 The Pope was taken prisoner; he d. shortly after his liberation.

305–14 CLEMENS V (formerly Archbishop of Bordeaux), the first in a line of Fr. popes, manifested the dependence of the Curia on France.

309 Transfer to Avignon. Jurisdiction in the trial of the Knights Templars was 1311/12 taken from the Council of Vienne (p. 191). During the 'Babylonian Captivity' the Church lost much of its authority because of its corruption and nepotism (the appointment to offices of papal relatives).

316–34 In his conflict with the Franciscans over the question of poverty, JOHN XXII condemned the teaching of the poverty of Christ and his Apostles. Final papal interference in questions relating to the succession to the Ger. throne (p. 195):

324 excommunication of LOUIS THE BAVARIAN. Urged by St BRIDGET of Sweden (1303–73) URBAN V returned to Rome in 1367; however, it was St CATHERINE OF SIENA (p. 184) who persuaded GREGORY X in 1377 to return definitively to Rome. The Vatican became the new residence.

ecularization and Decay of the Church

Exiled in Avignon, the popes maintained an extravagant court and admin. The eccles. scal system burdened Christianity; the Curia demanded *spolia* (the personal estates of the clergy), **annates** (the annual income of an ffice), fees for confirmation in office and bestowal of the *pallium* (papal vestment bestowed on archbps); it charged fees for privileges and letters of absolution, for investitures and 'reservations' for future investitures. **Indulgences** brought ample income (absolution from purgatory, not from sin): at first they were granted conditionally (as a reward for crusades and pilgrimages); later they could be bought.

The 'Rock of Christ' was split by the dual election of URBAN VI (Rome) and CLEMENT VII (Avignon).

1378–1417 The Great Schism. Europe divided into 2 camps. Heresy and superstition (fear of witches) increased (p. 230).

The Reform Movement within the Church

To reform the Church in 'head and members', the Paris professors D'AILLY and GERSON demanded a general council. They claimed that not the Pope, but the 'totality' of the faithful represented the will of God. This **Conciliar Theory** gained support.

1409 At the Council of Pisa the cardinals of both factions elected a 3rd pope.

1414–18 The Council of Constance (33 cardinals, 900 bps, 2,000 doctors). Presided over by the Emperor, the council voted according to 4 'nations' (the Fr., Eng., Ital. and Ger.). It claimed jurisdiction over:

1. The unity of the Church (*causa unionis*): deposition of the present popes and election of MARTIN V (1417–31).
2. The reform of the Church (*causa reformationis*), which had to be postponed.
3. The purity of the teachings (*causa fidei*): despite the Emperor's safe conduct

1415 JOHN HUSS (p. 184) and HIERONYMUS OF PRAGUE (1416) were burned as heretics (p. 197). After the fruitless

1423 Council of Pavia,

1431–49 the Council of Basle resisted its dissolution by the Pope.

1433 The *compactata* of Prague: compromise with the Hussites. The reform decrees (among them, the curial fiscal system) were accepted by France by the

1438 Pragmatic Sanction, which est. the Fr. (Gallican) nat. Church. EUGENE IV (1431–47) initiated the vict. of the idea of **papal supremacy** with the

1438 opposing Council of Ferrara (after 1439 at Florence). While the extreme reformers elected FELIX V as (last) anti-pope in 1439 (to 1449), the moderates under NICHOLAS OF CUSA (p. 184) sided with EUGENE.

1439 Decree of union with the Eastern Church (p. 207). Concordats granted the princes eccles. privileges.

1448 Concordat of Vienna. FREDERICK III discontinued reforms in Germany (p. 197). PIUS II (ENEA SILVIO, p. 218) declared

1459 the Conciliar Theory heretical.

Results of the reform movement: (a) elimination of the schism; (b) failure of internal reforms; (c) strengthening of the secularized papacy (p. 217); (d) development of territ. and nat. churches.

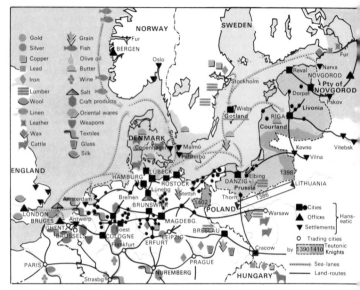

The Baltic trade, *c.* **1400**

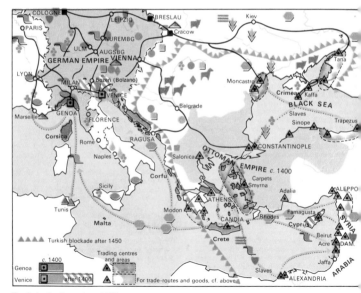

Trade in the Levant, *c.* **1400**

The Baltic Trade of the Hanseatic League

Corporate associations of Ger. merchants abroad (*Osterlinge*) had existed since the 11th cent. Their main contribution was

1150–1250 to est. an econ. sphere of the countries surrounding the Baltic Sea. Their *Koggen* (100 gross register tons) were superior to the oared Scand. vessels.

1161 A Ger. **Hanse** (group) est. at **Wisby.** As the ancient practice of itinerant trade was replaced by modern methods (book-keeping, sales on credit and commissions), trade activity shifted to **Lübeck** (founded 1158), which became the transit port for E.–W. trade and the port of embarkation for emigrants to Livonia and Prussia.

1259 Trade league of Lübeck, Hamburg, Wismar, Rostock. General union

1358 in the **League 'van der düdeschen hanse'** (= of the German Hanse) to secure trading advantages: the right to provide storage for their own goods; the obligation on the part of other merchants to maintain an adequate store of goods, and other privileges. The most effective weapon was the **Verhansung** (boycott of the goods of a port or a country), which was decided at league meetings (**Hansetage**) of the **cities.** They were organized in **quarters** according to region; individual cities were in control of subordinate cities (called *Vororte* = 'suburbs'). The Wendish quarter, with Lübeck as its head, became the leading quarter. The rather loosely organized league did not have a constitution; its membership (over 200 cities) changed periodically. Foreign offices (**Kontore**): Novgorod (Peterhof); London (Steelyard); Bergen (German Bridge) *et al.*; annual herring markets at Schonen (Falsterbo). Its main enemy was Denmark:

1361–2 WALDEMAR IV (p. 199) defeated the Hanse. Allied with Mecklenburg, Holstein, Jutland and **Cologne,**

1367–70 victorious counter-attack.

1370 Peace of Stralsund: election of the Dan. king only with the approval of the Hanse. Struggle against pirates (**Vitalienbrüder,** also *Likendeeler* = 'equalizers'), who

1389–95 supplied Stockholm, which was under siege, with food (*vitalia*) and plundered Wisby in 1392.

1402 Vict. by Hamburg at Heligoland and execution of leader KLAUS STÖRTEBECKER. After renewed war with Denmark (1420–35)

1435 peace of Vordingborg: the Wendish cities were freed from the Dan. **customs duty** imposed on the **Sound.**

1468–74 Support for the Eng. pretender EDWARD IV (p. 189) in exchange for confirmation of trading privileges. In 1470 Denmark was forced to prohibit Dutch and Eng. navigation in the Sound.

15th/16th cents. Decline of the Hanse because of: (a) the strengthening of the northern nat. states following the Union of Kalmar in 1397 (Sweden, p. 199; Russia, p. 203); (b) the migrating herring failing to return to the North Sea; (c) trade shifting to the Atlantic seaboard (p. 225).

1494 Closing of the Peterhof in Novgorod.

1598 Closing of the Steelyard in London.

The Levant Trade of Venice and Genoa

From the 11th cent., Arab. domination of the Mediterranean was disrupted by the *Reconquista* (p. 187) and the Crusades (p. 153). Trade with the w. fell to Genoa, Pisa, Naples; the eastern Levant trade to Sicily and Venice. Silk, brocade, damask and Gaaze materials, cotton, camelhair, ivory, porcelain, dyes, spices, perfumes, medicine, pearls and precious stones were desirable **orient. goods.** They came to the Levant *via* the Asiatic caravan routes (Silk Road) controlled by the Arabs, or by the Ind. Ocean trade, and were exchanged for textiles and other products of the Eur. provinces engaged in crafts (Milan, Florence, s. Germany, Flanders, Brabant).

The city-republics of Venice and Genoa gained wealth and power through: (a) carrier business during the Crusades; (b) increased demand for currency (deposit and credit banking); (c) experience in the Byz. and Arab. trade; (d) the collapse of Sicily (p. 173) and the decline of Byzantium (p. 207).

Both trading powers suffered owing to the Ott. advance; at first they avoided war and negotiated for privileges. Their importance declined with the shift of trade to the Atlantic seaboard (p. 225).

Venice: because of its key position between w. (control of the Alp. passes) and E. (connection with Byzantium, p. 175), the aristocratic republic became the **foremost naval and trading power.** The Venet. silver pennies (*denarius grossus: Groschen* = Ger. 10-cent piece), coined at the end of the 12th cent., and the gold coins (*ducatus Venetiae*) coined c. 1280, were internationally accepted.

1192–1205 The Doge Enrico Dandolo assumed the transportation of the 4th Crusade and, with the establishment of the Lat. Empire (p. 207), obtained harbours and bases of support between the Adriatic and the Black Seas, which, in part, became the 'principality of the *Nobili*'. The competition of Genoa was eliminated

1376–81 in the War of Chioggia. Food supply in Italy was secured against Milan by

1406–28 the construction of the **Terra Firma.**

Genoa: liberation with Pisa of the Western Mediterranean from the Isl. blockade.

1261 Extension of Genoan infl. to the Levant (Kaffa, Tana), allied with the Nicaean Empire; later trade rivalry with Venice.

1284 Vict. over Pisa: Corsica, Elba, Sardinia (until 1326) fell to Genoa. Feuds of the noble Doria, Fieschi, Grimaldi and Spinola families led

1339 to their being excluded from the position of the Doge.

1381 Defeat in the '100 Yrs War' with Venice. Polit. dependence on Milan or France.

1407 Establishment of the Casa di San Giorgio, the first public bank of Europe. Combating econ. decline, Gen. sailors participated in the discovery of the sea-route to India.

Late Scholasticism
Scholasticism found its poetic symbol in the relig. epic of the Florentine **Dante Alighieri** (1265–1321). In the *Divina Commedia* (**Divine Comedy**, 1311–21) the creator of lit. Italian traced the journey from hell (*Inferno*) to paradise as a vision of a universal last judgement.
Thomists (*via antiqua:* Dominicans) and **Scotists** (*via moderna:* Franciscans) combated each other within the scholastic movement. The conflict of the Spirituals (extreme minorities) with the Curia over the question of poverty had a fragmenting infl. In 1323, JOHN XXII declared the concept of Christ's earthly poverty (the ideal of St FRANCIS OF ASSISI, p. 141) to be heretical. The superior of the Order, MICHAEL OF CESENA, and WILLIAM OF OCCAM and others escaped papal captivity by fleeing to LOUIS THE BAVARIAN (p. 195). In the '*Defensor pacis*' ('Defender of the peace', 1324) LOUIS's adviser, **Marsilius of Padua**, advocated (with JOHN OF JANDUN) a purely sec. conception of the state: popular sovereignty, separation of Church and state, superiority of a council over the Pope (p. 181). **Roger Bacon** (1214–94) cal. for a critical examination of scholastic teaching authorities (ARISTOTLE), and a less restricted observation of nature through experimentation and experience.
The most important spokesman for the 'modernists' was **William of Occam** (*c.* 1285–1349). A pupil of DUNS SCOTUS, he regarded general concepts (*universalia*) only as 'names' (*nomina*) without real existence. **Nominalism** sharply distinguished unprovable truths of the faith, which were considered manifestations of the Divine Will, from knowledge (cognition). JOHN BURIDAN (d. 1358) and the naturalist philosopher NICHOLAS OF ORESME (d. 1382), who accepted the theory of the rotation of the earth around its axis and made mathematical calculations of its movements, belonged to the Paris school of the Occamists. Although the advocates of the *via moderna* and nominalism stimulated philosophical and theological reconsiderations, they spent themselves in petty conflicts.
All the intellectual currents of the time were embraced by **Nicholas of Cusa** (*Cusanus,* i.e. Krebs = cancer, 1401–64). His major work, *De docta ignorantia (Of learned Ignorance,* 1440) overcame scholasticism. The infinite universe has no centre (the earth), nor can it be comprehended rationally; each religion reflects a facet of Divine Truth. Religion can conceive of God only relatively because He incorporates all contradictions within Himself (*coincidentia oppositorum*). NICHOLAS's suggestions for a new calendar were based on his unprecedented astronomic researches, continued by his pupil, COPERNICUS (p. 221).

Mysticism
As a reaction to rationalistic scholasticism and the secularization of the Church, mysticism was an attempt (Gk *mystein* = to close one's eyes) to experience God through internal vision ('vision', contemplation) and to sub-

merge oneself in Him (*unio mystica*). The movement was stimulated by Neo-Platonism (which became known through the works of the Arab. philosophers AVICENNA and AVERROËS, p. 149), and the writings of DIONYSIUS AREOPAGITA (*c.* 500) and AUGUSTINE (p. 107). BERNARD OF CLAIRVAUX (1090–1153), HUGH OF ST VICTOR (d. 1141), HILDEGARD OF BINGEN (d. 1179), and MECHTHILD OF MAGDEBURG (d. 1280) were early mystics. St Catherine of Siena (1347–80) caused Pope GREGORY IX to return to Rome from Avignon (p. 181).
Embraced by the Dominicans and practised in convents and cloisters, mysticism was growing more intense esp. in Germany. The 'un-becoming' of man was taught by **Meister Eckart** (d. 1327) in (Ger.) writings and sermons; he conceived of the 'spark of the soul' as fusing with God in seclusion. His work influenced the Dutchman RUYSBROEK (1293–1381), JOHN TAULER (1300–61) and HEINRICH SEUSE (1295–1366), the lyric poet of Ger. mysticism.

The New Piety (Devotio Moderna)
Movements to internalize existence developed under the infl. of mysticism: the '**Friends of God**' (monks, urban dwellers and nobles along the upper Rhine), led by TAULER and the merchant RULMAN MERSWIN, wanted to 'undo' their worldliness through 'composure and tranquillity'. Most important tract: *Theologia deutsch* (*c.* 1400). Stimulated by GERT GROOTE (1340–84) clerics and laymen, without taking formal vows, joined as **Brethren of the Common Life** to study scripture and to conduct missions and schools. The major work of the circle, *De imitatione Christi* (*The Imitation of Christ*), attr. to THOMAS À KEMPIS (i.e. HAMERKEN, 1380–1471), gained wide distribution.
The Dutch **Beginen movement** was a precursor of lay activity: community (resembling an Order) of women (or men, the *Beghards* = Dutch for beggars) who aspired to an ascetic relig. life in the service of their neighbour. Exaggerated forms of asceticism manifested themselves *c.* 1350 in broad segments of the pop. as a consequence of the plague (p. 154): the flagellants roamed through Hungary, cen. Europe, England and Sweden; *c.* 1400 through the Lat. countries.

Reform Movements outside the Church
Opposed to the papacy and to the papal Church dominated by the clergy on nat. and relig. grounds, the **Lollards** (p. 189) spread in England. They were followers of the Oxford professor **John Wyclif** (d. 1384), who accepted nothing but the Bible as authority for Christ. dogma and ritual. For this reason he translated the Bible (*Vulgata*), denounced the hierarchy, celibacy, indulgences and the teaching of the Eucharist and demanded a nat. church founded on 'Christian poverty'. His teachings were suppressed in England; taught by the priest **John Huss,** they found new adherents in Bohemia (p. 181). HUSS's martyrdom and the excommunication of the **Hussites** (p. 197) caused nat., relig. and soc. crises for the Czechs.

Urban Life in the Middle Ages
Fortified customs and trading sites for long-distance trade in luxury goods (carried on by merchant guilds under royal protection) had existed since Frankish days (*Wiks*). With the econ. recovery of Europe during the 11th cent. (increase in pop. and trade, and the division of labour according to trades), the **castle (Burg)** became the **city** with **citizens** (burgess, bourgeois, *Bürger*). **Towns founded** by kings, bps and princes, or resulting from 'unplanned growth' ('wild roots'), added to the est. urban settlements (*Rom.* settlements, ancient sites of palaces, castles or bpcs). The growth of a city depended on its advantageous econ. and geographical location at the intersection of land, sea and river routes. In spite of the urban migration of rural craftsmen, a city was, above all, a **settlement of merchants with a permanent market** for the exchange of consumer goods (urban economy). Market days, usually connected with holy days, were important for the **guilds'** long-distance trade (Hanse, p. 183). ₃ne founders promoted the growth of the cities through **privileges** (liberties: 'City air makes free'). Expecting ample revenues, they surrendered sovereign rights (such as the ones to hold market, to fortify the city, coinage, and customs – *regalia*). The city became the most important source of revenue for the lord, who was represented by an overseer (*Vogt, Burggraf* (*castellan*), *Schultheiss*). **Urban privileges** (market, trade, and later rents, police, defence, finance, etc.) developed into **urban gvt** (urban courts and admin.) with councils chaired by officials (*podesta, Bürgermeister, maire,* mayor). Noble or prosperous families (**patricians**) played a major role.
Craft guilds, mandatory associations designed to control, plan and guide the production of the crafts (quality, price, distribution, profits) and to supervise the training, employment and social welfare of the craftsmen, developed in the 12th cent. In **struggles** with the patricians, these guilds (14th/15th cents.) often gained a share in the gvt of the cities.
The cities strove to increase their liberties and to extend their territ. sovereignty. Cities were classified acc. to the degree of their liberties:
1. Politically aut. cities: *communes* (sovereign city republics, p. 183) and *signoria* (p. 217) in Italy; consular cities in Provence; *free imp. cities* in Germany, and industrial centres in Flanders, Artois and Picardy.
2. Cities with limited self-admin.: royal cities in Western and Eastern Europe, cities of territ. states in Germany.
Importance: the law, the econ. life, the ctr. and the administrative organization of the cities gave direction to the development of the modern nat. or territ. state, which in turn developed the urban form of the **princely residence** as a centre of gvt and civilization.

The Ger. Territ. States
The impetus to the formation of 'states within the state' was rooted in the 'immunities', the feudal system, and the politics of the Empire. Steps in the development of territ.

princely sovereignty: mandatory investiture and the hered. character of fiefs; the transfer of Imp. privileges (*regalia*), esp. by **the decrees of 1220 and 1232** (p. 173) **governing the relationship of the Emperor to the princes;** the independence of territ. courts from the Empire during the Interregnum; the acceptance of complete jurisdiction and sovereignty of the electors in the **Golden Bull of 1356** (p. 195). **The Peace of Westphalia** (p. 255) granted complete polit. sovereignty to the estates.
Significance: the territ. states of the princes replaced the states based on personal ties, dissolved the Ger. Empire, determined the federal structure of Germany to the present. **Administration:** feudal offices (through which the princes had risen to power) were replaced by a system of uniform distticts administered by appointed *ministeriales* (later bureaucrats (*Vogts, prefects,* caretakers)). They were supervised by the state-wide centralized admin. with court offices controlled by the chancellor. From the 13th cent., the princes surrounded themselves with trained jurists (*counsellors*).
Areas 'immune' or exclusively subject to imp. authority existed within the territ. states (monasteries, cities, the territories of imp. knights, etc.). The policy of the princes therefore always aimed at rounding out their territories through territ. exchanges, purchases, the establishment of dependencies, inheritance and marriage contracts, and feuds.
The judicial system developed only gradually. It became a coherent organization headed by the High Court which was loc. at the prince's residence (Court of Appeals). Upper territ. courts (permanent courts of the nobility) and lower territ. courts existed side by side with local market, village, mining and other courts. To overcome the proliferation of legal systems and the increasingly materialistic nature of legal findings, but also because of new legal problems (e.g. the new methods of money exchange), the '**reception**' of the Rom. Law – taught at universities – became general. Considering it alien, the people rejected it (p. 233).
The fiscal system: based on eccles. or urban precedents, regular taxes (*stiura* = aid, Ger. *Steuern*) were levied, collected by tax-collectors in accordance with tax-rolls (therefore family names) and spent to sustain court, officials, judges and mercenaries, and to develop the country. An important source of revenue was the granting of **privileges** (customs, coinage, mining) to cities or corporations (p. 215); **Bede** (= Ger. request: *Bitte*) and **Ungeld** (direct and indirect taxes).
Estates: polit. participation in the gvt of the state and privileges (the right to hold special courts, exemption from taxation) were secured by noble landowners (knights), the upper clergy, and the cities at **territ. diets** at which they were granted the **right to levy taxes.** These forces strengthened their power during the 14th/15th cents., by alliances (against the prince; at times they had their own troops, admin. and fiscal systems). The result was a **dualistic estate–state** system that functioned up to the 17th cent.

The Spanish Reconquista

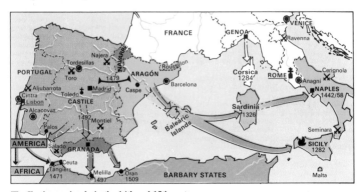

The Iberian peninsula in the 14th and 15th cents.

The Christ. Border States

Minor independent states continued to exist in Northern Spain:

The kdm of Navarre: SANCHO III (1000–35) in 1029 inherited the county of **Castile** and divided the kdm into Aragón, Castile and Navarre (in the Fr. power sphere from 1234).

The County of Barcelona developed as an outgrowth of the Sp. march of CHARLEMAGNE (p. 123).

The kdm of Asturia (also cal. **León**). After the wars of the Caliph ABD AR-RAHMAN III (912–61), the Vizier **al-Mansur** (the Victor) overran the states, weakened by disputes, in 978.

The Reconquista, 1085–1340

1008–28 Major civil war of the Arabs (dissolution of the Omayyad Caliphate); beginning of the Christ. assaults.

The Cluniacs strengthened the nat. Orders of knights and brought the Church into close contact with Rome. Popes (GREGORY VII, INNOCENT III) supported the Crusades by propaganda and funds; Orders of knights (Knights Templars, Knights of St John, p. 153) rendered aid.

Aragón: ALFONSO I THE WARRIOR (1104–34) conquered Saragossa in 1118.

1137 Union with Catalonia. Completion of the *Reconquista* (exc. Granada, see below) with the

1229–35 seizure of the Balearic Islands and (1238) Valencia by JAMES I (1213–76).

1276–85 Under PETER III Aragón extended its grasp to Italy; after the

1282 Sicil. Vespers (p. 173), he obtained **Sicily.** Under JAMES II (1286–1327) a compromise with the papal feudal lord was reached in the

1295 peace of Anagni. Another war over Sicily was terminated without papal approval.

1323–5 Struggles with Pisa and Genoa over **Sardinia** and Corsica. The 'union' of the nobility dominated the state. It granted the succession in Aragón to FERDINAND OF CASTILE.

Portugal: the county around Porto in

1094 obtained independence. After the vict. of

1139 Ourique, ALFONSO I proclaimed himself king. Rapid expansion to the s.

1179 Papal recognition of the kdm.

1279–1325 DINIZ (DIONYSIUS I) THE WORKER promoted development through forestry, mining, trade and navigation. Succession struggles with Castile until the

1385 vict. of Aljubarrota. After the accession of JOHN I (1385–1433) to the throne, extension to Africa:

1415 conquest of Ceuta (p. 243).

Castile: FERDINAND I THE GREAT (1035–65) obtained León in 1037.

1085 Conquest of Toledo. The hero of the struggle was RODRIGO DÍAZ, cal. **El Cid** (Arab.: Lord). He entered the Moors' service, becoming master of Valencia in 1094.

1126–57 ALFONSO VII – as Emperor – exercised sovereignty over all the Christ. states of the Iberian peninsula; however, this union was of short duration.

1185 The defeat of Alarcos again brought about a new coalition. After the

1212 vict. of Navas de Tolosa, the Almohad state (in existence since 1145) dissolved.

1217–52 FERDINAND III THE SAINT conquered the s., incl. Córdoba (1236), and completed the *Reconquista.*

Granada: the last Arab. state on the Eur. continent experienced a period of cult. brilliance during the 14th cent. (the Alhambra).

The Results of the Reconquista

The *Moriscos* (converted Moors) were not entirely deprived of their rights, but were settled in sep. districts of the cities. Jews enjoyed the protection of the law in exchange for fees; slavery increased (Moors, N. Africans). Royal officials guided Christ. settlement. The high nobility (grandees), politically represented in the *Cortes*, opposed the monarchy (and the reception of Rom. law). Feuds that led to the dissolution of the state (Castile) ensued. The crown was backed by the cities, which, granted sovereignty over urban provinces, formed leagues (*Hermandades*).

Church and civilization: strong infl. of the well-endowed Church (Franciscans, Dominicans); Goth. architecture (the cathedrals of Toledo and Burgos); infl. on the new universities of Arab. science (mathematics, medicine, philosophy).

The Development of the Sp. State

The mar. of the 'Cath. monarchs' (1469)

1474–1506 Isabella of Castile and

1479–1516 Ferdinand II of Aragón initiated a new epoch.

1474–9 The Castil. War of Succession against France and Portugal. The latter was

1476 defeated in the b. of Toro.

1479 Peace of Alcacovas: **union of Castile and Aragón;** both states for the time being retained their special institutions.

Castile: the fact that the king held the hered. dignity of the grand master over the Orders of knights strengthened the crown; development of a modern state through legal reforms, service obligations of the nobility and urban militias; the grandees were deprived of power and obliged to serve at the court. A **royal council** (jurists) and urban commissioners governed the state.

Church: although its privileges were acknowledged, the absolute primacy of the crown was preserved. Cardinal XIMENEZ DE CISNEROS (1436–1517), Archbishop of Toledo, reformed the clergy.

1481 Renewal of the Inquisition. Under the Grand Inquisitor TORQUEMADA (1483–98), Spain became a country of relig. fanatics, where agricultural work and the crafts were considered labours unworthy of a Christian. Expulsion of the Jews and Moriscos after the

1492 conquest of Granada. Attacks on N. Africa: conquest of Medilla, 1497; of Oran, 1509.

1496 Archduke PHILIP THE FAIR mar. JOANNA THE MAD. Their son CHARLES succeeded to the Sp. inheritance in 1516 (p. 237).

Battles of the Wars of the Roses (1272–1485)

Peasant revolt (Wat Tyler) 1381 (Lollards)

★ **Universities**

SHETLAND ISLANDS
Scottish 1468

HEBRIDES

Highlands

(Gaelic clans)

SCOTLAND

Perth Scone
Dumbarton Stirling St Andrews
Bannockburn Falkirk Edinburgh
1316 1306–29 1314 Berwick
Hedgeley
1405
Hexham
Carlisle

ULSTER

Belfast

1317/40
CONNAUGHT

PALE
1494
Dublin

KILDARE

IRELAND

Waterford

Cork

Caernarvon
Shrewsbury
1278–84
WALES
1400–8
Milford Haven
HENRY VII
1485

1399
LANCASTER
1296 York
Towton
Wakefield

Blore Heath
Bosworth
Ludlow Lutterworth Stamford
Warwick Northampton
Edgecote Cambridge
Tewkesbury Oxford St Albans
Redcot Bridge Eton Tower of London
Barnet London

Southampton

Hundred Years War 1339–1453

The British Isles in the 14th and 15th cents.

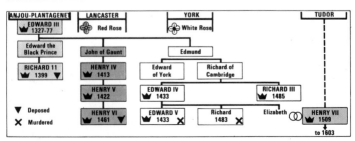

ANJOU-PLANTAGENET	LANCASTER	YORK		TUDOR
EDWARD III 1327–77	⚜ Red Rose	⚜ White Rose		
Edward the Black Prince	John of Gaunt	Edmund		
RICHARD II 1399 ▼	HENRY IV 1413	Edward of York	Richard of Cambridge	
	HENRY V 1422	EDWARD IV 1433	RICHARD III 1485	
	HENRY VI 1461 ▼	EDWARD V 1433 ✕	Richard 1483 ✕	Elizabeth ∞ HENRY VII 1509 ▼
▼ Deposed ✕ Murdered				to 1603

The struggle for the English crown

Domestic and Foreign Policy under Edward I
1272–1307 Edward I strengthened the crown by reforms.
1290 Expulsion of the Jews; their privileges were granted to foreign merchants (the Hanse). Two campaigns led to the annexation of
1284 Wales (Celt.), which became the principality of the Eng. crown prince (from 1301 Prince of Wales).
Scotland: conflicts over the succession of the throne after the extinction of the royal family. Recognized as overlord, EDWARD I appointed JOHN BALLIOL (1292–6) ruler. Later on EDWARD claimed the throne for himself and occupied the country.
1297 Popular uprising: WILLIAM WALLACE, the nat. hero (*c.* 1270–1305), was victorious at Stirling. Defeated at Falkirk, he continued to skirmish without the nobility. In
1304 the nobility had deserted the cause. WALLACE was executed.
1306–29 Robert Bruce obtained nat. independence for the people by his vict. in the
1314 b. of Bannockburn. ROBERT II est. the
1371–1714 Stuart Dynasty.

England during the Hundred Years War
1327–77 Edward III began the
1339 war with France and initially was militarily successful (p. 191); however, a shortage of funds made concessions to Parliament necessary. A severe econ. crisis was brought about
1349/50 by the **Black Death** (p. 154).
1369 Resumption of the war by EDWARD THE BLACK PRINCE.
1377–99 Prolonged conflicts over the throne began under RICHARD II. Setbacks in France, the introduction of a head-tax, and dislike of the corrupt gvt (JOHN OF LANCASTER) brought about the great
1381 Peasant Uprising of WAT TYLER and JOHN BALL, which collapsed after an assault on London. RICHARD II was deposed by Parliament because of his despotic rule.
1399–1413 HENRY IV and the **House of Lancaster** asserted himself against the high nobility, but only after difficulties.
1403/5 Revolts of the nobility in the N. (HENRY PERCY, cal. HOTSPUR). The king was aided by the clergy (persecution of the Lollards, the followers of WYCLIF). To divert attention
1413–22 HENRY V renewed the war with France in 1415; it ended in failure (p. 191). Still, the Hundred Years War strengthened Eng. nat. consciousness; Eng. ctr. became distinct from the Fr.
1362 Introduction of Eng. as official language in courts of law.
1387 Beginnings of a distinctively Eng. literature with the *Canterbury Tales* of **Chaucer** (1340–1400).
The Church: 'Fr. popes' and the fiscal claims of the Curia were rejected.
1351 Statute of Provisors: the granting of papal benefices and legal appeals to the Curia were prohibited (1353 Statute of *Praemunire*). JOHN WYCLIF, professor at

Oxford, struggled against the secularization of the Church (p. 184).
1380 1st Eng. translation of the Bible by WYCLIF.
The law: judicial cases that until then had been processed orally were collected from the time of EDWARD I. the 'Eng. Justinian', in 1292 in the 'Yearbooks'; thus Eng. law (common law) developed as customary law.
1327 Justices of the Peace, drawn from the gentry (lower nobility) with police and judicial authority (foundation of Eng. local admin.), were appointed to serve alongside sheriffs (royal county officials).
Parliament: SIMON DE MONTFORT (p. 161) expanded the Council of the Barons by 2 knights per county and 2 burgesses per city and created
1265 the 1st Parliament.
1295 The Model Parliament made the exception the rule under EDWARD I, since the gentry and the cities levied the taxes and the king needed their approval. The **Commons** (representatives of the communities) met jointly with the barons.
1297 Confirmation of the right of Parliament to approve taxation and customs duties. Parliamentary petitions approved by the king became law (legislative initiative). After the time of EDWARD III, convocation at regular intervals and gradual separation into a **House of Lords** (supreme court) and a **House of Commons** (lower house).
Milit. affairs: the yeoman (free peasant) carried the newly invented weapon, the longbow. War became the concern of all the people ('companies' were recruited from all classes). Enriched by the wool trade, the barons during the 14th/15th cents. purchased partisans in the conflicts over the throne.
1455–85 The Wars of the Roses between the houses of Lancaster and York. Public law and gvt were completely disorganized. 'Companies' of the Fr. war provided the soldiers; the people were hardly disturbed. The growth of commerce and the crafts continued; the position of Parliament was weakened because of bribery. In his position as regent RICHARD OF YORK claimed the crown; he arrested the mad
1422–61 HENRY VI. However, RICHARD d. in
1460 b. of Wakefield.
1461 The vict. of Towton gained the throne for
1461–83 Edward IV of York. RICHARD NEVILLE, Earl of Warwick ('Warwick the Kingmaker'), restored HENRY to the throne. But Warwick d. in
1471 b. of Barnet. HENRY and the adherents of the House of Lancaster were murdered. After the death of EDWARD
1483 RICHARD III (d. 1485) usurped the throne by, it was said, having his nephews EDWARD V (12 yrs of age) and RICHARD strangled in the Tower.
1485–1509 After landing in Wales, HENRY VII, heir of the House of Lancaster, defeated RICHARD in the
1485 b. of Bosworth and founded the strong monarchy of the **House of Tudor** (to 1603).

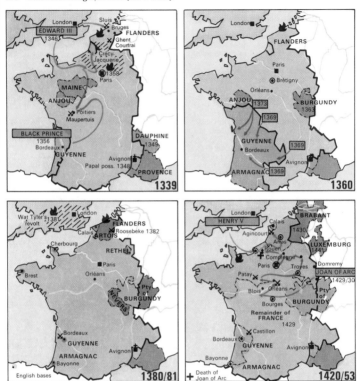

The Hundred Years War in France

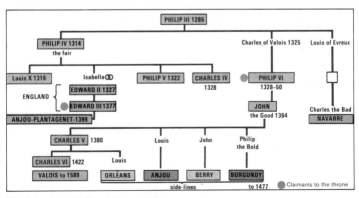

The claimants to the French throne, 1328

The Development of the Fr. Nat. State

1285–1314 PHILIP IV THE FAIR strengthened the monarchy by his prudent financial policies: establishment of a treasury (*Chambres de comptes*); exchange of feudal service obligations for money payments for the recruitment of mercenary knights; persecution and

1307 dissolution of the Knights Templars; their fortune was confiscated by the 'forger-king'. He compelled the Pope to

1309 transfer the papal residence to Avignon (p. 181), and expanded the estates of the crown in the E. by the addition of Champagne and other areas.

1297 Occupation of Flanders. Orientated towards England because of its imports of wool, this industrial area, with its prosperous urban civilization, defended itself. Urban dwellers for the first time defeated an army of knights in the

1302 b. of the Spurs at Courtrai. After confirmation of his Fr. royal fief of Guyenne (Aquitaine) in the

1303 Treaty of Paris EDWARD I of England ceased to support Flanders, which had to submit to PHILIP in 1305.

The dualism between the Fr. monarchy and its strongest vassal reached a crisis when

1328 the Capetian family became extinct with the death of CHARLES IV. According to the Salic Law (male succession) the

1328–1498 House of Valois succeeded. EDWARD III advanced claims against

1328–50 PHILIP VI. Although EDWARD pledged the oath of fealty, he attempted to utilize an anti-Fr. uprising in Flanders. The

1339–1453 Hundred Years War began with the victories of the Eng. people's army (archers and 'bombards' (early cannons)) over the Fr. levies of knights. The French were hindered from establishing a corresponding army in that they lacked:

1. Fixed taxes: hence there was frequent dilution of the coinage and convocation of the Estates General (**États-Généraux**).

2. Adequate yields from the land: from 1348 the Black Death precipitated econ. crises (p. 154); the first mercenaries (Armagnacs) plundered to provide for themselves and became a plague upon the country.

3. A sense of nat. consciousness: king and *seigneurs* exerted themselves only on behalf of their own estates.

1346 Defeat at Crécy. After a heroic defence by its citizens

1347 Calais fell; it became the basis of operations for the Eng. armies until 1559. The Fr. crown prince obtained

1349 Dauphiné (hence the title of Dauphin) by inheritance. The **Black Prince**'s vict. and JOHN THE GOOD's capture in the

1356 b. of **Maupertuis** plunged France into severe internal struggles.

1358 Paris uprising (ÉTIENNE MARCEL). The estates demanded that the Dauphin surrender control over the royal admin.

1358 The Peasant Uprising (*Jacquerie* der. from Jacques Bonhomme = 'good James'), caused

by the burden of taxation and corvées. Both risings were suppressed by the nobility.

1360 Peace of Brétigny: EDWARD III abandoned claims to the Fr. crown in exchange for sovereignty over south-western France.

1364–80 CHARLES V THE WISE. War was renewed in 1369. Avoiding major battles the French weakened the Eng. enemy in skirmishes (BERTRAND DU GUESCLIN) and forced them back to a few fortified bases. But after 1378 there was unrest in the heavily taxed Flanders cities (PHILIP VAN ARTE-VELDE). The citizens were defeated in the

1382 b. of Roosebeke. PHILIP II OF BURGUNDY, the victor, received Flanders (p. 193).

Struggles for power between the Dukes of Burgundy and Orléans – who had been appointed regents for the mad king CHARLES VI – and their supporting factions, the Cabochiens (the guilds of Paris) and the Armagnacs (mercenaries of the Count of Armagnac) brought about another crisis of state after the English had again landed.

1415 b. of Agincourt: Normandy and Paris were occupied; Burgundy allied with England; HENRY V was given a share in the gvt of France. However, the Armagnacs and the clergy proclaimed the Dauphin king.

1422–61 CHARLES VII lost the crown lands around Paris. At this point the 'Maid of Orléans' came to the rescue. **Jeanne d'Arc** (*c*. 1412–31), a peasant girl from Domrémy in Lorraine, followed her divine inspiration, traversed France and, through her faith, stimulated a nat. spirit of resistance which forced the English to

1429 raise the siege of Orléans; she escorted CHARLES VII to Reims to be anointed. Captured near Compiègne by the Burgundians and surrendered to the English, the nat. heroine was condemned as a heretic by the Inquisition and

30 May 1431 burned at the stake in Rouen. 1456 revocation of the judgement; 1920 canonization.

1435 Treaty of Arras: reconciliation of the king with Burgundy (p. 193);

1436 conquest of Paris. The Fr. unitary state now received its foundations.

1438 The Pragmatic Sanction of Bourges (p. 181): the **Gallican Church** est. Regular revenues to pay for the standing army to come from the yields of the crownlands;

1439 introduction of a direct property and head-tax (*taille royale*), from which the nobility, the clergy and the citizens of certain cities were exempted.

1449–53 Invasion of Normandy and Guyenne; the war petered out after the

1453 Fr. vict. of Castillon.

Results: despite the great power still wielded by the 'Princes of the Blood' (side-lines of the royal house), the war brought about the development of the nat. state. CHARLES THE BOLD remained a threat to

1461–83 LOUIS XI until 1477.

1483–98 CHARLES VIII began the Ital. wars in

1494 because of the claims of the house of Anjou to Naples (p. 219).

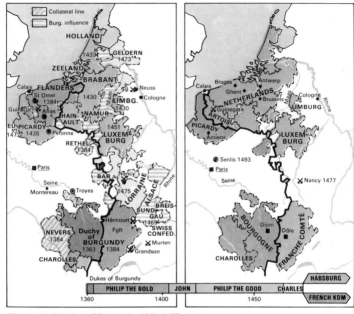

The interim kingdom of Burgundy, 1363–1477

Key labels (left map): Collateral line / Burg. influence

HOLLAND
GELDERN 1473
ZEELAND
BRABANT
1433
Calais · St Omer · FLANDERS
Guinegate 1384 · Neuss × · Cologne
Arras 1430 · LIMBG. 1430
EU 1472 · PICARDY 1435 · HAIN-AULT · NAMUR 1451
Péronne · LUXEM-BURG
RETHEL 1384?
BAR · Nancy
Paris · Seine
Montereau · Troyes
NEVERS 1384 · Duchy of BURGUNDY 1363 · 1384
CHAROLLES
Héricourt × · Fgft
ALSACE · BREIS-GAU · SUNDGAU 1469 · SWISS CONFED. × Murten × Grandson 1475
Dukes of Burgundy

(Right map):
Calais · Bruges · Antwerp · Ghent · NETHERLANDS · Brussels · Cologne
Guinegate · ARTOIS · LIMBURG
PICARDY · Amiens · LUXEM-BURG
Senlis 1493 · Paris · Seine · Nancy 1477 ×
BOURGOGNE · Dijon · Dôle · FRANCHE COMTÉ
CHAROLLES
HABSBURG · FRENCH KDM

Timeline: PHILIP THE BOLD — JOHN — PHILIP THE GOOD — CHARLES
1360 — 1400 — 1450

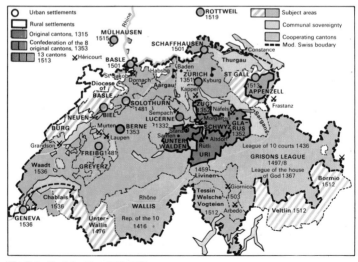

The Swiss Confederation, 1315–1513

Legend:
○ Urban settlements
□ Rural settlements
Original cantons, 1315
Confederation of the 8 original cantons, 1353
13 cantons 1513
Subject areas
Communal sovereignty
Cooperating cantons
--- Mod. Swiss boundary

Labels:
ROTTWEIL 1519
MÜLHAUSEN 1515
Rhine
SCHAFFHAUSEN 1501
Thurgau · Constance
BASLE 1501 · St Jakob · Habsbg · Baden · ZÜRICH 1351 · ST GALL
Diocese of BASLE · Dornach · Aargau · Kyburg · 1513 APPENZELL × Frastanz
SOLOTHURN 1481 · Sempach 1386 · Kappel · ZUG 1352 · Näfels × Sargans
NEUEN-BURG · BIEL · Murten · BERNE 1353 · LUCERNE 1332 · Morgarten · GLA-RUS 1352 · Altdorf
Grandson × · Laupen · Stans · SCHWYZ · Rütli · URI
FREIBG 1481 · UNTER-WALDEN · Samen
Waadt 1536 · GREYERZ · League of 10 courts 1436 · GRISONS LEAGUE 1497/8 · League of the house of God 1367 · Bormio 1512
Chablais 1536 · Rhône · 1459 · Livinen · Tessin Welsche Vogteien 1512 · Veltlin 1512
GENEVA 1536 · Unter-Wallis 1476 · WALLIS · Rep. of the 10 1416 · Giornico 1503 · Arbedo · Veltlin 1512

The Swiss Confederation (1291–1513)

After the extinction of the Zähringen family (1218), the Alp. Swiss region disintegrated into small, politically aut. territories. While enlarging their territ. sovereignty (connecting their possessions on the Upper Rhine with Tirol) the Habsburgs encountered after 1278 the resistance of the peasants of **Schwyz** (which had come under the immediate jurisdiction of the Empire since 1231) and Uri (1240) (p. 195). The **3 original cantons** – incl. Unterwalden – joined

1291 in the 'Eternal Union' to protect their liberties. (The 'Oath of the Rütli', Gessler's 'hat', and Tell's target of the 'apple' belong to legend.) The **confederation** was recognized by the enemies of the Habsburgs (ADOLF OF NASSAU, 1297; HENRY VII, 1309). The peasants repulsed the attack of an army of knights under LEOPOLD I of Austria in the

1315 b. of Morgarten.

1332 Lucerne became the first urban settlement to join the confederation, which

1353 expanded into the 'Confederation of the 8 original cantons'. The popular levy of the Swiss was victorious in the 'War of the Cities' in the

1386 b. of Sempach.

1415 Conquest of the Habsburg Aargau, which became the first Swiss subject area; expansion to the s. to control the passes to Italy continued until the

1422 defeat at Arbedo. Cooperation between the rural cantons (peasants) and the urban cantons (patricians, guilds) was endangered by the conflict between Schwyz and Zürich.

1440–46 The 1st ('Old') War of Zürich: the city allied itself with the Emperor FREDERICK III, who brought the undisciplined Fr. Armagnacs into the country (p. 191); a compromise between the confederation and France was reached, however, despite the

1444 defeat of St Jakob on the Birs. Zürich now again joined the confederation; the city and chapter of St Gallen joined in 1451 as cooperating cantons ('*zugewandte Orte*' = cantons 'turned to' the confederation).

The Habsburgs subs. lost their possessions (Thurgau), exc. Rheinfelden, and therefore sought to secure the assistance of CHARLES THE BOLD (see below). Disquieted by his actions, the enemies reconciled their differences with Fr. mediation and allied for mutual assistance in

1474 The 'Perpetual Peace'. Campaigning against Bern, CHARLES THE BOLD suffered

1476 the defeats of Grandson and Murten; he was killed in the b. of Nancy in

1477 (see below). Confident as a result of their successes, the members of the confederation resisted the imp. reform of MAXIMILIAN I (p. 219). The 'Swabian War' ended with the

1499 Peace of Basle: technically 'related to the Empire', Switzerland received polit. independence and separated from the Empire. Enlargement into the

1513 'Confederation of the 13 cantons' and expansion to the s. (Veltlin, Bormio, Tessin) until the

1515 defeat of Marignano. With the *lansquenet* (*Lands* (lance) *Knecht*), the Swiss introduced a new method of warfare. Swiss mercenaries became the most sought after soldiers of the day.

The 'Interim' Kdm of Burgundy (1363–1477)

A branch of the House of Valois formed a complex of territories resembling Carol. Lorraine in the border regions of France and Germany (p. 125).

1363–1404 PHILIP THE BOLD was invested with the Duchy of Burgundy (Bourgogne) by his father JOHN THE GOOD (1363). By inheritance and purchase he and his successors obtained

1384 the County of Burgundy (Franche Comté), also, the inheritance of the Wittelsbach family (Holland to 1433), and that of the Luxemburgs (to 1451).

Vassals simultaneously of the Ger. and the Fr. crowns, the dukes of Burgundy were among the wealthiest princes of Europe, for, with Flanders and Brabant, they had control over the economically strongest region of Europe (p. 245). Their court saw a late flowering of chivalric ctr.; Burg. court-ceremonial became a model of the absolutist state (p. 243). The added territories retained their regional privileges. Inspired by the spirit of a self-assured bourgeoisie, the realistic school of Flemish painting developed in the Netherlands with JAN VAN EYCK (1386–1440), ROGIER VAN DER WEYDEN (1400–64) and others.

1419 Murder of Duke JOHN by adherents of the Dauphin at Montereau.

1419–67 PHILIP THE GOOD by the

1420 Treaty of Troyes aligned with the Eng. party (p. 191); but the

1435 Peace of Arras which ended feudal dependence on France, brought about reconciliation with CHARLES VII. A politically independent position was also aspired to by PHILIP's son

1467–77 CHARLES THE BOLD. He won England, Castile and Aragón to his side in an alliance to encircle his bitter enemy LOUIS XI (p. 191). SIGMUND OF AUSTRIA pledged to CHARLES the Aust. territories on the Rhine (Alsace) in the hope of Burg. aid against the Swiss Confederation. In exchange for granting the royal dignity to CHARLES the Emperor demanded the hand of MARIA, heiress of Burgundy, for his son. After the futile

1474 siege of Neuss, CHARLES agreed to the marriage proposal. Following the

1475 conquest of Lorraine, Bern (NIKOLAUS VON DRESSBACH) induced Switzerland to enter the war (see above). CHARLES was killed in the

1477 b. of Nancy. MARIA mar. MAXIMILIAN I of Austria. Warring with LOUIS XI over the Burg. inheritance, MAXIMILIAN was victorious at the

1479 b. of Guinegate. It was not until

1489 that Flanders recognized MAXIMILIAN's claims. With the division of the legacy

1493 in the Peace of Senlis, the sec. conflict between France and Austria began.

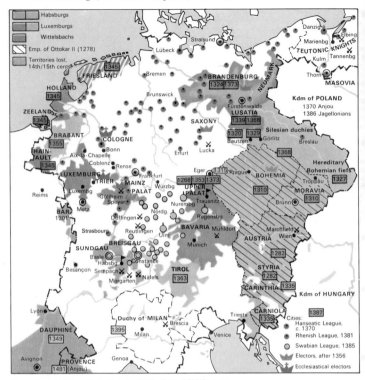

Dynastic policies and city leagues in the Late Middle Ages

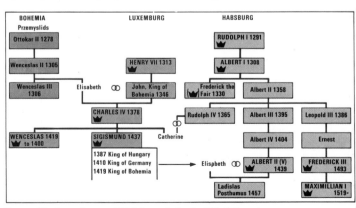

Przemyslids, Luxemburgs and Habsburgs during the 13th–16th cents.

The Elective Ger. Monarchy (1273–1356)
Intermittent feudal warfare and breaches of the law during the **Interregnum** made necessary the renewal of imp. authority by means of the **elective monarchy**; with the dual election of 1257 (ALFONSO OF CASTILE, to 1284; RICHARD OF CORNWALL, to 1272), the principle of the elective monarchy finally triumphed. **Consequence:** establishment of the electoral estate; the right to vote was limited to 3 eccles. and 4 sec. electors, who demanded special privileges (capitulations) and polit. rights from the candidate and wished for a weak monarchy; the dynasties wearing the crown were therefore alternated.
The dyn. policies of the kings: depending for their power on their personal estates, the kings sought to enlarge them. This resulted in conflicts between the interests of the Empire and the policies of dyn. power.
Separation from the Papacy: as a consequence of its Ital. policy, the 'Holy Roman Empire of the Ger. Nation' (pp. 145, 217) abandoned the concept of a universal empire, but did not find the strength necessary to realize a nat. state.

◀ **1273–91 Rudolf of Habsburg,** elected over OTTOKAR II of Bohemia (p. 169), demanded the return of the alienated imp. estates. OTTOKAR paid homage to the king, but refused to return the imp. fiefs, was placed under the ban and
◀ **1278 d. in the b. of the Marchfeld.** His son WENCESLAS II retained only Bohemia and Moravia. **Establishment of the power of the House of Habsburg** through investiture of the sons of RUDOLF with Austria and Styria (temporarily Carniola (as security) and Carinthia went to MEINHARD OF TIROL, 1335 to the Habsburgs).
◀ **1287 Diet of Würzburg:** a general peace decreed. The dyn. policies of
◀ **1291–8 ADOLF OF NASSAU** (Misnia (Meissen) and Thuringia) failed. He was deposed and d. in the
◀ **1298** b. of Göllheim fought against
◀ **1298–1308 Albrecht I of Habsburg.** The son of RUDOLF
◀ **1301** broke the opposition of the Rhenish electors and confiscated Bohemia as an expired fief of the crown. With the murder of the king by his nephew JOHN PARRICIDA the plan for a hered. Habsburg monarchy failed. The Fr. vassal and brother of Archbishop BALDWIN OF TRIER (1307–54),
◀ **1308–13 Henry VII of Luxemburg** (p. 217), whose son JOHN (1310–46) obtained the kdm of Bohemia through marriage, was elected Ger. king.
◀ **1314–47 Louis the Bavarian** fought against his Habsburg enemies with the aid of the Swiss (p. 193) and was victorious in the
◀ **1322** b. of Mühldorf: capture of FREDERICK THE FAIR (co-regent to 1330). Papal appeals were rejected in the
◀ **1324** Appellation of Sachsenhausen; LOUIS's excommunication was no longer effective (p. 181).
1327–8 Ital. campaign and Imp. coronation.

Urged by BALDWIN OF TRIER
1338 'the Day at Rense' (*Kurverein*) determined that the election of a king no longer needed confirmation by the Pope.
1346–78 Charles IV made Bohemia, which was well administered, the basis of his power. The cap., Prague, was enlarged through building projects (the Veits Dome, the Hradcany Castle); and by
1348 the establishment of the 1st Ger. university. The imp. chancery promoted the written language (Prague Chancery German). By prudent negotiations, CHARLES achieved a reconciliation with the Curia (1355 Imp. coronation) and the electors:
1356 The Golden Bull: by virtue of his election by majority vote at Frankfurt and his coronation at Aix-la-Chapelle, the king was considered to have been 'elected Rom. Emperor' (title used from 1508).
Significance of the basic law of the Empire: securing of hered. election by the Luxemburg family (after 1437 by the Habsburg family) and the **dualistic estate organization** with a division of power between 'the Emperor and the Empire'. The princes aspired to electoral privileges: e.g. Austria in the
1359 *Privilegium maius,* a forgery of RUDOLF IV OF AUSTRIA (1358–65).
Dyn. policies: CHARLES acquired the Upper Palatinate in 1353 and by 1368, Silesia and Lusatia. By the Treaty of Fürstenwalde, he purchased Brandenburg (1373).
The S. Ger. Leagues of Cities in the 14th Cent.
1254 The Rhenish League of Cities est. to secure the peace during the *Interregnum.* Later leagues were est. to protect urban liberties. They were directed against:
The knights: feuds and plunder of merchants *en route.*
The princes: constant struggle over the rights of citizens dwelling outside the city walls, who were under the protection of the cities and obstructing princely territ. expansion.
The kings: the granting of power over cities to princes for polit. or fiscal reasons.
1356 The Golden Bull prohibited leagues of cities. Nevertheless, in
1376 14 cities est. the Swabian League of Cities (in opposition to Count EBERHARD, THE GREINER, OF WÜRTEMBERG).
1377–89 The s. Ger. War of Cities, the cities winning
1377 victs. over CHARLES IV at Ulm, and over Würtemberg at Reutlingen. A Swabian–Rhenish League became
1381 the s. Ger. League of Cities, which allied with the Swiss Confederation in 1385. The army of the princes defeated the league in the
1388 b. of Döffingen (and Worms). With the surrender of the claim to the right to form special leagues in the
1389 Pacification of Eger, the period of the independent polit. activities of the Imp. cities was ended; however, as the 3rd 'collegium' (arranged separately in Swabian and Rhenish 'benches') they participated regularly in the Imp. diets from 1489.

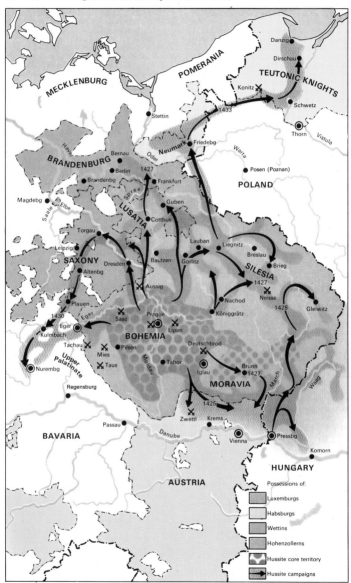

The Hussite Wars, 1419–36

Germany under the Sons of Charles IV
To realize the planned Greater Slav. Empire,
SIGISMUND acquired Brandenburg in 1378 (king
of Hungary, 1387), and WENCESLAS, Bohemia,
Silesia and the Ger. crown (1378).

1373–1419 Wenceslas, king of Bohemia.
Because of his arbitrary rule – he had St
JOHN OF NEPOMUK, vicar of the Archbishop
of Prague, slain by drowning – a league of
barons opposed to him was formed under
the leadership of his cousin JOBST OF
MORAVIA (1375–1411). Defeats of WENCES-
LAS (twice taken captive, 1394 and 1402).
Public order in Bohemia disintegrated.

Ger. Empire: WENCESLAS ('the Lazy', 1378–
1400) endeavoured to bring about
1383 the Imp. Peace of Nuremberg; but he
was powerless against princes, knights and
league of cities (p. 195), and was deposed.
1400–10 RUPRECHT OF THE PALATINATE was
also unable to raise the fallen prestige of the
crown. Claims to the throne by JOBST OF
MORAVIA were rejected in favour of those of
1410–37 Sigismund, who brought about the
convocation of the Council of Constance
(p. 181). **Rise of new territ. powers:**
1415 Burgrave Frederick I of Hohenzollern was
granted the Electorate of Brandenburg.
1432 Investiture of FREDERICK THE QUARREL-
SOME' of the **Wettin family** with the Electorate of **Saxony.** The **Hussite Wars** prevented imp. reform (1419–36).

The Hussites in Bohemia in the 15th Cent.
John Huss (1369–1415), executed in
1415 (p. 181), became Bohemia's nat. martyr.
When his 'murderer', SIGISMUND, claimed
the Boh. crown, the **Hussites** vented their
hatred of Germany in
1419 by an uprising (1st defenestration of
Prague). The principles of their faith were
contained in the
1420 Articles of Prague: liberty to preach;
communion '*sub utraque*' (under both
species); apostolic poverty of the clergy.
Relig. split into **Calixtines** (cup-users) or
Utraquists (university, nobility and bourgeoisie) and **Taborites,** followers of WYCLIF
(p. 180), who rejected all forms of worship
and dogma which lacked biblical authority
(peasants, low clergy, petit bourgeoisie).
Led by **Jan Ziska** (1360–1424) and **Andreas
Proscop** (1380–1434), the Hussite people's
army repulsed 5 assaults by imp. and
crusader armies. After the disastrous
1431 defeat of FREDERICK OF BRANDENBURG
at Taus, the Council arrived at a compromise
1433 with the Utraquists in the **Compactata of
Prague** (p. 181). The Utraquists defeated the
radical Taborites in
1434 b. of Lipan and
1436 recognized SIGISMUND at the Diet of
Iglau. Renewed struggles and
1448 Seizure of Prague by **George Podiebrad,**
leader of the Utraquists. Regent in
1452, Bohemian king in 1458, PODIEBRAD was
excommunicated after the papal dissolution
of the Compactata in 1466, and defeated by
Matthias Corvinus (p. 201), who

1468/9 in turn occupied Moravia, Silesia and
Lusatia. The Boh. Estates chose
1471–1516 VLADISLAV OF POLAND as successor.
He came to an agreement with MATTHIAS
CORVINUS in the
1478 Peace of Olmütz and became king of
Hungary in 1490. Taborites and Waldensians evolved after 1467 into the **Community
of the Boh.-Mor. Brethren.**
1485 The Peace of Kuttenberg led to a compromise between Catholics and Utraquists,
the latter retaining their eccles. organization.
Results: weakening of the crown, the Church
and the Ger. element in Bohemia; at the
same time, the upper nobility enriched itself
by acquiring eccles. estates, but was unable
to realize a Czech nat. state.

Germany under the Early Habsburgs
After the extinction of the Luxemburg line,
the crown, incl. Hungary and Bohemia, fell
to the Habsburg
1438–39 Albrecht II of Austria.
1440–93 Frederick III became regent for
LADISLAUS POSTHUMOUS (1440–57), the posthumous son of ALBRECHT II. FREDERICK'S
adviser, ENEA SILVIO, won him over to
the side of Pope EUGENE IV; the Conciliar
movement was terminated with the
1448 Concordat of Vienna (p. 181). The
Emperor remained inactive while the
princes struggled for power. General law-
lessness was countered – esp. in Westphalia –
by the
Vehme or Vehmic Justice: the chairman of the
court (cal. Lord of the royal 'ban of blood')
invested the **Free Count** (*Freigraf*) with
secret judicial power. Count and **free jurors**
(*Freischöffen,* also peasants) – as the
'knowing' – pronounced the judgement
(either freedom or the death penalty), which
was executed immediately.
1471 Diet of Regensburg: **prohibition of the
right to feud.** To preserve peace,
1488 the **Swabian League** (princes, knights and
cities) was est. **Decay of the Empire:** after
the death of LADISLAUS
1457 native kings were raised to the thrones
of Hungary (MATTHIAS CORVINUS) and
Bohemia (GEORGE PODIEBRAD); imp. losses
to Poland (p. 201) and Burgundy (p. 193).
1471–80 Turk. campaigns of plunder in
Styria; divisions of the Habsburg inheritance, and, from 1477, Hung. attacks on
Austria (MATTHIAS CORVINUS).
1485 Seizure of Vienna and occupation of
Lower Austria, Carinthia and Styria.
Dyn. policies: despite all their failures the
Emperor had confidence in the strength of
the Habsburgs. His inheritance and marriage
contracts laid the foundation for **Habsburg
power of world-wide dimensions.**
1463 Inheritance treaty with Hungary. The
marriage contract of FREDERICK'S son
MAXIMILIAN led to the acquisition of:
1477 Burgundy (p. 193);
1490 relief of Vienna; inheritance of Tyrol;
1491 inheritance treaty with Bohemia and
Hungary.

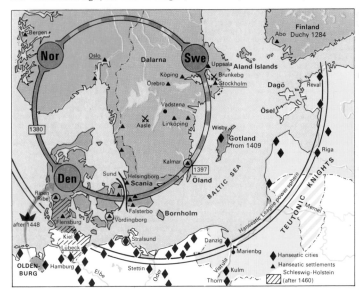

The Baltic states, *c.* **1400**

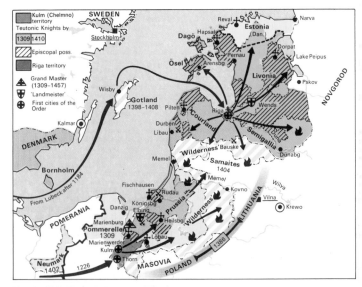

The rise of the Teutonic Knights, 1226–1410

he Teutonic Knights (1226–1410)

.ivonia: the master of the Bremen Cathedral Chapter, ALBERT VON APPELDERN, Bishop of Livonia (1199–1229), assembled an army of Crusaders, founded Riga in 1201, and set up the Order of the Brethren of the Sword (a red cross on a white cape).

3y 1230: Livonia and Kurland (Courland) subj.; settlement of the nobility; Ger. cities and bpcs est.; but no settlement by peasants. After the

.236 defeat by the Lithuanians and Semigalians at Saule

.237 union with the Teutonic Knights. An advance towards Novgorod ended with the

242 b. of Lake Peipus.

.346 The Order acquired Estonia from Denmark.

Prussia: Duke CONRAD OF MASOVIA asked the Order for aid against the heathen Prussians; he gave the territory of Kulm to the Order.

209–39 Prussia was granted as the territory of the Order to the **Grand Master Hermann von Salza** by FREDERICK II (p. 173), acting acc. to the

.226 Golden Bull of Rimini: Prussia was declared subject to the Pope in 1234. Proceeding from Thorn (1231) and Kulm (1233), Landmeister (Land Master) HERMANN VON BALK began the Crusades against the Prussians. After setbacks and uprisings

.283 the conquest of Prussia was completed.

.351–82 Winrich of Kniprode brought the Order to its zenith.

.370 Defeat of the Lithuanians at Rudau; systematic colonization (over 1,400 villages est.); the new cities (organized on the basis of the law of Kulm), with their facilities for trade, belonged to the Hanseatic League.

.393–1407 To protect the Baltic trade CONRAD VON JUNGINGEN drove

.398 the Vitalian Brethren (p. 183) out of Gotland (Wisby). Greatest extension of the Order after the seizure of the Neumark (1402) and Samagotia (Samaiten, 1404).

From 1386 the state was surrounded by a superior enemy owing to the Pol.–Lith. union; at the same time its miss. task was abandoned.

Constitution: the Order (p. 153) consisted of noble brethren (knights) and priests, who were served by non-noble brethren. The **statutes of the Order** (monast. vows, rule and laws) were supplemented by decisions of the chapters and decrees of the **Grand Master,** who was 'associated with the Empire' ('*reichszugehörig*') and who resided in the **Marienburg** (after 1309). Elected by the General Chapter, he governed with **'5 men of authority',** the marshal (war), the *Grosskomtur* (admin.), the *Spittler* (welfare), the *Trappier* (clothing), and the *Tressler* (finances), and the **Land Masters** of Prussia and Livonia.

Scandinavia in the Late Middle Ages

Sweden: during the reign of weak kings, the power of the nobility increased (developed from families owning and working large estates; not socially distinct from the free peasantry). In exchange for confirmation of their privileges and the establishment of a crown council, the 'Great Men' transferred the crown to

1319–63 MAGNUS ERICSSON. The first ruler of the Swed.–Nor. Union lost Schonen, Öland and Gotland to Denmark.

Norway: MAGNUS surrendered the country to

1355–80 HAAKON VI. In 1363 HAAKON mar. MARGARET, who after 1387 was queen of both Denmark and Norway.

Denmark: Count GERHARD III OF HOLSTEIN, elected regent of the realm, put an end to the conflicts between crown, nobility and clergy. He arranged for the election of WALDEMAR III, Duke of Schleswig, as king, and in return inherited Schleswig. GERHARD was murdered in 1340.

1340–75 Waldemar IV Atterdag. His campaigns against Öland and Gotland (Wisby) led to

1361–70 war with the Hanseatic League. Denmark was forced to submit to the financially superior enemy.

1370 Peace of Stralsund. Domination of the Baltic was secured by the Hanseatic League. WALDEMAR'S daughter compelled the election of her son OLAF (5 yrs old) as king of Denmark and Norway (1380). After his death

1387–1412 the Regent **Margaret,** 'the mighty woman and keeper of the House', became queen of Denmark and Norway. Noble opponents of the Swed. king summoned the 'Semiramis of the N.' into the country; the Swed. king ALBRECHT

1389 was taken prisoner at Aasle. Supplied by the **Vitalian** brethren (p. 183), Stockholm resisted until 1395. The crown councils of the 3 countries finally joined in the

1397 Union of Kalmar. A second projected Greater Northern Empire did not become a reality because Sweden rejected the idea of a united Dan. monarchy.

1412–39 ERIC OF POMERANIA favoured Dutch and Eng. trade; because of his

1423 customs levies in the **'Sund'** he came into conflict with the Hanseatic League and Holstein and was forced to confirm the privileges of the Hanseatic League in

1435 the Peace of Vordingborg.

1434–6 Popular uprising in Sweden under the nat. hero, ENGELBRECHT ENGELBRECHTSSON (c. 1400–36). After his murder KARL KNUTSON BONDE was regent until 1441 (king as CHARLES VIII, 1448–70).

1439–48 CHRISTOPH III of Bavaria was able to preserve the union. His successor

1448–81 CHRISTIAN I of the **Oldenburg Dynasty** was elected

1460 Duke of Schleswig and Holstein by the estates. The 2 duchies were joined in 'Realunion' ('forever indivisible') which lasted to 1863.

1464 Uprising in Sweden: the regent STEN STURE I (1470–1504) defeated the Danes

1471 in the b. of the Brunkeberg. The constant unrest and struggles taking place also during the reign of JOHN (1481–1513) led to the dissolution of the Union of Kalmar (p. 249).

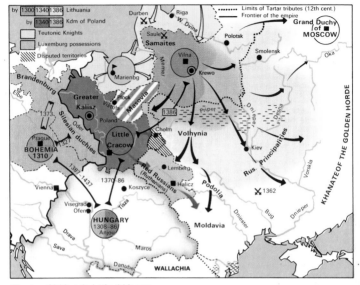

The rise of Lithuania in the 14th cent.

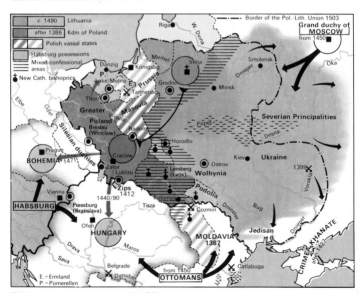

The Polish-Lithuanian state in the 15th cent.

Lithuania as Dominant Power in the E.

United by language and a pagan ctr., the Baltic branch of the Indo-Europeans dwelled in the forest and swamp lands of the Memel and Dvina (Düna). Attacks by the Teutonic Knights forced the clans *c.* 1250 to form a state.

1316–41 GEDYMIN built castles and cities.

1345–77.OLGERD defeated the Tartars in the

1362 b. of the Blue Water, and fought with Poland over Galicia and Podolia. The Rus. (Orth.) pop. predominated in the Lith. state; they were culturally superior to the pagan Lithuanians. After his conversion to Catholicism

1386 JAGIELLO (1377–1434), as king of Poland, est. the **Union with Poland**; however, by the treaties of Ostrow (1392), Horodlo (1413) and Grodno (1432) Lithuania remained an autonomous Grand Duchy under Poland.

1392–1430 VITOVT (WITOLD) expanded Lith. power along the Black Sea despite

1399 the Tartar vict. at the Vorskla.

The Stabilization of Poland in the 14th Cent.

1306–33 VLADISLAV I LOKIETEK was able to bring about nat. unification with papal aid. With a base of power in Hungary,

1333–70 Casimir III the Great was able to strengthen the kdm.

1335 Treaty of Visegrad: abandoning claims to Poland, Bohemia was given Silesia.

1343 Peace of Kalisch (Kalisz) with the Teutonic Knights. The king acquired

1366 the principality of Halisz.

1347 Codification of Pol. Law. In exchange for exemption from taxation, the nobility consented to personal union of the crowns of Hungary and Poland.

1370–82 Under the rule of LOUIS THE GREAT (ANJOU), the 'Barons of Cracow' broadened their power.

1374 The Charter of Koszyce (Kaschau): initial grant of polit. privileges to the nobility, which in turn affirmed the right of succession by the female line and assured that of the king's daughter

1382–99 JADWIGA (HEDWIG); who, in the Treaty of Krewo (1385), dissolved her engagement to a Habsburg prince and accepted the courtship of JAGIELLO OF LITHUANIA. After his conversion to Catholicism, marriage, and coronation at Cracow, **1386 personal union of Lithuania with Poland.**

The Pol. Jagiellonian State in the 15th Cent.

1386–1434 VLADISLAV II JAGIELLO encountered resistance during the christianization of Lithuania. The split between the Cath. and Orth. faiths burdened the Pol.–Lith. state. The common enemy was the **Teutonic Order,** the decline of which began with the

1410 b. of Tannenberg. HENRY OF PLAUEN (1410–13) defended the Marienburg.

1411 Subsequent to the (1st) Peace of Thorn, he attempted to introduce reforms and was deposed. Hungary confirmed peace in the

1412 Treaty of Lublau, and as security placed 12 cities along the Zips under Pol. rule.

The Council of Constance charged Poland with the spread of the Cath. faith in the E.

1422 Peace of Lake Melno: the Order permanently abandoned its claims to Samogitia.

1454 Because the Prus. estates placed themselves under Pol. rule, war was renewed.

1457 The Marienburg was stormed.

1466 (2nd) Peace of Thorn: Ermland and w. Prussia (Pomerellen, the Kulm territory) fell to Poland; Prussia had to acknowledge the feudal sovereignty of Poland. Special privileges for Danzig (the 'corridor' est.).

1434–44 VLADISLAV III, Hung. king after 1440, d. during the Turk. Crusade in the devastating and fateful

1444 b. of Varna (p. 209). He was succeeded by the Lith. Grand Duke

1447–92 CASIMIR IV, who depended on the support of the lesser nobility (*Szlachta*). The *Szlachta* convoked diets after 1454, and formed the Lower House of the Diet (*Sejm*) after 1468. As a result of the 2nd Peace of Thorn, Greater Poland stretched from the Baltic to the Black Sea. CASIMIR's son VLADIMIR became

1471 king of Bohemia; 1490 king of Hungary.

1497 Defeat of Cozmin. During the reigns of JOHN I ALBRECHT and ALEXANDER the Jagiellonian state was encircled by the Habsburgs (p. 249), Muscovy (p. 203) and the Turks (up to 1506).

End of the Hung. Kdm

Following the extinction of the Arpads (p. 169), the kdm underwent internal conflicts until the renewal of the power of the crown by the **House of Anjou** (1307–82).

1342–82 Louis I the Great deprived the magnates of power; bourgeoisie and cities fl. A belt of Turk. vassal states (Moldavia, Wallachia) was formed in the s.

1387–1437 Sigismund, king of Germany 1410, king of Bohemia 1419, Emperor 1433, planned a Greater Slav. Empire under the Luxemburgs.

1396 The b. of Nikopolis (p. 209) terminated his Turk. campaign. The magnates obtained feudal privileges for themselves.

1446 Election of JOHN HUNYADI as regent. He contested Habsburg claims (LADISLAUS POSTHUMOUS, p. 197);

1456 vict. over the Turks at Belgrade. HUNYADIS's son

1458–90 Matthias I Corvinus conquered the hered. Luxemburg territories from the Habsburgs; and seized Styria and Carinthia.

1485 He moved his residence to Vienna (p. 197). The Danubian state rapidly declined under

1490–1516 VLADISLAV II OF BOHEMIA, who in the

1491 Peace of Pressburg confirmed the Habsburg inheritance claims. Struggles with the nobility and peasant uprisings; advance of the Turks.

1515 Inheritance treaty with the Habsburgs, who received Hungary upon the death of LOUIS II (1516–26) in the

1526 b. of Mohacs (p. 209).

Russia, c. 1600

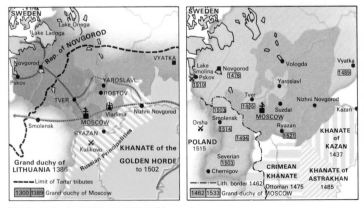

The Grand Duchy of Moscow, 1300–1533

The Rise of the Grand Duchy of Moscow

Divergent polit. and cult. developments led to the dissolution of the ancient union of the Rus. people into **Ukrainians** under Pol. sovereignty, **White Russians** under Lith. sovereignty and **Great Russians** under Tartar (Mongol) sovereignty. The Rus. territ. states descended into polit. anarchy. **Moscow**, mentioned for the first time in 1147, advantageously loc., protected by forests and relatively densely populated, became the heart of a new Rus. Empire. The princes unscrupulously expanded their possessions.

1325–41 IVAN I KALITA (Moneybag) is considered the first 'joiner of the Rus. earth'. He gained the favour of the Tartars by paying him tribute. After his

1328 vict. over Tver, he became Grand Prince. The Metropolitan THEOGNOST transferred his residence from Vladimir to Moscow; his successor ALEXEI used his power to work for nat. unification under Moscow.

1359–89 DMITRI DONSKOY. Renewed struggles with Tver and Ryazan, which were supported by Lithuania, ended in 1375 with the polit. predominance of Moscow.

1380 1st Rus. victory over the Tartars at Kulikovo on the Don.

1439 The Union of Florence (p. 207) was rejected. Separation of the Rus. Church from the Gk; the fall of Constantinople was considered deserved punishment.

The 'Joining of the Rus. Lands'

1462–1505 Ivan III the Great, who was mar. to the Byz. princess ZOË, cal. himself 'sole ruler (Tsar) of all Russia'; Ital. architects transformed the **Kremlin** (castle) into his residence. With the aid of immigrating Boyars, IVAN shaped the Muscovite state into a united nat. state. The autocratic concept of the state and its symbols (the twin-eagle, the court ceremonial) were of Byz. origin; the myth of Moscow as the '3rd Rome' and fount of the true faith (the monk PHILOTHEOS) est. a sense of mission for the Rus. people and their ruler, who was welcomed by the Orth. Church as God's deputy (Abbot YOSIF OF VOLOKOLAMSK, c. 1480). This concept was rejected in favour of a mystical internalization of the Church by the movement of the 'unselfish' (NEIL SORSKY, 1433–1509).

1478 Destruction of the republic of Novgorod.

1480 Disengagement from the sovereignty of the Golden Horde (p. 179), which disintegrated into partial Khanates and was dest. by the Crimean Tartars in 1502. Tver, Pskov, Smolensk and Ryazan were included into the 'patrimony of Moscow'.

1502 Fruitless attack on Livonia.

1533–84 Ivan IV Grozny (the 'Terrible') (Tsar at 3 yrs of age) had, as a child, experienced humiliations, acts of violence, and intrigues inflicted and instigated by rival groups of nobles. After his

1547 coronation as Tsar: renewal of the Empire through absolute autocracy.

Domestic policies: reform of the cen. admin.

(*Prikasy*), the law (Codex Sudyebnik, 1550) and the army with the aid of personal advisers (Prince KURBSKY), the service nobility (*Pomeschchiki*) and the **Streltsy,** the standing army of the Tsar. The people and the Church supported IVAN IV.

1551 Reform Synod of the Metropolitan MACARIUS: introduction of the calendar of saints and canon law (*Stoglav*).

1553 Opening of the White Sea route by the Brit. captain CHANCELLOR and the start of trade with England.

1584 Founding of Archangel, the only Rus. seaport.

1565–72 The **Oprichnina:** partition of the Empire into territories of the Tsar (*Oprichnina*) and of the Boyars (*Zemshtshina*); though the Boyars' power was broken by dispossession, deportations and the redistribution of land to the Dvoryane (a new class of warriors), the state was in the process exposed to awesome terror: liquidations, elimination of whole cities (1570 Novgorod), decline of agriculture, mass flight of peasants despite a decree tying them to the soil (Cossacks, p. 273). The arbitrariness and distrustfulness of the Tsar were indicative of mental illness.

Foreign policy: expansion to the s. through the

1552–6 subjugation of Kazan and Astrakhan; counter-attack by the Crimean Tartars:

1571 seizure and burning of Moscow.

1581 Beginning of the conquest of Siberia (p. 273). The establishment of an Orth. empire failed because of

1558–82 the war over Livonia (p. 249). IVAN d. leaving a distraught Empire.

1589 Moscow became an ind. patriarchate.

The Time of Troubles (Smuta 1605–13)

During the power struggles over the succession, the boyar BORIS GODUNOV

1588 became regent. Following the

1591 murder of the Tsar's son DEMETRIUS and the death of the last, mentally deranged, member of the Rurik Dynasty,

1598–1605 BORIS GODUNOV was elected Tsar.

1601–3 The 'FALSE DEMETRIUS', a polit. adventurer posing as the son of the Tsar, arrived with Pol. assistance on the scene following famine and unrest.

1605 Pol. troops occupied Moscow. During the reign of SHUISKY

1606/7 the first soc. upheaval of Cossacks and peasants brought to the fore a 2nd (PSEUDO-) DEMETRIUS, the 'rascal of Tushino'. With Swed. assistance, the Boyars' party was able to withstand him, but had to abandon Livonia by the terms of the

1609 Treaty of Vyborg. However, Poland now laid claim to the throne of the Tsars (p. 249) and took Smolensk in 1611, but was forced by an anti-Pol. uprising

1612 to give up Moscow. An assembly of the Empire elected a new Tsar,

1613–45 MICHAEL, the 1st

1613–1762 **Romanov Dynasty,** overcame the 'troubles' and arrived at a polit. settlement with Sweden and Poland (p. 249).

The Second Greater Bulgarian Empire, _c._ 1240

The Greater Serbian state, _c._ 1355

The 2nd Greater Bulg. Empire in the 13th Cent.

Assimilated by the Slavs, the Bulgars experienced a brief rise in power during the period of the Lat. Empire (p. 175). Taking advantage of the events of the 3rd Crusade IVAN and PETER ASEN in

1186 est. the 2nd Greater Bulg. Empire, with its cap. at Tirnovo. INNOCENT III bestowed the royal dignity upon its rulers in

1203/4 the state, in alliance with the Cumans, expanded.

1205 Vict. over the Lat. Empire at Adrianople.

1218–41 Ivan Asen II defeated Epirus in the

1230 b. of Klokotnitsa and, in alliance with Nicaea, launched an attack on the Lat. Empire; he was unable however to realize a Bulg.–Byz. Empire.

1235 Establishment of a Bulg. Patriarchate.

1242 Mongol. incursions, Hung. advances and dyn. and relig. conflicts with Byzantium weakened the state. Under Tartar sovereignty (NOGAI KHAN), the Empire after

1285 disintegrated into feudal territories which, after

1330 the b. of Küstendil (Velbuzhde), were absorbed by the Greater Serb. state. After the destruction of Tirnovo (1393)

1396 Bulgaria became a province of the Ott. Empire (to 1878).

The Greater Serb. State in the 14th Cent.

The first state formed during the 11th cent. (King·MICHAEL OF ZETA) soon fell apart into tribal groups. The Grand-Zhupan

1151–96 Stephen Nemanja united the tribes, threw off Byz. sovereignty and est. the Serb. Empire (the Nemanjian Dynasty). Opposed to the Western orientation of his brother, STEPHEN II (1196–1228), who was granted

1217 the royal dignity by the Pope, St Sava (1169–1236) est.

1219 the Serb.–Orth. Nat. Church, which became the unifying element for all Serbs and remained so even during the time of alien Turk. rule. The monasteries of St SAVA became centres of Serb. ctr. During the 13th cent., conforming to the Western model, the tribal state became a feudal state and formed a nobility; the free peasantry descended into serfdom, and the cities were granted special privileges (in the w. following the Ital., in the s. the Gk. model). Byzantium being incapable of effective opposition (p. 207), the state expanded southwards (the Morava).

1330 Vict. over the Bulgarians and Greeks at Küstendil (Velbuzhde): rise to dominant power in the Balkans.

1331–55 Stephen Dushan (UROSH IV), following policies aiming at major-power status, had himself

1346 crowned 'Tsar of the Serbs and Greeks' at Skopje and est. the Serb. patriarchate.

1349 Codification of the law in the 'Zakonik'; admin. of the Empire, after the Byz. model, under the direction of the Serb. nobility; the Church became the most prosperous landowner. STEPHEN was unable to conquer Constantinople (Slav. Zarigrad), and with it

the imp. crown. Plans for a Turk. crusade did not materialize because of Hung. opposition. Under UROSH V (1355–67) the dynasty fell apart and the state disintegrated into feudal principalities ('despoties'). LAZAR OF RASCIA vainly attempted to stem the Turks. Defeat of the s. Slav. peoples in the

1389 b. of Kossovo ('Field of the Blackbirds'); annihilation of the Serb. nobility.

1396 Serbia became a Turk. vassal state; GEORGE BRANKOVICH (1427–56) moved the cap. to Smederevo; but he was unable to prevent

1459 Serbia being incorp. into the Ott. Empire.

Culture: flowering of church construction (5-domed structure) in the 13th/14th cents.; gold embroidery; mosaics, icons and frescoes; national epics (the Kossovo cycle centring on STEPHEN DUSHAN and the nat. hero MARKO KRALJEVICH); greatest poet: IVAN GUNDULIC (1588–1638).

Albania: nomadic Vlachs (Wallachians) migrated during the 11th cent. from the NE. (Nish) into the territory populated by the remnants of the Thrac.-Ill. Albanians. Ott. advances were met by

1443–8 the nat. uprising under GEORGE KASTRIOTIS, cal. SKANDERBEG. During the period of Turk. control, approx. 70% of the population converted to Islam.

The Balkan Border States

Croatia: during the struggles with Venice and the Hungarians in the 10th/11th cents., a state was formed in the area between the Drave and the Adriatic Sea (924 King TOMISLAV).

1074–89 DEMETRIUS ZVONIMIR threw off Byz. overlordship; his coronation by the Pope in 1076 strengthened the orientation towards Rom. Cath. and Western ctr.

1102 Personal union with Hungary (*Pacta conventa*); self-admin. under a *Ban* (commander of a Hung. frontier march).

Bosnia: the 13th cent. saw crusades against the **Bogomils** (Slav. friends of God), a Manichaean sect (p. 149) who, despite their struggle against the Hungarians, Serbs, Croats and Venetians, est. their own state. Under the 'King of the Serbians and Bosnians',

1353–91 STEPHEN TVRTKO, a brief period of predominance by the Bogomils (until the conquest by the Ottomans in 1463).

Herzegovina (after 1448): withstood the Turks until 1483.

Moldavia/Wallachia: Mongol. vassals, the Vlachs moved in during the 11th cent.; subs. these areas became Hung. *Banates* (frontier marches); they est. themselves as ind. principalities *c.* 1365. After 1394, Walachia became a dependency of the Ott. Empire. In Moldavia

1457–1504 Stephen III the Great played his neighbours off against one another.

1512 Recognition of Ott. overlordship.

The Latin Empire, 1204–61

Byzantium after 1261

The Ottoman advances in the 14th and 15th cents.

The Lat. Empire (1204–61)

Venice provided the fleet to transport the 34,000 Flem. and Fr. crusaders raised by INNOCENT III (p. 153); in spite of the papal prohibition, Venice demanded

1202 the conquest of Zara. A request for aid by the Byz. pretender ALEXIUS IV, who promised the unification of the Church and subsidies, diverted the

1202–4 4th Crusade (originally directed to Egypt) to Constantinople. ALEXIUS did not keep his promise and was deposed.

1204 (2nd) Conquest of Constantinople: the Latins' hatred for the Greeks found expression in barbaric cruelties; the most extensive plunder of relics, works of art, and other precious articles of the Middle Ages. The Empire was partitioned into **feudal crusader states:**

The Lat. Empire: BALDWIN I OF FLANDERS (1204–15); BALDWIN II (1216–61).

The Kdm of Thessalonica (HENRY OF MONT-FERRAT); the principality of Achaea, the duchy of Athens, and other states. Venice secured bases to build a colon. trading empire. The subordination of the Gk Church to Rome intensified the Greeks' dislike of alien Lat. rule. Establishment of the **Byz. successor states:**

The Empire of Trapezus: expansion to Armenia with the aid of Georgia; the Christ. outpost in Asia Minor remained in existence until 1461.

The Despotate of Epirus: THEODORE I (1215–30) came into conflict with Nicaea after

1224 the conquest of Thessalonica.

The Empire of Nicaea: THEODORE I LASCARIS (1204–22) continued the Byz. tradition and in alliance with the Bulgars (p. 205) attempted to overthrow Lat. rule. Byz.–Bulg. vict. in the

1205 b. of Adrianople; peace with the Latins in 1214 fixed the respective borders.

1222–54 JOHN III VATATZES wrested border provinces from the Lat. Empire, occupied Thessalonica (in 1246), and defeated all rivals (Epirus, Bulgaria). Allied with Genoa (p. 183),

1258–82 Michael III Paleologus put an end to the Lat. rule of BALDWIN II.

1259 Vict. at Pelagonia over the coalition of Epirus and Sicily; decline of Frank. knight-hood; **Mistra** on the Morea developed as the centre of renewed Byz. power.

1261 Dissolution of the Lat. Empire. Genoa est. herself as the second commercial power in the Levant.

Byzantium under the Paleologi

The new Byzantium did not recover from the destruction of the last Christ. bulwark against Islam. Venice maintained herself in the islands, the Latins held on in Greece. MICHAEL therefore sought diplomatic relations with France, the Golden Horde and, above all, the Papacy. His hope for the reunification of the Church at the

1274 Council of Lyon was not fulfilled.

1281 The newly contracted alliance of Orvieto between Venice and CHARLES OF ANJOU, intended to restore Lat. rule, was countered by the Emperor, who formed an alliance with PETER III OF ARAGÓN and the Sicil. nobility (p. 187). The Emperor's restorative work later suffered under his successor

1282–1328 ANDRONICUS II. Increasing infl. of the Orth. Church and its monasteries (monast. community of Athos) over the state, which decayed completely during the

1321–54 Epoch of the Civil Wars.

1328 Following struggles over the succession, policy came to be determined by JOHN CANTACUZENE. Supported by the Hesychasmic (Gk = quietly resting) mystical monast. movement, he set himself up as anti-emperor. Serbs, Bulgars and Seljuks were drawn into the civil war which ensued with the social-revolutionary party of the Zelots. JOHN was able to regain the throne in 1347 with the aid of the Ott. Emperor ORKHAN (1326–59).

1349 Conquest of Epirus; but the Ottomans occupied almost all of Asia Minor and, in

1354, Gallipoli, their first Eur. possession. JOHN became a monk after his deposition; his son MATTHAEUS was able to maintain his position at Mistra until 1382; here there was a late flowering of Byz. civilization.

1354–91 JOHN V.

1362 subsequent to the **Fall of Adrianople** JOHN became a dependant of the Ottomans. Vain appeals for help made to LOUIS OF HUNGARY and Rome. After the failure of the Turk. crusade before Nicopolis in 1396,

1399–1402 MANUEL II (1391–1425) undertook a journey to Europe to enlist aid; it was in vain (Rome, Paris, London). Only the Ott. defeat by the Mongols in 1402 (p. 179) delayed the destruction of the state.

1422 1st Ott. siege of Constantinople.

1425–48 JOHN VIII, hoping to gain support by negotiating with the Church, converted to Catholicism and, after the Council of Ferrara (p. 181), concluded

1439 the Union of Florence with Pope EUGENE II (p. 181). It did not result in help against the Turks and was rejected by the Gk Church. After recognition of the Union by ISIDORE, Metropolitan of Kiev, the Rus. Church declared itself independent. The last hopes for relief vanished with the

1444 defeat of Varna (p. 209). Defended by Byzantines, Genoese and Venetians, on

29 May 1453 Constantinople fell after a siege. End of the E. Rom. Empire.

Significance: establishment of an Asian–Eur. Turk. Empire, which became an immediate threat to the Christ. Occident. The heritage of Antiquity removed by Gk scholars to Italy (development of European **Humanism,** p. 212); transfer of the legal succession of Byzantium and leadership of the Orth. Church to **Tsardom and the 3rd Rome** (Moscow) (p. 203). By losing access to the Black Sea (Sea of Asov), Europe was deprived of the land route to India; the search for a new sea route brought about the discovery of the New World.

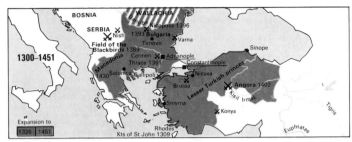

The rise of the Ottoman Empire, 1300-1683

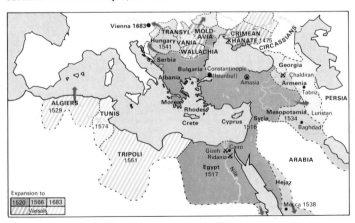

The Ottoman Empire, 1683

The Beginnings of the Ott. Empire (1300–1402)
As a result of the advance of the Mongols (p. 179), nomads began to migrate w. from Turkestan. Among them were Turk. Moslems, who, retreating from the assault of the Mongols, settled

after 1243 in Asia Minor. The Emir (ruler) of a community of warriors (*Ghazid*) in the service of the Rum Seljuks (p. 137), OSMAN I

1281–1326 proclaimed himself Sultan and est.

1301 the Ott. Empire.

1326 Conquest of Brussa. OSMAN's son ORKHAN (1326–59) completed the subjugation of Bithynia by the

1337 seizure of Nicomedia (Ismid). He introduced a new currency and – as a nat. symbol – the fez (a smooth cap of felt). The army was organized into 'light troops' (*akindschi*) and feudal cavalry (the Sultan's guard of pashas). This army of élite soldiers became the terror of Europe: the *spahis* (riders), composed of renegades (converts to Islam), and the *janissaries* (Christ. children raised as slaves to become fanatical Moslems), fought with iron discipline for the 'Master of all the faithful'. Numbering up to 100,000 men, they eventually formed a 'state within the state'. Summoned by a Byz. faction (p. 207), they crossed to Europe:

354 Ott. base at Gallipoli.

1359–89 MURAD I advanced into the Byz. Empire and, after the

1361 Conquest of Adrianople, reduced it to the city of Constantinople. The resistance of the Christ. peoples of the Balkans was broken in the

389 b. of Kossovo ('Field of the Blackbirds').
The area of Ott. control was extended to the Danube and the Euphrates (1393 Bulgaria, Wallachia). A crusade of Emperor SIGIS-MUND (p. 201), intended to free Byzantium, ended with the

396 b. of Nicopolis; however, the fall of Constantinople was delayed by the incursion of TIMUR (p. 179).

1402 b. of Angora (Ankara) and collapse of the Empire of Asia Minor.

Rise and Flowering of the Empire (1413–1566)
Not threatened in the Eur. part of their empire, MOHAMMED I (1413–21) and MURAD II (1421–51) were able to overcome the crisis of the state. A crusader army under JOHN HUNYADI (p. 201) was dest. in the

444 b. of Varna.

451–81 Mohammed II the Conqueror. His dyn. law determined that, for the sake of world order, each Sultan must kill his brothers.

453 Siege and fall of Constantinople (p. 207), which from then on was, as Istanbul, Turkey's cap. Serbia and Bosnia became Ott. provinces. GEORGE KASTRIOTIS (cal. SKANDERBEG), the nat. hero of Albania, resisted until 1468. MOHAMMED subj. 12 kdms. and 200 cities. Venice lost its possessions in the Morea.

461 Trapezus the last Christ. bastion to fall.

512–20 SELIM I gained Syria, Arabia and Egypt.

1520–66 Suleiman II the Magnificent developed the power of the Ottomans to its greatest extent. Three vics. marked his success:

1521 conquest of Belgrade;

1522 capitulation on Rhodes of the Knights of St John (Turk. control of Gen. and Venet. trade);

1526 b. of Mohacs: upon the death of King LOUIS II, Hungary lost its independence until 1918 (p. 237). The defence of the Occident fell to Austria; the Poles and the Venetians were allies in the defence against the Turks; France concluded treaties with the Ott. Empire.

1529 1st siege of Vienna; 1533 armistice and partition of Hungary: the Ott. vassal JOHN ZÁPOLYA of Transylvania received the e.

1541 Turk. Hungary became an Ott. province. After the abdication of the last Caliph of the Abbasid Dynasty (p. 137), SULEIMAN took

1534 Persia; Baghdad declined to the rank of a provincial city. The Pers. Shi'ites became the Ottomans' bitter enemies.

The State: successes were due to the autocratic power of the sultans and the effectiveness of the army. For this reason, 20,000 Rus. and Afr. slaves were imported annually; added to this was the 'toll of boys' (every 5th Christ. boy had to be surrendered to supplement the ranks of the janissaries). Administered by grand viziers (often of Slav. or Gk origin), the conquered country was divided into milit. fiefs and exploited by pashas. The natives (*rajas*) were not molested so long as they were obedient and paid taxes; they were not converted by force. Not gifted in trade or the crafts, the Turks tolerated Armenians and Greeks as merchants, seamen, administrative aides (*fanariotes*) and interpreters (*dragomans*). In spite of certain reforms, there was no internal strengthening of the state; intellectually undemanding, the corruptible pashas easily succumbed to their craving for wealth.

The Start of the Empire's Disintegration (1567–1661)
1566 Storming of the fortress of Szigeth, defended by the Hung. nat. hero ZRINYI;

1568 Peace of Adrianople in exchange for annual payment of tribute by the Habsburgs.

1571 The naval b. of Lepanto (p. 243) broke the dominance of the Turk. fleet.

1593–1606 renewed war with Austria; for the first time, however, the Sultan was forced to negotiate with the enemy in the

1606 Peace of Zsitva-Torok. Baghdad and Mosul defected; palace intrigues and corruption weakened the state. Mustering incredible energy, MURAD IV (1623–40) suppressed the uprisings of the janissaries and took a bloody retribution for the defections in the e.

1639 Peace with Persia; the border arrangements remained in effect until 1918.

1645–69 War with Crete again shook the Empire; however

1656–61 the Alb. Grand Vizier, MOHAMMED KÜPRÜLÜ, was once again able to prevent the disintegration of the Empire.

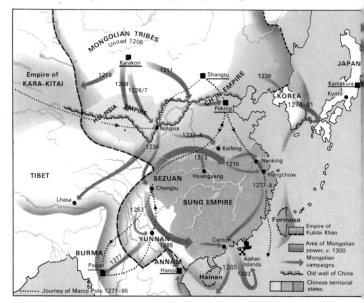

China during the Mongolian period (Yuan Dynasty), 1205–1368

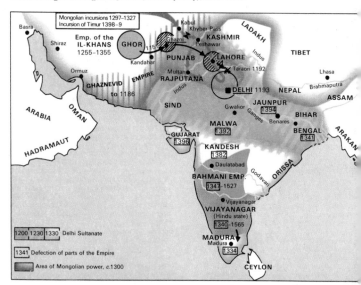

The Sultanate of Delhi, 1206–1526

Mongol. Rule in China (1264–1368)

211–15 GENGHIS KHAN's invasion of the Ch'in Empire (p. 179), which he systematically devastated.

215 Peking was taken. The Great Khan died after

227 the destruction of the Hsi-Hsia Kdm. The Mongols and the Sung Dynasty concluded an alliance to subjugate and

233/4 partition the Ch'in Empire. After the conquest of Sezuan and Yunnan, **Kublai** (1214–94), grandson of GENGHIS KHAN, in 1257 transferred his residence to Chengtu; to Peking (Chanbalik) in 1264.

258 Attack on the encircled Sung Empire. Proclaimed Great Khan, KUBLAI redistributed the Mongol. Empire and then completed the

268–79 conquest of the Sung Empire (use of cannons and guns). He est. the **Yuan Dynasty** (1280–1368) and as Emperor SHIH-TSU reigned over a vast empire. Advances to Burma and Java failed.

281 Naval attack on Japan; however, a typhoon (*kamikaze* = 'wind of the gods') saved the islands (cf. the Armada, p. 243).

Government: division of the land into 12 provinces and of the pop. into 4 classes: (a) Mongols (dignitaries, tax-exempt landowners); (b) natives of Cen. Asia (Turk. peoples and Europeans serving in admin. and trade); N. Chinese and Koreans (lower middle class); and Sung Chinese (barbarians without rights or permission to trade). Religiously tolerant, the Mongols allowed the penetration of Islam in the W.

307 1st Cath. archbpc in Peking.

Econ. life/trade: experimentation with technical inventions (flying machines, submarines, the torpedo, the telescope) which were later to be rejected by Chin. ctr. as too crude. Extensive manufacture of porcelain for export. Peking became the trade metropolis of Eurasia; vigorous trade with Europe.

The **extensive travels** of the Venetian **Marco Polo** (1254–1324) brought him to the Imp. Court; at the request of his host, he undertook travels within China. His accounts formed Europe's geographical ideas of Asia throughout the 14th/15th cents.

325 Famine: 8 mil. of 45 mil. Chinese succumbed. The Yuan Empire's cult. inferiority as well as nat. Chin. resistance hastened its disintegration (p. 227).

Literature: excluded from administrative service, former Chin. officials turned to popular writing (novels) and playwriting, which had up to then been neglected.

The 1st Isl. Incursions into India

During the 'Holy War', Arabs conquered

712–45 the Indus Area (Sind), incl. Multan; they were prevented from advancing further.

999–1030 Mahmud the Great of Ghazni (W. Turkestan), 1st Turk. Sultan. **Firdausi** (939–1020), the greatest Pers. writer of epics, resided at his court (*The Book of Kings*); so did the mathematician AL-BIRUNI (973–1048: descriptions of the Ind. countryside).

1001–26 17 predatory campaigns of the Sultan against India (superiority of cavalry over Ind. infantry with elephants). The Ghaznevids est. themselves in the Punjab (Lahore); in 1160 they were pushed out of Ghazni by the Sultan of Ghur.

1162–1206 Mohammed of Ghur, who in

1186 dest. the Ghaznevid Empire and defeated the *Rajputs* (territ. Hindu princes) in the

1192 b. of Taraori.

The Sultanate of Delhi (1206–1526)

Elevated to the position of general by slaves, AIBAK expanded Isl. power, murdered MOHAMMED, and made himself

1206 Sultan of Delhi (the so-called 'Slave Dynasty').

1221 Advance of GENGHIS KHAN to the Indus.

1296–1316 ALADAIN KHALJI broke the power of the Rajputs and repulsed Mongol. incursions in the NW. of the Sultanate.

Government: milit.-theocratic despotism of the Sultan, but without order of succession (dyn. struggles fraught with murder); there was no hered. feudal nobility; rather, the state was led through the **Jagir system:** high officials (Turks, Arabs, Indians, Mongols, and others) were granted fiefs to exploit for a limited period. A severe system of taxation did not prevent great prosperity: textiles (Bengal), shawls (Kashmir), carpets (Lahore), sugar. Vigorous trade with the Isl. world (Egypt). Sharp social contrast between Isl. (incl. Ind.) lords, Arab.-Ind. merchants (relatively prosperous), and Ind. craftsmen and artisans (poor as a result of taxation that could amount to 50% of income).

Destruction of Ind. Buddhism: destruction of monasteries, temples and writings. The excessively large numbers of Hindus, called 'men of the book' (non-heathen), were obliged to pay a special tax (*jizya*). The relationship between Moslems and Hindus was at all times determined by the Sultan.

c. 1330 Greatest extension of the Sultanate under MOHAMMED IBN TUGHLUK (1325–51), the '2nd Alexander'; conquest of S. India (Deccan); dissolution began simultaneously.

c. 1340 The Hindu Empire of **Vijayanagar** ('City of Victory') became the independent centre of resistance to Islam. Constant warfare against the

1347 Bahmani state of the Moslem rebel ZAFAR KHAN; *c.* 1490 it disintegrated into the '5 Deccan Sultanates' (until 1527).

1351–88 FIRUZ III attempted to halt the decline of Delhi through the support of agriculture (irrigation projects). With his death the power of the sultans declined further.

1398/9 Invasion of Timur (p. 179): Delhi dest., the Punjab pillaged and annexed. During the 15th cent. the sovereignty of the Sultan was limited to Delhi (p. 229). Because of the Port.

1498 discovery of the sea route, India became an area of Eur. interest (p. 221).

Humanism

(Lat. *humanitas* = humanity; from '*studia humanitatis*'.)

Italy: in schools and universities, the '*studia humanista*' (grammar, rhetoric and poetics) were traditionally taught by '*Oratores*', '*Poetae*' or '*Humanistae*'. The study of the literature of antiquity was an innovation. The superior knowledge of the humanists found expression in the critique of scholasticism (ignorance of Lat. authors and Lat. style). The movement was stimulated by Neo-Platonism: scholars migrating from Byzantium (MANUEL CHRYSOLORAS, BESSARION) taught Gk from 1400, and est. the **Platonic Academy** at Florence in 1440. The unhampered intellectual development of man, who was considered able to perfect himself through the study of classical literature, was advocated. Strong impulses came from the poet **Petrarch** (1304–74). Familiar with AUGUSTINE, SENECA and CICERO, he sought the 'wisdom of the enlightened heathen' – to develop intellect and soul, and to renew the mission of Rome and Italy – in pastoral solitude. With the **Decameron**, his friend Boccaccio (1313–75) composed the first mod. short story collection. The ideal of the cultured and simultaneously politically active individual was portrayed by LEONARDO BRUNI in the *Cicero Novus* (Florence, 1415). **Ficino** (1433–99), a physician and interpreter of PLATO, advocated a religion of aesthetics (God as the expression of beauty). **Pico della Mirandola** (1463–99) projected a concept of the world based on Christ., classical and Jew. cult. values. The first of the papal humanists, **Nicholas V** (1447–55), founded the **Vatican Library** at Rome. His secretary **Lorenzo Valla** (1405–57) introduced **philological humanism** by the critical study of texts and Scripture: comparison of the Vulgate with the original Gk text; proof of the forgery of the 'Donation of Constantine'. The new poetic style of PETRARCH was adopted by LUIGI PULCI, ARIOSTO and **Torquato Tasso** (1544–95). By the mid 15th cent., humanism, disseminated by students, printers (CAXTON, London; BADIUS, Paris; etc.), Ital. clerics and diplomats attending the councils, spread throughout Europe.

Germany: brief prelude c. 1350 at the court of CHARLES IV at Prague as a result of the Chancellor JOHANN VON NEUMARKT's acquaintance with PETRARCH (JOHANN VON SAAZ: *Ackermann aus Böhmen*, 1400).

1348 Establishment of the University of Prague. Prepared by mysticism and the *Devotio Moderna* (p. 184), Ger. humanism was characterized by relig. earnestness.

Philological direction: utilization of classical and early Christ. works to deepen the understanding of life; conflicts with scholasticism. **Rudolf Agricola** strove for a reform of the Lat. schools (Schlettstadt, Deventer). The new learning captured almost all universities by 1500. MAXIMILIAN I invited **Conrad Celtis** (1459–1508), who had been proclaimed '*Poeta Laureatus*', to Vienna as the first teacher of rhetoric and poetics.

John Reuchlin (1455–1522) promoted the study of Gk and Heb. Attacked by Cologne Dominicans because of this, he was supported by the **Erfurt Circle** of MUTIANUS RUFUS. The ensuing so-called Reuchlin feud (1515–17) produced the satirical **Letters by Obscure Men** (CROTUS RUBEANUS, HUTTEN) aimed at scholastic ignorance. As '*Praeceptor Germaniae*', **Philip Melanchthon** (1497–1560) created the humanistic Gymnasium and endeavoured to forge synthesis of the Reformation and humanism (p. 231).

Nat. orientation: the discovery and collection of outstanding works of Ger. literature awakened a feeling of **nat. consciousness** which resulted in attempts to repel accusations of Germ. barbarism through historical scholarship. CELTIS edited the first **edition of Tacitus** (*Germania*); **Jakob Wimpfeling** (1450–1528) composed the first Ger. historical study in 1505; **Ulrich von Hutten** (1488–1523) struggled against the abuses of the Rom. Church and Curia and for a new Ger. empire (p. 231).

Cosmopolitan orientation: Europe's most renowned scholar, **Desiderius Erasmus of Rotterdam** (1467–1536), strove for a compromise between the humanistic spirit and Christ. piety. His scholarly work found its climax in the **Gk ed.** of the **New Testament of 1516.**

Neo-Lat. poets and translators were, among others, WILLIBALD PIRCKHEIMER and EOBANUS HESSUS; historians, BEATUS RHENANUS, JOHN TURMAIR (cal. AVENTINUS) and PEUTINGER.

England: spreading of the 'New Learning' from Oxford. FICINO's pupil **John Colet** (d 1519) founded St Paul's School, London; like HENRY VIII's chancellor, **Thomas More** (1478–1535), he was a friend of ERASMUS. In his **Utopia** (1516) More conceived an ideal state after that modelled on PLATO's *Republic* (see also p. 238). WYATT and HOWARD utilized the poetic forms of PETRARCH in English. First **flowering of literature** with the works of LYLY, SIDNEY and EDMUND SPENSER, and the **dramatists** CHRISTOPHER MARLOWE (1564–93), BEN JONSON, JOHN WEBSTER. Outstanding was the work of **William Shakespeare** (1564–1616) of Stratford-on-Avon (tragedies, comedies, histories, sonnets).

France: the *studia humanitatis* became a firm part of tradition by the end of the 15th cent. ROBERT GAGUIN introduced PLATO. The heritage of Rome and Gaul. Jacques Lefèvre (*Faber Stapulensis*) translated the Gk Testament in 1523; the scholar of Graecism, **Guillaume Budé**, est. the Collège de France and the Bibliothèque Nationale. François **Villon** (1431?–1489?) continued to write in the manner of the vagrants; **Rabelais** (1495–1553), the satirist, already wrote in the new style (*Gargantua and Pantagruel*), as did the poets of the Pléiade: among others Ronsard, PELLETIERS and DU BELLAY (who developed theory of language stressing Rom. traditions). MALHERBE strove for a purification of the nat. language; **Michel de Montaigne** (1533–92), the moralist, developed the genre of the essay.

The Renaissance in Italy (15th/16th Cents.)

The Fr. conception of the Renaissance (Ital. *inascita, rinascimento* = rebirth) was introduced c. 1550 as an art-historical classification by the painter VASARI and has been widely disseminated since MICHELET and BURCKHARDT after 1860).

The 'turning to the world' (p. 215) and humanism changed attitudes towards life fundamentally from the '*viator mundi*' ('pilgrim to the heavenly home') to the '*faber mundi*' 'creator and ruler of the world'). The writer CASTIGLIONE (1478–1529) created the image of the '**uomo universale**', the universally educated, great individual, who knows himself at one in beautiful) harmony with nature and 'is able to accomplish whatever he wills'. This ideal affected the conception of the Fr. '**gentilhomme**', the Eng. '**gentleman**' and the Sp. '**caballero**' and the Ger. '**Kavalier**'.

The breakthrough to the discovery of man and the world was most strongly expressed in **art**. The example of antiquity was to encourage **art. integrity**; to surpass antiquity was the highest aim. The ground was prepared during the 14th cent. (*trecento*) by CIMABUE, GIOTTO and GIOVANNI PISANO. Patronized by the city-republics of Venice, Florence (the Medici, p. 15), and the Sforza family (Milan), the Este family (Ferrara) and the Popes (p. 217), the **Early Renaissance** was a product of the 15th cent. (**Quattrocento**).

During the 16th cent. intensification led to the **High Renaissance (Cinquecento)**, which after 1530 developed into the **Mannerism** of the **Late Renaissance**.

Architecture: adoption of classical forms barrel-vaults, round arches, domed central structures); a new concept of space was illustrated by stress on vertical lines with balanced proportions; development of the -storeyed Ital. city-palace with structured façade, interior courts and arched promenades. The construction of **St Peter's** in Rome, commissioned in 1506 by Pope JULIUS II, saw the participation of **Bramante** (1444–1514), **Raphael**, **PERUZZI** and **Michelangelo** (the cupola).

Sculpture: the example of antiquity brought about the 'rediscovery of the human body'; figures in the round (busts, statues of nobles on horseback, tomb memorials). Direction was given by **Ghiberti**, his pupil **Donatello** 1386–1466) and **Michelangelo** (1475–1564): David', 'Moses'.

Painting: the striving for ideal natural beauty led to the **development of perspective**, the observation of anatomical **proportions**, the technique of **portrait painting** (oils), and the **fresco**. Early, religiously inspired works of MASACCIO, FRA ANGELICO, DOMENICO VENEZIANO, *et al.*; masterpieces by **Sandro Botticelli** 1444–1510); **Raphael Santi** (1483–1520): Madonnas; **Michelangelo**: Last Judgement; **Leonardo da Vinci** (1452–1519): The Last Supper, Mona Lisa (also writings on the theory of art); **Titian** (1477?–1576).

Music: with the adaptation of polyphonic vocal music (mass, motet) to instruments (lute,

cembalo), pure **instrumental music** developed. Masters of the imitative style were **Orlando di Lasso** (1532–94) and **Palestrina** (1525–94).

The Late Gothic in Europe

Despite princely commissions (FRANCIS I of France) to Ital. artists (LEONARDO DA VINCI) and study by Eur. artists in Italy (DÜRER), the Renaissance did not spread until the 16th cent. and late Goth. styles remained in use. The princely **palace** and residence took the place of the castle; the artist freed himself from the ties of artisans still maintained by some of the schools of painters, dome-builders and masons. **Germany**: the bourgeois character of the period is reflected in the urban patrician homes and city-halls, some built of lath and plaster with bays, staircases and clock-towers (Nuremberg, Rothenburg). City-halls and palaces were built after the Ital. model – esp. in the s. (Heidelberger *Schloss*) – during the so-called Weser Renaissance (c. 1600). The realism of traditional Ger. woodcarving and painting was intensified in the works (altar decorations) of, among others, STEPHAN LOCHNER (Cologne school), KONRAD WITZ, MARTIN SCHONGAUER (d. 1491) and HANS HOLBEIN THE ELDER. The period found its fulfilment in the 'last artist of the Gothic', **Matthias Grünewald** (d. 1528) of Würzburg (the Isenheim Altar-piece).

Albrecht Dürer (1471–1528) combined Late Goth. tradition and Ger. feeling with the Ital. viewpoint. Utilizing perspective and proportion he became the teacher of a new generation of painters with his self-portraits, religious tableaux, water-colour landscapes, woodcuts, copperplate engravings and etchings.

Ital. influence is also evident in the portraits of **Hans Holbein the Younger** (1497–1553), the paintings of ALBRECHT ALTDORFER and the drawings of LUKAS CRANACH THE ELDER.

A flowering of **sculpture** was reflected in the Franconian carved altars of **Tilman Riemenschneider** (d. 1531), and the work of the Nurembergers **Veit Stoss, Adam Kraft** and **Peter Vischer.**

Netherlands: grandiose unfolding of the 'soft style' of realistic mood painting (early portraits, landscapes) by, among others, the brothers **van Eyck** (the Ghent Altar-piece, 1432) and **Rogier van der Weyden** (p. 193). The grotesque representations of **Hieronymus Bosch** (d. 1516) influenced **Pieter Breughel the Elder** (d. 1569).

France: the Late 'Flamboyant Gothic' concealed architectural form in a wealth of decorative features. Brief flowering of Renaissance architecture in the **Loire châteaux** of FRANCIS I and in Paris in the work of LESCOT (a wing of the Louvre, 1556–64) and DELORME (façade of the Tuileries, begun 1564). In **painting** transition from the miniature to the tableau by **Jean Fouquet** (d. 1481) and the 'school of the Loire'.

England: indigenous development of Goth. in the **Perpendicular style** c. 1350–1530 (fan vaults, flat arches, vertical decorations). Fused with Renaissance influences, it became the **Tudor style** (before 1600): Hampton Court.

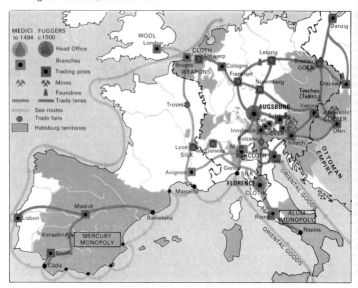

Early capitalist trade associations

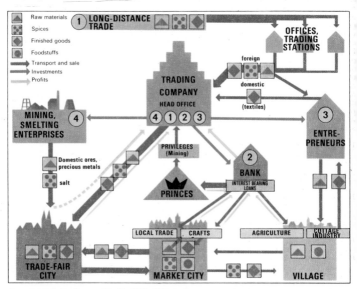

A company's development in the 15th–16th cents.

Early Capitalism

The gradual change from a barter to a money economy began with the **Crusades** (p. 153) and spread from Cen. and Upper Italy (p. 183) by way of s. Germany, France and the Netherlands through all Europe. Man's freedom to strive for calculated profit was the symptomatic expression of the change in attitude in the mode of man's **gainful employment**. Talent and ability, not origin and estate, were the qualifying factors for membership in the aristocracy of money.

Trade and the crafts: to expand long-distance trade, important merchants est. private **trading companies** (e.g. the Ravensburger trading company, 1380–1530) and invested capital to finance the transport of goods (ship-building) and trading stations abroad. Merchants used new techniques of accounting and granted credit. Clerical prohibitions of interest (usury) were evaded by the Church itself through the **rent system.** Grown to the top rank of Eur. financial power (p. 181), the Church used merchants (and also the Knights Templars, p. 153) to secure its income; in exchange for advances, they were granted privileges (**rents**). Sec. princes imitated the system by farming out the rights to customs, coinage, the holding of markets, mining and the use of the soil.
Banks were est. in Genoa, Florence (the Bardi and Strozzi families et al.), Augsburg (the Welsers) and Antwerp (p. 245). The **merchant banker** est. his own **export shops** (textiles, metal articles), which produced on the basis of the **'putting-out'** system. The entrepreneur provided domestic workers, who were paid wages, with raw materials and tools, but he distributed the finished articles himself.
Large capitalists (merchants, bankers, entrepreneurs) strove for monopolies and polit. influence through the control of one branch of the economy (mining), export trade, or the credit business. The state was often their competitor, seeking monopolies as part of its sovereign right (Spain, p. 243). In the 16th cent., privileged **associations of merchants,** which carried out the colon. policies of the state, developed in France and England (p. 275).

The Medici in Florence: enriched by trade with the Orient and the **alum monopoly** granted by the Curia, GIOVANNI est. the greatest Eur. trading and banking company, which in the production of textiles alone occupied 300 firms with 10,000 workers.
1434–64 As 'father of the fatherland', COSIMO THE ELDER exercised monarchical powers in an urban régime with republican forms. He patronized PETRARCH and BOCCACCIO (p. 212) and founded the
1440 Platonic Academy. Important as a writer and statesman,
1462–92 Lorenzo il Magnifico ('the Magnificent') pursued a policy of peaceful reconciliation in Italy and led Florence to its highest flowering. Renaissance artists worked at his court, incl. BOTTICELLI and MICHELANGELO (p. 213).

1513–21 Pope Leo X. (Tomb of the Medici in Florence; the frescoes in the Sistine Chapel; the cupola of St Peter's.) The expenses incurred in the support of the arts and in financial speculation finally exceeded the financial power of the Medici company.

The Fuggers in Augsburg: rise of the peasant family of weavers during the 15th cent. through trade and transactions in money. As banker to the Habsburgs and the popes
1511–25 JAKOB FUGGER THE RICH financed the election and wars of CHARLES V, controlled Eur. lead, silver and copper production, and obtained a **monopoly in quicksilver.**
1525–60 ANTON FUGGER had trading concessions in Chile, Peru and Moscow. The company declined by the end of the 16th cent. because of state bankruptcies in Spain, family conflicts and lack of interest on the part of the heirs.

Agriculture: increased urban demands for foodstuffs and raw materials brought about a change of structure:
1. Transition to the production of specialities (rye and wheat on suitable land, dairy farming).
2. Decline of the patriarchal feudal system (p. 126) because of the change from labour services to rents (lease-holders).
3. Development of new forms of landowning: hered. peasant leases (France); free agricultural wage labour (England); leasing of the feudal estate to the 'Meier'; descent of the serf into personal bondage; direct admin. of noble estates.
4. Establishment of manorial estates **(Gutsherrschaft)** in the E. (agricultural production by the landlord, incl. corvées and bonded serfdom (*Gesindezwang*)).

Soc. crises and upheavals: production for profit increased the money in circulation; owing to the over-production of silver, currencies were devalued continuously and prices rose. In the cities an early form of the proletariat (wage-earning artisans) developed, which urged the guilds to challenge the patricians for control of the city. The gap between wealth and poverty increased; this, together with diseases and epidemics (p. 155), caused socio-relig. crises:
after 1302 continuous artisan unrest in Flanders (p. 191); in France
1357/8 uprising of the Paris guilds and the Jacquerie (p. 191);
14th/15th cent. factional urban struggles in Italy;
1378 uprising of the wool carders in Florence;
1381 uprising of the peasants (WAT TYLER) and the Lollards in England (p. 189);
1419–36 the Hussite wars of the Czech proletarians against the Ger. bourgeoisie;
15th cent. guild struggles and peasant unrest in Germany (p. 233);
16th/17th cents. peasant and Cossack uprisings in Poland (p. 249) and Russia.

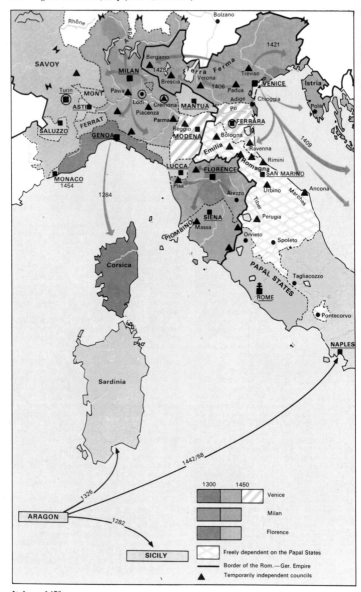

Italy, c. 1450

The **Holy Rom. Empire** lacked the strength to control Italy politically after the decline of the Hohenstaufen Dynasty (p. 173). The Curia resided at Avignon (p. 181); France was at war with England (p. 191).

The Twilight of Ger. Imp. Policy

1310–13 HENRY VII in Italy. Hailed by DANTE (p. 184) as 'Liberator', he made the Visconti (Milan) and Scaligers (Verona) his vicars.

1312 Following his coronation, HENRY d. at Siena as he was planning a campaign against Naples.

1324 The final conflict between Emperor (LOUIS IV) and Pope (JOHN XXII; p. 181) occurred because of the dismissal of a vicar.

1327–30 LOUIS's journey to Rome: alliance with Sicily against Naples; coronation by representatives of the Rom. people (Colonna); however, the concept of a secular empire (MARSILIUS OF PADUA, p. 184) was unrealized. **Charles IV** abandoned imp. activity and journeyed to Rome only on the occasion of his

1355 coronation, and in 1368/9 when he accompanied the Pope back to Rome.

The Ital. States in the 14th/15th Cents.

Signoria (city-states) developed alongside the existing feudal states: factional struggles between the imp. **Ghibellines** and the papal **Guelphs**, between artisans, patricians and noble families, usually resulted in the rise of polit. leaders. By means of cunning or force, the **Podestà** often became hered. **Signore.** They enlarged the *Signoria* to include other cities, cared for the people, and patronized the arts and sciences. Despite continual unrest, Italy experienced a period of econ. advance and cult. brilliance (Renaissance, p. 213).

The new concept of the state: econ. considerations (p. 215) determined politics and admin. The **autonomous state** was governed by paid officials in accordance with '*ragione di stato*' **(reason of state).** Warfare was conducted by the **Condottiere** (an entrepreneurial mercenary); he avoided the capital outlay of battles by manoeuvring and using siege techniques; possessing 'the nose of a stock-market speculator', he often switched allegiance and entered the polit. arena. The **theory** of the new, purely sec. state based on power was developed by the Florentine **Niccolò Machiavelli** (1469–1527); principal work: **The Prince** (1513). From the mid 15th cent. (1451 Peace of Lodi) a measure of balance existed between the medium-sized Ital. states:

Venice: the constitution of the aristocratic republic was completed by the

1291 Curtailment of the Great Council and the establishment of the

1310 Council of 10 (to prevent conspiracies). Following the

1381 vict. over **Genoa** (p. 183), extension of the **Terra Firma** in rivalry with Milan.

Florence: a democratic constitution was

1228 put into effect by the republic. The guilds alone governed the *Signoria*. By the

1293 'Ordinance of Justice' the patricians were excluded from all polit. activity.

1409 Subjugation of Pisa. The ALBIZZI family lost power to the **Medici** (p. 215) during the unsuccessful war with Milan.

Milan: HENRY VII decided conflicts between the nobility in favour of the **Visconti.**

1385–1402 GIANGALEAZZO expanded the state as a step towards becoming king of Italy.

1450 The condotierre **Francesco Sforza** obtained power during the struggles with Florence, Naples and Venice.

The Papal States: ind. *Signorias* were est. during the exile of the Popes at Avignon. Subsequent to conflicts between the ORSINI and COLONNA families in Rome and the abortive democratic upheaval

1347 under the 'popular tribune' COLA DI RIENZI

1353–68 Cardinal ALBORNOZ regained the city for the Curia; his code of laws (the Aegidian Constitutions) remained in effect until 1816.

The Renaissance popes saw themselves as sec. princes, artists or scholars, but hastened the internal decay of the Church (p. 181).

1447–55 NICHOLAS V est. the **Vatican Library.** The diplomat, humanist and *littérateur*

1458–64 PIUS II (ENEA SILVIO PICCOLOMINI) unsuccessfully advocated a crusade against the Turks at the

1459 Congress of Mantua. The papal court deteriorated (nepotism, simony) with the reign of the great patron of architecture SIXTUS IV (1471–84). Excessive moral decay occurred in the reign of INNOCENT VIII (1484–92) and

1492–1503 ALEXANDER VI (BORGIA), whose son CAESARE (1475–1507) dest. the sep. polit. entities of the state.

1503–13 JULIUS II distinguished himself as commander in the field and statesman.

1513–21 The learned aesthete, patron of the arts and lavish spender LEO X (Medici) promoted the construction of St Peter's through a system of indulgences which set the Reformation into motion; a development to which he was blind (p. 231). With the capture of CLEMENS VII during the

1527 Sacco di Roma (p. 237), the Renaissance papacy came to an end.

Naples: allied with the Curia,

1309–43 **Robert the Wise** obtained hegemony over Italy. In 1347/8 LOUIS I of Hungary (p. 201) occupied the kdm., but was unable to halt the decline of the House of Anjou. ALFONSO V OF ARAGÓN conquered Naples in 1442.

Sicily: ruled by a branch of Aragón since the days of FREDERICK III (1296–1337), the state fell apart as a result of wars with Naples and baronial feuds.

1442–58 Union with Naples;

1479 Sicily fell to Spain (p. 187).

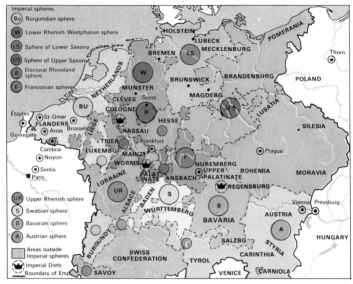

Organization of the German Empire into Imperial districts, 1512

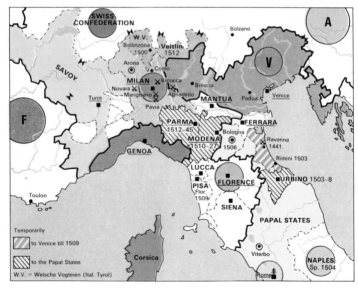

The struggle for Italy, 1494–1519

Imp. Reforms (c. 1500)

1493–1519 As ruler of all the hered. Habsburg lands, **Maximilian I** (king since 1486) held a key position in Europe, which gained him in **Burgundy** (p. 193) and **Upper Italy** the enmity of France. Beloved leader of lansquenets (mercenary soldiers) and master of gunnery, as well as 'last knight' and patron of the humanists, he was an impatient and inconsistent politician who, at times, pursued unrealistic aims (succession to the Fr., Swed. and papal thrones), but who successfully represented the **policies of the Habsburg family:** his son PHILIP THE FAIR mar. the heiress of Spain (p. 187).

1515 Marriage and inheritance contracts with Bohemia and Hungary (p. 201) formed the **basis for Habsburg world power.** The **imp. reforms** were the work of the constant opposition to the Emperor within the Empire, led by the Archbishop of Mainz,

1484–1504 Berthold von Henneberg. At the Council of Basle (p. 181) Cardinal **Nicholas of Cusa** (CUSANUS, 1401–64) advocated the concept of joint action by Emperor and the estates in legislation and gvt – a concept based on natural law – by disseminating his work

1433 De Concordantia Catholica ('Of the Unity of the Church'). Demands for reform had been voiced at imp. diets from the mid 15th cent. These included the **Gravamina** (complaints) **of the German Nation** and the *Reformatio Sigismundi,* a widely distributed anonymous pamphlet. The work of reform began with the

1495 Diet of Worms: proclamation of the **Perpetual Public Peace.** The **Imp. Chamber of Justice,** the supreme court of the land, was est. at Frankfurt (after 1527 at Speyer) to eliminate feuding privileges. To cover expenses, the 'common penny' was levied (1st imp. tax, not permanent). Switzerland rejected the decisions and obtained its independence in the

1499 Swabian War.

1500 Diet of Augsburg: a permanent 'Council of Regency' (*Reichsregiment*) was est. (dissolved 1502; reintroduced 1521).

1512 Diet of Cologne: supreme power was granted to the **Imp. Diet,** which deliberated the Emperor's propositions in 3 **Colleges** (Electors, Princes, Imp. Cities). Its decisions were proclaimed as **Imp. Mandates** (*Reichsabschiede,* from 1663 *Reichsschlüsse*). Establishment of 10 **Imp. Circles,** each under the *directorium* of 2 princes, each for the preservation of the public peace and the raising of the imp. tax and the **imp. army** (under commanders of the circles).

1521 Imp. Diet of Worms: Imp. Ordinance of Registration (*Reichsmatrikelordnung* = Roll of territ. income to determine the basis for troop and tax levies).

Results: the beginnings of framing an **Imp. Constitution** and of eliminating tribally based particularism was not continued because the imp. diets met only irregularly.

The Struggle over Italy, 1494–1516

1483–98 With the object of re-creating the Byz. Empire, **Charles VIII of France** claimed the Kdm of Naples as an Anjou inheritance. The Treaty of Étaples with England (1492) and

1493 the Treaties of Senlis with the Habsburgs (confirmation of the Burg. inheritance) and Barcelona with Spain (Roussillon) were concluded in preparation for the ·conquest. In alliance with Duke LUDOVICO SFORZA ('*Il Moro*') (1480–1508)

1494 the Conquest of Naples was accomplished. The Ital. state system collapsed.

Florence: expulsion of the Medici; the preacher of penance and prophet of doom **Savonarola** (1452–98) est. a democratic theocracy, was excommunicated by ALEXANDER VI and burned as a heretic.

To maintain the balance of power

1495 the League of Spain and the Habsburgs – joined by England and the Ital. states – forced CHARLES to retreat.

1498–1515 As heir of the Visconti, **Louis XII of France** renewed the attack.

1500 Occupation of Milan. For its support (vict. at Novara), Switzerland received Tessin (Bellinzona) in the

1503 Treaty of Arona. **Naples'** loss of independence to Spain was recognized by LOUIS

1504 in the Treaty of Blois: beginning of **Sp.-Habsburg dominance over Italy.** MAXIMILIAN and LOUIS concluded the

1508 League of Cambrai to check **Venice,** which lost Terra Firma by the defeat of Agnadello. Pope JULIUS II left the league after the conquest of Romagna and, with Spain, Venice and Switzerland, formed the

1511 'Holy League to Liberate Italy'. MAXIMILIAN and HENRY VIII (of England) joined the league and encircled LOUIS, who in turn was able to incite Scotland to attack England (1513 b. of Flodden, p. 247); LOUIS was forced

1513 to vacate Milan after the defeats of Guinegate and Novara. However,

1515–47 Francis I was able to regain the duchy by the

1515 Vict. of Marignano over Switzerland. Switzerland abandoned its claim to major-power status and has ever since followed a **policy of strict neutrality.**

1516 Concordat of Bologna: confirmation of the Gallican Nat. Church by Pope LEO X.

1516 In the Treaty of Noyon, Spain guaranteed France's possession of Milan. However, the new Sp. king, CHARLES I (V) (Habsburg, 1516–56) refused to recognize the agreement. The rivalry was intensified by the claims of both kings to the Ger. imp. crown. It entered a new stage with the election of CHARLES in 1519 (p. 237).

Significance: until the 18th cent. the Habsburg–Fr. conflict was to remain the cen. problem of the w. Eur. community of states. The fundamental polit. principle of the **balance of power** was worked out in the struggle over Italy with its continually alternating coalitions.

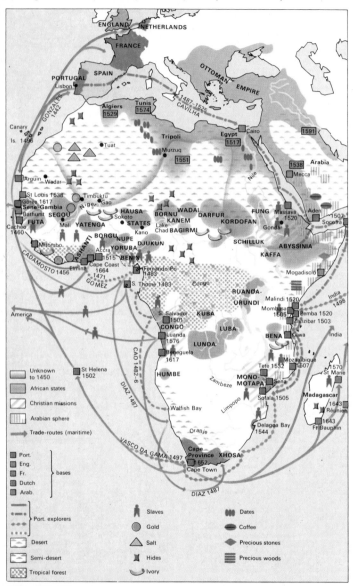

ENGLAND NETHERLANDS
FRANCE
PORTUGAL SPAIN
Lisbon
OTTOMAN EMPIRE
GONZALES 1442
Algiers Tunis
1529 1574
1487-1525
CAVILHA
Canary Tuat
Is. 1496
Tripoli Egypt Cairo
Murzuq 1517
1591
1551
Arabia
1538
Mecca
Arguin
Wadar
St Louis 1638 Timbuktu Niger Gao
Gorée 1617 Sene-Gambia SEGOU HAUSA BORNU WADAI Massaua Aden 1507
Bathurst Mali Sokoto STATES KANEM DARFUR FUNG 1520 Socotra
FUTA YATENGA Lake BAGIRMI KORDOFAN Gondar
Cachéo BORGU Chad Kano
1460 Mitombo ASHANTI NUPE DJUKUN SCHILLUK ABYSSINIA
Accra YORUBA KAFFA
CADAMOSTO 1456 Elmina BENIN Fernando Pó
Cape Coast 1515 1493 Mogadiscio
1664 1471
GOMEZ S. Thomé 1483 Congo
America RUANDA- India
URUNDI 1498
Malindi 1520
S. Salvador KUBA Mombasa Pemba 1520
1501 1505 Zanzibar 1503
CONGO LUBA
Luanda Kilwa India
1576 LUNDA BENA
Benguela
1617 Tete 1532 Mozambique
HUMBE 1507 1570
St Helena St Marie
1502 Zambeze Sena
MONO- Madagascar
MOTAPA 1643
CAO 1482-6 Sofala 1505 Réunion
DIAZ 1487 Walfish Bay 1643
Limpopo Fr Dauphin
Oranje Delagoa Bay
1544
VASCO DA GAMA 1497 Cape
Province XHOSA
1652
Cape Town
DIAZ 1487

Unknown
to 1450
African states
Christian missions
Arabian sphere
Trade-routes (maritime)

Port.
Eng.
Fr.   bases
Dutch
Arab.

Port. explorers

Desert
Semi-desert
Tropical forest

Slaves Dates
Gold Coffee
Salt Precious stones
Hides Precious woods
Ivory

Africa, 15th–17th cents.

New Findings in the Natural Sciences

Humanistic studies, the observation of nature and a fresh spirit of exploration replaced the traditional Aristotelian conception of the universe (p. 58). Man through Gk writings (ARISTARCHUS OF SAMOS, p. 71) was again made aware of the **global shape of the earth.** The Nuremberg astronomer and printer, REGIO-MONTANUS (JOH. MÜLLER), calculated the daily position of the heavenly bodies in the **Ephemerids** (yearbooks, after 1475). MARTIN BEHAIM designed the 1st globe in 1492. Influenced by CUSANUS (p. 184) and the teachings of PYTHAGORAS, the physician and canon **Nicholas Copernicus** (1473–1543) of Torun discovered the mathematically yet unproven **heliocentric solar system** (published 1543 in *De revolutionibus orbium coelestium*). **Giordano Bruno** (1548–1600; burned as a heretic) expanded the Copernican system with his pantheistic conception of an infinite universe without centre. The Dane TYCHO BRAHE (1546–1601) erected the 1st observatory (Kassel) and, as KEPLER's teacher (p. 256), furthered the development of modern astronomy.

George Agricola (1494–1555) was the founder of mineralogy and metallurgy; a physician, botanist and chemist, THEOPHRASTUS BOMBASTUS VON HOHENHEIM, cal. **Paracelsus** (1493–1541), reformed medicine. He recognized the chemical and physical sources of life and attempted to explain it on its own terms.

Technical Inventions

Gunpowder was utilized for firearms (p. 191) from the 14th cent.; the **compass,** and navigational instruments (the 'Jacob's staff' used to fix position at sea). Coastal shipping became **seagoing shipping.** The pocket-watch ('the Nuremberg egg') was invented by PETER HENLEIN in 1500; LEONARDO DA VINCI (p. 213) was a pioneer in the sciences of hydraulics and mechanics. The most important invention was that of **Johann Gutenberg** (GENSFLEISCH, *c.* 1400–67) of Mainz: **c. 1445 printing** with movable metallic type; printing press, printing double-faced on **linen-paper** (in use in Europe for woodcuts since the 13th cent.). GUTENBERG's 1st great production: the '42-line Bible' (c. 1455). Printing spread rapidly throughout Europe and opened unexpected possibilities in education and communications (cf. Humanism, p. 212).

Geographical Discoveries

The previously separate civilizations of Asia and Europe met through geographical discoveries. As a result of the achievements of the seafaring Eur. nations, the **epoch of universal history** was begun.
Turk. customs tolls had made the Arab. transit trade more costly since the advance of the Ottomans into the Levant (p. 209). The Port. prince **Henry the Navigator** (1394–1460) est. the 1st navigational school in the world and planned the circumnavigation of Africa:
1. To combat Islam (completion of the *Reconquista*, p. 187).

2. To conquer the Holy Land with the aid of the kdm of 'Prester John', supposedly loc. in Abyssinia.
3. To establish direct trade connections with the gold and slave markets of E. Africa.
Port. explorers reached
1419 the Madeiras; 1431 the Azores; 1445 Cape Verde; 1482 the mouth of the Congo.
1487 **Bartholomew Diaz** circumnavigated the southern tip of Africa (**Cape of Good Hope**).
1498 Vasco da Gama in command of 3 ships and 150 sailors **found the sea route to India.**

Africa: the Sudan (Arab. = 'Land of the Blacks') and the E. coast were opened up by Arab. traders and islamized from the N. and E. from the 7th cent.
11th–15th cents. **States were est.** by Isl.–African peoples: among them, **Kanem** (centre of Islam and Arab trade), Bornu, Wadai, Ashanti, Darfur. Details are little known since to go by there are only oral traditions, a few datable artefacts and scant reports by Arabian travellers (IBN KHALDUN, 1332–1406).

Mali (city at midcourse of the Niger): *c.* 1235 SUN DIATA KEITA est. a large state. It reached the pinnacle of its power under emperor
1312–37 GONGO MUSA; but fell apart during the 15th cent. after the destruction of Timbuktu by the **Songhai** successor state.
1493–1528 The new state (cap. Gao) was brought to full flower by ASKIA MOHAMMED. It was subj. by Morocco in 1590.

The Congo Kdm (est. during the pre-Eur. period):
1490 King NZINGA NKUWU accepted Christianity. Decline after King NZINGA MPANGU (ALPHONSO I, d. 1541), whose son HENRIQUE, as the 1st African bp, vainly attempted to establish a distinct Church.

The Monomotapa Kdm: there are indications that gold-rich Rhodesia had an extended cult. tradition (ruins of **Simbabwe** w. of Sofala, dating to 5th/6th cents.). This, however, has not been historically substantiated (connection with the biblical Ophir?). After conquering it at the end of the 16th cent., the Portuguese est. a protectorate and exploited the goldmines.
During the 15th/16th cents. **Port. coastal fortifications** secured the sea route to India against Arab attack. At the same time they were storage and trading stations, and esp. **slave markets.** Up to the beginning of the 19th cent. Africa 'supplied' approx. 11 mil. slaves. About the same number probably succumbed *en route.* The econ. exploitation of the continent was confined to occasional raids.

India: between 1505 and 1515 the viceroys ALMEIDA and ALBUQUERQUE est. a **Port. commercial empire** in Goa, Ceylon, Malacca and the E. Indies. It yielded enormous profits (*c.* 400%); however, after *c.* 100 yrs it largely fell victim to Eng. and Dutch attacks.

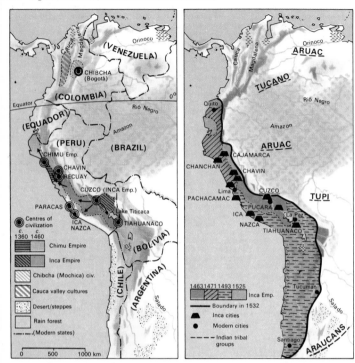

Ancient civilizations in South America

The Inca Empire, 1460–1532

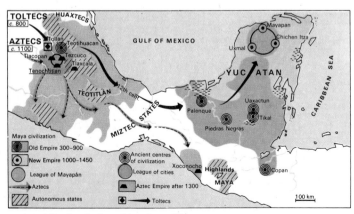

Ancient civilizations in Central America to 1520

After 15,000 B.C. (?) settlement of America by waves of immigrants from Asia (Bering Straits): fishermen in the N. (Atlantic); hunters in the northern forest and steppe areas; agricultural settlers in the S., which saw the beginnings of higher ctrs. (burial and temple mound ctrs. on the Ohio and Lower Mississippi).

c. A.D. 200–500 Agricultural peoples (Olmecs) made inroads into Mexico. They formed the basis (cultivation of corn, pottery, weaving) for the (early Toltec?) **Teotihuacan ctr.**

Ind. Civilizations in Cen. America

Technologically, the early Amer. ctrs. belong to the Younger Stone Age; metalworking was only in its beginnings (copper, gold, silver). In spite of many theories, Eur. (viking) infl. cannot be substantiated; infl. from E. Asia is possible. The **Kon-Tiki journey** of HEYERDAHL in 1947 once again raised the problem of a cult. connection with Polynesia.

The Toltecs

Emigration to Mexico (c. 800) and establishment of their ctr. at **Tollan.** Development of the crafts, art, calendar calculations. Veneration of the major deity (feathered snake) by sacrifices not involving slaughter.

The Aztecs

Adoption of more advanced forms of ctr. from the Toltecs, Mixtecs, Zapotecs, etc.

c. 1200 development of small polit. entities.

1325 (?) Establishment of **Tenochtitlan** in the lake of Mexico. Residence of the major tribe which – under its leader **Itzcoatl –**

c. 1430 forced other tribes to pay tribute and est. the 3-city league of Tenochtitlan–Tetzcoco–Tlacopan to gain polit. control.

1502–20 Montezuma II expanded the Empire, which was soon dest.

1519–21 by **Hernan Cortés** (after the murder of the prince).

Religion: Quetzalcoatl created man and the earth out of the primeval chaos (a disk with 9 to 13 heavens and netherworlds); he consumed himself in flames, but will return as a 'white cloud' to save man. The sun-gods were supposed to live from the heart-blood of man; cruel sacrificial rites were therefore performed for the watching populace (the tearing out of hearts and the eating of those sacrificed).

Culture: rebus-like pictographic symbols on stone, deer-skin or bast; writings on matters relig. and magical, as well as urban plans and accounts. The yr had 18 months (of 20 days each) and 5 'nameless' days; 52 yrs made up a 'time-cycle'.

Architecture: temples erected on massive pyramids, decorated with reliefs and sculptures.

Soc. organization: the Empire was made up of tribes of 20 clans each; leadership was provided by 4 elected leaders; the pop. was organized into classes of priests, nobles, free men, dependants and slaves.

Econ. life: joint ownership of the land by the clan; road and bridge construction. Respected as diplomats, merchants traded by barter.

The Maya Ctrs.

The Maya possessed a pictographic form of writing (only partially deciphered) and were advanced in astronomy and arithmetic.

4th–7th cents. The Old Empire: city-states with local dynasties. Their ctr. disintegrated during the

9th/10th cents. and (because of the Toltecs?) the inhabitants migrated to Yucatán: flowering of the **New Empire.**

15th cent. The League of Mayapan (Toltecs) formed to subjugate the Mayan cities.

1436 Uprising to drive out the Toltecs; the Maya migrated back to Guatemala.

The Ancient Peruvian Ctrs. of S. America

Mt. Indians were the representatives of the most ancient ctrs. discovered so far (sculptures in stone, ceramics) at **Chavin** (c. A.D. 100), **Tiahuanaco** and **Recuay.** Coastal peoples est. their own centres c. A.D. 500.

The Inca Empire of the Quechua Mt. Indians

13th cent. Establishment of the cap. Cuzco by the 1st Inca, MANCO CAPAC.

1438–1531 The development of the conqueror-state began with the 9th Inca, PACHACUTIC.

1470 Destruction of the Chimu state.

1471–93 TUPAC YUPANQUI advanced far to the S.

1513 HUAYNA CAPAC subj. the land of Quito (Equador).

1527–32 Struggles over the succession to the throne between his sons HUASCAR (Cuzco) and **Atahualpa** (Quito) who as a result of deception

1532 was captured at Cajamarca by **Francisco Pizarro** and killed.

1533 Conquest of Cuzco by the Spaniards.

Religion: 11 temples were dedicated to the sun-god, personified by the Inca, to whom animal (and at times human) sacrifices were rendered. In addition, local deities were venerated on *huacas* (mounds of stones).

Art: temples, fortresses and roads of blocks of stone (without mortar); small-scale sculptures made as sacrificial gifts, plain ceramics. No writing; *quippus* (colourful knotted cords) used to record statistics and messages.

Government: absolute theocracy. The Inca (mar. to his sister) disposed of over two thirds of the income of the state; his family provided all milit. commanders. The land was divided into areas belonging to the Inca, the temple and the community. Public storage places, terraces, irrigation systems and roads were cared for by the people, who were controlled by officials and obliged to perform labour services. Collective cultivation of the soil (corn, potatoes), no private property. Over 10,000 kms. of **Inca roads** with suspension bridges. Chains of runners and carriers.

The Chibcha Ctr.

The tribes of the plateau of Bogotá were ruled by a priest-king. Because of their trade in salt, fruits and esp. gold they influenced the area of the Magdalena river. 1536–41 destruction by the Spaniard QUESEDA (p. 225).

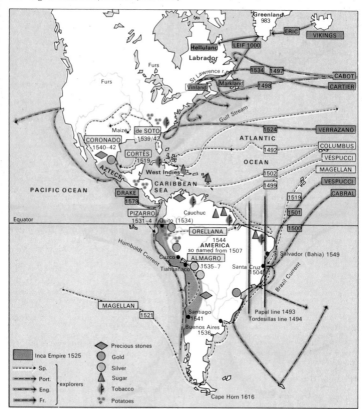

The discovery of America

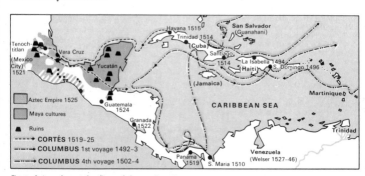

Central America at the time of the explorations

The Discovery of America by the Vikings

984 ERIC THE RED of Iceland reached **Greenland** and est. colonies.
c. 1000 His son LEIF ERICSON landed on the coast of N. America (Vinland). Permanent settlement was not possible. Because contact with Greenland was broken after 1400 (climatic changes), the discovery faded from memory.

Discovery and Initial Exploration of America

A map by the Florentine TOSCANELLI (1397–1482) inspired the Genoese **Christopher Columbus** (1451–1506) to seek the westward sea route to India in the service of ISABELLA OF CASTILE (p. 187).
1492 After a journey of 61 days, America was discovered and landings made at Guanahani (San Salvador), Cuba and Haiti. Appointed Viceroy, COLUMBUS between then and 1504 undertook 4 more journeys to 'West India', in 1498 discovering the mainland (the mouth of the Orinoco; later Panama).
1499–1502 Coastal excursions of the Florentine **Amerigo Vespucci** (1451–1512). His travel reports made the new continent known; following a suggestion of the Ger. scholar MARTIN WALDSEEMÜLLER, from 1507 it was cal. **America**. Travelling to India, the Portuguese **Pedro Alvares Cabral** (1460–1526)
1500 discovered Brazil. By crossing the Isthmus of Panama
1513 the Spaniard BALBOA was the first European to reach the **Pacific Ocean.** The Continent of North America was (before COLUMBUS) discovered
1497 by the Florentine **John Cabot** (GIOVANNI CABOTO), who, in the service of England, was seeking the sea route to India.
By 1542 northern Mexico had been explored by the Spaniards DE VACA, DE SOTO, ALVARADO and CORONADO. Proof of the global shape of the earth was provided by
1519–21 its **1st circumnavigation by Ferdinand Magellan** (c. 1480–1521). A Portuguese in the service of Spain, he discovered the Moluccas, but was killed en route by Philippinos: Captained by SEBASTIAN DEL CANO, one of his 5 ships returned to Lisbon in 1522.
577–80 2nd circumnavigation of the earth by the Eng. naval hero **Francis Drake** (c. 1545–96). S. and Cen. America were explored and subj. by **conquistadores**, frequently feuding Sp. nobles (hidalgos), priests and adventurers, who were driven by their craving for gold, miss. zeal and ambition for honour and fame. **Hernán Cortés** (1485–1547) founded Vera Cruz and advanced into **Mexico.**
1519–21 Bloody conquest of the Aztec Empire.
1531–4 Subjugation of the Inca Empire by **Francisco Pizarro**, who founded **Lima** in 1535; he had his rival ALMAGRO, conqueror of Bolivia, killed in 1538; was killed in turn by the latter's adherents in 1541.
1535–8 QUESEDA conquered Colombia.
1544 ORELLANA crossed the continent (via the river route Marañon–Amazonas).
1540–54 VALDIVIA explored Chile.

The Establishment of the Sp. Colon. Empire

Shortly after the original discoveries
1494 Treaty of Tordesillas: partition of the world into Sp. and Port. colon. empires. Pope ALEXANDER VI fixed a line of demarcation (c. 370 mi. w. of the Azores). True to the principle, 'To God the souls, the land to the king', the state counteracted the individual ambitions of the conquistadores by establishing a colon. régime controlled from Spain.
1524 Seville was made exclusive port for trade with the colonies and the seat of the **Council of the Indies,** the cen. authority for the admin., the law and the Church. **Viceroyalties** – New Spain 1535, Peru 1542 (later New Granada 1718, La Plata 1776) – were organized under the governorship of captains-general, who had judicial autonomy (audiencias). The **cities** were given limited autonomy (cabildo). Universities were founded in Mexico City 1553; Lima 1551; Bogotá 1592; Caracas 1642.
1527 Leasing of Venezuela to the Welsers (p. 215). Explored (1530–39) by FEDERMANN, this 1st Ger. colony was given up in 1546. Distribution of the land to the conquerors in the form of encomiendas (latifundia); the Indians were obliged to render goods-in-kind, but were to be cared for in a Christ. spirit. The 'Apostle of the Indians', **Las Casas** (1474–1566), fought against their exploitation and obligation to forced labour. To ease the lot of the Indians
1510–11 beginnings of the importation of Negro slaves from Africa (see p. 221). Protective legislation
1542–5 culminated in the New Laws, which made the Indians free vassals of the crown. Establishment of protected areas (reductiones).

Consequences of the Discoveries

Economic life: shift of emphasis from the N. and Baltic seas and the Mediterranean to the Ocean (Atlantic trade). Lisbon, Seville and Rotterdam took the places of the hitherto leading ports of Lübeck, Venice and Genoa (p. 183). The introduction of colon. products (potatoes, corn, tobacco) and intensive cultivation on plantations led to an enormous **increase in world trade** and large enterprises (the colonies as customers). Increased demand for money (capital for entrepreneurs, the formation of monopolies) promoted large capitalistic enterprises, which also gained polit. importance (p. 215).
Politics: rise in power of the countries along the Atlantic seaboard of Europe; decrease in the polit. importance of Cen. Europe. **Portugal** and **Spain** became major powers. The Dutch, French and English turned to the sea, first as merchants and then as pirates (1555 Guild of **Merchant Adventurers).**
Culture: beginnings of the **Europeanization of the earth;** shifting of peoples and mixing of races (slave transportation, colonization); expansion of the intellectual horizon (knowledge of other civilizations) and the sciences.

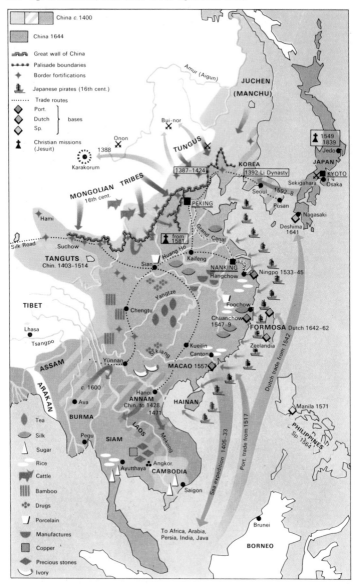

China c. 1400

China 1644

Great wall of China

Palisade boundaries

Border fortifications

Japanese pirates (16th cent.)

Trade routes

Port.
Dutch } bases
Sp.

Christian missions (Jesuit)

Amur (Aigun)

JUCHEN (MANCHU)

Bui-nor

Onon

1388

Karakorum

TUNGUS

1549
1839

Jedo

JAPAN

KOREA

1387–1424   1392 Li Dynasty

KYOTO

MONGOLIAN TRIBES
16th cent.

Seoul   Sekigahara

1592–8   Osaka

PEKING   Pusan

Nagasaki

Hami

from 1581   Grand Canal   Deshima 1641

Silk Road

Suchow   Huang Ho

TANGUTS   Sian   Kaifeng   Ningpo 1533–45

Chin. 1403–1514

NANKING

Hangchow

Yangtze   Foochow

TIBET   Chengtu   Chuanchow
1547–9   FORMOSA   Dutch 1642–62

Lhasa

Tsangpo   Si-kiang   Zeelandia

ASSAM   Yünnan   Kueilin

Canton

MACAO 1557

c. 1600

ARAKAN   Hanoi   ANNAM   HAINAN

Ava   Chin. to 1428
1471   Manila 1571

BURMA   PHILIPPINES
Sp. 1564

Pegu   LAOS

SIAM   Mekong

Ayutthaya   Angkor

CAMBODIA   Saigon

To Africa, Arabia,
Persia, India, Java   Brunei

BORNEO

Tea

Silk

Sugar

Rice

Cattle

Bamboo

Drugs

Porcelain

Manufactures

Copper

Precious stones

Ivory

Sea expedition 1405–33

Port. trade from 1517

Dutch trade from 1542

China during the Ming Dynasty, 1368–1644

China: The Ming Dynasty (1368–1644)

Poor harvests and floods led to peasant uprisings. 'Prophets' of the secret 'Cult of the White Lotus' proclaimed the appearance of an 'Enlightened One'.

1368–98 CHU YUAN-CHANG, a Buddhist monk, drove the last Mongol Emperor from Peking and est. a new nat. dynasty at Nanking, which continued in existence until 1644. The Empire was divided into 13 provinces and centralized (departmentalization of gvt, censorship and judicial authorities, development of public schools – the Imp. Academy – with lit. examinations for officials). Trade and industry were controlled because, according to Confucian teachings, they were considered morally questionable. Increasing bureaucratization strengthened the power of the Mandarins (the highest caste of officialdom): even palace eunuchs were therefore given polit. tasks. Their rivalry with the officials showed itself in corruption and harem intrigues.

The security of the Empire became the leading task. China reacted to the advances of Europeans, the constant incursions of Mongol. peoples and Jap. pirates with increasing isolationism.

1403–24 To improve the defence of the northern frontier, YUNG-LO moved the cap. to Peking in 1421. The Great Wall was extended to 2,450 km.; it was 16 m. wide and 8 m. high.

1405–33 Naval expeditions as far as Africa opened new trade routes and directed Chin. emigration towards SE. Asia.

c. 1500, famines, plagues and floods weakened the Empire.

1516 1st Port. base at Canton; in exchange for the payment of tribute

1557 Eur. trade was limited to Macao.

1522–66 During the reign of KIA-TSING – more poet than ruler – Tungusian raids reached Peking.

1563 Elimination of the Jap. pirates.

From 1581 the miss. activity of the Jesuits was encouraged by WAN-LI (1573–1619) (Fr RICCI). Their mathematical and technical skills gained them infl. at the Imp. Court.

The decline of the dynasty began in 1622 owing to activities of the 'Cult of the White Lotus'. A refined style of life and polished manners were characteristic.

Literature: the philosopher WANG YANG-MING (1472–1528) criticized Sung scholasticism; the collection of lit. works, *Yung-lo ta tien*, included 23,000 vols.; cartographic representations of the Empire were made and realistic novels written.

Art: Imp. tombs at Nanking and Peking; extension of the Imp. residence (the Heavenly Altar, 1420, the Summer Palace). Perfection of coloured **Ming porcelain** and Chin. gardens with pagodas, arched bridges, singing birds, tea-houses and images of dragons.

Medicine: development of scientific diagnosis and **acupuncture** (treatment with extremely thin needles).

Japan: The Ashikaga Shogunate (1338–1573)

Residences of the Mikado were loc. at Kyoto and Yoshino.

1392 End of the schism by the Shogun YOSHIMITSU; however, the creation of 2 new gvtl offices (*Kanryo*) resulted in the involvement of the noble families in a civil war which lasted 150 yrs.

1478–1573 Epoch of the Warring Countries (Sengoku period of the 'Knights and Heroes'). The state almost disintegrated. Social transformation of the people by the decline of old and the rise of new clans. The *Daimyo* (= great name), numbering c. 1,500, became hered. princes; their vassals rose to become the warrior caste of the **Samurai** (retainers). The Confucian spirit further developed in the **Bushido** ('the Warrior's Way') to become the ideal of the Jap. knight; besides training for battle (bowmanship, fencing, wrestling), he must aspire to specific virtues: loyalty to the Tenno (*Shu*) and to parents (*Ko*) were the highest ideals. Disputes involving questions of honour were not settled by duels, but by suicide (**Sappuku**) governed by ceremonial rules. Movements to protect Jap. cult. accomplishments (porcelain, the culinary arts, fencing) and secret rites to enhance the relig. quality of Shintoism were developed (p. 177). The tea ceremony became important with its aesthetic meditation ('illumination') as a means to relieve man from his urges.

1542 Introduction of Eur. firearms; soon imitated, they took the place of bow, lance and sword.

1549 Establishment of successful Jes. missions in the S. (FRANCIS XAVIER).

The Shogun-less Age (1573–1603)

It witnessed the work of the 3 great creators of the new Jap. Empire:

Oda Nobunaga (1534–82), the 'Jap. Attila', who fought the opponents of the Tenno, occupied Kyoto and eliminated the last Ashikaga Shogun in 1573. To weaken the position of the Buddhist monk-warriors (*Sohei*), he supported the Christ. missions.

Hideyoshi Toyotomi (1535–98), Japan's most brilliant commander and statesman, broke the reign of the *Daimyo*. Chancellor in 1582, he est. a new cen. admin. composed of 5 *Tairos* (representatives of the Shogun) and 5 *Bugyos* (administrators of the Empire).

1592–8 Campaign to subjugate Korea.

Ieyasu Tokugawa (1542–1616) defeated the successor HIDEYORI TOYOTOMI in the

1600 b. of Sekigahara; he secured his power by eliminating all the Toyotomi, redistributing the fiefs and establishing a police state.

1603–1867 Tokugawa Shogunate. Edo (Tokyo) flowered as the cap.

1637–8 The uprising of the Shimabara resulted in the annihilation of Christians.

1639 Closure of all ports (until 1854); the only trade channel was by way of the artificially created island of Deshima.

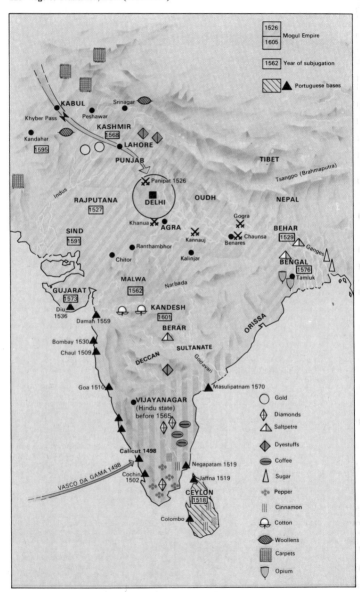

The Mogul Empire in India

The Mogul Empire in India (1526–1658)

The final Isl. advance into Hindustan (India) was led by the Timurid

1494–1530 Babar, a descendant of GENGHIS KHAN and TIMUR, who had been master of Kabul since 1504. Using artillery and conquering Agra, he decisively defeated Sultan IBRAHIM LODI of Delhi in the

1526 b. of Panipat.

1526 Vict. at Khanua over a Rajput confederacy; subjugation of Northern India.
1530–40 HUMAYUN attempted to preserve his father's empire;
1535 successful campaign against Gujarat; however, he was defeated at
1539 Chaunsa and 1540 at Kanauj by the Afghan usurper
1539–45 SHER-SHAH, who est. an interim empire of brief duration.
2nd conquest of India by
1556–1605 Akbar (13 yrs old), the greatest of the Mogul emperors. Hindu rebels were defeated by the regent BAYRAM HAN in the 2nd
1556 b. of Panipat. After 1559 AKBAR conducted campaigns of his own; by 1576 he had, with his professional army, seized control of Northern India (exc. Sind).
1591–1601 He subj. Sind, Kandahar, Berar and Kandesh.
Domestic policy: marriages with Hindu princesses to **stabilize the empire;** Hindus were accepted into state service.
1563 Discontinuation of special Hindu taxation; reorganization of the cen. admin. with provisions to prevent fraud or opposition by the officials (supervisors).
1582 The attempt to establish a pantheistic cult of sun-worship was unsuccessful. Open-minded in questions of religion, the ruler maintained personal contacts with Jesuits and Parsees.
1583 Edict of Toleration for all religions. During the reign of AKBAR's son
1605–27 JAHANGIR, who was a drunkard, policy was influenced by the latter's favourite wife NUR JAHAN (1611–22). The income of the state was squandered on luxuries.
1612–13 Initiation of Eng. colon. policies.
Following the customary conflict between brothers
1628–58 Shah JAHAN ascended the throne and expanded the Empire into the Deccan.
1636 The sultans of the Deccan became vassals of the Great Mogul. AURANGZEB (p. 275) usurped power while his father was still alive.

Isl. Ctr. in India (15th–17th Cents.)

Fusion of Ind. and Arabian–Pers. elements. The Isl. aristocracy adopted Ind. customs; sl. infl. led to strict isolation of women (incl. Hindu), an increase in child marriages and he burning of widows. **Urdu,** based on Hindu grammar and Pers.–Arab. vocaulary, became he language of the state. New Ind. popular dialects were developing: **Hindi,** Bengali, Panjabi, Mahrati, etc. The sultans of Delhi attracted Pers. poets, historians and scholars

to their court. A well-educated man, **Babar** composed *Memoirs* which rival those of CAESAR (p. 95). **Akbar** reorganized the educational system and est. libraries and universities. The poets URFI (1555–91) and ABUL FADL and the historian BADAUNI worked at the Mogul court.

Literature

Europe received its initial knowledge of Ind. literature through the Pers. trans. of the *Upanishads* (p. 43) of DARA SHOKOH. The Hindi re-creation of the **Ramayana** epic by **Tulsi Das** (1532–1625) became the **'house-bible' of the Hindus.**

Architecture

Similarities in the style of relig. edifices facilitated the fusion of Pers. and Hindu architectural traditions (interior courts and pillared walks). The palaces and mosques of AKBAR's new residence, Fathpur Sikri, nr Agra (1569), reflected pure Mogul art; the same may be said of AKBAR's mausoleum at Sikandra and the Go-Mandal Temple at Udaipur (1600), built in the Rajput style. The high-point was found in the **Taj Mahal,** the mausoleum built for Shah JAHAN's favourite wife (1632–52): decorated with encrusted precious stones, the domed edifice with its 4 minarets (of white marble), arranged to harmonize with the gardens and water basins, is considered to be among the world's most beautiful buildings. Citadels and pearl mosques at Agra, as well as the **peacock throne** (today in Teheran), were also created.

The Development of Hindu Sects

The Pashupata and Lingayat sects belonged to the Shiva group, which advocated asceticism as the way to salvation. The Vishnu group sought salvation through loving dedication **(Bhakti)** to the gods: the **Bhagavatas** relied on the sacred book of worship **Bhagavad Gita** ('The Song Celestial'), interpreted by RAMANUJA (1055–1137) with emphasis on divine grace. The **Mahdvas** of MAHDVA ANANDATIRTHA (1199–1278) advocated a dualistic doctrine of God and the world; VALLABHA (1479–1531) and his **Maharajas** sect, on the other hand, spoke of sexual love between God and the soul. CAITANYA (1485–1534) preached ecstatic love of God through song, music and dance. Modern Hinduism was shaped through **Tantrism,** which had mystical-magical rules and a ceremonial based on the sacred Tantra books. **Syncretistic sects** (fusion of Hindu and Isl. concepts): RAMANANDA (c. 1400–70) est. a Bhakti sect at Benares; all castes were admitted, so were Moslems. His pupil KABIR (1440–1518) connected Isl. monotheism with the transmigration of souls (*Karma*). Wearing distinctive clothing, hair styles and beards, the relig. community of the **Sikhs** (Ind. = apostles) formed around NANAK (1469–1538). Adoption of the conception of the 'holy war' against the unbelieving Moslems; a milit. theocracy est. The Sikhs have ever since provided the élite of Ind. soldiers.

Church and State in Germany

The weakness of cen. polit. power (p. 197) prevented a nat. Church, as in England, France and Spain, being est. Although the reform decrees of Basle were accepted 1439 by the Diet of Mainz, the Curia (NICHOLAS V) was able to deal with the princes 1447 by concluding sep. concordats, which strengthened the **eccles. authority** of the territ. princes (appointments to eccles. offices, supervision over Church properties). 1448 By the terms of the Concordat of Vienna (p. 181), FREDERICK III gave up his project of eccles. reforms in the Empire. At a time of growing needs for funds, the Curia increased the contribution demanded from Germany, because the income from these countries with nat. Churches was no longer forthcoming.

Mid 15th cent. Pamphlets called for an **'Gravamina** (complaints) **of the German Nation'** at the occasion of imp. and prov. diets. Pamphlets called for an '*Endzeitkaiser*' ('Ultimate Emperor') who would protect the 'good law of old' and the Ger. Church from exploitation by the Walisians (i.e. Ital., Fr., foreign control); humanists protested against the theological tutelage of laymen and criticized papal judicial decisions and cravings for profit. General dissatisfaction and bitterness because of:

1. The **wealth of the Church**, which led to a levelling of spiritual values and the moral decline of the clergy, incl. many monasteries.
2. The **upper clergy**; considering their properties to be 'wards of the nobility', the '*Junkers* of God' looked upon them as the means to a standard of living in keeping with their social position. The upper clergy left spiritual functions to be carried out by vicars, lived opulently or pursued scholarly works, while the lower clergy suffered neglect and lived in theological ignorance.
3. The deterioration of the **eccles. means of salvation into legalisms** (indulgences, confession, penance); scholastic formalities and impersonal liturgical services.

Ger. Popular Piety

At a time of increasing prosperity, internal unrest and anxiety were caused in simple people by the incomprehensible changes in the conception of life and the world (see Renaissance, p. 221). **Edificatory literature:** pamphlets containing instructions concerning confession, the Mass and the problems of death; evangelical proclamations, the lives of saints, editions of the Bible (18 translations by 1521). **Popular preachers** (often mendicants), advocating the simple life in evangelical poverty, were very popular, as were **fraternities** dedicated to common prayer and charitable works. JOHANN GEILER VON KAISERSBERG (1455–1510) protested against the imperfect versions of the Bible that were being distributed; SEBASTIAN BRANT (1457–1521) called for reforms; WESSEL GANSFORT and JOHANN RUCHRAT fought against the traffic in indulgences (*c.* 1480); however, the reformers lacked power or theological training.

Donations and votive gifts: hospitals and orphanages were founded. Surrounded by chapels adorned with altar-paintings, figures of saints and sacred vessels, churches and cathedrals resembled richly furnished museums. Cologne (pop. 30,000) possessed 19 churches, 100 chapels, 22 monasteries and 12 hospitals; every 9th inhabitant of Germany was a cleric; brilliant unfolding of eccles. splendour on c 100 annual Sundays and feast days in the form of processions, passion plays and pageants of the Dance of Death. **The cult of relics:** innumerable relics were venerated, recorded in catalogues, collected and traded at any price. Business sense joined with pious fraud to catch the credulous. In 1520 FREDERICK THE WISE possessed 19,013 relics which provided him with 2 mil. years' indulgence. **The veneration of saints:** churches, cities, crafts, estates, every adversity, even animals had patron saints and helpers; among them, MARY and her mother, St ANNE, received special veneration. Penitential journeys and **pilgrimages** multiplied.

Even so, these eccles. means to grace did not prevent belief in miracles, superstition, visions of devils and hell. **The persecution of witches** based on the Bull (1484) and the trial regulations provided by the Cologne Dominicans KRAMER and SPRENGER (*Malleus Maleficarum = The Hammer of Witchcraft*, 1489); more than 1 mil. fell victim to the witch persecutions by the 18th cent.

The Life of Luther to 1517

The comprehensive and initially purely relig. movement of the Reformation cannot be understood without insight into its founder's theological development and decisions of personal conscience.

1483–1546 Martin Luther, b. Eisleben, raised at Mansfeld. Following his basic education at Magdeburg, Eisenach and Erfurt, he obeyed his father's wish and took up the study of jurisprudence.

1505 The experience of conversion (in a thunderstorm); entrance into an August monastery at Erfurt and theological training in the scholastic school of OCCAM (p. 184).

1508 Transfer to the University of Wittenberg.

1510 journey to Rome under orders by the vicar of the Order, JOHANN VON STAUPITZ.

1512 doctor of theology and *magister* (professor) of bib. interpretation.

1513–17 Lectures on the Psalms and the Epistles of PAUL. Wrestling with the 'problem of the merciful God' and striving for relief from the painful consciousness of sin led to doubts about the eccles. means to salvation and to the intensive study of the Bible, esp. the Epistles of PAUL.

1512–13 Decisive relig. revelation (the so-called experience in the tower): justification of man not through efforts of the will or good works, but through the grace of God alone (Romans 1: 17). A circle of theologians concerned with the study of the Bible and AUGUSTINE formed around LUTHER NICHOLAS VON AMSDORF, KARLSTADT (p. 233).

The Beginnings of the Reformation (to 1521)

1514 LEO X renewed the indulgence for the reconstruction of St Peter's (p. 217).

31 Oct. 1517 Luther's 95 theses, posted at the castle church of Wittenberg (in Lat.), calling for a disputation on the abuses of the traffic in indulgences, were directed against TETZEL, the business-wise indulgence commissary of the Archbishop of Mainz. Rapid spread of, and vigorous echo to, the theses all over Germany. Accused by Dominicans, LUTHER was asked to appear at a trial of heretics in Rome; however, he was protected by FREDERICK THE WISE (1486–1525). Polit. circumstances (the imp. election) prompted the Curia to give way.

1518 Questioning at the Imp. Diet of Augsburg by the Papal Legate CAJETAN: LUTHER did not retract the theses and, having fled, called for a general council.

1519 Leipzig disputation between KARLSTADT, LUTHER and his main opponent JOHANN ECK (1486–1543), professor at Ingolstadt: **break with Rome,** because LUTHER denied papal primacy, the tradition of the Church and the infallibility of councils.

1520 Breakthrough of the Reformation: Luther composed 3 **programmatical essays:**

Aug. on polit. questions: 'To the Christian Nobility of the German Nation: On the Improvement of the Christian Estate' – written in the style of the *Gravamina* (p. 230), it was addressed to the Emperor and the Imp. estates. It appealed for reforms through a **nat. council,** since all Christians were considered to be of the spiritual estate (priesthood of believers);

Oct. on questions of dogma: 'The Babylonian Captivity of the Church' (in Lat.) – of the 7 sacraments it accepted only the 2 which could be justified on a scriptural basis (baptism and communion);

Nov. on questions of ethics: 'The Freedom of a Christian Man' – which could be found only in faith (*sola fide*) through the grace of God (*sola gratia*).

Dec. Burning of the Bull *Exurge Domine* (threatening excommunication) at Wittenberg.

Consequences: enormous impact of LUTHER's writings and action; sudden increase in the production of books; pamphlets (woodcuts) excited enthusiasm for the reformer in the broadest circles. Among the humanists joining the movement were MELANCHTHON, HUTTEN and ZWINGLI.

1521 Diet of Worms (p. 237): LUTHER appeared under a pledge of safe conduct and based his position on Holy Writ, but was placed under the ban of the empire by CHARLES V through the Edict of Worms.

The Spreading of Luther's Teachings (1521–5)

Granted refuge under the name of 'Junker Jörg' by FREDERICK THE WISE, LUTHER translated the N.T. from the original Gk text at the Wartburg. The **September Bible** of 1522 made LUTHER the creator of the **New High Ger. lit. language.** ('Luther-German' was

accepted in Cath. regions only in the 18th cent.) Complete translation of the Bible in 1534.

Wittenberg: Unrest caused by excessive fervour (p. 233) forced LUTHER to intervene in Wittenberg in 1522. Subs. the city and the university became the **centre of the Reformation** (the 'Ger. Rome'). Besides LUTHER there were, among others, **Johannes Bugenhagen** (1485–1558), the author of ordinances governing Prot. eccles. and educational organization, **George Spalatin** (1484–1545), the judicial advisor of the Elector, the painter **Lukas Cranach,** and, above all, **Philip Melanchthon** (p. 212): 1st theological formulation of Luth. doctrine in the *Loci communes* (1521).

Early focal-points of the Reformation:

Strasbourg with **Martin Bucer** (1491–1551), whose teachings on communion influenced **Calvin** (p. 238). Union with Lutheranism in the 'Concordat of Wittenberg' (1536).

Nuremberg: Andreas Osiander (1498–1551) proclaimed the new doctrine; the circle of artists around **Albrecht Dürer** and **Hans Sachs** joined LUTHER. Ulm, Nördlingen, Magdeburg and Bremen opened their gates to the Reformation. Dissolution of convents and monast. orders; rejection of celibacy (in 1525 Luther mar. the former nun KATHARINA VON BORA); confiscation of eccles. properties (secularization) by territ. princes who had become Prot.

Relig. pamphlets composed in the 'Grobian' (ruffian) style of the period: **Thomas Murner** (1469–1537), 'Of the Great Lutheran Fool' (1522). Many humanists turned from LUTHER after (in *De Servo Arbitrio*, 1525) he brusquely denied the freedom of the will which ERASMUS had advocated.

The Reformation in Switzerland

Ulrich (Huldreich) Zwingli (1484–1531), a humanist, pastor and milit. chaplain, was after

1518 a priest at Zürich. Like ERASMUS and LUTHER, he came to criticize the Church as a result of his humanistic studies. After

1522 public protest against eccles. abuses. The city council accepted his

1523 Programme of Reform, presented in 67 **theses:** prohibition of all Cath. forms of worship: processions, relics, images; control of attendance at church, morality, and care of the poor; emphasis on predestination. Orientated in a more practical and rational manner, the movement est. itself in, among other places, Basle (ÖKOLAMPADIUS), Bern, St-Gallen, and later on Constance and Strasbourg (BUCER). Setback after the

1526 Disputation with ECK at Baden. The

1529 Marburg Colloquy with LUTHER failed over the question of **communion.**

1531 ZWINGLI d. in the b. of Kappel near the Zürich war with the Cath. cantons of Switzerland. His successor **Heinrich Bullinger** (1504–75) rejected the union of Lutherans and Zwinglians advocated by BUCER.

1539 The Helvetic Confession; to counteract it, union with CALVIN's Church of Geneva was achieved

1549 in the *Consensus Tigurinus.*

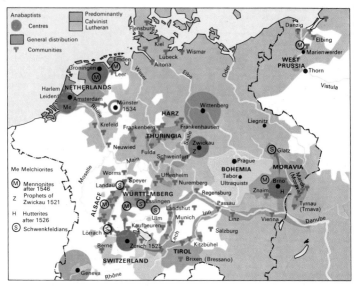

The Anabaptist movement in the 16th cent.

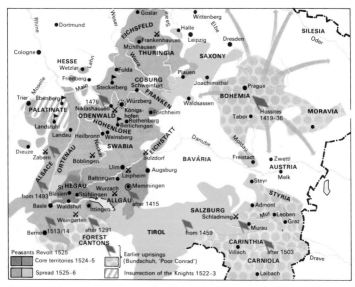

The Peasants' Revolt, 1525

Tributary Currents of the Reformation

LUTHER's struggle against the authority of the Church and for a renewal of Christ. life awakened fervent feelings and ideas. The '*Evangelium* of the little man' unleashed radical outbreaks and jeopardized the Reformation. Unclear in their teachings, the **Anabaptists** and '**Schwärmer**' ('enthusiasts') rejected any kind of gvtl and eccles. organization; they believed in personal revelation, prophetic calling, the 'inner light' and the sanctification of man through rebaptism.

ANDREAS BODENSTEIN, cal. **Karlstadt** (1480–1541), introduced radical reforms (marriage of priests, dissolution of Orders) in Wittenberg during LUTHER's absence (Wartburg). His assault on images became the rallying-cry of the Anabaptists (p. 231).

Boh. Hussites and KARLSTADT were an infl. on the 'Prophets of Zwickau', THOMAS MÜNZER and NICHOLAS STORCH. Under the infl. of relig. visions, they preached communistic upheavals and incited those with social grievances. Itinerant preachers, such as BALTHASAR HUBMAIER (Waldshut), JOHANNES DENK (Nuremberg) and SEBASTIAN FRANCK (Donauwörth), spread their visions and prophecies of the end of time (eschatology) throughout the entire Empire. KASPAR SCHWENKFELD est. a mystical sect in Swabia and Silesia. Having been persecuted in the most cruel fashion, the followers of JAKOB HUTTER of the Tirol est. their Mor. communities.

Whereas many Anabaptists conceived of their sufferings as martyrdom, MELCHIOR HOFFMANN preached the destruction of the godless and proclaimed the beginning of the 'Millennium of Christ' for the year 1533. In the Netherlands the **Melchiorites** found their leaders in JAN MATTHYS, a baker of Harlem, and JAN BOKELSON, a tailor of Leiden. In 1534/5 they est. the reign of the **Anabaptists in Münster**. Won over to the Reformation in 1532, the city came under the infl. of the Melchiorites. Under siege, the relig. fanaticism in the 'Kingdom of Zion' intensified (communally held property, polygamy). All those 'disposed to Anabaptism' were persecuted after the conquest. The fact that from then on they lived as 'the quiet ones in the country' was owed to the work of the Frisian preacher **Menno Simons** (1492–1559). Peaceful, but imbued with the conviction of their salvation, Mennonite communities spread to Russia and N. America.

The Rising of the Imp. Knights (1522/3)

An 'unemployed caste of warriors', the Imp. Knights became embittered and joined together in their struggle against the lowering of their soc. position. They hoped that the new doctrine would bring imp. reform, incl. the confiscation and distribution of the eccles. territories and their own elevation to princely rank. Won over to the cause of 'Ger. evangelical liberty' by ULRICH VON HUTTEN (p. 212), the leader of mercenaries, FRANZ VON SICKINGEN (1481–1523), began the '*Pfaffenkrieg*' (*Pfaffe* =

priest) against the archbpc of Trier. Excommunicated, he was mortally wounded during the bombardment of his fortress. The Imp. Knights lost their polit. influence.

The Great Peasant War (1525)

Prosperous as a result of the secure markets for their products, and militant and self-confident because of their service as lansquenets, the peasants of the splintered territories of s. and cen. Germany resisted pressures to make financial contributions and perform labour services exerted on them by the impoverished landlords. The reintroduction of Rom. Law had further limited their rights to the commons, their personal freedom and their self-admin. Secret societies and unrest developed from the 15th cent.

1476 Revolt of the 'PIPER OF NIKLASHAUSEN' (Franconia);
1493 *Bundschuh*-uprising (Upper Rhine);
1514 Uprising of 'poor Conrad' (Swabia). The Reformation was reinterpreted in a spirit of fervent enthusiasm and found its strongest echo in the countryside. Appealing to the Bible, divinely founded natural law and LUTHER's (misunderstood) essay *The Freedom of a Christian Man*, the peasants demanded the elimination of class differences and labour services.
1524 Beginning of the Peasant War in Waldshut and Stühlingen.
1525 Sudden spread to Thuringia and Upper Austria; however, the 'peasant-hordes' lacked uniform aims, planning and leadership. Some imp. cities (Rothenburg) and Imp. Knights joined voluntarily (such as the 'idealist of the movement', **Florian Geyer**) or under coercion (GÖTZ VON BERLICHINGEN). The 'Chancellor of the Peasants', **Wendelin Hippler**, developed a moderate programme in the '12 Articles'. Luther's 'Appeal to maintain the Peace' was directed at princes and peasants. After initial successes, the upheaval deteriorated into pillage, murder and burning. THOMAS MÜNZER proclaimed the coming of a 'Kingdom of God'.
May 1525 LUTHER's *Against the Murderous and Thieving Hordes of Peasants* appeared. It was a severe appeal to the princes to destroy the peasants so as to preserve divinely appointed authority, to which man owed obedience. Militarily superior, the Swabian League (TRUCHSESS OF WALDBURG) defeated the Swabian and Franconian hordes with terrible punishment.

Consequences:
1. Conditions of the agricultural sector 'ossified' until the early 19th cent.; the peasant became the personal property of the landlord and was deprived of polit. rights.
2. Strengthened by LUTHER's doctrine of 'obediently suffering authority', the territ. state became, by its victory, the determining power of the Modern Age.
3. The popular relig. movement of the Reformation changed to a polit. movement, led by the princes.

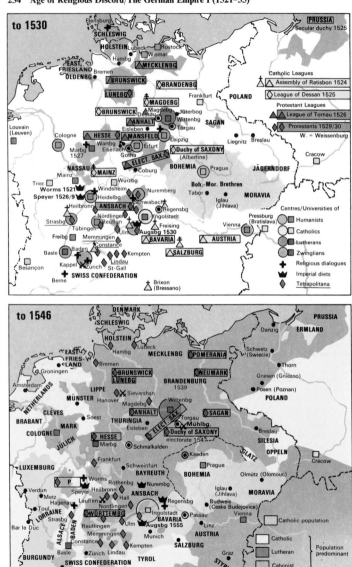

The Reformation in Germany

Polit. Aspects of the Reformation (1521–55)

The Reformation spread despite the Edict of Worms; its expansion corresponded to the lengths of thé Emperor's periods of absence from the Empire (p. 237).

1524 Imp. Diet of Nuremberg. The territ. princes promised the Papal Legate CAMPEGGIO to observe the Edict 'as far as possible'. The Convention of Regensburg in 1524 and the 1525 League of Dessau led to the establishment of special confessional leagues aimed at stamping out the new doctrine. The leaders of the Prot. princes, PHILIP OF HESSE (1518–67) and JOHN FREDERICK OF ELECTORAL SAXONY (1525–54), responded with the League of Torgau.

1525 Introduction of the Reformation into Prussia: the Grand Master ALBRECHT OF HOHENZOLLERN (1513–68) made the state of the Teutonic Knights into a sec. duchy.

1526 The Diet of Speyer decided that each member of the Imp. estates should conduct himself 'in a way he hoped would enable him to justify himself in the eyes of God and his Imp. majesty'.

1529 2nd Diet of Speyer. The Prot. estates appealed to conscience in matters of faith, protesting against the Edict of Worms. In the face of the Emperor's successes in foreign affairs, PHILIP OF HESSE urged the '**Protestants**' to join together; he mediated the fruitless

1529 Marburg Colloquy between LUTHER and ZWINGLI. The s. Ger. Protestants came to agreement in the Convention of Schwabach.

1530 **Diet of Augsburg.** The Emperor endeavoured to preserve the unity of the faith. The Protestants presented their confessional positions in the **Confessio augustana** (composed by MELANCHTHON), the *Tetrapolitana* (BUCER, CAPITO), and the '*Fidei Ratio*' (ZWINGLI). Cath. theologians opposed them by the *Confutatio* (ECK, FABER); CHARLES V rejected the *apologia* of the *Confessio* and confirmed the Edict of Worms.

1531 The Prot. Imp. estates thereupon formed the **Schmalkaldic League** with a joint army and treasury seeking ties abroad (France).

The Establishment of Prot. Territ. Churches

During the Peasant War LUTHER decided in favour of the territ. princes as the sec. authority (p. 233); considered as 'provisional bps', they were entrusted with the task of establishing distinct eccles. organizations. The basis of Prot. worship was developed by LUTHER himself in the

1526 **German Mass,** and the

1529 catechisms, marriage and baptismal booklets (communion, sermon and communal singing). MELANCHTHON and BUGENHAGEN composed handbooks for ministers.

1526–9 Church and school visitations in Electoral Saxony; its eccles. organization became the model of a Luth. territ. church. Advised by the *Consistorium* (supreme territ. eccles. authority) and the superintendents, the prince appointed the ministers (now married) and supervised eccles.

priest) against the archbpc of Trier. Ex-education. Future theologians were educated at Lat. or *Fürsten* (princely) schools.

1527 The 1st Prot. university est. at Marburg (Königsberg 1544, Jena 1558). Church authority strengthened the territ. state, and confiscated the former Cath. possessions.

The Successes of the Schmalkaldic League

Since the Turk. danger had forced the Emperor to conclude the

1532 Relig. Peace of Nuremberg (postponing final settlement), the League, by the

1534 Peace of Kaaden, forced the return of Duke ULRICH OF WÜRTTEMBERG, driven out in 1519. Doctrinal differences within the League were reconciled by

1536 the Concordat of Wittenberg (BUCER, MELANCHTHON). The 'Enthusiasts' were attacked (p. 233) and new adherents gained.

1539 The Reformation reached the Duchy of Saxony and Electoral Brandenburg. Tied down by foreign affairs, CHARLES V attempted to reach a peaceful compromise. Futile relig. discussions at

1540/41 Worms and Regensburg. However, the Emperor was able to win over PHILIP OF HESSE (morally burdened by his bigamy), and

1521–53 Duke MAURICE OF SAXONY (driven by dyn. egotism); the League was thus paralysed.

1545 At the Diet of Worms the Prot. Imp. estates declined to participate in the Council of Trent (p. 239).

The Crisis of Protestantism

Allied with the Pope, Bavaria and a number of Prot. princes (incl. MAURICE OF SAXONY), the Emperor was victorious in the Schmalkaldic War (p. 237). He now determined to settle the relig. question by force.

1548 The Interim of Augsburg: until clarification of the matter by a council, the Prot. estates were permitted only lay communion and priestly marriage. Magdeburg ('the Lord's Chancery') refused to accede and was placed under the Imp. ban. MAURICE OF SAXONY (the 'Judas of Meissen') became the saviour of Protestantism (p. 237).

1552 The Convention of Passau: the *status quo* was recognized.

1555 **The Relig. Peace of Augsburg.** Its vagueness led to future conflicts. Principal conditions:

1. The Peace was valid only for the Luth. and Cath. confessions.

2. Subjects were obliged to follow the confession of the prince (*Ius reformandi: cuius regio, eius religio*); only Imp. cities were granted relig. toleration.

3. Eccles. territories were placed under the 'reservation' (*Reservatum ecclesiasticum*: upon changing his personal confession, an eccles. prince was obliged to resign his offices).

4. The *Declaratio ferdinandae* guaranteed relig. liberty to the nobility and to the cities in eccles. territories.

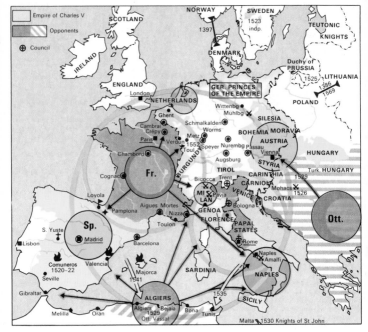

The empire of Charles V

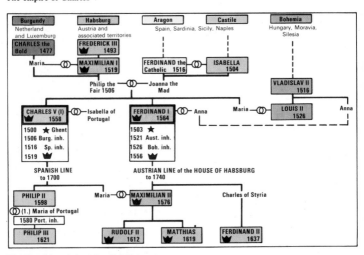

The Spanish and Austrian Habsburgs

1519–56 Charles V born at Ghent 1500, educated in the courtly manner (the future Pope HADRIAN VI was his tutor), he became Duke of Burgundy in
1515 and, with Spain,
1516 inherited an empire on which 'the sun never set'. A reform of the Sp. gvt led to the fruitless
1520–22 Revolt of the Comuneros (urban communities). The crisis strengthened the state. Spain became the core of the Empire. Its army commanders (the Duke of Alba) and mercenaries served the Emperor, whose wars were financed by the taxation of Spain and Italy (Naples).

The Struggle for Predominance in Europe
Aided by the Fuggers and Welsers (p. 215), CHARLES won the election as
1519 Ger. Emperor against FRANCIS I OF FRANCE (1515–47); he was, however, obliged to respect the 'Ger. liberties'. The so-called **'capitulation of election'** required: observation of the princely privileges; electoral approval of legislation, treaties, taxes and Imp. policy; the prohibition of the use of foreign mercenaries, etc. Advised by Grand Chancellor GATTINARA, CHARLES saw his task as emperor being to restore – by modern means (mercenaries, officials) – the **medieval universal empire**. His opponents were therefore the Eur. nat. states, esp. **France;** the Ger., esp. the Prot., **territ. princes;** the **Turks;** but also the Pope. After the establishment of an Imp. gvt for the duration of his absence, based on the estates and headed by his brother FERDINAND (1503–64), CHARLES was promised aid against France by the Empire at the
1521 Diet of Worms. CHARLES transferred the hered. Habsburg lands within the Empire to FERDINAND and thereby est. the Aust. branch of the dynasty.
1521–6 1st War against FRANCIS I.
1525 The b. of Pavia gave vict. to the Sp. and Ger. mercenaries. By the
1526 Peace of Madrid, the captured king lost Milan, Genoa, the Duchy of Burgundy and Naples. After his release, he repudiated the conditions and concluded the
1525 'Holy League' of Cognac with Pope CLEMENS VII, Milan, Florence and Genoa.
1526–9 The 2nd War with France was caused by the League.
1527 Sacco di Roma: the Imp. army plundered Rome; (Luth.) mercenaries ridiculed the captured Pope.
1529 The 'Ladies' Peace' of Cambria was more in the nature of an armistice.
1529 1st Siege of Vienna by the Turks (p. 209). Following the (last)
1530 Imp. coronation at Bologna, CHARLES intervened in the Ger. relig. struggle:
1530 Diet of Augsburg (p. 235): without an army and short of funds, he was forced to allow the conclusion of the
1532 Relig. Peace of Nuremberg so as to obtain help against the Turks. The Turk. vassal and pirate KHAIREDDIN BARBAROSSA (c.

1475–1546) raided the Sp. and Ital. coasts in agreement with FRANCIS I.
1535 N. African campaign against BARBAROSSA. Seizure of Tunis.
1536 Franco-Turk. alliance and 3rd war by CHARLES V against FRANCIS I.
1538 Armistice of Nice.
1541 A punitive expedition to Algiers failed; with the loss of Budapest, Hungary fell to the Turks. Forming a new coalition, FRANCIS I initiated the
1542–4 4th war against the Emperor. At the 'deceitful'
1544 Diet of Speyer, CHARLES promised a nat. council and, with the assistance of Prot. territ. princes, could advance on Paris.

Charles V at the Height of his Power
1544 Peace of Crespy: FRANCIS I promised assistance against the Prot. estates of the Empire and gave up Naples; CHARLES V returned Burgundy. Urged by the Emperor, PAUL III called for a
1545 council to meet at Trent to settle the relig. question (p. 239). The Prot. estates of the Empire refused to participate.
1546–7 The Schmalkaldic War in s. and cen. Germany. After the
1547 b. of Mühlberg, arrest of the banned Prot. leaders PHILIP OF HESSE and JOHN FREDERICK OF SAXONY (of the Ernestine line), whose electoral dignity was granted to
1541–53 MAURICE OF SAXONY (Albertine line) upon the
1547 Capitulation of Wittenberg. At the
1547/8 'fortified' Diet of Augsburg, CHARLES dictated the so-called **Interim** (p. 235).

The Failure of the Imp. Policy of Charles V
Concerned for their 'liberties', the princes resisted Imp. reform and the so-called Sp. succession plan: transfer of the Imp. dignity to PHILIP, even though FERDINAND had been elected king of Rome in 1531. Entrusted with the execution of the
1551 Imp. Ban of Magdeburg, MAURICE OF SAXONY placed himself at the head of a secret conspiracy of princes and, by the
1552 Treaty of Chambord, obtained the aid of HENRY II OF FRANCE, who was promised control of Metz, Toul and Verdun. Deceived, the Emperor was forced by MAURICE to flee from Innsbruck to Villach. The Council of Trent was dissolved. While FERDINAND negotiated the
1552 Convention of Passau and the
1555 Relig. Peace of Augsburg (p. 235) with the princes, CHARLES,
1552–6 at war with France, attempted in vain to regain Metz, Toul and Verdun.
1556 Embittered, CHARLES abdicated, and d. (1558) at San Yuste. His brother FERDINAND became Emperor; his son PHILIP (II) received the Sp. inheritance.
Consequences: the nat. state triumphed over the idea of a universal empire. The dualism within the Empire was decided in favour of the princes; confessional discord was perpetuated.

The Reformation in Geneva (Calvinism)

1509–64 John Calvin (JEAN CAUVIN), born in Noyon (Northern France); humanistic and juristic studies at Paris, Orléans and Bourges. After turning to the Prot. faith

1534 flight of the itinerant preacher from Paris to **Basle**. His principal work, the

1536 Institutio Religionis Christianae (*Instructions in Christianity*), a systematic text of Prot. doctrine, was created here.

Doctrine: God's omnipotence and honour demanded unconditional obedience. Man was **predestined** to salvation or damnation. Entitled to hope to be chosen were those who sanctified their lives by fulfilling their duties on earth in accordance with the law of Holy Writ (incl. the O.T.). The Eucharist was neither symbolic commemoration (ZWINGLI) nor bodily substantiation of CHRIST (LUTHER), but a spiritual contact with CHRIST. Travelling through **Geneva** CALVIN was

1536 persuaded to stay for his first appointment there by the reformer WILLIAM FAREL (1489–1565). For polit. reasons, Geneva had joined the Swiss Confederation and the Reformation.

1538 Expulsion of FAREL and CALVIN as a result of their over-severe demands. At BUCER's invitation, CALVIN assumed leadership of the Fr. Strasbourg comm. (p. 231).

1541 Recall to Geneva and

organization of the Genevan Church: destined to worship God and to sanctify its members, the community was to govern itself (principle of the **relig. community**) through the election of representatives for:

1. **4 spiritual offices:** pastors (sermons, spiritual care), doctors (doctrine), elders (church discipline) and deacons (care of the poor).
2. **2 committees** to elect the ministers and to lead the community by means of the **Consistorium (Synod).** It supervised conduct, punished relig. offences or called for their punishment by the state, which in its turn was obliged to aid the relig. community (theocratic gvt). Attendance at church obligatory, severe morality: prohibition of gambling and dancing; removal of images, altars and candles from churches ('prayer barns') to centre the concentration of the community on the **sermon, prayer** and the singing of psalms. The image of the diligent, thrifty worker, considering profit and success to be signs of his election, developed into a new (capitalistic) **ethic of economics.**

Resistance to the Genevan 'City of God' was broken with great severity (58 capital sentences by 1546).

1553 Execution of the freethinker MICHAEL SERVETUS (p. 221), after which **Geneva became the leading centre of the Prot. world.** To spread Calvinism in Europe (p. 241)

1559 the Genevan Academy was est. CALVIN's successor THEODORE BEZA (1519–1605) taught there. The militant manifestations of the new and the old faiths, **Calvinism** and the **Jes. Order,** became the protagonists of the subsequent religio-polit. struggles.

The Anglican Church in England

The anti-clerical revolution is explained by:

1. The **special position of the Eng. Church,** which, without representation in the House of Commons, had little contact with the nation. Appointed by the king, the upper clergy had anti-papal tendencies;
2. The clergy's envy of the **bourgeois laity,** which, with its humanistic training at Oxford and Cambridge, assumed intellectual leadership. Criticism of the wealth of the Church since WYCLIF (p. 189); parliamentary proposals for secularization to the advantage of Crown and Parliament.
3. The **financial and moral bankruptcy of the crown.** Humanistically and theologically educated, but unscrupulous and tyrannical,

1509–47 Henry VIII in 1521 obtained the papal title '*Defensor fidei*' ('Defender of the Faith') with his pamphlet against LUTHER. A special legate of the Pope, his ambitious adviser **Cardinal Wolsey** was in charge of Church affairs without restriction and involved the king in expensive but politically futile undertakings. The king's main concern was over the succession; but the *Curia* rejected his proposal to divorce CATHERINE OF ARAGON.

1529 Fall of Wolsey; the clergy was coerced to

1531 recognize the king as the supreme head of the Church; 1533 divorce from the queen, marriage to the lady-in-waiting **Anne Boleyn** (executed 1536). Altogether, HENRY VIII contracted 6 marriages.

1534 The Act of Supremacy: confirmation of the Anglican state-church by Parliament. Advised by THOMAS CROMWELL, the king cruelly suppressed all opposition. He forced THOMAS MORE (p. 212) to resign the lord-chancellorship and had him executed in 1535.

1534–9 Dissolution of the monasteries. Their extensive properties were sold to the gentry and the bourgeoisie: greatest shift of property in the modern history of England. The make-up and doctrine of the Church remained Cath. because of

1539 the '6 Articles' (the 'bloody statute'). Still, Prot. trends entered England. These were intensified during the reign of

1547 EDWARD VI (9 yrs old); promoted by the first Anglican primate and Archbishop of Canterbury, THOMAS CRANMER (1489–1556). Introduction of the Anglican Liturgy in the

1549 Book of Common Prayer, and of a mixed Luth.-Calv. confession in the

1552 '42 Articles' (retaining Cath. forms of worship). Sharp reaction under **Mary I** ('Bloody Mary', mar. to PHILIP II of Spain, p.243). Persecution of Protestants, *c.* 300 executions, among them CRANMER in 1556. Polit. opposition to Spain made the Reformation a matter of nat. concern.

1558–1603 Elizabeth I renewed royal supremacy over the Church, short of control of scripture and the sacraments, by the

1559 Oath of Supremacy and the **Acts of Uniformity:** restoration of the Liturgy.

1563 '**39 Articles':** a new, refined, Calv. confession formed the basis of the state-church.

The Catholic Renewal

The Cath. Church stabilized itself by:
1. **Internal reforms** (without conflict in **Spain** and **Italy**) in response to relig. discord at the **Council of Trent.**
2. **Resistance** to and **campaigning** against Protestantism: the **Counter-Reformation.** From the mid 16th cent. both currents were fused in the **reform papacy.**

Spain: a nat. consciousness tied to relig. conviction, the Inquisition and internal reforms (p. 243) prevented the advance of Prot. teachings. In **Francisco de Vitoria** (to 1546), **Soto** and **Cano** Christ. humanism developed a distinct Sp. ctr. and brand of scholasticism (p. 243). Perfected by the Jesuits VÁZQUEZ, **Molina** and **Suárez** (p. 243), **neo-Thomism** became an important force in the reconstitution of Church doctrine, in natural law and in int. law. With **St Teresa of Avila** (1515–82), Sp. **mysticism** took on its own distinctive character: reform of the (barefoot) Carmelites and mystical writings. St **John of the Cross** (1542–91) was her pupil.

Italy: a charitable movement expressing lay piety, the **Oratorian** movement spread from Vicenza after 1494; one of its members was Cardinal **Contarini** (1483–1542), the mediator between the old and the new faiths. The **Theatines** (clericals) 1524; **Capucines** (spiritual care) 1525; **Paulans** (charitable work) 1530; **Ursulines** (education) 1535 and other Orders and schools were est. – also by the Protector of Switzerland, Cardinal-Archbishop BORROMEO (1538–84) and Bishop FRANCIS DE SALES. Neri (1515–95) was dedicated to the ideal of charity; the Order he founded, the Congregation of the Oratory (1576), became a stage in the training of priests and provided new impetus for sacred music (the oratorio).

The Jes. Order

1491–1556 Ignatius Loyola (INIGO LÓPEZ DE LOYOLA), a Basque nobleman.
1521 A severe wound incurred in the defence of Pamplona transformed him into a 'Knight in the service of Jesus'. Mystical visions and ascetic self-examination, recorded in **Exercitia Spiritualia** (*Spiritual Exercises*).
1523 Pilgrimage to Jerusalem; 1526 beginning of theological studies (Alcala, Salamanca); following conflicts with the Inquisition, in 1528 he studied at the Sorbonne in Paris.
1534 Foundation of the Societas Jesu (S.J.): LOYOLA and his (7) companions wanted to do miss. work or to place themselves unconditionally at the disposal of the Pope.
1540 Confirmation of the order by PAUL III.
Constitution: the elected Superior General (the 'Black Pope') governed the provinces and houses of the Order in military-absolutist fashion. He was assisted by an admonitor (cautioner) who had to give constant criticism. Monastic vows of the members (who wore the garb of sec. priests); élitist selection through exercises and mutual supervision. The *Professi* (the professed), pledging a special 4th vow

('cadaver obedience'), were recruited from coadjutors who had proved their worth. Sole purpose: the conversion of heretics and heathens; to this end, concerted efforts at the courts of princes as tutors and **confessors; at** schools and universities (Jes. colleges, Jes. preparatory schools (Gymnasia)) as teachers, preachers and missionaries.

Significance: most important order in the renewal of the **Papal Church** (BELLARMINE); **struggle against heresy** (FABER, CANISIUS, p. 251), and **world-wide miss. activity**, esp. in America (p. 277), India, Japan, China (Xavier, RICCI); they frequently attracted hostility and suspicion because of their methods.
1541–56 As 1st Superior General of the Order, LOYOLA shaped the '*Compania Jesu*'.
1549 The Order was made directly subject to the Pope; theological seminaries were est.:
1551 Collegium Romanum; 1552 Collegium Germanicum. Noteworthy successors were **Lainez** (1558–65) and **Aquaviva** (1581–1615). Initial rapid spread in Lat. countries.

The Reform Papacy

1536 PAUL III (1534–49) convoked a 'deputation of reform' (CARAFA, CONTARINI).
1542 Reintroduction of the Inquisition. In the person of **Paul IV Carafa** (1555–9), the first active reformer became Pope.
1566–72 PIUS V rigorously attacked simony. Revised version of the Rom. Catechism: 1568 the Breviary; 1570 the Mass.
1582 Reform of the calendar during the pontificate of GREGORY XIII. After Sixtus V (1585–90) periodic reports on visitations and reform of the College of Cardinals.
1590 New ed. of the **Vulgate.**

The Council of Trent (1545–63)

Cal. by PAUL III to safeguard the unity of the faith and the Church and conducted by papal legates:
1545–7 1st Session: differences between the Emperor (reform) and the Pope (doctrine):
1547–9 Transfer of the Council to Bologna.
1551–2 2nd Session included Prot. representatives on the orders of CHARLES V; after his defeat, dissolution (p. 237).
1562–3 3rd Session: conducted in masterful fashion by MORONE, the 'saviour of the Council'; papal centralism owed its vict. in part to the Jesuits LAÍNEZ and SALMERÓN.
Provisions: doctrinal decrees, clearly distinguished from Prot. teachings, concerning the sacraments, Church tradition, the sacrifice of the Mass, the priesthood, original sin and confession; **reform decrees** concerning the training, dress, duties and celibacy of the clergy; elimination of the abuses related to benefices and indulgences.
1564 The clergy sworn to the **Tridentinum** (the Provisions of Trent); the **index librorum prohibitorum** (index of books prohibited by the Church, maintained by the Congregation of the Holy Office) est.
Significance: the basic theological and eccles. reorganization shaped the entire development of modern Catholicism.

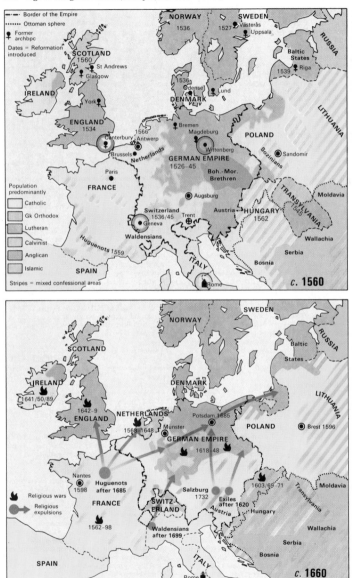

Map legend (c. 1560):
- –·–·– Border of the Empire
- ········· Ottoman sphere
- ♱ Former archbpc
- Dates = Reformation introduced

NORWAY 1536
SWEDEN 1527 Västerås ♱ Uppsala
RUSSIA
SCOTLAND 1560 ♱ St Andrews ♱ Glasgow
IRELAND
York ♱
Baltic States
1539 ♱ Riga
LITHUANIA
DENMARK 1536 ♱ Odense ♱ Lund
ENGLAND 1534 ♱ Canterbury 1566
Antwerp Brussels ♱ Netherlands
♱ Bremen ♱ Magdeburg
POLAND
Sozimira
Sandomir
Paris ●
FRANCE
GERMAN EMPIRE 1526–45
♱ Wittenberg
Boh.-Mor. Brethren
● Augsburg
Austria
TRANSYLVANIA 1545
Moldavia
Switzerland 1536/45 Geneva
Waldensians
Trent ♱
HUNGARY 1562
Wallachia
Huguenots 1559
SPAIN
ITALY
♱ Rome
Serbia
Bosnia

Population predominantly:
- Catholic
- Gk Orthodox
- Lutheran
- Calvinist
- Anglican
- Islamic

Stripes = mixed confessional areas

c. 1560

Map (c. 1660):

NORWAY
SWEDEN
RUSSIA
SCOTLAND
IRELAND 1641/50/89
ENGLAND 1642–9
Baltic States
LITHUANIA
NETHERLANDS 1568–1648
Münster
DENMARK
Potsdam 1685
POLAND
Brest 1596
GERMAN EMPIRE 1618–48
Nantes 1598
Huguenots after 1685
FRANCE 1562–98
SWITZERLAND
Salzburg 1732
Exiles after 1620
Austria
1603/69–71
Transylvania
Moldavia
Hungary
Wallachia
Waldensians after 1699
ITALY
Serbia
Bosnia
SPAIN
Rome ♱

- Religious wars
- Religious expulsions

c. 1660

The religious schisms in Europe, 16th–17th cents.

Proceeding from Germany and Switzerland, the Reformation affected all Europe with the exception of Spain, Italy and the Gk. Orth. territories; but only northern Europe became purely Luth., and Scotland purely Calv.

Denmark/Norway: FREDERICK I (1523–33) allowed Prot. worship in Schleswig.
1527 Diet of Odense: toleration granted to Lutherans.
1536 Introduction of the Reformation under CHRISTIAN III. BUGENHAGEN shaped the eccles. organization, which became effective also for Norway. Eccles. properties fell to the crown.
From 1539 gradual acceptance of Luth. doctrine in Iceland.

Sweden: hoping for a strengthening of royal power through the Reformation, GUSTAVUS VASA compelled acceptance of the Reformation against the will of the people at the
1527 Diet of Vasteras. Cath. forms of worship were retained, the state church was made subject to the king. As a Catholic, SIGISMUND VASA was obliged at the
1594 Church Assembly of Uppsala to pledge to respect the Luth. confession. The Counter-Reformation failed with his defeat (p. 249).

The Baltic States: proceeding from Riga, the new faith spread by
1539 into the state of the Teutonic Order; after its dissolution, the Pol. and Swed. (later Rus.) parts remained Luth.

Poland/Lithuania: all Prot. confessions made inroads in the confessionally mixed state (Catholics, Eastern Orthodox, Jewish).
Starting in 1540 JOHN LASKI (1499–1560) disseminated Calvinism; expelled Boh.–Mor. Brethren est. new communities. The Prot. groups concluded the
1570 Union (Consensus) of Sandomir; all relig. denominations were granted relig. toleration by the
1573 *Pax Dissidendum.* A Unitarian (denier of the Trinity), FAUSTUS SOZZINI (1539–1604) est. the
1579 Socinian Church. Initiated by Cardinal **Stanislaus Hosius** (1504–79), Bishop of Ermland, the Counter-Reformation began during the reign of SIGISMUND VASA with persecutions, esp. of the Socinians. Protestantism was reduced through the efforts of the Jesuits by the middle of the 17th cent. Owing to the efforts of the preacher PETER SKARGA (1536–1612), a compromise was reached with part of the Orth. Church in **1596 the Union of Brest.**

Transylvania: JOHANN HONTER (1498–1549) was a relig. reformer and the founder of the Luth. nat. church of the Saxons; exc. the Wallachians, all nationalities became Prot.

Hungary: Prot. doctrines gained acceptance among the nobles (Magnates), and in the cities through the work of MATTHIAS BIRÓ.

After 1562 the *Confessio helvetica* was the determining factor. However, a distinct church was not est. While Turk. Hungary remained Prot., Aust. Hungary became Cath. again during the 17th cent. despite the resistance of the Magnates.

The Hered. Aust. Possessions: Luth. doctrine had a strong effect on nobility, *bourgeoisie* and peasantry, except for the Tirol. A Prot. Church existed in
1561–99 Carniola; its writings laid the basis for Slovenian literature.
1572 Introduction of the Jes. Order and formation of the
1579 Reform Commission under Cardinal MELCHIOR KHLESI (1552–1630) to carry out the re-catholicizing of Austria. FERDINAND II led the Counter-Reformation in Styria, Carinthia and Carniola. Ultimately, expulsion of Prot. subjects (*Exulanten*) through Archbishop FIRMIAN of Salzburg.

France: although he was indifferent in matters of religion, FRANCIS I did not tolerate heretics because he needed the income derived from the Cath. Church. Though persecution increased under HENRY II, Calvinism spread.
1559 1st nat. synod at Paris. After the conversion of the Bourbon and Châtillon families, the Huguenots (confederates pledged to one another by oath) became a polit. party,
1562–98 Huguenot Wars. The Huguenots were granted toleration by the
1598 Edict of Nantes (p. 247). Cardinal RICHELIEU was to destroy their strongholds (La Rochelle, 1628).
1685 Revocation of the Edict by LOUIS XIV: half a million Huguenots left (p. 261).

The Netherlands: Lutherans and Anabaptists (p. 233) severely persecuted by CHARLES V.
1523 First burning of heretics of the Reformation at Brussels. Calvinism later reinforced resistance to Spain.
1566 Synod of Antwerp: foundation of the Calv. Church, which became the state church of the Dutch Republic.

Scotland: CALVIN's pupil, the reformer **John Knox** (1505–72), united the Protestants.
1547 They were overwhelmed at St Andrews. However, the nobility converted and, in 1557, to safeguard 'God's Word', formed the Covenant and in
1560 est. the Scottish Nat. Church. After the forced abdication of MARY STUART, JAMES VI (JAMES I of England) made it
1567 the state-church. The church property fell to the nobility.

England: (see p. 238).

Ireland: EDWARD VI and ELIZABETH I forced an Anglican clergy on the country; but despite persecutions and punitive campaigns, it remained Cath. (exc. Ulster).

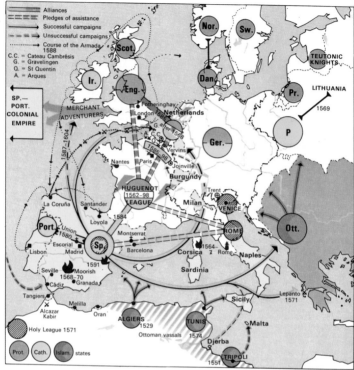

Spain, c. 1580 (Philip II)

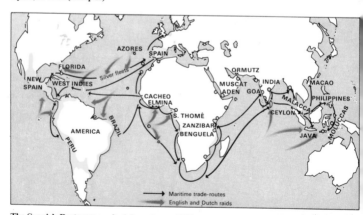

The Spanish-Portuguese colonial empire, c. 1580

The Port. Empire in the 16th Cent.

1495–1521 MANUEL I THE GREAT founded Port. commercial power with settlements in India, E. Asia (spice monopoly), Africa and Brazil, making Lisbon the largest Eur. port. The brief period of flowering, described by Portugal's greatest poet, CAMÕES (1524–80), in *The Lusiads* (VASCO DA GAMA's journey to India, p. 221), strained the nat. resources. Colon. prosperity demoralized people and state.

1557–78 A theatrical crusade to Morocco was undertaken by SEBASTIAN I, who, with a high proportion of the Port. nobility, was killed in the

1578 b. of Alcazar-Kabir. During the

1580–1640 Personal Union with Spain, the colon. empire was almost entirely lost to the Dutch and English.

1640 Liberation from Spain under the leadership of the new royal house of **Braganza** (JOHN IV).

The Age of Philip II of Spain

Serious and self-confident, while suspicious, pedantic and slow to make decisions,

1556–98 Philip II ruled over his inheritance by means of written orders. Isolated from his subjects by the introduction of

1548 Burg. court ceremonial, PHILIP, as **Spaniard, Habsburg** and **Catholic**, conceived his mission to be the reunion of Christianity under the Cath. faith and under Sp. leadership. The **Escorial** (begun 1557), residence, monastery and mausoleum of the Sp. kings, became the symbol of his will to power.

Domestic policy: the relig. and polit. unity of all hered. lands was accomplished through:

1. An unscrupulous Inquisition, incl. *autos de fe* (burnings of heretics) and suppression of the *Moriscos* (Moors) and *Marranos* (pigs: Jews), the mainstays of trade and crafts (1568–70, *Morisco* rising in Granada).

2. Absolute authority over the nat. church with royal *placet* (approval) of all papal edicts; the rights of the estates were curtailed.

3. Control of the economy and the colonies. The goal was achieved at the price of

1581 the defection of the Netherlands (p. 245); the grandees were deprived of power, the *hidalgos* (lesser nobility) migrated to the colonies and the economy was shaken by public bankruptcies, importation of silver (p. 277), prohibition of trade and inflation; decline of agriculture and crafts. Capital accumulated in the hands of the Fuggers (p. 215). Fame came to the army and its leaders: the Duke of Alba (1507–82); ALEXANDER FARNESE (1545–92); JOHN OF AUSTRIA (1547–78, step-brother of the king); SPINOLA (1569–1630).

Foreign policy: France and England opposed the Sp. striving for hegemony.

1556–9 War against **France** with victs. at St-Quentin and Gravelingen.

1559 Peace of Cateau-Cambrésis: the Free County (Franche-Comté) of Burgundy and Naples were gained. After the death of PHILIP's 2nd wife (and aunt), MARY TUDOR,

a severe anti-Cath. reaction set in in **England** under

1558–1603 Elizabeth I, who postponed a response to the courtship of PHILIP, but clandestinely promoted the piracy of the merchant adventurers against Sp. shipping (p. 247). In the struggle against the Turks, the 'Holy League' broke Turk. domination of the Mediterranean with the brilliant

1571 naval vict. of Lepanto. The conquest and

1580 Union of Portugal with Spain crowned the successes of PHILIP.

1584 Alliance with the Cath. party (League) of France (p. 247).

To conquer England, which often supported the Dutch rebels, a fleet of galleys, consisting of about 130 ships with 27,000 men, was assembled under the command of Admiral MEDINA SIDONIA.

1588 Destruction of the Great Armada, in part by artillery battles in the Channel (DRAKE), in part by storms. The guns of the easily manoeuvrable Eng. sailing vessels (galleons) saved the principal Prot. power of Europe and initiated a change in Sp. power politics and naval warfare.

The Decline of Sp. Power

1590 Sp. interference in the Huguenot War reinforced Fr. nat. resistance. England and the Dutch Republic joined

1595 War of France against Spain.

1598 Peace of Vervins: Spain abandoned all interference in France.

1598–1621 PHILIP III left the management of the exhausted state to his favourite, Count LERMA, the 'greatest thief of Spain'.

1610 The unscrupulous expulsion of the *Moriscos* completely dest. the land's prosperity. Under PHILIP IV (1621–65) the gvt was carried on by

1621–43 Duke OLIVARES. Participation in the 30 Years War and the

1621–48 renewal of the war with the Dutch quickened the decline of power. Portugal and Catalonia (reunited 1652) defected in 1640.

1648 Recognition of the Netherlands; loss of the predominant power position to France by the

1659 Peace of the Pyrenees (p. 259).

Ctr. during the Age of Spain

Sp. mores and customs spread across Europe, as did Sp. court ceremonial and the knightly romances of the **Amadis stories.** Poetry and painting achieved their most brilliant flowering. **Cervantes'** (1547–1616) satiric masterpiece *Don Quixote* and the dramas of LOPE DE VEGA (1562–1635) and CALDERÓN (1600–81) took their places in world literature. The painters **El Greco** (1541–1613) and MURILLO (1617–82) used relig. themes, while VELÁZQUEZ (1599–1660) portrayed life at court. The Jesuit SUÁREZ (1548–1617) developed a theory of int. law.

The Dutch War of Independence, 1568–1648

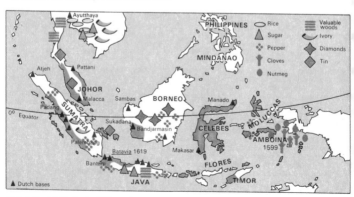

Dutch East India in the 18th cent.

The Netherlands under the Habsburgs (1477–1568)

1477 The southern provinces, incl. Holland, fell to MAXIMILIAN I with the **Burg. inheritance** (p. 193); by 1543 the Habsburgs had also inherited the northern provinces.

1512 Formation of the Burg. Imp. Circle, transferred by CHARLES V to the Sp. line in 1551.

Make-up of the 17 provinces: (a) ethnic contrasts between the Lat. s. (Walloons) and the Germ. N. (Flemish); (b) econ. differences between the impoverished country nobility and the prosperous urban *bourgeoisie*; (c) relig. differences between the Cath. s. and the N., which early turned to Lutheranism, and to some extent to Anabaptism (p. 233), and, after 1563, to Calvinism; (d) polit. differences as a result of traditional local privileges. Every city and province defended its **ancient liberties**.

Constitution: self-admin. of each province with a royal governor and a representative body of the 7 estates; loose gvtl supervision by the Governor-General, the Council of State and the United Diet (Estates General).

Significance: with more than 200 cities, the most thriving industrial-commercial area of Europe brought in taxes 7 times the amount of America's silver to the crown. Rotterdam and Antwerp, the 'turnstiles of trade', handled c. 50 % of world trade. The Bourse of Antwerp was the centre of the Eur. money market. The 'citadel of Europe' was also a major factor in terms of power politics (encircling France). Leading polit. personalities were MARGARET OF PARMA, Governor-General (1559–67), and her counsellor, Cardinal GRANVELLA. His pro-Sp. policy offended the people, who were led by the *stadholders* EGMONT, HOORN and William of Orange (1533–84).

PHILIP II tolerated neither relig. nor polit. liberties; to hispanicize the Low Countries, he ordered

1565 an intensification of the Inquisition and a reduction of the size of bpcs. Protests (petitions) were rejected, the Dutch noble leaders ridiculed as **Geuzen** (beggars).

1566 Unrest and iconoclasm were opposed by EGMONT and WILLIAM OF ORANGE. Nevertheless the king delegated 'pacification' to the 'Iron Duke' of ALBA.

1567 Establishment of a milit. dictatorship with special courts (the 'Council of Blood' at Brussels) to try the rebels.

1568 Execution of EGMONT and HOORN.

The Dutch War of Independence (1568–1648)

WILLIAM OF ORANGE assembled mercenaries in Nassau, but he was no match for ALBA in open battle. Successful raids, however, by the **'Water geuzen'** on Sp. naval transports and bases.

1572 Seizure of Briel and Vlissingen.

1573 Recall of ALBA. To combat plunder and terror by the Sp. military, all provinces joined in the

1576 Pacification of Ghent. Politically adroit, the new Governor-General

1578–92 **Alexander Farnese** confirmed the southern Cath. provinces in their liberties and won them back to Spain by the

1578 Union of Arras. Formed in opposition, the

1579 **Union of Utrecht** of the northern provinces split the Low Countries. PHILIP II placed WILLIAM OF ORANGE under the ban.

1581 The Union's **Proclamation of Independence** from the Sp. 'tyrant and lawbreaker'.

1584 Murder of WILLIAM OF ORANGE at Delft.

Constitution of the United Provinces: representatives of the 7 republics met under the chairmanship of **Holland** (designation also used to refer to the entire country) at The Hague; Holland appointed the 'Pensioner of the Council' (or Permanent Advocate of the Netherlands) for 5-yr terms. First occupant of the office and polit. leader: OLDENBARNEVELDT (1547–1619).

New assault by FARNESE: recapture of Flanders and Brabant. After the fall of

1585 Antwerp, England (LEICESTER) openly supported the United Provinces (p. 247). Raids on Sp.-Port. overseas trading stations led to the **Dutch Colon. Empire** being est. Spain, forced to trade 'with the enemy', helped to finance the war against itself. Neither could the United Provinces be overcome on land. The Sp. army was diverted by England and France (p. 243). In

1585–1625 **Maurice of Nassau** the Dutch had a brilliant organizer and tactician.

1591–8 Counter-attacks pushed the Spanish back in the E. and s.

1609 Conclusion of a 12-yr truce. Factional struggles between MAURICE and the Pensioner ended with the

1619 execution of OLDENBARNEVELDT.

1621 Final struggle with Spain, which was forced to recognize the new republic in

1648 the Peace of The Hague.

The Flowering of the Netherlands in the 17th Cent.

Commerce and the crafts shifted to the N. during the 80-yr struggle (Amsterdam). Holland became the world's foremost commercial power. Providing their own armies and enjoying polit. privileges, the **East India Company** (1602) and the West India Company (1621) assumed the task of colon. exploitation. England became a superior opponent to Dutch naval power by the mid 17th cent. (p. 267). Pre-eminence in **painting led to general cult. flowering**: the Flem. School with Peter Paul Rubens (1577–1640), and VAN DYCK (1599–1641): Baroque allegories, portraits. More realistic portraits of manners and customs, the sea and landscapes, were provided by the Dutch School of FRANS HALS (1580–1666), JAN STEEN, RUYSDAEL, Vermeer, etc.; **Rembrandt** (1606–69): portraits, group paintings; etchings as a distinct form of portraiture. **Science**: SPINOZA (p. 256) and **Hugo Grotius** (1583–1645), the 'Father of International Law', became better known than the philologist LIPSIUS and the natural scientist LEEUWENHOEK.

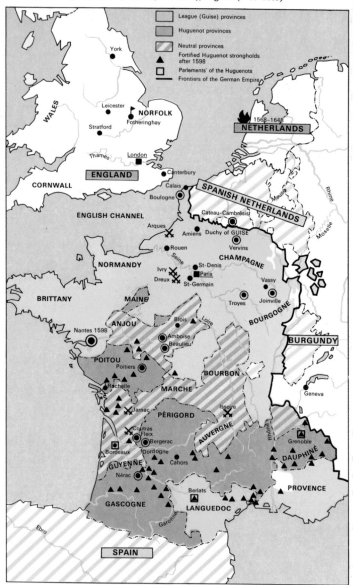

France during the Huguenot Wars, 1562–98

The Civil Wars in France

1547–59 Henry II. Struggling with the Habsburgs (p. 243), he allied himself with the Prot. princes of the Empire (p. 237); none the less he persecuted the Fr. Huguenots (p. 241); his death in a tournament led to a crisis.

1559–60 Francis II (15 yrs old), mar. to Mary Stuart, was under the infl. of his wife's relatives, the Cath. Guise family.

1560–74 Charles IX (10 yrs old) was dominated by his Regent mother, **Catherine de' Medici,** who played off the Bourbons (Anthony of Navarre) against the Guises. Conditionally recognized by the Edict of St-Germain, the Huguenots were attacked by the Guises in

1562 the Massacre of Vassy. A total of 8

1562–98 Huguenot wars were fought. Spain supported the Guises, England the Huguenots (milit. aid also from the Electoral Palatine and Hesse). In consequence of the theory of the **Monarchomachi,** which condoned tyrannicide (subscribed to by Beza (p. 238) and the Jesuit Mariana among others), the leaders of both noble factions, Francis of Guise and Louis Condé, were murdered. Henry of Guise and Admiral Coligny continued the struggle. Jean Bodin (1530–96), author of the *De la République* (1576), belonged to a third party, the 'party of the politicians'. His doctrine of the **sovereignty of the state** laid the foundation for absolutism (p. 259).

1570 Peace of St-Germain: the Huguenots were granted 4 fortified places. Coligny won the king over to a nat. and anti-Sp. policy. Catherine therefore used the marriage of her daughter to Henry of Navarre to eliminate Coligny and the Huguenots.

1572 The **Massacre of St Bartholomew:** murder of *c.* 20,000 Huguenots (3,000 in Paris). The Huguenots, however, maintained their position at **La Rochelle** and est. their own milit. organization in the s. Henry III (1574–89) yielded to their pressure with the Edict of Beaulieu of 1576. When the Huguenot Henry of Navarre became legitimate heir to the throne, the **Cath. League** (Henry of Guise) allied with Spain.

1585–9 'War of the 3 Henrys' over Paris. The king had Henry of Guise murdered and was himself assassinated.

1589–1610 Henry IV of Bourbon fought the League and the Sp. armies; in

1593 he converted to the Cath. faith ('Paris is well worth a mass'), which ended the wars.

1598 The Edict of Nantes: the Huguenots were granted freedom of conscience, limited freedom of worship, polit. equality and fortified strongholds.

Consequences: France remained Cath., but integrated the Prot. minority, politically and culturally. The crown was victorious over the nobility; Henry IV realized the nat. unitary state. His minister **Sully** put agriculture and the finances of the state into order; trade and the crafts improved; the 1st Fr. colony was est. in Canada (p. 277).

England under the Tudors

1485–1509 Henry VII restored law and order with the aid of the **Star Chamber** (a special royal court); he transferred local admin. to justices of the peace and, with the marriage of his daughter to James IV of Scotland (1488–1513), prepared the ground for the later union of the whole island (p. 267).

1509–47 Henry VIII let himself be led into wars with France and Scotland by Cardinal Wolsey (to 1530).

1513 b. of Flodden Field: destruction of the Scottish army. The king strengthened his authority at the expense of the Church (p. 238) and proclaimed himself

1542 king of Ireland. The Duke of Somerset (Seymour) governed as Protector during the reign of Edward VI (9 yrs old); after his fall, his rival, the Duke of Northumberland (Dudley), succeeded; he wished to alter the order of succession to the throne and was executed.

1553–8 Mary I (p. 238) entrusted her polit. destiny to Charles V, involved England in Spain's struggle with France and lost Calais in 1558. Spain and the Cath. Church (the Jesuits) henceforth considered nat. enemies.

1558–1603 Elizabeth I (acc. to Cath. views the illegitimate daughter of Anne Boleyn), astute in her politics and eccles. policy, asserted her ideas with the aid of Lord **Burghley** (William Cecil, 1520–98) (p. 238).

1559–60 Intervention in Scotland in favour of the Calv. noble opposition (p. 241). Educated at the Fr. Court

1542–67 Mary Stuart returned, mar. Bothwell, the murderer of her husband (Darnley), was forced to abdicate, fled to England in 1568 and, encouraged by the Cath. party (Norfolk), asserted claims to the throne. Mary was taken prisoner.

1587 Her execution led to open conflict with Spain (until 1604). Previously England had already assisted the Dutch (p. 245) and conducted privateering warfare through her naval heroes **John Hawkins, Francis Drake,** Frobisher, Cavendish, etc.

1588 Destruction of the Spanish Armada (p. 243); renewed Sp. attacks in 1596/7 and 1599 no longer threatened the island.

Trade and econ. life: the unavailability of previous ports of destination owing to blockade by Spain, France and the Hanseatic League promoted the search for new markets. The **merchant adventurers** (trade and piracy on their own account) formed trading stock companies: 1554 the Muscovy Company, 1581 the Levant Company;

1600 the East India Company (p. 275). The Eng. capitalist economy had its beginning in

1571 with the opening of the London Stock Exchange.

1584 The 1st Eng. colony est. in **Virginia** by Sir **Walter Raleigh** (1552–1618). The offices of the Hanseatic League in London were closed in 1598 (p. 183).

Consequences: England broke Sp. hegemony and became the leading Prot. power; she experienced a flowering of her civilization (p. 212) and est. her basis as a colon. power.

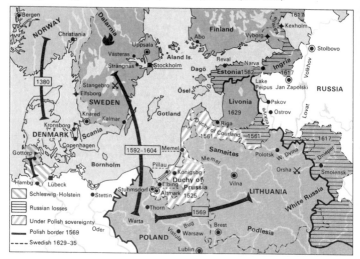

The Baltic area in the 16th cent.

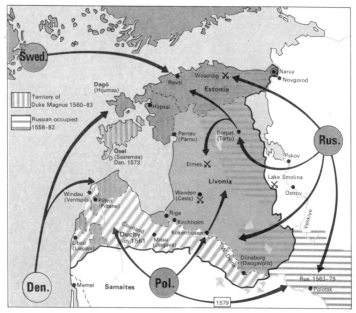

The struggle for Livonia, 1558–82

The Republic of the Pol. Nobility

1506–48 SIGISMUND I.

1515 At the Congress of Pressburg and Vienna he gave up Bohemia and Hungary; MAXIMILIAN I (p. 219) in exchange confirmed Pol. feudal sovereignty over Prussia, which became a sec. duchy in 1525 (p. 235).

Threatened by Russia, the Ottomans and Sweden, Lithuania surrendered her independence in the

1569 Union of Lublin; a common diet est.; compromise between the Lith. and Pol. nobilities.

Constitution: the **Szlachta** (lesser nobility) obtained the privileges of the magnates. Transformation of the manorial system (payments and contributions in kind by free copyholders) into an **estate economy** (p. 215); autonomous cities without representation in the **Sejm** (diet), which consisted of the king, the magnates (in the senate) and the *Szlachta*.

1572 *Articuli henriciani* (after HENRY OF VALOIS, Pol. king 1572–4): the right to resistance, electoral and relig. liberty of the nobility.

Culture: the 'Golden Age of Poland' began under the last Jagiellonians: relig. toleration (p. 241); flowering of the 'Vistula Gothic'; introduction of the Ital. Renaissance into the 'Cracow School of painting'; infl. of Ger. and Flem. artists (VEIT STOSS). CONRAD CELTIS and COPERNICUS (p. 221), the scholars of jurisprudence PAUL WLODOWIC and JAN OSTOROK, and the poet JAN KOCHANOWSKI (1530–84) worked at the University of Cracow, a centre of humanism.

After the expiration of the Jagiellonian Dynasty (1572)

1574 dual election. By the efforts of the Pol. statesman JAN ZAMOYSKI (1542–1605) MAXIMILIAN II (p. 251), the candidate of the Habsburg party, was excluded in favour of

1575–86 Stephen Bathory, who strengthened the army by the introduction of Cossacks, and conducted 3 successful campaigns against IVAN IV.

1587–1632 SIGISMUND III VASA (also Swed. king 1592–1604), promoted the Counter-Reformation (p. 241).

1607–9 Uprisings of the nobility against his '*absolutum dominium*'; struggles against the Turks in the Principality of Moldavia.

1610 Vict. of Hetman ZOLKIEWSKI at Klushino and occupation of Moscow; but Pol. claims to the throne of the Rus. Tsars led to nat. Rus. and Swed. resistance and the

1618 Armistice of Deulino.

1621 Peace of Chotin with the Turks after the loss of Livonia to Sweden.

Sweden under the Vasas in the 16th Cent.

1513–23 CHRISTIAN II (1481–1559) defeated the regent STEN STURE II and, after his coronation, was revenged on his enemies by the

1520 Stockholm massacre. Popular uprising at Dalarne.

1523–60 Gustavus I Vasa, with financial aid from Lübeck, removed the last Dan. king of the united state (1523). Elected king at the diet of Strängnäs, VASA est. the Swed. nat. state despite domestic opposition. The admin. was reorganized by the introduction of offtcials, a chancery and an exchequer; taxes were approved by the diet. To end financial dependence on Lübeck, the property of the Cath. Church was confiscated after the

1527 introduction of the Reformation (p. 241). Support of Denmark against Lübeck. Having become Burgomaster in the wake of a revolution, JÜRGEN WULLENWEYER (1492–1537) provoked the

1534–6 'Feud of the Counts' to renew the power of the Hanseatic League; he was deprived of his office and executed. The marriage of

1568–92 JOHN III est. the Cath. branch of the Pol. Vasas. His son

1592–1604 SIGISMUND united the crowns of Poland and Sweden; however, he was attacked because of his Cath. policies, defeated in the

1598 b. of Stangebro and deprived of his throne by the diet. CHARLES IX (1604–11) was succeeded by Sweden's greatest king,

1611–32 Gustavus II Adolphus (17 yrs old). He achieved his successes with the aid of the nobility.

1621 The 'Articles of War', making milit. service obligatory for the peasantry, created the most modern army in Europe.

The Struggle for the Baltic in the 16th Cent.

The 1st Rus. advance to the Baltic was repelled in the

1502 b. of Lake Smolina by the Master of the Order of Livonia

1494–1535 WOLTER VON PLETTENBERG. However, he was unable to restore the state of the Order. IVAN IV (p. 203) initiated the

1558 struggle for Livonia, which placed itself under Pol. protection. Sweden intervened when FREDERICK II OF DENMARK (1559–88) bought the bpcs of Ösel and Courland for his brother Duke MAGNUS OF HOLSTEIN. Reval and Estonia paid homage to MAGNUS. Out of the collapse of the Order, Master GOTTHART KETTELER salvaged Courland as a sec. duchy under Pol. sovereignty. Courland's Pol. vassalage brought Poland into conflict with Russia: allied with Denmark

1563–70 'War of the 3 Crowns' against Sweden.

1582 Armistice of JAN ZAPOLSKI: Russia gave up Livonia and Polotsk. The struggle over the '*Dominium maris Baltici*' was won by **Gustavus II Adolphus.** He ended the

1611–13 'War of Kalmar', fought over the Nor. provinces in Lapland, by entering into the Peace of Knäred with CHRISTIAN IV OF DENMARK (p. 253), whose policy of union failed. Russia lost access to the Baltic Sea by the

1617 Peace of Stolbovo.

1621 Conquest of Livonia by GUSTAVUS II ADOLPHUS. With the Armistice of Altmark (1629) Poland was forced to give up Livonia and important ports to Sweden.

The Counter-Reformation in Germany, 1555–1648

Centralized Imp. Authority (1555–1619)

The most extended period of peace in Cen. Europe was rather a respite of exhaustion. Germany was removed from the avenues of world trade; her cities were increasingly impoverished, the crafts deteriorated; imp. authority declined; there was a lack of outstanding individuals.

1556–64 Ferdinand I was concerned with safeguarding the relig. peace. Last attempt at confessional reconciliation in

1557 relig. discourse of Worms. The Prot. princes refused to recognize the 'eccles. reservation', the Cath. princes the 'secret declaration'. Leaning towards Protestantism,

1564–76 Maximilian II refused to have the decisions of the Council of Trent (p. 239) proclaimed and declared himself neutral in questions of religion. Protestantism reached its widest expansion (conversion of the N. Ger. bpcs).

1576–1612 Rudolph II. Educated by Jesuits in Spain, he introduced the Counter-Reformation into the hered. lands of the Habsburgs. Residing at the Hradčany Castle in Prague, the shy eccentric surrounded himself with alchemists, grooms and astronomers (Kepler, p. 256), leaving gvt to court officials. His brother

1612–19 Matthias attempted to restore imp. authority under Habsburg domination.

The Development of the Territ. Principalities

Without obstruction by the Empire, the princes stabilized their power through police ordinances and administrative reorganization. Their foreign policy aimed at rounding out their possessions (marriage, inheritance contracts, judicial proceedings and purchase of eccles. foundations). The establishment of territ. churches broadened the public services rendered by the state to include education and welfare (p. 235); the patriarchal conception of the prince as the deputy of God gained acceptance. Confessional problems determined the policies of the 'Christ. welfare state'.

Division within Protestantism

As the reconsiderations and discussions of the doctrines of the faith by court theologians intensified, the more extreme dogmatic viewpoints asserted themselves. These brought about the disintegration of Luth. doctrine and the dissolution of the unity of the Prot. territ. princes. Theological righteousness took the place of forceful religiosity, esp. in the conflict between the 'Philipists' (the adherents of Melanchthon's *Variata* of 1540) and the Orthodox who gathered around Flacius Illyricus.

The compromising formula of the Luth. Concordat of 1577 (devised by J. Andreae, Chancellor of the University of Tübingen) was adhered to by most Luth. princes. On the other hand, their opposition to the Calv. states was that much more severe. The Calv. states found their main support in the **Electoral Palatinate** and their denominational identity in the **Heidelberg Catechism** (1563). The Palatinate became the link between Ger., Fr., Dutch and Boh. Protestantism.

Electoral Saxony was the heartland of Lutheran orthodoxy. Of conservative orientation and politically feeble, Electoral Saxony was more disposed to unite with the Cath. emperor than with the Prot. Palatinate. Lutheranism became the pietism of the families of the common folk, who served authority obediently (Lutheran quietism).

The Cath. Counter-Reformation

Divisions within Protestantism promoted Cath. rest., esp. the work of the **Jesuits** (p. 239). They gained infl. over Cath. princes, in universities, and over education in general, and, by means of magnificent Baroque churches, processions and relig. plays, over the people as well. Est. in 1552 at Rome, the Collegium Germanicum provided the training of priests. **Peter Canisius** (1511–97), writer of popular catechisms, became the '2nd Apostle of Germany'. By the establishment of the

1573 *Congregatio Germanica* (a committee of cardinals for Ger. affairs) the Curia intervened directly in Ger. church affairs; permanent nunciatures were set up (Vienna, Cologne).

1563 Beginning of the Counter-Reformation in **Bavaria,** the predominant Cath. power in Germany.

1579 The Cath. reaction in **Austria** took on more severe forms (Cardinal Khlesl).

1583 War within the bpc of Cologne was decided in favour of the Cath. party. The archbp, who had become Prot., was expelled. After 1596 brutal extermination of heretics in Styria, Carinthia and Carniola by Archduke Ferdinand (p. 241). On the other hand, Rudolph II was forced to grant relig. liberty to the Hung. estates in 1606, and to the Boh. estates in

1609 by a 'Letter of Majesty' (p. 253).

An alliance of the Prot. princes, aspired to by Frederick IV of the Palatinate (1583–1610), became possible only after the

1607 occupation of Donauwörth by Maximilian of Bavaria (1597–1623). Placed under the ban because of interference with Cath. processions, this Prot. Imp. city of Bavaria was confiscated and re-catholicized by the Elector, entrusted with the execution of the Imp. decree. This breach of the relig. peace led to the

1608 disruption of the Diet of Regensburg and the establishment of the **Prot. Union** (Christian of Anhalt) which est. ties with France, England and the United Provinces.

1609 Establishment of the **Catholic League** by Maximilian I of Bavaria in association with Spain.

1609–14 Conflict over the succession in Jülich and Clèves.

1614 The Treaty of Partition of Xanten prevented a fresh clash: after the claimants changed their denominations, Brandenburg (now Calv.) received Clèves, Mark and Ravensberg; the Prince of Newburg (now Cath.) received Jülich and Berg.

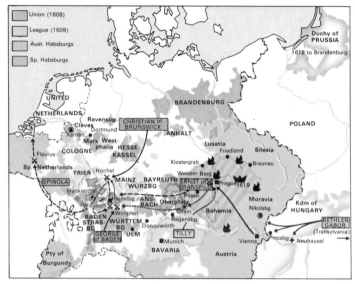

The Bohemian phase, 1618–23

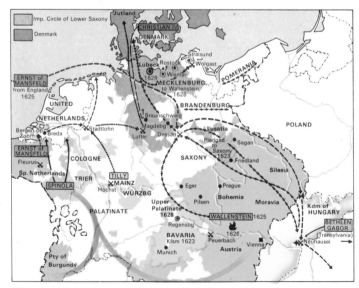

The Danish phase, 1625–9

1618–48 The Thirty Years War. Beginning as a relig. conflict, it ended as a Eur. power-struggle. Existing tensions between Cath. and Prot. states, estates and princes, Imp. cities and the Emperor, the Habsburgs and France exploded during the war.

Immediate Cause: Habsburg Family Conflict
During the fraternal conflict between RUDOLPH (p. 251) and MATTHIAS, both sides courted the estates. The Aust., Hung. and Mor. estates elected MATTHIAS king in 1608. The Boh. estates were granted relig. liberty by RUDOLPH's
1609 Letter of Majesty. MATTHIAS granted them the right freely to elect their king.
1617 The Treaty of Prague gave PHILIP III of Spain claim to the Habsburg possessions in Alsace in exchange for his surrender of hered. rights in Bohemia in favour of Archduke FERDINAND (p. 251), who became king of Bohemia without the approval of the estates. Unrest over the destruction of Prot. churches and the violation of privileges brought about the (2nd)
1618 Defenestration of Prague (of imp. deputies). General uprising (Count THURN) and establishment of a gvt of the estates with milit. assistance from the Count VON MANSFELD, a mercenary leader of the Duke of Savoy.

The Boh. Phase (1618–23)
THURN advanced on Vienna; the Aust., Sil., Mor. and Hung. estates joined, as did those of Transylvania (BETHLEN GABOR).
1619–37 FERDINAND II, elected Emperor, was not recognized by Bohemia. Bohemia made FREDERICK V OF THE PALATINATE (23 yrs old) king. Papal subsidies, the assistance of Spain, the League (MAXIMILIAN I OF BAVARIA) and Luth. Electoral Saxony made the Imp. counter-attack possible. While Saxony conquered Lusatia and Sp. troops (SPINOLA) invaded the Palatinate, the army of the League (TILLY) was victorious over Bohemia in the
1620 b. of the White Mountain. The 'Winter-king', FREDERICK OF THE PALATINATE, fled to Holland; the Union dissolved itself.
1622 A separate peace was concluded at Nicholsburg with BETHLEN GABOR. TILLY stormed Heidelberg (transfer of the library (the Palatina) to Rome); was victorious at Wimpfen (over GEORGE FREDERICK OF BADEN), at Höchst and in the
1623 b. of Stadtlohn (over CHRISTIAN OF BRUNSWICK); occupation of Westphalia and Lower Saxony.
1623 Bavaria received the electoral dignity of the Palatinate and Upper Palatinate; Lusatia was pledged to Saxony. **Bohemia** experienced terrible punishment, incl. executions and the confiscation of half the nobility's landed property. Coerced re-catholicization (150,000 emigrants) and re-germanization laid the foundation for Czech hatred of the Germans.
1627 Bohemia, hitherto a hered. Habsburg

possession, was given an absolutist form of gvt by the 'renewed constitution'.

The Dan. Phase (1625–9)
Strengthened by Eng., Dutch and Fr. subsidies, CHRISTIAN IV OF DENMARK (p. 249), Duke of Holstein and 'Superior of the Imp. Circle of Lower Saxony', entered the war.
Albrecht von Wallenstein (1583–1634) placed an army at the disposition of the Emperor. A member of the Boh. nobility, he turned Cath., entered the service of the Emperor and became wealthy through marriage and the purchase of confiscated Boh. estates; in
1624 he became Duke of Friedland. WALLENSTEIN defeated VON MANSFELD in the
1626 b. at the Bridge of Dessau and pursued him into Hungary (Neuhäusel).
1626 TILLY's vict. at Lutter am Barenberge over CHRISTIAN IV. Together with WALLENSTEIN he pushed the king back to Jutland. WALLENSTEIN subj. northern Germany (exc. Stralsund), became 'Generalissimo of the Baltic and the Ocean Seas'.
1629 Peace of Lübeck: CHRISTIAN IV abandoned all intervention and was allowed to retain his possessions. FERDINAND II now had 3 polit. options: (a) to est. universal Habsburg power (the plan of CHARLES V, opposed to France and Sweden); (b) to institute imp. reforms along absolutist lines (the plan of WALLENSTEIN, opposed by all territ. princes); (c) to recatholicize Germany (opposed by the Prot. princes).
1629 The Edict of Restitution: return of all eccles. territories which had come into Prot. possession after 1552 (p. 235).
1630 Meeting of the electors at Regensburg. Concerned about their 'liberties', the princes forced the removal of WALLENSTEIN.

The Character of the War
Since their maintenance was expensive, the armies were kept small and reluctantly risked in battle (strategy of attrition). The duration of campaigns depended on finances. Mercenaries were freed of their obligations if their pay was in arrears. They allowed themselves to be hired by others, and pillaged and suppressed the pop. Among those fighting were:
1. Mercenaries armed in varying fashion (lance, arquebus, pike) led by mercenary captains (VON MANSFELD). The Cath. army of the League under TILLY took a distinct form.
2. The Sp. army, with its disciplined battle-formation, the 'Sp. Quadrangle' (p. 243).
3. The army of WALLENSTEIN without confessional ties; severe discipline in camp and field, but freedom to pillage. The occupied country had to bear all the burdens of the war. The principle that 'war sustains the war' then made large armies and prompt payment possible, but at the cost of terrible devastation.
4. The nat. Swed. army, with flexible battle-formation and strong fire power (light muskets, culverins). In the beginning it fought for its king and the Luth. faith; later it deteriorated and became the scourge of the war.

The Swedish and the Franco-Swedish phase, 1630–48

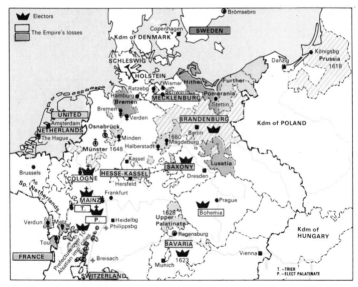

The Peace of Westphalia, 1648

The Swed. Phase (1630–35)

Following the conclusion of peace, mediated by RICHELIEU (p. 249, 259),

1630 Gustavus II Adolphus of Sweden landed on Usedom to protect the Prot. cause, but also to safeguard the Swed. power position and to round out Swed. possessions in the Baltic.

1631 France, the driving power in the struggle with the Habsburgs, concluded with Sweden the Treaty of Bärwalde, promising subsidies. The Prot. pop. welcomed the Swed. king; the Prot. estates (Brandenburg, Saxony) joined the 'Lion of the North' only after

1631 the destruction and pillage of Magdeburg by TILLY and PAPPENHEIM. Ridiculed as the 'Snow King' at Vienna, GUSTAVUS ADOLPHUS saved N. Ger. Protestantism by destroying the Imp. army under TILLY in the

1631 b. of Breitenfeld; crossing Thuringia and Franconia, he liberated the Palatinate and set up winter quarters in Mainz.

1632 Vict. at Rain on the Lech; TILLY killed; Munich and Nuremberg opened their gates. Recalled as commander-in-chief '*in absolutissima forma*' ('with special powers'), WALLENSTEIN drove the Saxons from Bohemia and forced GUSTAVUS ADOLPHUS to abandon a planned advance on Vienna and his secure camp at Nuremberg.

1632 b. of Lützen: Swed. vict., but GUSTAVUS ADOLPHUS killed. His milit. successors were BERNHARD OF WEIMAR and the Swed. generals HORN and BANÉR, and later TORSTENSSON and WRANGEL. Polit. leadership was assumed by the Swed. Chancellor OXENSTIERNA (p. 271).

1633 The League of Heilbronn 'for Ger. liberty and the satisfaction of Sweden'. BERNHARD OF WEIMAR received the Duchy of Franconia and conquered the Upper Palatinate and Bavaria to the Danube. Although WALLENSTEIN took Silesia, he left MAXIMILIAN I OF BAVARIA in the lurch.

1634 By the Declaration of Pilsen he ensured the loyalty of his officers and initiated ind. peace negotiations with Sweden and Saxony. He was removed from office, placed under the ban and (in Feb.) assassinated at Eger by a force under command of the Irish General BUTLER. As a result of the

1634 b. of Nördlingen Sweden lost s. Germany. Abandoning the claims of the Edict of Restitution, FERDINAND concluded the

1635 Peace of Prague with Saxony, which was acceded to by almost all the Prot. estates.

The Franco-Swed. Phase (1635–48)

Allied with BERNHARD OF WEIMAR, France now actively entered the war, which was conducted in unrestrained fashion in 2 sep. theatres. With the accession of

1637–57 FERDINAND III, the general will to peace increased.

1638 The Franco-Swed. Alliance, however, prolonged the war and the people's sufferings.

Saxony/Bohemia: relief for Sweden and renewed advance after the

1636 vict. of BANÉR at Wittstock. An advance on Vienna was given up (TORSTENSSON).

1643 Declaration of war by Denmark (p. 271).

1644 Beginning of extended peace negotiations at Münster and Osnabrück; armistice between Sweden and Brandenburg, joined by Saxony.

S. Germany: with the seizure

1638 of Breisach, BERNHARD OF WEIMAR conquered the Duchy of Alsace. After his death the Fr. advance was halted by the Bav. General MERCY

1643 at Tuttlingen. Franco-Swed. victs. at

1645 Alerheim (TURENNE) and Jankau (TORSTENSSON). A pincer attack on Bavaria ended the war.

1648 The Peace of Westphalia was concluded with the 2 powers 'protecting the peace' (France at Münster, Sweden at Osnabrück).

The Conditions of the Peace of Westphalia

1. Relig. terms: confirmation of the Relig. Peace of Augsburg (1555), now to include the Calvinists. The year 1624 was to be considered the point-in-time determining the state of eccles. possessions and denomination. Changes in denominations were to be tolerated by the authorities (exceptions: the Upper Palatinate and the hered. lands of the Emperor, where the Cath. faith alone was acceptable).

2. Constitutional terms: Imp. privileges (legislation, treaties) were made conditional on the approval of the Imp. Diet (*Reichstag*; after 1663 a permanent diet of delegates, p. 263); full sovereignty of the Imp. Estates granted by the *Ius foederationis* (the right to form alliances, so long as they were not directed against Emperor and Empire). Bavaria remained an electorate; the Palatinate was again granted the electoral dignity.

3. Polit. terms: France received the Sundgau (southern part of Upper Alsace), the vicariate over the bpcs of Metz, Toul and Verdun; the gvt of 10 imp. cities in Alsace; – and with it the border of the Rhine, secured by the bridgeheads of Breisach and Philipsburg.

Sweden received Hither Pomerania with Stettin, Wismar and Rügen; the Duchy of Bremen and Verden; and thereby control over the mouths of the Weser, Elbe and Oder.

Bavaria received the Upper Palatinate; **Saxony,** Lusatia.

Brandenburg received Further Pomerania, the bpcs of Halberstadt, Kammin and Minden, and the candidacy to the archbpc of Magdeburg.

Switzerland and the **United Provinces** left the Empire.

Significance: beginning of the era of the secularized state with relig. toleration. The danger of Habsburg hegemony in Europe was eliminated. Other powers rose to great-power status (France, Sweden, the United Provinces).

In Germany, the 'Germ. liberties' of the princes prevailed over centralized imp. power; the Empire disintegrated into a confederation of states; the future polit. and milit. impotence of Germany was thereby determined. 1st separation of Austria from the Empire.

The Baroque (1600–1750)
As an epoch of courtly style, the Baroque (Port. *barocco* = 'irregular pearl') reflected the prevalent mood of the Counter-Reformation and absolutism; it grew out of the Renaissance, proceeding as the latter from Italy (MICHEL-ANGELO) and spreading at first in the Cath. s. It then moved into the Netherlands (painting, p. 245), and eventually became the first universal style, being mostly represented in eccles. and aristocratic structures.
Architecture: the 'grand style' (according to H. WÖLFFLIN) was aspired to. Therefore sculptures and painting (picturesque forms) inspired massiveness, and decorative adornments were employed to saturation point.
Church construction (model: the Gesù in Rome, 1585) brought together the central-plan and cupola structures on foundations stressing an oval outline; the main area was kept in light colours (white and gold), with ceiling frescoes, sculptures, decorative ornamentation and clustered spiralled columns. Surrounded by geometrically designed parks, the **princely palace** (model: Versailles, p. 261) showed similar elements: a decorated centre part with staircase, side-wings, galleries and raised corner pavilions. The city in which a princely residence was loc. was shaped to correspond to the palace (e.g. Karlsruhe). Leading architects in **Italy** were **Borromini** (1599–1667) and **Bernini** (1598–1680); in **Franconia** there were the **Dientzenhofer** family and **Balthasar Neumann** (1687–1753), the builders of the Prince Bishop of Schönborn. The ASAM brothers were active in Bavaria, SCHLAUN in Westphalia, BÄHR in Saxony (Austria p. 265; Dresden, Berlin p. 263). **Inigo Jones** (1573–1652) and **Sir Christopher Wren** (1632–1723) represented a more severe **Palladian style** in England.
Music: mus. style was altered in Italy through a synthesis of old with newly invented forms (fugue, suite, cantata, concerto grosso, sonata). **Monody** asserted itself over polyphonic compositions (counterpoint); church music was reduced to major and minor keys with an emphasis on melody and harmony (thorough bass). FRESCOBALDI (1583–1643), **Corelli** (1653–1713), and **Vivaldi** (*c.* 1685–1741) developed the *ars nuova* (organ, vocal and instrumental music), which was introduced into England by Purcell (1659–95). A mus. creation combining lyrical and epic qualities was developed in the relig. **oratorio;** the **opera** was developed out of dramatic recitals and lyrical arias by **Monteverdi** (1567–1643), CAVALLI and ALESSANDRO SCARLATTI. Ital. conductors brought it to the courts of Eur. princes. **Lully** (1632–87) created heroic opera; **Rameau** (1683–1764) the nat. Fr. opera. The way prepared by SCHÜTZ (1585–1672) and BUXTEHUDE (1637–1707), **Ger.** music reached its first climax with the cantor of St Thomas's in Leipzig, **Johann Sebastian Bach** (1685–1750). **George Frideric Handel** (1685–1759) worked in England from 1712. After 1750 **Vienna** became the centre of the **classical period** (sonata, symphony, *Lieder*, opera) with GLUCK (1714–87), **Haydn** (1732–1809) and **Mozart** (1756–91).

Literature: (Spain p. 243, France p. 261). In Germany a movement was started to purify the Ger. language by endeavouring to eliminate foreign Fr. infls.; **Martin Opitz** (1597–1639) provided rules of style for courtly poetry. The Thirty Years War shaped the works of GRIMMELSHAUSEN (d. 1676) and ANDREAS GRYPHIUS.
Philosophy: the search for a rational method for understanding the 'real' world free of eccles. or relig. dogmatism led **Francis Bacon** (1561–1626) to found Eng. **empiricism:** experience, leading from the observation of particulars to universal laws (inductive method), brought man knowledge, and hence power. **John Locke** (1632–1704) denied the existence of 'innate ideas'. Only internal and external senses convey knowledge. René Descartes (CARTESIUS, 1596–1650), on the other hand, asserted **rationalism:** truth is arrived at only through thought and universal and logical principles (deductive method). Nature and spirit are absolutely distinct (dualism). **Spinoza** (1632–77) arrived at the unity of God and nature (monism) via the rationally deduced identity (oneness) of thought and existence. His pantheism had as much infl. on the Enlightenment as did the mediating system of **Leibniz** (1646–1716): the world consists of an infinite number of **monads** (dynamic units of energy), which are arranged by God in pre-established harmony in steps rising qualitatively from inanimate matter to the central monad, God. Morally free and potentially perfect, man was meant to learn to understand the rational order of this 'best of all possible worlds'.
Polit. science: BACON developed the model of a perfectly organized state in his utopian work *Nova Atlantis;* **Campanella** (1568–1639), on the other hand, envisioned his ideal 'city of the sun' (1602) in totalitarian-communist fashion. Proceeding from a rational conception of **natural law, Hugo Grotius** (1583–1645) saw the state as an institution resting on a free contract made by men to provide for their security. In his *De jure belli ac pacis* (1625) he called for **int. law** to secure general peace. Only defensive war has moral justification; the oceans were to be free for the use of all nations. The theory of a **soc. contract** was also used by **Hobbes** (p. 259) and PUFENDORF (p. 263) to justify the absolute authority of the princely state. They considered the soc. contract to be indissoluble; **Locke** (p. 269), on the other hand, asserted the people's right to dissolve it should the ruler disregard the natural law.
Science: by his demand 'to read the book of nature with the aid of mathematics' **Galileo Galilei** (1564–1642) initiated the **classical period of physics.** He discovered the law governing bodies in free fall, which was complemented by **Johann Kepler's** (1571–1630) laws of planetary motion and explained with mathematical precision by **Isaac Newton's** (1642–1727) law of gravitation. The new scientific conception of the world was confirmed by many discoveries and inventions (p. 279).

The Enlightenment (18th cent.)

Proceeding from Western Europe, this most important intellectual development after the Reformation was based on humanism (p. 212) and the philosophical and scientific concepts of the world of the 17th cent.; amplified to a generally accepted view of the world, and applied to all situations of life, its implications were perceived by the *bourgeoisie*, which had been made self-confident by its prosperity and demonstrated capacities. **Enlightenment,** acc. to **Kant,** is 'man's emergence from his self-imposed nonage'. **Reason,** the courage to be **critical, freedom of thought** and **relig. toleration** must overcome relig. dogmatism, eccles. and gvtl authority (absolutism), and moral and class prejudices. Man raised in natural (= rational) fashion and educated to honour **humanitarian principles** is the guarantor of progress and the promoter of **brotherhood (citizenship of the world** = cosmopolitanism), the welfare of all, and 'eternal peace' (KANT), as well as personal happiness (eudemonism). The cities and universities were the focalpoints of the Enlightenment. To propagate the ideals of the Enlightenment, the secret int. association of the **Freemasons** was est. in England (1717 foundation of the Grand Lodge of London); its polit. influence has been grossly overestimated.

Philosophy: Enlightenment philosophy in England was marked by the prevalence of **Deism:** God left his creation to developmental laws, and did not interfere with it by miracles or revelation. Rational worship consists of moral action. This 'natural religion' (renewed by CHRIST) is the core of all religions. Deistic **freethinkers** incl. CHERBURY, COLLINS and SHAFTESBURY (1671–1713), the latter desiring to fuse the beautiful with the good to arrive at genuine morality.

The limitations of Enlightenment thought were revealed by **David Hume** (1711–76), who doubted (scepticism) all certain knowledge. The 'soul' – an 'associative apparatus' – connects sensations only, acc. to psychological laws. Man is a *tabula rasa* (an empty page) at birth; experience impresses on him its 'symbols'.

The uncompromising champion of the freedom of thought and religion, **Pierre Bayle** (1647–1706), prepared the way for the **Fr. Enlightenment.** A famous satirist and brilliant stylist, **Voltaire** (F.-M. AROUET, 1694–1778) assaulted faith and Church. He was an admirer of England (Anglophilia) and a friend of FREDERICK II OF PRUSSIA. Among those contributing to the **Encyclopédie** (1751–77), edited by D'ALEMBERT and DIDEROT and intended to demonstrate and propagate the knowledge of the time in an enlightened spirit, were the **materialist** and **atheist** CONDILLAC, the physician LA METTRIE ('Man a machine') and D'HOLBACH (religion a product of fear and a nonsense of priests). Another contributor was **Jean-Jacques Rousseau** (1712–78), who, as a critic of ctr., had already gone beyond the Enlightenment: good by nature, man becomes corrupt because he does not allow himself to be guided by **feelings.** Deliberate reason leads

to the distortions of civilization (envy, dishonesty, hypocrisy). It is necessary for man to 'return to nature' and find the simple 'culture of the heart'. Proposals for education adjusted to the needs of children in the spirit of this 'evangelium of Nature' were contained in *Émile* (1762), while the 'justification of the great passion' was asserted in the epistolary novel *La Nouvelle Héloise* (1761).

The Ger. Aufklärung (Enlightenment), with predominantly pedagogical intentions, was represented by **Christian Wolff** (1679–1754), who propagated the ideas of LEIBNIZ. **Gotthold Ephraim Lessing** (1729–81) championed tolerance (*Nathan the Wise*, 1779), natural reflection on the self and humanitarianism (*On the Education of the Human Race*, 1780). His friend MOSES MENDELSSOHN (1729–86) worked for equal rights for the Jews.

The greatest thinker of the age was **Immanuel Kant** (1724–1804) of Königsberg. His *Critiques* perfected and transcended the Enlightenment. **The Critique of Pure Reason** (1781): empirical perception and rational thought are dependent on *a priori* (preconceived) categories (basic forms: time, space, the laws of logic). The world, therefore, can be understood only 'as it appears to us', and not 'as it is' (rigorous separation of belief and knowledge). **The Critique of Practical Reason** (1788): the moral law postulates the existence of God, freedom and immortality. The *dicta* of ethics are in consonance with morality only when they are set up by man himself as **categorical imperatives** (obligatory laws) and free from considerations of personal interest (success, personal preference), and freely obeyed (moral autonomy of the individual). The **philosophy of Ger. idealism** began with KANT; his work influenced Ger. classicism (SCHILLER).

Religion and churches: within the Cath. Church the enlightened current of **Febronianism** developed (led by the Suffragan Bishop J. N. VON HONTHEIM), criticizing the hierarchy and the dependence of the episcopate on Rome. The Curia dissolved the Jes. Order in 1773 (it continued to be tolerated in Russia and Prussia). Protestantism witnessed alongside Luth. orthodoxy (p. 251) the development of **Pietism,** an irrational counter-current to the Enlightenment. Those 'quiet in the land' realized a practical and active form of evangelical Christianity. **August Francke** (1663–1727) founded the Orphanage of Halle and the Luth. Mission to the Heathen. Count **Zinzendorf** (1700–60) settled expelled Boh.–Mor. Brethren (p. 197) (the Herrnhut Community of Brethren), composed tracts for relig. edification and est. missions and schools. The persecution of witches was abandoned.

Influenced by Pietism, the free **Methodist Church** developed in England *c.* 1770 under WHITEFIELD and **John Wesley** (1703–91); Methodism entailed the experience of conversion, personal consecration, popular miss. activity and the care of the poor. Great successes in N. America; SHARP and Wilberforce assaulted the institution of slavery, which was abolished in England in 1807.

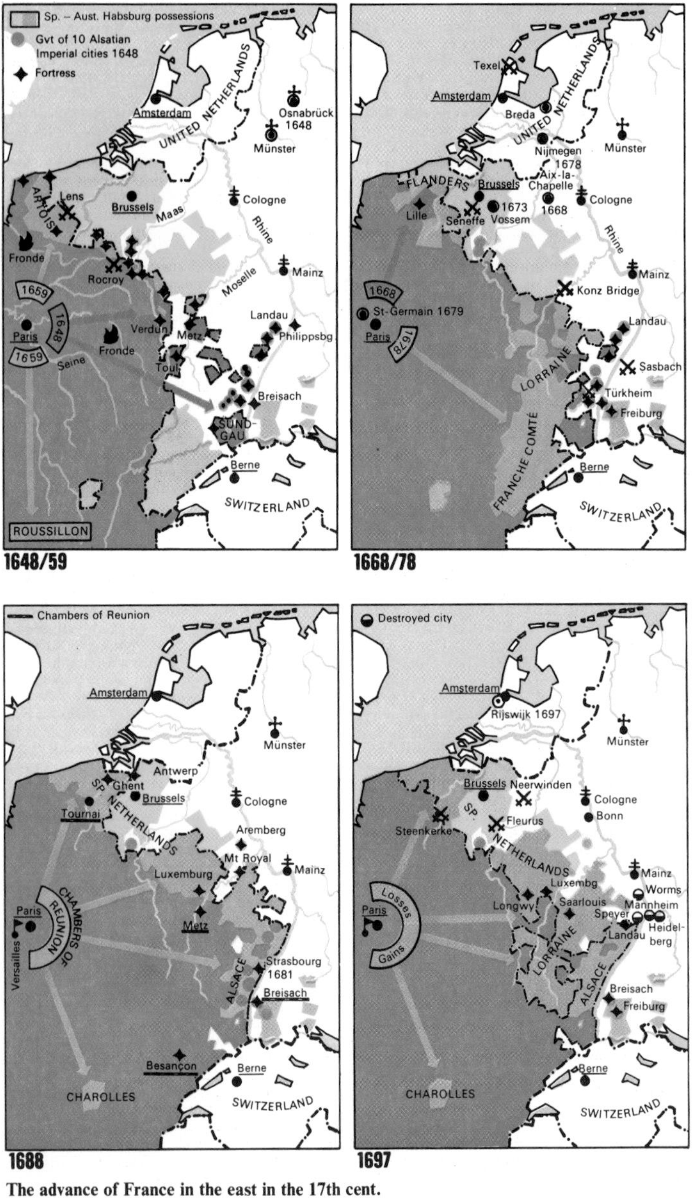

1648/59

Sp. – Aust. Habsburg possessions
Gvt of 10 Alsatian Imperial cities 1648
Fortress

UNITED NETHERLANDS
Amsterdam
Osnabrück 1648
Münster
ARTOIS
Lens
Brussels
Maas
Cologne
Rhine
Fronde
Rocroy
Moselle
Mainz
1648
1659
Verdun
Landau
Paris
Metz
Philippsbg
1659
Seine
Fronde
Toul
Breisach
SUND-GAU
Berne
ROUSSILLON
SWITZERLAND

1668/78

Texel
Amsterdam
Breda
UNITED NETHERLANDS
Münster
FLANDERS
Nijmegen 1678
Aix-la-Chapelle
Brussels
1673
Cologne
Lille
Seneffe
Vossem
1668
Rhine
Mainz
Konz Bridge
1668
St-Germain 1679
Landau
Paris
Sasbach
1679
LORRAINE
Türkheim
Freiburg
FRANCHE COMTÉ
Berne
SWITZERLAND

1688

Chambers of Reunion
Amsterdam
Münster
Antwerp
SP. NETHERLANDS
Ghent
Brussels
Cologne
Tournai
Aremberg
Mt Royal
Luxemburg
Mainz
Paris
CHAMBERS OF REUNION
Versailles
Metz
Strasbourg 1681
ALSACE
Breisach
Besançon
Berne
CHAROLLES
SWITZERLAND

1697

Destroyed city
Amsterdam
Rijswijk 1697
Münster
Brussels
Neerwinden
Cologne
SP. NETHERLANDS
Fleurus
Bonn
Steenkerke
Mainz
Worms
Luxembg
Mannheim
Losses
Longwy
Saarlouis
Speyer
Heidelberg
Paris
Gains
LORRAINE
Landau
ALSACE
Breisach
Freiburg
CHAROLLES
Berne
SWITZERLAND

The advance of France in the east in the 17th cent.

The Establishment of Absolutism in France
Theoretically justified by **Jean Bodin** (p. 247)
and **Thomas Hobbes** (1588–1679, *Leviathan*,
1651), the absolute state was developed under
LOUIS XIII. Self-preservation forces all men to
conclude a **contract** with one another, because
a self-centred 'war of all against all' prevails
in the state of nature; by this contract they
surrender their rights unconditionally to the
state, which thereby has absolute (indivisible,
indissoluble) authority over all subjects, and
which is most perfectly expressed in one
person, the king **(absolute monarchy).** Jacques
Bossuet (1627–1704), the renowned eccles.
orator of the age of LOUIS XIV, reduced
absolutism to the formula '*Un roi, une foi, une
loi*' ('One king, one faith, one law'). He
stressed the prince's dependence on the **grace
of God;** as God's deputy he owed account
neither to the Church nor to the people.
1614 Last convocation of the Estates General
(États-Généraux). In the field of politics,
absolutism was enforced by
1624–42 Cardinal Richelieu (39 yrs old). As
chief minister to the crown, he fought the
opposition of the upper nobility and the
polit. (not the relig.) privileges of the
Huguenots (p. 247), taking their last fortified
stronghold (La Rochelle) in 1628. Development of a standing army and a royal
provincial admin.: the aristocratic **governors**
were replaced by **intendants** (royal officials).
The elimination of the purchase of offices
and of courts based on class (*parlements*)
was not possible.
1635 Establishment of the **Académie Française**
for the promotion of the arts and sciences.
Foreign policy: extrication of the state from
Habsburg encirclement and rest. of the
'natural frontiers of Gaul', the Pyrenees and
the Rhine; for this reason, assistance was
rendered to the Prot. princes of Germany.
Mediation in the Baltic conflict between
Poland and Sweden (1629, Armistice of
Altmark); financial assistance to Sweden
(GUSTAVUS ADOLPHUS).
1635 Intervention in the Thirty Years War
(p. 255).
1643–61 Cardinal Mazarin (41 yrs old) continued
RICHELIEU's policies in the governing of the
state.
1648 Gains of the Peace of Westphalia (p. 255).
War with Spain was continued until the
1659 Peace of the Pyrenees. Significance:
descent of Spain from, and rise of France to,
the position of predominant Eur. power.
Beginning of the 'Age of France'.
1648–53 Last revolt of the nobility, the
'*Fronde*', joined by the Paris *parlement* (the
highest Fr. court with jurisdiction over
royal edicts). The upper nobility was
deprived of polit. power.

The Foreign Policy of Louis XIV
1661 LOUIS XIV (22 yrs old) assumed the
reins of gvt. His aims: **Eur. hegemony** and
rounding out the state's frontiers in the w.
and N. (the Rhine). LOUIS was able (a) to lean
on the anti-Habsburg Rhenish Alliance (p.

263); and (b), with the object of encircling the
Empire, to attempt to gain the support of the
'neighbours of the neighbour': Sweden,
Poland, Hungary, even Turkey, the 'chained
dog of Europe'.
Subsidies were the usual means of diplomacy.
1667–8 The War of Devolution against Spain,
provoked by dubious claims to Brabant.
By the Peace of Breda (p. 267) England and
Holland reached agreement and concluded
a triple alliance with Sweden, forcing LOUIS
XIV to accede to the Peace of Aix-la-
Chapelle (1668). The 'revenge on Holland'
(econ. competition) was prepared by
alliances with CHARLES II of England (1670),
with Sweden (1672) and with some of the
Imp. bps (Cologne, Münster).
1670 Fr. occupation of Lorraine.
1672–8 War against Holland: JAN DE WITT,
leader of the 'regent's party', was toppled
from office and **William III of Orange** (22
yrs old) was named Stadtholder-General for
life. The land was defended by the opening
of sluices and the cutting of dykes.
1672–3 Anti-Fr. alliance under the leadership
of Austria (LISOLA); LOUIS met it by supporting the pro-Fr. candidate for the Pol.
throne (JAN SOBIESKI) and the uprisings of
the Hung. nobility (p. 265); Brandenburg
was tied down by a Swed. attack (p. 271).
1678 Peace of Nijmegen: Holland did not
incur territ. losses; Spain had to give up
the Free County of Burgundy (Franche-
Comté); despite her milit. successes,
1679 Brandenburg by the Peace of St-Germain
had to give up Swed. Hither Pomerania,
incl. Stettin; embittered over Imp. policies,
the Great Elector concluded a subsidy
treaty with LOUIS XIV and tolerated his
'Policy of Reunion' for the 'peaceful conquest
of the Rhine frontier'. Fr. 'Chambers of
Reunion' (courts) advanced claims to Imp.
territories. Climax of this policy:
1681 Annexation of Strasbourg and formal
entry of LOUIS XIV.
1684 Occupation of Luxemburg. Fortifications
systems to secure the border. Tied down by
the advance of the Turks (p. 265), Emperor
and Empire recognized the Reunions in
1684 the Truce of Regensburg. But anti-Fr.
resistance continued in the League of
Augsburg (1686); even so, LOUIS XIV made
inheritance claims to the Palatinate on
behalf of his sister-in-law (ELIZABETH
CHARLOTTE = 'LISELOTTE').
1688–97 War of the League of Augsburg (the
War of the Palatinate).
1689 The **Grand Alliance** (WILLIAM III OF
ORANGE) to maintain the Eur. balance of
power was formed after the Fr. invasion of
s. Germany. Devastation of the Palatinate,
incl. the destruction of Worms, the Imp.
tombs at Speyer and the castle of Heidelberg.
1692 Naval b. of La Hogue: decisive defeat of
the new Fr. fleet. Deterioration of the
alliance by the time of the
1697 Peace of Rijswijk: 1st losses of LOUIS
XIV; but Strasbourg and the Alsatian
'Reunions' were retained.

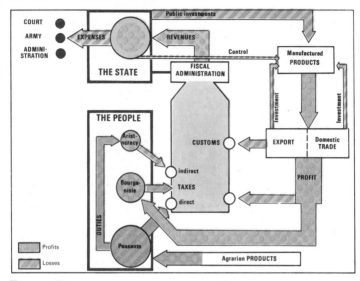

The mercantilist system

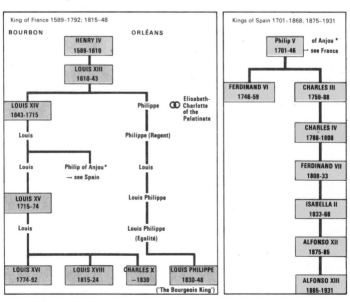

House of Bourbon-Orléans

House of Bourbon

The Perfection of Absolutism in France

(1643) 1661–1715 Louis XIV, the 'Sun King'. Of delicate figure, courteous and restrained, yet of majestic bearing, pervaded by the dignity of his office ('*L'état c'est moi!*'), he felt called to increase and represent the glory of the state.

Gvt: executed by decree, the gvt was under the sole authority of the king, who was assisted by a 'secret' Council of State and departmental ministers, the Cabinet (small, private chamber). Interference in legal processes by royal orders of arrest (*lettres de cachet*), secret police and polit. detention (the Bastille).

The army: Louvois (1641–91), minister of war after 1668, increased the standing army to 170,000 men (pop. 18 mil.); he introduced uniforms, improved equipment (bayonet), organized the troops functionally (infantry, cavalry, artillery) and fixed ranks. The king appointed and paid the (aristocratic) officers. Led by the marshals TURENNE, CONDÉ and LUXEMBOURG, the Fr. army became the largest and best in the world. **Vauban** (1633–1707) revolutionized fortress construction by means of star-shaped bastions, which eliminated the 'dead angle' of shooting; the techniques of siege and of warfare in general were thereby altered.

Admin.: further development of the royal intendencies in the provinces and the royal magistracies in the cities; the aristocratic landlords (*seigneurs*) retained administrative and police powers in the countryside.

The economy and finances: as minister of finance **Colbert** (1619–83) developed the first nat. economy of the modern age. This state-guided economy included statistical planning of the budget and regularized bookkeeping. **Mercantilism** (also 'Colbertism') created the financial basis for the development of absolutism, because customs duties, direct (the Taille) and indirect (excise) taxes provided the state with profits to maintain the army, the admin. and the court. Since, according to the concept of the day, wealth consisted of money, mercantilism aimed at a favourable balance of trade through the export of valuable finished products (luxury and fashion articles, glasswares, perfumes, porcelain, etc.). Consequently elimination of interior customs duties, development of roads and canals, establishment of state monopolies, subvention of **manufactures** (large craft enterprises with division of labour); promotion of navigation and of trading associations (colon. policy, p. 277); protective tariffs, fixed prices for agricultural goods; encouragement of marriage, prohibition of emigration. While mercantilism promoted commerce and the crafts and thereby increased the prosperity of the *bourgeoisie*, the peasants were not stimulated to increase their production.

Soc. organization: the class structure based on estates was retained, but without polit. privileges. The clergy and the nobility were privileged as a result of their ownership of land, exemptions from taxation and special judicial status. The upper *bourgeoisie* took part in the econ. rise and was able, through the purchase of offices, to advance into the (service) nobility (*noblesse de la robe*). *Petits bourgeois* and peasants shouldered the econ. burden of the state by paying high taxes.

Church policy: safeguarding of a Cath. state church by royal privileges (appointments to eccles. positions) and censorship of papal decrees by the 'Gallican Articles' (BOSSUET), which were confirmed by the **Nat. Council of Paris** (1682). To restore the unity of the faith the Protestants were harassed by the 'Dragonades' (milit. billeting).

1685 Revocation of the Edict of Nantes prompted *c.* ½ mil. Huguenots to flee the country; the mercantilistic economy was thereby severely damaged and criticism of absolute gvt began (FÉNELON). Acceptance of the refugees, esp. by Holland, the 'suburb of the Enlightenment' (BAYLE, p. 257), and Brandenburg (p. 263).

After 1710 persecution of the **Jansenists** (named after CORNELIUS JANSEN, Bishop of Ypres), an anti-clerical movement advocating inner renewal of Catholicism in the spirit of AUGUSTINE. The convent of Port-Royal, nr Versailles, was its centre. Jansenism continued to exist in Italy, the Low Countries (the Church of Utrecht) and Austria (Josephism, p. 287).

Absolutism at Court: the opulent palace of **Versailles,** designed by MANSART (1598–1666), erected 1624–1708, became the symbol of the absolutist state; luxuriously decorated (interior decoration by LEBRUN (1619–90)), wasteful in material, uncomfortable but representative, surrounded by the 'green architecture' of geometrically planned parks (LE NÔTRE, 1613–1700) with fountains and radial axes pointing to the centre of the palace (the king's bedroom). The Fr. palace and park became as much Eur. fashion as the Fr. language, customs and courtly ctr., with parades, opera and ballet, the *Allongewhig* and *culotte* (breeches). The ideal of the day was the 'galant cavalier' (the polished gentleman). The Fr. Age succeeded the Sp. Age.

Literature: it was **Boileau** (1636–1711) who provided the **Classical Period** of Fr. literature with a formal book of rules in his *L'Art pòétique*. The Classical ethos of the period was also reflected in the tragedies (often modelled after themes of Rom. and Gk antiquity) of **Corneille** (1606–84) and **Racine** (1639–99), as well as in the comedies of **Molière** (1622–73) and the fables of **LA FONTAINE** (1621–95).

Art: the paintings of **Poussin** (1594–1665), **Claude** (1600–82) and **Rigaud** (1659–1743) presented decorative 'heroic' landscapes or prominent people in the guise of antiquity or mythology. The king was the supporter and leading patron of courtly art.

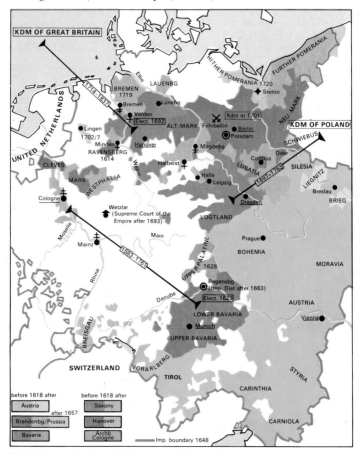

The territories of the German Princes after 1648

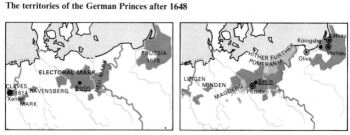

Brandenburg to 1620

Prussia to 1740

The Ger. Empire after 1648

Despite severe war damage (devastation, reduction of the pop. from 15 mil. to 10 mil., in some areas as much as 70%) and general degeneration (widespread robbery, brutality, dissipation and delusions about witchcraft) recovery was rapid – an accomplishment of the princes. By centralizing the admin., army and taxation, they became the focal points of polit. and cult. life ('Frenchification'). Alongside the absolute states (Brandenburg, Bavaria) there developed states with constitutions based on the estates (Würtemberg, Mecklenburg).

Constitution: the Empire consisted of c. 300 sovereign parts, most or all of which lacked the consciousness of belonging to an imp. entity; in his *De statu Imperii Germani* (1667) the teacher of int. law, SAMUEL PUFENDORF (1632–94), referred to it as a 'Gothic (feudal) monstrosity' with absolutist members.

The governing bodies of the Empire were divided between the Emperor and the Empire in accordance with the dualistic principle of an order based on estates: the Court Chancery at Vienna and the Chancery of the Empire at Mainz; the Council of the Imp. Court at Vienna (1664) and the Supreme Court of the Empire (*Reichskammergericht*) at Wetzlar (after 1693); after

1663 permanent Imp. Diet **(Reichstag)** at Regensburg; it was a congress of delegates structured into the 3 *curiae* of the electors (8), the princes (165) and the Imp. cities (61), all again subdivided according to confession.

1658 Imp. election of LEOPOLD I (to 1705); opposing candidate: LOUIS XIV.

1658 Rhenish anti-Habsburg alliance (the electorates of Mainz, Cologne and others).

The Rise of the Ger. Territ. Princes

Bavaria (House of Wittelsbach)

1597–1651 MAXIMILIAN I. Leader of the Cath. League (1609), he received the electoral dignity of the Palatinate in 1623 (and retained it after 1648). His brother initiated the Wittelsbach candidacy for the archbpc of Cologne (1583–1761), henceforth to be under Bav. archbps. Under

1651–79 FERDINAND MARIA, build-up of Munich as an electoral residence (Nymphenburg Palace, Church of the Theatines (Theatinerkirche)).

1679–1726 MAXIMILIAN II EMANUEL, victor over the Turks and ally of LOUIS XIV during the War of the Sp. Succession (p. 269); Munich became the centre of the s. Ger. Baroque.

Saxony (House of Wettin)

1697–1763 Under the reign of AUGUST II, THE STRONG (1694–1733) personal union with the Kdm of Poland. Development of Dresden through the architecture of DANIEL PÖPPELMANN (1662–1736) (the Zwinger).

Hanover (House of Brunswick–Lüneburg)

1692 Duke ERNST AUGUST (1697–8) became the 9th elector; from 1701 candidacy to the Eng. throne (Act of Settlement, p. 269).

1714–1837 Personal Union with Britain.

Brandenburg–Prussia (House of Hohenzollern)

1608–19 JOHANN SIGISMUND obtained Clèves, Mark and Ravensberg (by the Treaty of Xanten, 1614); he received E. Prussia as a Pol. fief by inheritance (1618).

1640–88 **Frederick William I, the Great Elector.** He became the creator of the Brandenburg–Prus. nation-state by depriving the estates of power (i.e. the right to consent to taxation) and by granting privileges to the nobility (exemption from taxation and autonomous manorial estates). Strongest opposition by the E. Prus. estates; their polit. support in Poland was lost as a result of the Swed.–Pol. War (1655–60, p. 271). Sovereignty over E. Prussia was recognized by Sweden in the Treaty of Labiau (1656), and by Poland (after a change of sides) in the Treaty of Wehlau (1657), and confirmed by the

1660 Peace of Oliva.

1661–3 Perpetual Diet of Königsberg. The leaders of the estates executed or imprisoned.

Admin.: officials who collected the *Kontributionen* (direct real-estate or head tax) and the *Akzise* (indirect excise tax on urban consumers); establishment of fiscal authorities for the country (*Kriegskammern*) and for the royal domains (*Domänenkammern*). The admin. was under the direction of a Privy Council.

Mercantile economy to increase prosperity and taxable income: road, dyke and canal construction; model farms; colon. policy following the Dutch example:

1683 establishment of the settlement Gross-Friedrichsburg in w. Africa (Prus. to 1720).

The army: increase of the standing army from 8,000 to 23,000 led to successes in the war against France and Sweden (1672–8, p. 271).

1675 b. of **Fehrbellin** and pursuit of the Swed. army to Riga. With this vict. over the leading milit. nation of Europe, the Prus. milit. tradition was initiated.

Foreign policy: constant manoeuvring by the major powers; gains in the Peace of Westphalia (p. 255); however, Hither Pomerania with Stettin remained Swed.; even so Brandenburg was, with the exception of Austria, the strongest Ger. state and a new power factor in Europe.

1688–1713 FREDERICK (III) I Prussia's courtly 'Baroque King'.

1701 Coronation at Königsberg as 'King in Prussia'.

Berlin: residence of the court, with buildings by EOSANDER (1670–1729) and ANDREAS SCHLÜTER (1664–1714): the Zeughaus, the Royal Palace (Schloss), and Old Bridge. Under the protection of Queen SOPHIE CHARLOTTE (cf. Charlottenburg) the Academy of Art (1696) was est. and – following a suggestion by LEIBNIZ – the Academy of Sciences (1701).

Halle: through the work of CHRISTIAN WOLFF and A. H. FRANCKE it became the centre of the N. Ger. Enlightenment and Pietism.

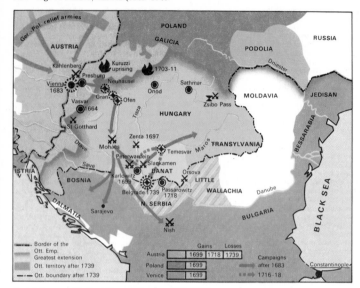

Austria's wars with the Ottoman Empire, 1633–1739

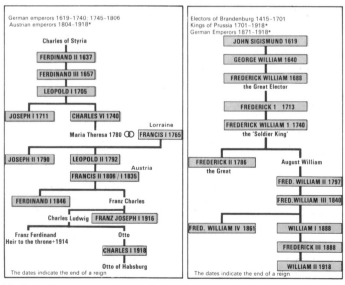

The House of Habsburg (from 1637)

The House of Hohenzollern (from 1619)

Austria's Rise as a Major Power

After the Ott. Empire had been stabilized under the Grand Vizier MOHAMMED KÜPRÜLÜ (1656–61)

1663–99 2nd **Turk. assault on Cen. Europe** (MOHAMMED IV (1648–87)).

1663/4 1st Turk. War, caused by Aust. and Turk. intervention in the polit. confusion in Transylvania.

1664 Battle of St Gotthard/Raab (MONTECUCCULI, SPORCK) and the (humiliating) Peace of Vasvar (Eisenburg); partition of Hungary and tribute payments by Austria.

1669–71 Conspiracy of the Magnates of the Hung. nobility owing to the cruel persecution of Protestantism by dragonades, executions and galley slavery – which also led to the **Kuruzzi uprising** under Count IMRE TÖKÖLY (1656–1705), who cal. for Turk. assistance.

1683–99 2nd **(Great) Turk. War.** Advance to (by Grand Vizier KARA MUSTAFA) and

1683 **Siege of Vienna.** Defender: Count RÜDIGER VON STARHEMBERG (anti-Turk. clerical orator: ABRAHAM A SANTA CLARA). A Eur. (esp. Ger.–Pol.) relief army, led by the Pol. king JAN SOBIESKI, was victorious at the **Kahlenberg** under the command of CHARLES V OF LORRAINE: end of Turk. pressure on Europe.

1684 Holy Alliance (Austria, Poland, Venice and after 1686 Russia) against the Turks under the Protector Pope INNOCENT XI. Despite attacks by LOUIS XIV in the w., (1st occurrence of the 2-front problem in Ger. history, p. 259), the Emperor took the offensive. MAX EMANUEL OF BAVARIA (p. 263) and LOUIS OF BADEN beat the Turks.

1686–97 Lib. of Hungary, incl. the conquest of Belgrade (1688).

1687 **Imp. Diet of Pressburg:** the estates transferred the Hung. crown to the House of Habsburg (in the male line). Development of the Austro-Hung. Dual Monarchy.

1691 Victs. at Nish and Salem Kemen; lib. of Transylvania; uprisings of the Christ. Balk. peoples.

1696 Tsar PETER I conquered Azov.

1697 **Prince Eugene of Savoy** (1663–1736) became supreme commander of the Imp. army. A grand-nephew of MAZARIN, he had been in the service of Austria from 1683, after having been rejected by LOUIS XIV because of his small stature.

1697 b. of Zenta; seizure of Sarajevo.

1699 **Peace of Karlowitz:** Austria became a major power. Venice received the Morea; but it was reconquered in 1715, which led to

1716–18 the 3rd Turk. War. Victs. of Prince EUGENE (Peterwardein, Temesvar) and

1717 **conquest of Belgrade.**

1718 **Peace of Passarowitz:** greatest extension of the Habsburg Empire.

Austria–Hungary 1700–40: Prince Eugene was milit. commander and leading statesman of the newly risen major power ('Austria above all!'). The **multi-nat. state**, with a core of 11 peoples, was kept together by (a) the Turk. threat in the Danube area; (b) the Habsburg dynasty (*Domus* Austria); (c) the Cath. confession; (d) the Habsburg court nobility drawn from all the hered. lands; (e) the absolutist and centralized admin. (with Lat., later Ger., as the official language).

Vienna became the polit., econ. and cult. centre of the Empire. Among its masters of Baroque architecture were FISCHER VON ERLACH (1656–1723: Palaces of the nobility, the Karlskirche, the Court Library (Hofbibliothek) and plans for the Schönbrunn Palace); LUKAS VON HILDEBRAND (1668–1745: the Belvedere); and JAKOB PRANDTAUER (1660–1726: the abbey church of Melk).

Admin.: the supreme administrative organ, the Privy Conference (Geheime Konferenz, 1709), consisted of the Court Chancery (domestic affairs), the Privy Council and the State Chancery (foreign affairs), the Court Council of War (the army) and the Court Chamber of the Exchequer (finances). Strict organization was lacking and waste, protectionism and imperfect planning of the state budget weakened state and army (cf. the defeat of 1739).

Econ. life: monopolies of salt, tobacco, iron and of the manufacture of textiles (Silesia, Linz, Graz), silk (St Plöten) and glass (Bohemia) failed to improve the finances of the debt-ridden state.

1718 Establishment of a factory producing porcelain in Vienna. W. VON HÖRNIGK (1640–1712): 'Austria can accomplish anything she sets her mind to' (1684).

Settlement policy: a so-called adjustment agency (*Einrichtungswerk*) provided the foundations for the resettlement of the areas depopulated because of Turk. domination.

1711–40 **Charles VI.** Following uprisings by the nobility, the

1711 Peace of Sathmar: self-admin. for Hungary subject to laws of the Imp. Diet.

Foreign policy: participation in the War of the Sp. Succession brought a hegemony to Italy which, however, remained uncertain (p. 269). The Emperor's policy was determined by the

1713 **Pragmatic Sanction:** succession to the throne in the female line (MARIA THERESA, born 1717) was safeguarded; to this end treaties with Spain (1725), Prussia (1728), Great Britain (1731) and France (1738). Attempts to establish a distinct colon. policy by the foundation of an Orient Co. (Trieste, 1719) and

1722 an E. India Co. (Ostend) failed because of Brit. resistance. Following congresses at Cambrai (1724) and Soisson (1728), the trading companies were dissolved by the

1731 Treaty of Vienna; Great Britain recognized the Pragmatic Sanction.

1737–9 4th (Austro-Rus.) Turk. War;

1739 Peace of Belgrade: loss of Northern Serbia and Little Wallachia; Austro-Rus. Balk. rivalry began. In 1740 MARIA THERESA assumed the reins of a state which lacked inner strength and prestige abroad.

1643
Begin. End Monarchy (Cavaliers)
Parliament (Roundheads)

Scotland
Edinburgh 1643
'Covenant with God' 1638
1603
Ulster 1641
IRELAND
Marston Moor 1644
York
Hull
Chester
Newark
Lichfield
Edgehill
Eastern Association
WALES
Gloucester
Oxford
Pembroke
Landsdown
1642
London
Lyme
Poole
Portsmouth
Plymouth

1645-8
End Monarchy (Cavaliers)
Begin. End Parliament (Roundheads)

SCOTLAND
Edinburgh 1648
Newcastle
IRELAND
Preston 1648
York
Hull
Chester
Newark
WALES
Worcester
Naseby 1645
Gloucester
Oxford 1646
Pembroke
London
Plymouth
Lyme
Poole
Winchester
Corfe Castle

The struggle between Parliament and the Crown, 1642–8

1649-60
Eng. naval victories
Dutch naval victories 1652-4

COMMONWEALTH
1645 Edinburgh
Dunbar 1650
1649 IRELAND (confiscation of landed property)
Drogheda
Dublin
Wexford
Cromwell's punitive expeditions
WALES
Worcester 1651
London
CHARLES I 1649
Dunkirk 1658-62
Channel Islands

Cromwell's dictatorship

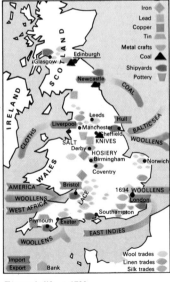

Iron
Lead
Copper
Tin
Metal crafts
Coal
Shipyards
Pottery

SCOTLAND
Glasgow
Edinburgh
Newcastle
COAL
IRELAND
Leeds
Hull
Liverpool
Manchester
BALTIC SEA
CLOTHS
Sheffield
WOOLLENS
SALT
KNIVES
Derby
HOSIERY
Birmingham
Norwich
Coventry
AMERICA
WOOLLENS
Bristol
LACE
1694 WOOLLENS
WEST AFRICA
London
Southampton
Plymouth
Exeter
EAST INDIES
WOOLLENS

Wool trades
Linen trades
Silk trades
Import
Export
Bank

Economic life, c. 1700

England under the Stuarts (1603–48)

1603–25 JAMES I (37 yrs old). As JAMES VI of Scotland and heir to the Tudors, he called himself 'King of Great Britain' (1604); he leaned for support on the Anglican state church. The Hampton Court Conference of Bishops condemned Puritanism and Catholicism (1604); which led to the

1605 Gunpowder Plot of the Catholics (GUY FAWKES). A parliamentary opposition was formed of gentry and the middle classes to preserve ancient rights in the face of the absolutist tendencies of the 'British Solomon' (tax levies, the purchase of titles and offices).

1625–49 CHARLES I (25 yrs old). Intensification of the conflict because of royal judicial procedures (Star Chamber) and demands for taxes (1635, ship money for naval construction).

1628 Petition of Rights. Despite repeated dissolution, Parliament demanded safeguards against arbitrary arrest and taxation.

1629–40 Gvt without parliament; persecution of all polit. and relig. opponents (dissenters, Nonconformists), esp. of the **Puritans** (the 'pure ones'). This Calv. movement, based on a free form of evangelical Christianity and incl. the communal principle (p. 238) and an ascetic mode of life, sought to purge the church of Cath. influences. The **radical independents** among them demanded unconditional autonomy for the communities.

1638 Uprising of the Scots, who joined in the 'Covenant' (the 'League with God' of the Presbyterians) to defend themselves against the introduction of the Anglican Church into Scotland by WILLIAM LAUD, Archbishop of Canterbury.

1640 Convocation of the 'Short' – later the 'Long Parliament' – to provide the means for the 'Wars of the Bishops' against the Scots. Dominated by Puritans (JOHN PYM), it imposed controls on the gvt (1641 summary of grievances in the 'Grand Remonstrance'); trials and execution of the royal advisers STRAFFORD (1641) and LAUD (1645).

1642–8 The English Civil War between Crown (Cavaliers) and Parliament (Roundheads: closely cropped hair), caused by an uprising of Irish Catholics (massacre of Ulster, 1641) and the arrest of JOHN PYM. Decisive factors were the intervention of Scotland (1643) and the new Parliamentary army under **Oliver Cromwell** (1599–1658), who, convinced of his mission, was able to forge his 'God-possessed Ironsides' into a Puritan élite.

1648 CROMWELL'S victory over the Scots (persuaded by CHARLES I to join his side) at Preston. Following 'purification' by the army, the 'Rump' brought charges against CHARLES. The trial was followed by

1649 execution of Charles I and the abolition of monarchy.

England under the Commonwealth (1649–60)

The Rump governed the Commonwealth without a House of Lords and Council of State. Vigorous revival of relig. sects (levellers). Puritan 'clean-up' of Cath. Ireland (1649) and Scotland (1650–51) by CROMWELL, incl. complete confiscation of Irish landed property (beginning of Irish repugnance); following the dissolution of the Rump, CROMWELL became

1653 Lord Protector (milit. dictatorship by the Puritans). Brilliant successes against Holland and Spain in foreign policy.

1651 Navigation Act: directed against the Dutch carrier trade, it provided that all goods shipped to and from England were to be transported in Eng. ships; to this end

1652–4 1st Eng.–Dutch Naval War (Eng. fleet led by Admiral ROBERT BLAKE).

1654–9 War with Spain: capture of Jamaica (1655) and Dunkirk (1658). Strict Pur. rule in England, incl. the supervision of everyday conduct (observation of the Sabbath). With his epic *Paradise Lost* (1667) CROMWELL'S former secretary **John Milton** (1608–74) gave expression to the Eng. Puritans' sense of mission as 'God's own people'.

1658 Death of CROMWELL. His incompetent son RICHARD abdicated. General MONK restored the monarchy.

The Stuart Restoration (1660–88)

1660–85 Charles II (30 yrs old) had been educated at the court of LOUIS XIV. His imitation of Fr. absolutism, persecution of the Puritans and rest. of the Anglican state church (Act of Uniformity, 1662) led to renewed tensions between Crown and Parliament.

1665 the plague and 1666 London dest. in the Great Fire.

1665–7 2nd Eng.–Dutch Naval War (with victories by the Dutch Admiral DE RUYTER). By the Peace of Breda of 1667 New Amsterdam (New York) was exchanged for Surinam (Dutch Guiana). Assisted by the Cabal (1667–73), the king concluded

1670 the secret Treaty of Dover with LOUIS XIV and launched the unpopular

1672–4 3rd War against the Dutch (p. 259). Parliament responded to the royal Declaration of Indulgence favouring Catholics and Dissenters with the

1673 Test Act: exclusion of all non-Anglicans from gvtl offices, and the

1679 Habeas Corpus Act: protection from arbitrary arrest and safeguarding of personal liberty ('my home is my castle!'). Parties were formed in Parliament: **Whigs** (nickname for Scot. peasants): middle-class opponents of the Cath. Stuarts; **Tories** (Irish bandits): Conservative, Anglican and loyal to the king.

1685–8 James II (52 yrs old). A Catholic, he attempted a Cath. rest.; severe resistance by the Anglican Church and the Whigs (W. RUSSELL; SHAFTESBURY).

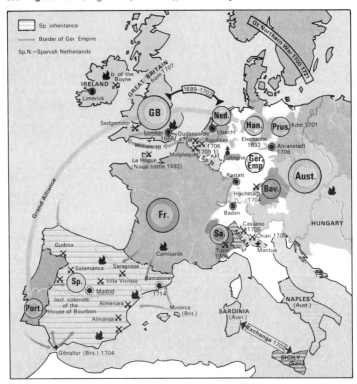

The power alignments of the War of the Spanish Succession

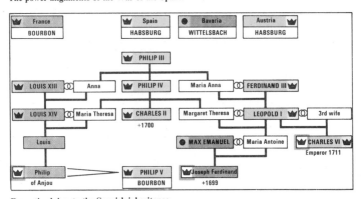

Dynastic claims to the Spanish inheritance
(Pretenders to the throne: Philip, Joseph Ferdinand, Charles VI)

The 'Glorious Revolution' (1688)
The unexpected birth of an heir to the throne (JAMES III) brought about the threat of a permanent Cath. dynasty for England. Whigs and Tories summoned WILLIAM III OF ORANGE ('For the Protestant faith and a free parliament').

1688 The Glorious Revolution followed a bloodless course; flight of JAMES II to France; campaign of WILLIAM III against the Cath. 'Jacobites' in Ireland: 1690, b. of the Boyne and capitulation of Limerick (1692).

Significance for England: 1. Right of parliamentary approbation granted to the gentry and the city by the

1689 Declaration of Rights (approval of taxation, freedom of speech, no standing army). To secure the personal liberty and property of the citizens JOHN LOCKE (p. 257) provided the theoretical justification for the division of the powers of the state into the legislative and executive branches in his *Two Treatises of Government* (1689). 2. Rise of England to the position of leading commercial and financial power of the world.

1694 The Bank of England est.

Significance for Europe: 1. Constitutional monarchy replaced absolutism. 2. Fr. hegemonic policies countered with the principle of the balance of power – resulting in war with France 1689–97 (p. 259).

Significance for the world: 1. Rivalry on the seas decided in favour of England (in Personal Union with Holland until 1702). 2. Development of Anglo-Fr. dualism in colon. affairs (p. 277).

Great Britain to 1742
1701 Act of Settlement to regulate the succession to the throne (House of Hanover).

1702–14 Queen ANNE (daughter of WILLIAM III). Participation in the War of the Sp. Succession; JOHN CHURCHILL, Duke of Marlborough (1650–1722), commander.

1707 Union of Scotland and England under the title **Great Britain.**

1714–1901 The House of Hanover (GEORGE I (1714–27); GEORGE II (1727–60)). Development of gvt by party: the parliamentary majority provided the ministry, headed by the **Prime Minister.**

1721–42 Period of peace under the Whig gvt of ROBERT WALPOLE, the 'ruler of the nation', with patronage, electoral corruption and censorship of the press (critical satirist: JONATHAN SWIFT, 1667–1745; *Gulliver's Travels*, 1726); increasing prosperity as a result of mercantilist colon. policies.

The War of the Sp. Succession (1701–13/14)
After 1665 Europe awaited the death of the last Sp. Habsburg, CHARLES II ('CARLOS THE BEWITCHED'), congenitally retarded as a result of Habsburg intermarriage. The Sp. inheritance could possibly create a new world power (France or Austria); to prevent this, WILLIAM III endeavoured to bring about a partition. 1st plan (1698): support for the son of the Bav. Elector as pretender

to the throne; dropped upon his death in 1699; 2nd plan (1700): backing the claim of the Archduke CHARLES (in line as pretender to the Habsburg *Sekundogenitur* (2nd line of dyn. inheritance)) to Spain and her colonies. Thanks to the joint efforts of LOUIS XIV, the Sp. Council of State and the Curia, the will of CHARLES II named PHILIP OF ANJOU sole heir. This solution endangered the Eur. balance of power; thereupon, formation of

1701 The Grand Alliance between Great Britain, Holland, Austria, Prussia, Hanover, Portugal (Methuen Treaty), the Empire (1702) and Savoy (1703). The House of Wittlesbach (Bavaria, Electoral Cologne) allied with LOUIS XIV.

1701–13/14 The War of the Sp. Succession, the first world war of modern times with theatres of war in Spain (civil war), Italy (Prince EUGENE), s. Germany (LOUIS OF BADEN), the Netherlands (CHURCHILL), on the oceans and in the N. Sea (Brit. naval blockade).

1703 Elevation of Archduke CHARLES (III) to be king of Spain.

1704 British seizure of **Gibraltar.** Brilliant victories by the allies: Blenheim (1704), Ramillies, Turin (1706), Oudenaarde (1708), Malplaquet (1709). Seven years of war, with the overburdening of the mercantilist system, the pressures of taxation and internal insurrections (the Camisard uprising of the Huguenots in the Cevennes), exhausted France. Austria was able to settle her problems with the rebels in Hungary (p. 265). Peace offers by LOUIS XIV to surrender Spain and vacate Alsace failed because of the excessive demands of the victors.

1711 Two accidents caused a polit. turn of events: (a) the fall of the Whig gvt and the beginning of the BOLINGBROKE (Tory) era in Great Britain, which led to the recall of CHURCHILL; (b) the death of the Emperor JOSEPH I, who was succeeded by CHARLES VI (p. 265). The connection of Spain with Austria now brought about the renewed threat of Habsburg world power; to meet it an agreement was reached between France and the maritime powers.

1713 Peace of Utrecht (the 2nd peace congress of the modern age) brought about the partition of the Sp. Empire: the country itself and the colonies went to Philip of Anjou; the Eur. territories to Austria, exc. for Sicily, which went to Savoy. The Barrière treaty secured Belg. strongholds for the Dutch. Great Britain obtained Gibraltar, Minorca, Newfoundland, Nova Scotia, the Hudson Bay territories and the monopoly of the slave trade with Latin America (the *Asiento*). After a milit. epilogue the Emperor recognized the new order in the

1714 Peace of Rastatt and Baden.

Consequences: triumph of (Brit.) balance-of-power policy. Great Britain became the 'arbiter of Europe' and the power able to grant the largest subsidies as a result of this 'most businesslike of all our wars' (SEELEY).

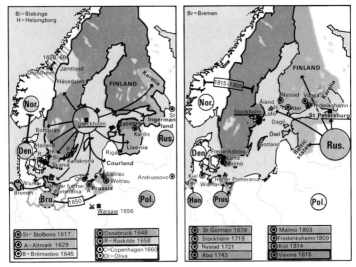

Swedish expansion to 1660

Sweden's losses to 1815

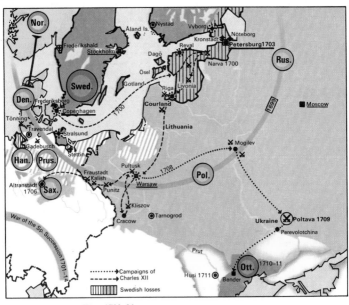

The Great Northern War, 1700–21

Sweden as Major Power

1632–54 CHRISTINA (6 yrs old). After converting to Catholicism she abdicated. Guided by its greatest statesman, Chancellor **Axel Oxenstierna** (1583–1654), Sweden became the leading power of the Baltic area after its

1643–5 war with Denmark and the advantageous

1648 Peace of Westphalia (p. 255). However, it lacked the econ. and fin. means to pursue independent great-power policies. Sweden's natural opponents were Denmark, Poland (dyn. claims to the throne by the Vasas), Brandenburg and later Russia.

1654–1720 The House of Pfalz–Zweibrücken.

1654–60 CHARLES X GUSTAVUS, the 'Nordic Alexander', invaded Poland (ruled by JAN CASIMIR, 1648–68), which had been weakened by the Zaropóg Cossack uprising (1654) and a Rus. attack.

1654–60 Swed.–Pol. War. After the occupation of Cracow and Dünaburg

1656 Victory at Warsaw with the aid of Brandenburg (Treaty of Labiau, p. 263). Denmark lost s. Sweden in the

1658 Peace of Roskilde. To maintain the balance of power the 'maritime powers' compelled the Baltic states to conclude the

1660 Peace of Oliva. Russia obtained Smolensk and the Eastern Ukraine by the

1661 Peace of Kardis (recognized by Poland in the Treaty of Andrussovo, 1667). Sweden financed the war by granting privileges concerning taxation and crown lands to the nobility, which as a result owned 72% of the land. Under

1660–97 CHARLES XI (4 yrs old) the state became dependent on Fr. subsidies (p. 259). Sweden was obliged

1675 to invade Brandenburg, was defeated at Fehrbellin, and retreated to E. Prussia (1678); at the same time she was

1675–9 attacked by Denmark (victory in the Bay of Kjöge, 1677). However, Sweden did not incur any losses in the peace treaties of Lund (Denmark) and St-Germain (p. 259) because of Louis XIV's interpellation.

1682 Introduction of absolutism to reorganize the state (as in Denmark, *Lex regia* of 1665), incl. the previously discontinued confiscation of crown lands. The distribution of landed property between the crown, the nobility and the free peasantry was balanced, the army and navy were reorganized.

1694 Opposition by the Livonian nobility under REINHOLD VON PATKUL to the discontinuation of gvt by the estates.

The Great Northern War (1700–21)

1697–1718 Charles XII (15 yrs old), the 'last Viking'; confirmed Lutheran, brilliant general, but headstrong politician. PETER I (p. 273) concluded against him

1699 alliances with Saxony/Poland (AUGUST II, p. 263) and Denmark (FREDERICK IV). PATKUL placed Livonia under Pol. protection; Denmark and Russia prepared to march on Sweden.

1700 Assisted by Brit. and Dutch naval forces

CHARLES XII landed on Zealand and defeated Denmark (Peace of Travendal).

1700 Victory at **Narva** over PETER I (against 5 times numerically superior forces); instead of destroying the Rus. army, the king (probably for reasons of personal dislike) turned against the convert AUGUST II and drove him from Poland. 1704 Election of STANISLAS LESCZINSKI as king of Poland. Subjugation of Saxony and the (dictated)

1706 Peace of Altranstädt: AUGUST II was forced to give up the Pol. crown and surrender Patkul. Sent as personal envoy of the Eng. king, CHURCHILL (p. 269) was able to avert CHARLES's intervention in the War of the Sp. Succession (by reference to the Swed. 'deliverance of Protestantism').

Meanwhile, PETER I had restored his army and recaptured Schlüsselburg (= Nöteborg), Ivangorod and Narva (1704).

1703 Foundation of St Petersburg in the swamps at the mouth of the Neva.

1708/9 Rus. campaign of CHARLES XII. Union with the Cossack Hetman MAZEPPA to liberate the Ukraine and advance on Moscow. The onset of winter, epidemics and Rus. raids decimated the weakened army; even so, CHARLES took on the

1709 b. of Poltava, which ended in total Swed. defeat and capitulation at Perevolotchina: 1st foreign catastrophe in Russia of modern times (as later NAPOLEON and HITLER). The wounded king escaped to Turkey and urged the Sultan to war (1711); the Rus. army was encircled on the Prut; but PETER I was by bribery able to obtain safe conduct in exchange for giving up Azov (in the Peace of Husi).

1713–20 Concentric attacks on the Swed. possessions along the N. Sea and the Baltic Sea;

Denmark: advance to Bremen and Verden; seizure of Tönning (1713);

Russia: occupation of the Aland Islands and Finland (1714); invasion of Sweden (1719/20);

Prussia and Hanover – joining the coalition after 1713 (Utrecht) – seized Sweden's Ger. possessions. CHARLES XII emerged from Turk. internment and, after a forced ride, appeared at Stralsund (1718); he was killed before the fortress of Frederickshald in 1718. Brit. and Fr. interest in the maintenance of the balance of power in the N. averted the complete dissolution of Swed. possessions.

1719–21 Peace treaties: at Stockholm with Hanover (Bremen, Verden) and Prussia (Hither Pomerania); at Fredericksborg with Denmark (customs duties for the Sund); at Nystadt with Russia (the Balticum, which, according to a special arrangement, retained the Lutheran Church, the Ger. language and administrative autonomy).

Victor: **Peter the Great.** After 1721 he called himself 'Tsar of all Rus'. Russia supplanted Sweden as the major power in the Baltic area.

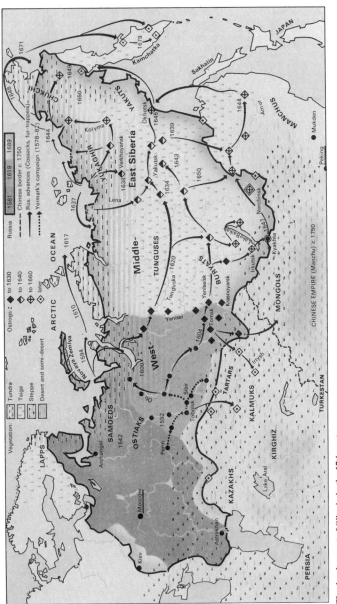

The development of Siberia in the 17th cent.

The Opening of Siberia in the 17th Cent.

1558 IVAN IV 'THE TERRIBLE' provided the Stroganovs, a family of merchants, with a document certifying their possession of Siberia, but obliging them to open up the continent through colonizing activity. Unnoticed by Europe, one of the greatest feats of conquest in human history thus had its beginning. It was executed by

Cossacks, escaped Rus. and Ukrainian serfs, who est. autonomous milit. communities on 'free (steppe-) fields' (*Sotnje*) under elected leaders (*Hetman, Ataman*). Recognized by the Tsars from .the 15th cent., they were used to protect the frontiers against Turks, Tartars and Poles. They were joined by merchants and peasant settlers (*Sibirjaks*) in the 'chase after the sable'.

1581–4 Commissioned by the Stroganovs, **Hetman Yermak** crossed Western Siberia with 800 men (without horses) to the Irtysh; the Khanate of Sibir was conquered. Siberian cities developed out of *Ostrogs* (simple fortifications to secure transit).

1610 The Cossacks reached the mouth of the Yenisey (from 1619 the river marking Russia's eastern border). Founding of Tomsk (1604), Yeniseisk (1619), Krasnoyarsk (1628), Irkutsk (1652). By

1640 cen. Siberia was penetrated to the Lena, Yana and Indigirka. Advances from Yakutsk (1632) and Verkhoyansk (1638): to NE. Siberia under Poyarkov and **Simon Dezhnev,** the discoverer of the Bering Strait (1648); to the Sea of Okhotsk (1645); to the Amur basin under Khabarov (1653); to the Kamchatka Peninsula (1679). A Russo-Chin. border conflict was settled by the 1st Chin.–Eur. agreement, the

1689 Treaty of Nerchinsk (the Amur border).

1727 The Kyakhta Treaty made provisions for a Rus. trading station to be est. at Peking. Siberia became the destination of exiled criminals and polit. prisoners.
Commissioned by the Tsar, the Dane **Vitus Bering** (1680–1741) undertook the first of a series of expeditions for the scientific exploration of Siberia in 1728.

1742 CHELYUSKIN discovered the N. Cape; Alaska was explored (Rus. from 1791).

1613–1762 The House of Romanov. It terminated the 'Time of Troubles' (p. 203). Owing to the (1652) reform of the Patriarch of Moscow NIKON to restore what was supposed to be the Gk rite), the Orth. Church split during the reign of the Tsar ALEXIS (1645–76). The persecution of the 'Old Believers' (burning of the Archpriest AVVAKUM 1682) followed. With the aid of the Streltsy (p. 203), SOPHIA, the Tsar's daughter, attempted to secure her Regency; but in 1689 she was overthrown by her halfbrother PETER, with whom Russia's modern age begins.

The Rise of Russia

1689–1725 Peter I, the Great (17 yrs old), 'the master craftsman on the throne', endea-

voured to europeanize the country with despotic energy ('Russians must be coerced!'). His travels abroad (1697/8; 1716/17) reflected admiration for the 'Germans' (a term used collectively for all foreigners). The Tsar had himself personally trained as a gunnery expert (Königsberg), shipbuilder (Amsterdam) and navigator (London). Resistance to his reforms was broken without scruple: extermination of the Streltsy 1698; death of his own son following torture in a prison (1718).

The reforms: carried out with the aid of foreigners (GORDON/Scottish; LEFORT/Swiss), these aimed at improving the public finances and strengthening the new fleet and the army (by Eur. training, regular levies (1 soldier per 20 serf households) and service obligation of the nobility).

Admin.: the resort ministries (11 resorts, 1718) were placed under the senate, the highest judicial authority; the Empire was organized in 11 'governments', 50 provinces (and districts); the bureaucracy was controlled through procurators (1722). (A reliable corps of officials failed to develop in Russia despite the 'eyes of the Tsar'.) Introduction of a direct (head) tax.

Eccles. policy: the Patriarchate was replaced by the Holy Synod (1721), presided over by the Tsar (Caesaropapism).

Soc. organization: prohibition of old Rus. traditions (incl. customs relating to apparel and beards); for the sake of adjustment, the nobility of birth and the nobility of office (ennoblement through service in high public office) were listed in the Table of Ranks (14 steps, 1722). ·

1714/22 Regulations governing the succession to eliminate palace revolutions.

Econ. life: state monopolies for the manufacture of tapestries and textiles, and for forestry and mining; construction of canals and ports; recruitment of foreign specialists (craftsmen, merchants, officers, artists). Advanced professional schools, incl. the Academy of Sciences, est. at St Petersburg (1725).

Foreign policy: access to the open sea (the window on Europe) was gained as a result of the Great Northern War (p. 271).

1722/3 Pers. campaign (Derbent, Baku).

PETER's accomplishments remain controversial in Russia. The revolution 'from above' europeanized the people only superficially; nevertheless it had a profound impact on Rus. history.

1725–40 CATHERINE I and ANNA represented the 'Ger. period', with their favourites at court: MENSHIKOV, BÜHREN, MÜNNICH, OSTERMANN; the court absorbed up to 50 % of state income; the situation of the peasantry was worsened by the arbitrariness of the nobility.

1735–9 War with Turkey, incl. victs. in the Crimea, before Ochakov and Chotin. By the Peace of Belgrade (1739, p. 265) Azov was annexed, and the Black Sea was thereby reached.

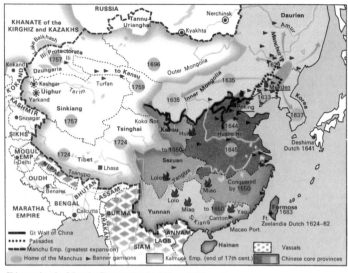

China under the Manchu Dynasty in the 16th and 17th cents.

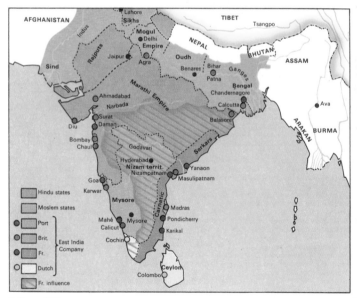

India, *c.* 1700

China under the Manchu Dynasty

c. 1600 NURHACHI (1583–1628) united Tungu tribes in SE. Manchuria to form the nation of the Manchu and gave it tight milit. organization in '8 banners' (1615).

1620 Seizure of Mukden (cap. after 1625); **1637** successful Korean campaign. As a result of rebel uprisings, the Empire disintegrated under the last Ming Emperor TSUNG-TSENG (1628–44). Summoned to their aid by Ming troops, the Manchu

1644 entered Peking and took over the gvt.

1644–1911 the Manchu Dynasty. After subjugating S. China, the regent DORGUN founded the Empire.

1662–1722 Emperor K'ang Hsi, the most important ruler of China because of his triple role as milit. commander, statesman and scholar; he tolerated the Jesuits for their scientific and technical capacities (not for relig. reasons); the Jesuit FERDINAND VERBIEST was his teacher.

1673–81 Unrest among the adherents of the Ming in the W. and S.; conquest of Formosa (1683).

Campaigns against W. Mongolia and the Tanguts in the Koko Nor region were undertaken to protect the 'Celestial Empire' by a circle of buffer zones; protectorates over Mongolia (1696) and Tibet (1724).

Domination over a giant empire by the small Manchu people was secured by police-state methods: (a) creation of a hierarchy of officialdom (qualification by a strict examination system) in accordance with the principle of dual-occupancy (Manchu/Chinese) of all offices; (b) retention of the est. army organization; (c) promotion of Eur. trade through Chin. companies (Hong merchants); (d) intellectual subjection of the masses (thus, also, obligatory introduction of the Manchu pigtail); (e) dogmatization of Confucianism as state-wide doctrine in the 16 rules of the *Holy Edict* (1671, modelled on Jes. practice). An extended period of domestic peace was made possible; pop. growth from 100 mil. (1680) to 76 mil. (1780) flooded the Chin. border areas colonization of Manchuria).

Ctr.: foremost period of Chin. philology (main representative KU YEN-WU). Geographical descriptions of the Empire, local chronicles, lit. collections (Book of Songs) and the 'Daily Commentaries' (mottoes) on the classical writings of Confucianism. The standard Chin.

716 encyclopedia of the Imp. Academy influenced LEIBNIZ and the Fr. Encyclopedists among others.

1736–96 Emperor Ch'ien Lung, an orthodox Confucian, prohibited Christ. miss. activity. The Manchu system began to ossify: lit. inquisition, incl. book-burnings; formation of secret societies; increasing distrust of 'foreigners' and opposition to the advances of the Eur. (opium) trade.

Demanding the utmost of her subjects (uprisings of the Miao, original people of S. China, and the Moslems in Kansu) China reached her greatest territ. expansion through successful colon. wars in the Ili region (Dzungaria: 1729–34; 1754–61), in Burma (1767–9) and in Tibet (1791–2).

During the 18th cent. China had a strong impact on Europe, reflected in the idealized fashion for things Chinese (*Chinoiserie*) of the Rococo (lacquered articles, porcelain; decorative Chin. gardens with tea-houses and pavilions).

Dissolution of Mogul Rule in India

1658–1707 Aurangzeb, the last significant Grand Mogul and a fanatical Moslem. After the conquest of Kandahar, Kabul and the Deccan,

1691 greatest extension of the Mogul Empire; but also beginning of internal dissolution owing to the politically unwise persecution of the Hindus (incl. the destruction of temples in N. India), reintroduction of the *jizya* (special tax on Hindus) and attacks on Hindu vassals (Jaipur). The Hindus responded with uprisings, the secession of the **Sikhs** (the militant relig. sect of the Punjab) and of the **Rajput** states (Hindu vassals).

Militarily united through **Shivaji** (1646–80), the **Marathi** (prob. the original inhabitants of the Deccan) became the leading proponents of Hinduism. Constant raids served to sustain the army.

1664/70 Pillages of Surat, the most prosperous trade-centre of the Mogul Empire. From 1681 annual campaigns by AURANGZEB against the Marathi, who became a major Ind. power under **Peshwas.**

Eur. Colon. Powers in India

The dissolution of the Mogul Empire and the bloody conflict between Moslems and Hindus facilitated the establishment of new Eur. trading centres.

The Dutch pushed the Portuguese out of Ceylon (1609), but experienced bitter conflicts with the English.

1615 Naval b. of Surat.

England: the **East India Company** (1600–1858) carried out Brit. colon. policy; Madras (1639), Bombay (1661) and Calcutta (1696), the centres of the future Brit.–Ind. world empire, were exposed to repeated attacks by the Marathi.

France; used mercantilistic methods to build its colon. empire and developed the India trade.

1664 COLBERT est. the Compagnie des Indes Orientales and promoted colon. expeditions by the state. Fort Dauphin on Madagascar (1643–72) and the Is. of Bourbon (Réunion, 1654) served to secure the sea lanes to India. Governor **Dupleix** met the competition of the Brit. East India Company successfully.

From 1746 Brit.–Fr. colon. struggles, the Fr. side represented with diplomatic adeptness by **DUPLEIX,** who took advantage of his cordial relations with S. Ind. princes.

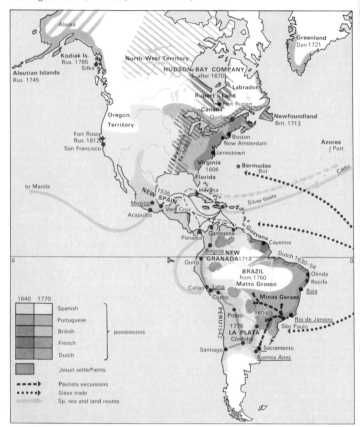

America in the 17th and 18th cents.

The West Indies in the 17th cent.

es. Miss. Activity in S. America

Spain left the 'jungle frontier' along the Paraná, Marañon and upper Orinoco rivers to the miss. Orders. Brilliant successes of the Jesuits (incl. econ. gains) – esp. in the **'Jes. state' of Paraguay**, the 'vision in the jungle'.

From 1607 Ind. missions (collectives excl. private property) est. They grew in spite of constant raids (*entradas*) by Braz. slave-raiders.

767 Expulsion of the Jesuits (p. 287); the squandering of the Order's properties led to a severe soc. and econ. crisis reflected in the 780–83 uprising of the 'last Inca' TUPAC AMARU.

The Exploitation of S. and Cen. America

Sp. colonies: Eur. plants (grains) and domestic animals (cattle, horses, sheep) spread rapidly; but the major econ. interest was the exploitation of precious metals, carried on regardless of the expense of transport by **silver fleets** (after 1561 in convoys as protection against Eng., Dutch and Fr. attacks).

546 Establishment of the silver-mining centre of **Potosi** (4,000 m. above sea-level) which was by 1600 the 2nd largest city in the world (London being the largest).

Consequences of Sp. silver imports into Europe: latent inflation, price rises, marketing crises, bankruptcies of gvts (decline of the Fuggers, p. 215). The Asiento Treaty of 1713 loosened gvtl supervision of trade; though Amer. trade was freed only in 1797. Introduced in 1782 and modelled on the Fr. system, the intendancy bureaucracy consumed 80% of the colonies' income from taxation.

Portugal: colon. interest centred on E. Indies; Olinda (1537) was est. as a base against pirates, Bahia (1549) as a port of transfer. The fertile coastal areas of Brazil were divided by the crown into 12 hered. captaincies (semi-feudal, virtually politically ind. territories). Armed bands were formed in the backwoods of São Paulo by the descendants of adventurers (Paulistas and Mamelucos). Stealing domestic animals and conducting slave-raids, the *Bandeitantes* advanced into the interior.

680 Establishment of the colony of Sacramento within the area of Sp. sovereignty. Gold finds in Minas Geraes (1693) and Matto Grosso (1720) led to the opening up of the hinterland; the boundary between the colon. powers was thereby pushed farther w. It was recognized by Spain in the 777 Treaty of Ildefonso.

The polit. rivalries of Europe carried over into the overseas territories.

The Netherlands: attacks by the Dutch West Indies Company (1609) against the kdm of **Spain and Portugal** (united 1580–1640), incl. piracy against silver fleets.

624 Conquest of Bahia and occupation of 6 captaincies with the aim of utilizing their products (sugar-cane, coffee) and taking over

their slave-trade. Recife (1630) assumed the protection of the NE. coast, but was recaptured by the Portuguese in 1654. Curaçāo (1634) and Guiana (1636) remained Dutch.

The West Indies: the **Fr. possessions in the Antilles** developed out of the settlements of groups of **filibusters**, among them the 'Company of the American Isles': San Christoph (1625); San Domingo, Guadeloupe, Martinique (1635); Haiti (1655); providing more than 25% of the colon. imports; and others. Trading stations of the Brit. **West Indies Company** were loc. on Barbados (1605), the Bahamas (1646–70), Bermuda (1612) and elsewhere.

1655 Jamaica became Brit. (p. 267).

Even Denmark and Courland temporarily played a role in founding colonies in the w. Indies.

Fr. and Eng. Colonization in N. America

France: beginning in 1603, the first governor of **Canada**, SAMUEL DE CHAMPLAIN (1567–1635), took possession of Newfoundland, Nova Scotia and New France.

1608 Foundation of Quebec (1643 Montreal); after 1625, miss. activity by Fr. Jesuits; fur and rum trade with the Indians. After 1674, promotion of the 1st Fr. colon. empire by COLBERT (p. 261), who applied the mercantilistic policies of the state; by 1690 there were over 10,000 settlers in Canada.

1682 Exploration and incorporation of the **Louisiana Territory** into the Fr. possession by LA SALLE; a series of forts linking with New Orleans protected the new colony.

England: colon. interest centred on E. Indies; **Virginia**, the 1st Eng. settlement in America (Jamestown 1607), was est. by **Walter Raleigh** 1584. Emigrants persecuted for relig. reasons est. the **New England** states during the 17th cent.; they were either crown colonies (with a royal governor and a popular assembly) or proprietary colonies (based on private contracts with the crown).

1620 Crossing of the **'Mayflower'** with the **Pilgrim Fathers** (Pur. separatists) to Massachusetts;

1632 Maryland est. by Catholics.

The state supported the colonies (by 1640 over 25,000 settlers) by means of charters and trade privileges (the Navigation Acts, p. 267), which were directed esp. against Dutch maritime and commercial rivalry.

1664 Attack on New Netherlands (Dutch from 1616); became Eng. by the Treaty of Westminster (1667; states: New York, New Jersey, Delaware). S. Carolina and Rupert's Land (Hudson's Bay Company) were taken after 1670.

1683 WILLIAM PENN founded Philadelphia and the Quaker colony of Pennsylvania.

1713 Great Britain received Newfoundland and Nova Scotia; Brit.–Fr. colon. conflict intensified (p. 283).

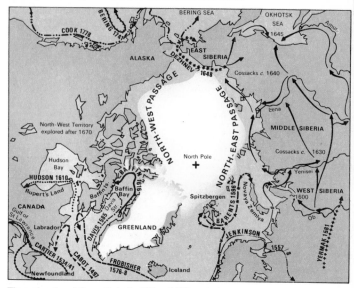

The exploration of the arctic in the 16th and 17th cents.

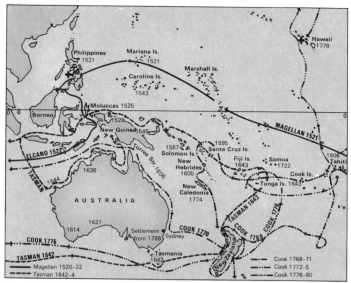

Discoveries in the Pacific Ocean to the 18th cent.

Geographical Discoveries in the 17th/18th Cents.
After the great discoveries of the turn of the 16th cent. the exploration of the world was continued (mainly by the Dutch and English):

1. The search for a northern passage from the Atlantic to the Pacific led to the discovery of the **Arctic** and the **NE. Passage** (DEZHNEV and BERING, p. 273; the **NW. Passage** was yet to be discovered): DAVIS/Davis Strait, 1585; HUDSON/Hudson's Bay, 1610 (1st Eng. trade settlement 1674); BAFFIN/Baffin Bay, 1616.

2. Expeditions to the presumed 'Terra Australis'. Exploratory journeys brought knowledge of important islands and sailing routes of the **Pacific Ocean.** Notable explorers were DE QUIROS and DE TORRES (Paumotu Island, the New Hebrides, Torres Strait, Tahiti).

1642–59 Journeys of the Dutchman ABEL TASMAN, who discovered Mauritius, Van Diemen's Land (Tasmania), New Zealand and NW. New Guinea. In 1721–2 ROGGEVEEN discovered Easter Island, Samoa and the Solomons; the circumnavigator of the world BOUGAINVILLE discovered Polynesia and Melanesia in 1766–8.

1768–79 Scientific expeditions by the Eng. seaman Captain **James Cook,** who explored the E. coast of Australia, New Caledonia, the Tonga and Sandwich Islands and others; he was killed in Hawaii in 1779.

Knowledge of the continents, but also of the land and water distribution of the earth, was extended by:

1. The worldwide miss. activity of the Jesuits (p. 239).

2. The illegal struggle of freebooters (pirates, filibusters, buccaneers) against Spain, often with gvtl support (p. 277); also FRANCIS DRAKE (p. 225).

3. Gvtl commissions to est. colonies or promote trade: DE VRIES in Japan, 1643; CHAMPLAIN and LA SALLE in N. America (p. 277); YERMAK in Siberia (p. 273).

4. Private excursions/scientific explorations in the 18th cent.: KÄMPFER/Japan 1690–92; TOURNEFORT/Armenia and Persia 1700–2; KOLBE/S. Africa 1710; GMELIN/Siberia 1733–4; NIEBUHR/interior of Arabia, 1765; THUNBERG/S. Africa 1772; *et al.*

c. 1600 *c.* 49 % of the surface of the earth (32 % of the land) known.
c. 1800 *c.* 83 % (60 % of the land) known.

Scientific Discoveries
Empiricism and rationalism advanced the natural sciences (p. 256).

Mathematics:

1614 Logarithms	NAPIER
1637 Analytical geometry	DESCARTES
c. 1665 Differential and integral calculus	NEWTON, also LEIBNIZ 1672
c. 1700 Theory of probability	BERNOULLI

Physics:

1609 The motions of falling bodies (kinematics) and the pendulum	GALILEO
1609–19 Laws of planetary motion	KEPLER
1618 Law of the reflection of light	SNELLIUS
1662 The physical properties of gases	BOYLE
1665 The diffraction of light	GRIMALDI
1666 The law of gravitation	NEWTON
1675 Calculation of the speed of light	RÖMER
1690 The wave theory of light	HUYGENS
1728 The aberration of light	BRADLEY
1738 Principle of hydrodynamics	BERNOULLI
1790 Contact electricity ('galvanism')	GALVANI

Biology and chemistry:

1618 Circulation of the blood	HARVEY
1677 Semen (spermatozoa)	LEEUWENHOEK
1727 Silver bromides	SCHULTZE
1735 The nomenclature of organic life	LINNAEUS
1766 Hydrogen	CAVENDISH
1771 Oxygen	SCHEELE
1772 Nitrogen	RUTHERFORD
1780 The law of combustion	LAVOISIER
1783 Carburetted hydrogen (pit coal)	MINCKELAERS
1791 Synthetic sodium carbonate	LEBLANC
1799 Cement	PARKER

Inventions of the 17th and 18th Cents.
New discoveries were in part made possible only after the development of new **instruments for observation and measurement:**

1590 Microscope	JANSSEN
c. 1605 Telescope (principle of)	KEPLER
1643 Mercury barometer	TORRICELLI
1657 Pendulum clock	HUYGENS
1663 Air pump	VON GUERICKE
1669 Reflecting telescope	NEWTON
1718 Mercury thermometer	FAHRENHEIT
1742 Centigrade thermometer	CELSIUS

Technical processes, tools, and instruments, at first often discovered accidentally by craftsmen and hobbyists, were from the 18th cent. increasingly the result of scientific research. The Industrial Revolution was thus initiated.

1642 Adding machine	PASCAL
1673 Calculating machine	LEIBNIZ
1693 Porcelain (Eur.)	TSCHIRNHAUS
1711 Three-colour printing	LE BLOND
1735 Cast steel	HUNTSMAN
1738 Roller loom for spinning	WYATT
1751 Breech-loading rifle	CHAUMETTE
1752 Lightning conductor	FRANKLIN
1754 Sheet-iron mill	CORT
1767 Spinning jenny	HARGREAVES
1769 Steam engine	WATT
1769 Steam car	CUGNOT
1778 Diver's helmet	SMEATON
1783 Hot-air balloon	MONTGOLFIER
1785 Mechanical power loom	CARTWRIGHT
1795 Hydraulic press	BRAMAH
1796 Lithography	SENEFELDER
1799 Paper manufacture	ROBERT
1804 Loom for pattern weaving	JACQUARD
1807 Steam ship	FULTON

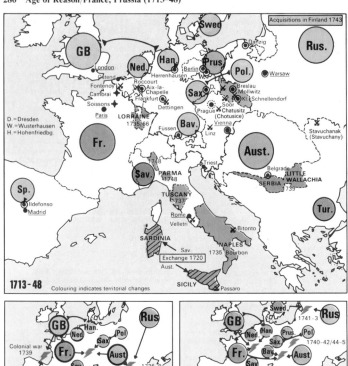

Alliances, wars and territorial changes in Europe, 1713–40

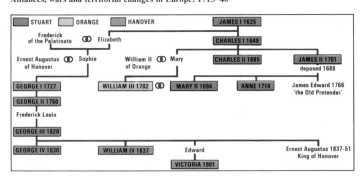

The Stuart (Orange) and Hanoverian dynasties in England

Eur. Cabinet Politics (1713–48)

A strong desire for polit. calm became evident after the War of the Sp. Succession (p. 269). Anglo-Fr. conflicts were avoided by compromises and maintaining the balance of power through agreements between cabinets. Congresses, alliances, partitions and territ. exchanges served **reasons of state**.

Spain: Cardinal ALBERONI, a minister of the crown, desired to re-establish Sp. hegemony over Italy. Taking advantage of the events of the Great Northern and Turk. Wars (p. 265), Spain

1717 occupied Sardinia and Sicily.

1718 Naval vict. of the Quadruple Alliance at Cape Passaro; Spain was placed under milit. pressure until ALBERONI's dismissal.

1720 Savoy exchanged Sicily for Aust. **Sardinia.**

Poland: During the

1733–5 Pol. War of Succession, Rus. troops forced the election of

1733–63 AUGUST III OF SAXONY, the Austro-Rus. candidate to the throne, over STANISLAS LESCZINSKI, the Fr. candidate. The French proved superior in the western theatre of war (Italy); 1735 preliminary peace;

1738 **Peace of Vienna:** STANISLAS LESCZINSKI (p. 271) received **Lorraine;** after he d. in 1766 it fell to France; FRANCIS OF LORRAINE, who had mar. MARIA THERESA in 1736, received **Tuscany;** Naples and **Sicily** were given to a Sp. Bourbon, Parma and Piacenza to a subordinate (*secundo geniture*) line of the Aust. dynasty.

Austria: Despite the pledges received to honour the Pragmatic Sanction, the

1740–48 **War of the Aust. Succession** broke out. It was caused by the invasion of **Silesia** by FREDERICK II OF PRUSSIA (p. 287). Saxony and Bavaria advanced claims to the Aust. throne. A Franco-Prus. alliance and the

1740–42 **1st Silesian War;** Prus. victs. at Mollwitz and Chotusitz; Franco-Bav. advance on Prague and Linz.

1741 The Diet of Pressburg brought **Maria Theresa** (p. 287) Hung. assistance. CHARLES ALBERT OF BAVARIA was elected Emperor as CHARLES VII (1742–5).

1742 **Separate Peace of Breslau:** Austria gave up Silesia, turned against Bavaria and formed alliances with Savoy, Saxony and **Great Britain.**

1743 The 'Pragmatic Army' defeated a Fr. army in the b. of Dettingen. 2nd Franco-Prus. alliance and

1744–5 **2nd Silesian War.** After Prus. victories at Soor and Hohenfriedberg,

1745 **Peace of Dresden:** Austria confirmed the cession of Silesia. With the Peace of Füssen, Bavaria recognized

1745–65 Emperor FRANCIS I (of Lorraine).

1748 **Peace of Aix-la-Chapelle:** France returned the Aust. Netherlands and Brit. colon. territories. Parma (Piacenza) fell to a subordinate Sp. Bourbon line (*secundo geniture*); Savoy received parts of Milan.

The Ancien Régime in France

1715–74 **Louis XV** (5 yrs old). Even though the state was heavily indebted because of the wars of LOUIS XIV (p. 269), the court of the Regent PHILIP OF ORLEANS (1715–23) was conducted in extravagant splendour. The Scotsman JOHN LAW attempted to improve the fiscal position of the state through the

1715 **establishment of the 1st public bank** (issuing notes) and of joint-stock companies (to exploit the colonies) (1718–19).

1720 **Inflation of paper currency** and public bankruptcy.

1726–43 **Cardinal Fleury** brought about what were to be the final polit. accomplishments of France under the Ancien Régime. Subs. the infl. of royal mistresses increased (Marquise DE POMPADOUR, Countess DU BARRY). Attempts at financial reform by the minister MACHAULT failed owing to the infl. of the privileged estates (clergy, nobility). After 1750 the faults of absolutism were criticized with increasing candour.

Culture: brilliant climax of the courtly and playful **Rococo** with its pastoral poetry and graceful musical dramas; ladies' fashions featured towering coiffures and hoop skirts; gentlemen's tailed wigs, courts, the galant's épée and the tricorn hat. Interior decoration with ornamental friezes, gilded mirrors, porcelain figurines, tapestries and *chinoiserie*. **Flowering of Fr. Rococo painting:** WATTEAU (1684–1721); BOUCHER (1703–70); FRAGONARD (1732–1806).

The Milit. Bureaucratic State of Prussia

1713–40 **Frederick William I,** the king most instrumental in Prussia's domestic development, was determined to 'govern his lands well'. Deeply religious, but rough and averse to the refined ctr. of the court, the 'drill-master of the Prussian nation' demanded unconditional obedience ('the soul is God's, all else must be mine'). Frugal and exemplary admin.: reform of the royal domains and the General Exchequer (to control finances). The king gave personal directions to the

1722 General Directory, the highest organ of centralized admin. Advancement of the mercantile system and agriculture.

1732 Settlement of 15,000 emigrants from Salzburg (p. 241). Elevation of the standards of public education (Edict of 1717). The aristocratic officer corps constituted the highest social class in the state. The **'soldier king'** was the first Eur. monarch to wear milit. uniform constantly. Increase of the professional army to 83,000 men (pop. 2·2 mil.). Prince LEOPOLD OF ANHALT-DESSAU (1683–1747) was the infantry's disciplinarian (drill, iron ramrod, marching in step).

1733 The Canton system: milit. service obligation of the peasant pop. Severe tensions between the king and crown prince **Frederick** (1712–86), who submitted in 1730 after an abortive attempt at flight and the execution of his friend KATTE. Trained in public service, the crown prince after 1736 had his own court at Rheinsberg and pursued lit. and philosophical studies.

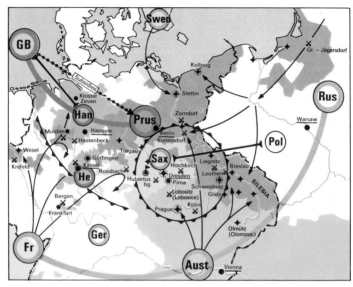

The Seven Years War in Europe

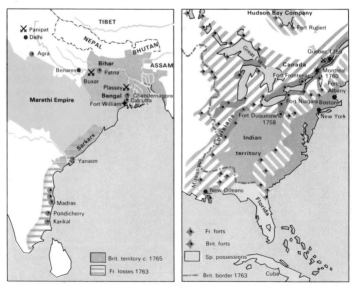

The British–French war in India

The British–French war in North America

The Seven Years War 1756–63
The Peace of Aix-la-Chapelle did not relieve int. tensions; the impetus to bring about a milit. resolution of the int. conflicts came from the colon. powers and Austria. Brit. interests accounted for the fact that the war was carried on simultaneously in Europe and overseas.

The Brit.–Fr. Colon. War (1754/5–63)
N. America (the Fr. and Ind. War): increasing immigration intensified the pressure exerted by the 400,000 Brit. settlers on the thinly settled but well-fortified Fr. colon. territories. Constant border conflicts became open warfare in the Ohio valley in 1754. Initial Fr. successes led to the fall of the Whig. gvt.
1757–61 William Pitt (the Elder, Earl of Chatham, 'after CROMWELL and WILLIAM III, the 3rd architect of the Brit. Empire') assumed polit. leadership; he strengthened the navy and the overseas army; Prussia received subsidies.
1758 Advance to the Ohio valley; seizure of Fort Louisburg and Fort Duquesne (Pittsburg).
1759 Advance to the St Lawrence river; **Quebec,** 'the heart of the enemy's power', was taken (General WOLFE defeated MONTCALM; both d. in battle); the breakthrough to the Great Lakes was made possible by the seizure of **Montreal** (1760).
The W. Indies: among other islands of the Fr. Antilles, Guadeloupe 1759 and Martinique 1762 were seized and, after Spain entered the war in 1761, Cuba (with the Philippines).
W. Africa: and the Atlantic coast. By 1760 all Fr. bases in Senegal were occupied; naval victs. (Lagos, Quiberon) and raids on Fr. ports ('breaking windows with guineas').
India: here too initial Fr. successes; but, with the exception of Madras, almost all s. India, incl. Calcutta, was lost.
Robert Clive (32 yrs old), an employee of the East India Company, strengthened Brit. resistance; utilizing the rivalries of Ind. princes, he regained Calcutta (Fort William). His
1757 vict. at Plassey, obtained by treachery over a 20-fold numerically superior enemy and with the loss of only 10 men, est. Brit. rule in India. Collapse of Fr. plans for India.
1763 Peace of Paris: Great Britain obtained Canada, Louisiana, Cape Breton and Senegal from France, Florida from Spain. It was the most brilliant Brit. vict. of modern history; North America became Anglo-Saxon.

The War over Silesia (1756–63)
Austrian Chancellor after 1753, Count KAUNITZ-RIETBERG won MARIA THERESA over to the idea of a polit. compromise with France (Marquise DE POMPADOUR) and the formation of a coalition against Prussia. FREDERICK II felt isolated; he therefore concluded the
Jan. 1756 Brit.–Prus. Convention of Westminster for the protection of Hanover. This defensive treaty initiated the 'diplomatic revolution' aspired to by KAUNITZ.
May 1756 Treaty of Versailles; the Franco-Aust. offensive alliance was joined by: Tsarina ELIZABETH (for reasons of a personal nature), Saxony, Sweden, and the Empire (with the exception of the territ. states of Hanover, Hesse-Kassel and Brunswick). After learning of their plans of attack, FREDERICK II acted to anticipate their joint action of 1757.
Aug. 1756 Incursion into Saxony (preventive war); after the capitulation of Pirna, Saxony became the base for Prus. operations.
The course of the war: facing an opposition 20 times superior (acc. to pop. figures), Prussia struggled for existence in a series of the 'classical battles' of the history of warfare. FREDERICK II endeavoured to utilize the advantage of his 'interior lines of communication' to strike a number of decisive offensive blows; he was, however, unable to prevent the allies from joining forces.
1757–8 FREDERICK II on the attack: victs. at Prague, **Rossbach** (Seydlitz), Zorndorf, **Leuthen;** defeats at Gross-Jägersdorf (Rus. occupation of E. Prussia), **Kolin** (the milit. decoration Order of MARIA THERESA created) and Hochkirch (Daun).
Brit. support for Prussia provided by PITT ('Canada will be won in Silesia'): fighting in the service of Great Britain, FERDINAND OF BRUNSWICK repulsed the Fr. attack in the w. with victs. at Krefeld (1758) and Minden (1759). After Great Britain had obtained her objectives overseas, and following the fall of PITT in 1761, subsidies to Prussia were discontinued.
1759–61 FREDERICK II on the defensive: the united Aust. and Rus. armies nearly dest. the Prus. army in the
1759 b. of Kunersdorf. The victors' disunity saved Prussia ('le miracle de la maison de Brandebourg'); pillages of Berlin; coinage of debased currency ('Ephraimites') to overcome the financial emergency. After the victs. of Liegnitz and Torgau (1760) there were signs of general exhaustion (the Aust. public debt rose from 49 to 136 mil. l.).
1762 After the death of the Tsarina, Russia quit the coalition; PETER III, an admirer of FREDERICK, was murdered; CATHERINE II (p. 287) terminated the war. A lack of resources forced France and Sweden to discontinue the war; Austria had to initiate negotiations.
1763 Peace of Hubertusburg – no territ. changes. Significance: as the 5th **major power,** Prussia complicated the Europ. balance-of-power system; Rus. infl. grew, while the failure of France intensified domestic criticism of the **Ancien Régime** (p. 281). Ger. politics were to be dominated by the Austro-Prus. power conflict (Ger. dualism) until BISMARCK's 'small Ger. solution' of 1866. The personality and accomplishment of FREDERICK THE GREAT brought about the development of early Ger. polit. self-consciousness and nat. feeling.

RUSSIA
Smolensk
Andrussovo
Wehlau
Prussia
Oliva
Warsaw
POLAND
Kiev
Ukraine
AUSTRIA
Vienna
1660/67

Poland in the 17th cent.

RUSSIA
Vitebsk
White Russia
West-Prussia
Danzig
POLAND
Thorn (Torun)
Warsaw
Radom
Galicia
Bar
Balta
Vienna
AUSTRIA
1st Partition 1772

Russian, Prussian and Austrian gains

Grodno
RUSSIA
PRUSSIA
Danzig
Thorn
POLAND
Warsaw
Posen
Dubienka
Polesia
Podolia
Targowice
Vienna
AUSTRIA
2nd Partition 1793

Prussian and Russian expansion

Lithuania
Vilna
Masovia
PRUSSIA
RUSSIA
Praga
Warsaw
Maciejowice
Volhynia
Cracow
Vienna
AUSTRIA
3rd Partition 1795

The dissolution of Poland

Tilsit
Danzig
PRUSSIA
Pultusk
Grand Duchy of Warsaw 1807
Warsaw
Radzyn
RUSSIA
1809
Vienna
Schönbrunn
AUSTRIA
1807/09

The Grand Duchy of Warsaw

PRUSSIA
Warsaw
Kalisz
Congress POLAND
RUSSIA
Rep. of Cracow
Vienna
AUSTRIA
1815

Congress Poland

Polit. Advancement of Russia after 1763

1764–80 Count PANIN conducted Rus. foreign policy under CATHERINE II.

1764 Alliance with Prussia, which supported the election of Russia's candidate for the Pol. throne, PONIATOWSKI.

Poland: interference in the conflicts over the succession to the Pol. throne by both parties led to the

1768–74 1st Russo-Turk. War. Opposing the Rus. occupation of Moldavia and Wallachia, Austria concluded an alliance with Turkey. As mediator in this 1st **Balkan conflict,** Prussia turned attention on Poland.

1772 1st Partition of Poland. Russia gave up the Danubian principalities and peace was preserved.

The Black Sea: the Rus. Baltic fleet

1770 with the aid of Eng. officers defeated the Turks at Chesmé, determining the decline of Turkey as a power (the 'sick man of the Bosporus'). The

1774 Peace of Kuchuk Kainarji: Russia obtained Azov and became protector of the Orth. Christians in the Balkans.

1783 Annexation of the Crimea. Development of **'New Russia'** by the Tsarina's favourite **Potemkin** (1736–91): construction of a Black Sea fleet; new villages and cities est. (Kherson, 1778, Sevastopol, 1784). Jointly with Austria,

1787–92 2nd Russo-Turk. War, under the direction of Count **Suvorov** (1730–1800). His book *The Science of Conquest* became instrumental in the shaping of Rus. tactics (loosening of infantry lines; surprise attacks with coordinated infantry and artillery).

1792 Peace of Iaşi: the coast between the Dniester and Bug rivers became Rus.

Austro-Prus. Dualism in Germany after 1763

The growth of Rus. power affected Prussia and Austria; they took turns seeking Russia's support.

1765–90 After the extinction of the Wittelsbach Dynasty in 1777, JOSEPH II endeavoured to strengthen the position of Austria within the Empire. The plan to exchange territories with CHARLES THEODORE of the Palatinate, the heir to the Bav. throne (Lower Bavaria and the Upper Palatinate for Lower Austria), led to the

1778/9 War of the Bav. Succession and a Prus. invasion of Bohemia. MARIA THERESA forced JOSEPH to capitulate. In the

1779 Peace of Teschen (Těšín), guaranteed by Russia, Austria settled for the Inn district. JOSEPH II now pursued his aims

1781 in alliance with Russia. FREDERICK II responded to the attempt to exchange Belgium for Bavaria (which would have upset the Peace of Westphalia) with the formation of the

1785 League of Ger. Princes (p. 255). Austria was no longer able to assert herself against Prussia in the Empire. The

1790 The Convention of Reichenbach forced Austria to give in to Prus. demands and to discontinue the

1787–91 war against Turkey.

1791 Although the Austrians were victorious at Focsani and conquered Belgrade, the Peace of Sistova brought no significant gains.

The Partition of Poland (1772–95)

1764–95 STANISLAS II PONIATOWSKI. Elected king under Rus. pressure, the favourite of CATHERINE II (p. 287) aspired to reform conditions described as 'anarchy tempered by civil war'. Russia placed the dissidents (non-Catholics) and the opposing nobility, who were represented in the

1767 Confederations of Slutsk and Radom, under its protection and prevented a curtailment of the '*Liberum veto*' (p. 249). Aided by Russia, the dissidents dest. in civil war the

1768 Counter-Confederation of Bar.

1769 Austria occupied the area along the Zips (p. 201), pledged to Poland since 1412. To avert war between Russia and Austria

1772 1st Partition of Poland (against the will of MARIA THERESA: 'Trust and faith are lost for all times!'). The partitioning powers demanded that Poland retain the elective monarchy, the prerogatives of the nobility and the '*Liberum veto*'. During the Rus. war with Turkey and Sweden (1788–90) the

1788–91 Four Years Diet decided to transform Poland into a hered. constitutional monarchy, which was proclaimed in the

1791 May Constitution. Influenced by Russia, the opposition thereupon formed the

1792 Confederation of Targowice, forcing the king to join. To 'restore order' the

1793 2nd Partition of Poland, recognized by the 'silent Diet' of Grodno. Uprisings at Wilna and Warsaw inspired a general

1794 popular uprising under the nat. hero TADEUSZ KOŚCIUSZKO (1746–1817), which was suppressed by Prus. and Rus. troops (SUVOROV).

1795 3rd Partition of Poland: dissolution of the state. Led by General DABROWSKI (1755–1818), Pol. legions fought under NAPOLEON; who est. the

1807 Grand Duchy of Warsaw, which was later at the Congress of Vienna joined to Russia in personal union as

1815 'Congress Poland', and after a futile

1830/31 Pol. revolution became a Rus. province. The poets **Adam Mickiewicz** (1798–1855), SLOWACKI (1809–49) and KRASINSKI (1812–59) and the composer **Frédéric Chopin** (1810–49) worked in Paris, the **centre of Pol. emigration,** for their homeland's liberation.

Consequences of the partitions: the Pol. nat. movement became irrepressible. During the 19th cent. Poland was a source of Eur. unrest (nat. anthem: 'Poland is not lost'). **Prussia** burdened herself with an ethnic minority and laid the foundations for tense Ger.–Pol. relations (20th-cent. consequences: Ger. policy of extermination; Pol. hatred of Germans). **Russia** advanced westward and became an immediate neighbour of Prussia and Austria in 1795.

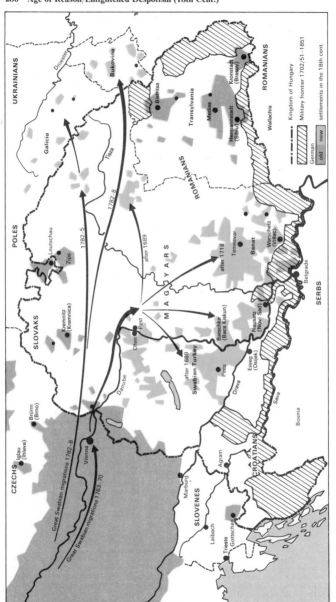

New settlements in the Danubian area after the Turkish wars of the 18th cent.

Enlightened Despotism in the 18th Cent.
The humanitarian ideas of the age also influenced the theories of the state and society. The enlightened ruler governed his subjects as the '1st servant of the state' in accordance with the principles of reason ('Nothing by the people, everything for the people!'). 'Revolution from above' created the absolute and sovereign welfare state with a modern bureaucracy and an ordered system of law.

Prussia: Frederick II the Great (1740–86)
Continuation of his father's reform work (p. 281): fixed budgets; state monopolies of coffee, tobacco, salt.
Colonization of the interior: drainage of the marshes of the Oder, Warthe and Netze valleys; road and canal construction; 900 villages with over 300,000 new settlers est.
Promotion of agriculture: rotation of crops, potato cultivation; improvement of animal husbandry, tree care and forestry.
Soc. organization: all estates were to serve the state: the **king** (personal gvt, aided by counsellors and secretaries) took active care through inspections and controls; the **nobility** (large landowners and proprietors of agricultural estates) provided officers for the army and high officials for the bureaucracy; the artisan and **bourgeois** classes (crafts and commerce) carried the burden of taxation, but were supported by the state (development of the silk, glass and porcelain industries); the **peasants** (agriculture) remained in hered. dependence (a specific form of serfdom). **Freedom of thought and religion** for all subjects.
Legal reforms were initiated by SAMUEL VON GOCCEJI (1679–1755): torture, royal intervention in legal proceedings and the purchase of offices eliminated. Introduction of **equality before the law** and autonomy of the judiciary (division of powers). Gvtl examination and pay for the legal profession. Uniform legal procedures regulating appeals, trial procedure, punitive measures and the prison system. Prussia changed from a police to a **constitutional state**. The **Prus. Law Code** came into effect in **1794.**

Austria: Maria Theresa (1740–80)
The Empress followed the example of her Prus. opponent. 'Internal rearmament' in Austria was made difficult by the soc., polit. and econ. differences among the various peoples of the state. Nevertheless, the Austro-Boh. part of the Empire was transformed into a modern bureaucratic state, organized in provinces (*Gubernia*) and districts; general tax obligation (incl. Church and nobility) based on the periodical census and the *Theresian Kataster* (land-register).
Legal system: Protestants and Jews were subject to legal restrictions; the state supervised the Church and had the right of '*placet regium*' (approval) over papal edicts.
Education: grammar schools and training schools for the crafts; milit., engineering

and commercial academies to raise the level of the practical knowledge of the people.
Colonization of the interior: after 1748 increased '**treks of the Swabians**' into the southeastern areas of the country (p. 265).
1765–90 Joseph II (co-regent with his mother in Austria to 1780). He introduced radical reforms, but was too hasty to realize his aim of a unitary state. Cen. admin. for the entire Empire with Ger. as official language.
1781 Abolition of serfdom and the guilds; an edict of toleration, but without equality for the denominations.
Church reform: dissolution of 'inactive' orders (1,300 monasteries); gvtl education and pay of priests; schools and welfare institutions (hospitals and orphanages; institutions for the insane and the blind); civil marriage.
Consequence of the reforms: the various peoples of the state resisted the disregard of their nat. traditions and prerogatives.
1787 An uprising of the Aust. Netherlands led to general unrest (Hungary) and the
1790 secession of the 'Republic of the United Belg. Provinces'. JOSEPH retracted most of his own reforms.
1790–92 To preserve the monarchy, his brother LEOPOLD II compromised cautiously.

Russia: Catherine II the Great (1762–96)
The cultured Tsarina of the House of **Anhalt-Zerbst** propagated Enlightenment ideas in Russia.
1767/8 A reform commission failed and was followed by
1775 autocratic gvt: organization of the country into **Gouvernements** with a degree of self-admin. headed by confederations of nobles. Following a suggestion of the chemist LOMONOSOV (1712–65)
1755 the **University of Moscow** est. Subs. plans were made for the creation of grammar and secondary schools. These attempts failed, as did those to change the Rus. way of life, because of a shortage of educated officials, and urban citizens. 'Letters of Majesty' granted to the nobility intensified the exploitation of the serfs (souls), and led to peasant unrest and the
1773/4 Cossack rising (PUGACHEV's rebellion).

Reform Activity in the Rest of Europe
Portugal: educational, financial and army reforms under POMBAL, a royal minister.
1755 The Lisbon Earthquake; reconstruction; many new industries among other things.
1759 Expulsion of the Jesuits from **Spain** by Count ARANDA, 1767.
Denmark: reforms pushed through by the Ger. physician STRUENSEE, who fell from power in 1772 and was executed.
1788 Count Bernstorff (1735–97) carried out the emancipation of the peasantry.
Baden: KARL FREDERICK (1746–1811), considered the model of an enlightened **Ger. territ. prince.** As early as
1760 he granted self-gvt to the rural communities.
1783 Abolition of serfdom.

Index

Index

This index contains only a selection of key entries. A full index will be found at the end of Volume 2. Bold figures indicate entries of central importance.